TECHNOLOGY, CURRICULUM AND PROFESSIONAL DEVELOPMENT

TECHNOLOGY, CURRICULUM AND PROFESSIONAL DEVELOPMENT

ADAPTING SCHOOLS TO MEET THE NEEDS OF STUDENTS WITH DISABILITIES

JOHN WOODWARD
LARRY CUBAN
EDITORS

The development of this book was supported in part by grants from the Office of Special Education Programs, U.S. Department of Education. Opinions expressed herein do not necessarily reflect those of the U.S. Department of Education or offices within it.

CORWIN PRESS, INC.
A Sage Publications Company
Thousand Oaks, California

For information:

Corwin Press, Inc.
A Sage Publications Company
2455 Teller Road
Thousand Oaks, California 91320
E-mail: order@corwinpress.com

Sage Publications Ltd.
6 Bonhill Street
London EC2A 4PU
United Kingdom

Sage Publications India Pvt. Ltd.
M-32 Market
Greater Kailash I
New Delhi 110 048 India

Printed in the United States of America

Library of Congress Cataloging-in-Publication Data

Woodward, John.
　　Technology, curriculum, and professional development: Adapting schools
　to meet the needs of students with disabilities / by John Woodward & Larry Cuban.
　　　p.　cm.
　　Includes bibliographical references and index.
　　ISBN 0-7619-7742-2 (c) — ISBN 0-7619-7743-0 (p)
　　1. Special education—United States—Computer-assisted instruction.
　I. Cuban, Larry.　II. Title.
　LC3969.5 .W66　2000
　371.9′04334—dc21　　　　　　　　　　　　　　　00-010002

This book is printed on acid-free paper.

01　02　03　04　05　06　07　7　6　5　4　3　2　1

Editorial Assistant:	Kylee Liegl
Acquiring Editor:	Robb Clouse
Production Editor:	Diane S. Foster
Editorial Assistant:	Candice Crosetti
Designer/Typesetter:	Marion Warren/Lynn Miyata
Cover Designer:	Michelle Lee

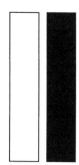

Contents

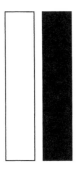

About the Editors

John Woodward is a professor in the School of Education at the University of Puget Sound in Tacoma, Washington. He received his bachelor's degree from Pomona College in Claremont, California, in 1973. He holds master's and doctoral degrees in special education from the University of Oregon in Eugene. He received his doctorate in 1985. From 1977 to 1982, he was a special education teacher at the elementary and secondary level in Kodiak, Alaska. His interest in technology began in 1980, when he had the opportunity on far too many evenings to write BASIC programs on a TRS-80 with 4 kilobytes of memory and, with occasional success, to save (and load) them on cassette tapes. That observation alone suggests that even though schools and classroom teaching may look the same after 20 years, technology seems to have made some progress.

Woodward's main professional interests include technology-based instruction, mathematics education, and school reform. He has conducted a number of research and curriculum development projects in these areas over the past 15 years. These projects have been funded by the U.S. Department of Education, Office of Special Education Programs; he is immensely grateful for their support. He has published more than 60 articles in professional journals on various topics, almost all of which address the instructional needs of students with disabilities.

Larry Cuban is a Professor of Education at Stanford University. He teaches courses in the methods of teaching social studies; the history of school reform, curriculum, and instruction; and leadership. He has been faculty sponsor of the Stanford/Schools Collaborative and Stanford's Teacher Education Program.

His background in the field of education prior to becoming a professor includes 14 years of teaching high school social studies in ghetto schools, directing a teacher education program that prepared returning Peace Corps volunteers to teach in inner-city schools, and serving 7 years as a district superintendent.

Trained as a historian, he received his bachelor's degree from the University of Pittsburgh in 1955 and his master's degree from Cleveland's Case Western Reserve University 3 years later. On completing his doctoral work at Stanford University in 1974, he assumed the superintendency of the Arlington, Virginia, public schools, a position he held until returning to Stanford in 1981. Since 1988, he has taught semester-long courses in U.S. history and economics three times in local high schools.

Cuban's major research interests focus on the history of curriculum and instruction, educational leadership, school reform, and the uses of technology in classrooms. His books include *Oversold and Underused: Reforming Schools Through Technology, 1980-2000* (in press); *How Scholars Trumped Teachers: The Paradox of Constancy and Change in University Curriculum, Research, and Teaching, 1890-1900* (1999); *Tinkering Toward Utopia: A Century of Public School Reform* (with David Tyack, 1995); *The Managerial Imperative: The Practice of Leadership in Schools* (1988); *Teachers and Machines: The Use of Classroom Technology Since 1920* (1986); *How Teachers Taught, 1890-1980* (1984); *Urban School Chiefs Under Fire* (1976); and *To Make a Difference: Teaching in the Inner City* (1970).

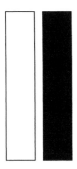

About the Contributors

Carmen Arreaga-Mayer, Ph.D., is the co-director of a Leadership Preparation Grant for Post-Doctoral Training at The Juniper Gardens Children's Project; associate research professor, Schiefelbusch Institute for Life Span Studies; and courtesy professor, Department of Special Education, University of Kansas. Her research work emphasizes the use of ecobehavioral approaches to the observational assessment of student behaviors in natural settings and the use of ClassWide Peer Tutoring procedures to increase the academic and oral engagement levels of culturally and linguistically diverse learners with and without disabilities in inclusive settings. Dr. Arreaga-Mayer serves as a consultant to a number of school districts in designing effective district and classroom options for the inclusion of special needs students.

Michael R. Benz is Professor of Special Education at the University of Oregon, involved in both teacher training and research and development activities. His areas of interest include secondary education and transition services, school-to-career systems, community development, youth at risk of school and community failure, and youth with disabilities. He is a former secondary special education teacher.

A. Edward Blackhurst is Professor Emeritus in the Department of Special Education and Rehabilitation Counseling at the University of Kentucky. He is the author of numerous articles, chapters, books, and monographs, and his 1965 article in *Exceptional Children* was the first in the professional literature to address the potential of technology for educating students with disabilities. Since that time, he has conducted seminal research on a host of technology applications in special education, including the delivery of instruction via communication satellites, computer-assisted instruction for teaching spelling and math, an expert system for selecting single-subject research designs, use of technology productivity tools to facilitate teaching, software tools to collect direct observational data, hypermedia programs for teaching about assistive technology, models for making assistive technology decisions and developing assistive technology programs in schools, and Web-based teacher preparation programs, among others. He also has directed master's, educational specialist, doctoral, and post-doctoral programs to prepare special education personnel for careers involving technology. He is Past President of the Association for Special Education Technology and the Teacher Education Division (TED) of the Council for Exceptional Children (CEC) and was the recipient of TED's Excellence in Teacher Education Award. In 1999, he received a Career Distinguished Leadership in Special Education Technology Award from the Technology and Media (TAM) Division of CEC. He continues to consult, conduct research, and write about technology topics.

Joseph Delquadri is Research Professor in the Schiefelbusch Institute for Life Span Studies at the University of Kansas and a Project Director at Juniper Gardens Children's Project. He holds academic appointments in the Departments of Special Education and Human Development. Dr. Delquadri is a former school psychologist and has an extensive record of research and program development focused on classwide peer tutoring and other curricular and instructional interventions.

Carol Sue Englert is Professor at Michigan State University in the Department of Counseling, Educational Psychology and Special Education. Her research interests include literacy instruction for students at risk for school failure with a specific focus on the examination of technology and oral discourse in literacy events, and the role of participation in a sociocultural community in the development of literacy performance. She continues to work closely with teachers to design and implement integrated literacy curricula that

emphasize the role of apprenticeship processes in multiage inclusion classrooms.

Ralph P. Ferretti is Professor of Education and Psychology at the University of Delaware. In his work, he seeks to promote students' proficiency in problem solving. Most recently, his research focuses on the design of inclusive technology-supported learning environments in the social studies.

Deborah Gallagher, Ph.D., is Associate Professor of Special Education at the University of Northern Iowa. Her research interests center on qualitative research, inclusive pedagogy, and sociological perspectives in special education.

Charles R. Greenwood, Ph.D., is Director of the Juniper Gardens Children's Project in Kansas City, KS. He is also Senior Scientist in the Institute for Life Span Studies and Courtesy Professor of Special Education and Human Development and Family Life at the University of Kansas. Previously a special education teacher, his research has focused on the development and validation of effective instructional intervention strategies for at-risk youth with and without disabilities.

Andrew S. Halpern is Professor of Education, Emeritus, at the University of Oregon. Throughout his career, he has focused on transition programs for adolescents and adults with disabilities. His research has focused on functional assessment, the design and evaluation of transition programs and curricula, and the articulation and evaluation of transition policy.

Liang-Shye Hou is Programmer/Analyst at the Juniper Gardens Children's Project (JGCP) in Kansas City, KS. With an interest in instructional and behavioral intervention electronic media development, she designs and develops software for the various research projects at the JGCP, and JGCP collaborative projects with other universities or with any other units within the Schiefelbusch Institute for Life Span Studies at the University of Kansas.

Charles A. MacArthur is Professor in the School of Education at the University of Delaware. His primary research interests are the social and cognitive processes involved in writing development, writing instruction for students with learning disabilities, and applications of technology to enhance literacy and independence.

David B. Malouf is Educational Research Analyst with the Division of Research to Practice in the Office of Special Education Programs in the U.S. Department of Education. His work currently focuses on technology for students with disabilities, research-to-practice issues, and standards-based reform and its impact on students with disabilities. He received his Ph.D. from the University of Oregon, and worked at the University of Maryland before coming to the U.S. Department of Education.

Cynthia M. Okolo is an Associate Professor and Interim Associate Director in the School of Education at the University of Delaware. She is a former special education teacher and has worked in the area of special education technology for the past 15 years. Her research program has focused on the impact of technology-based learning activities for students with mild disabilities.

Marleen C. Pugach is Professor of Teacher Education in the Department of Curriculum and Instruction at the University of Wisconsin-Milwaukee. Her scholarly interests include building collaborative relationships between special and general education teachers at the preservice and inservice levels and the intersection of inclusion and school reform. Dr. Pugach has authored and co-authored numerous books and articles, including *Collab-*

orative Practitioners, Collaborative Schools (with Lawrence Johnson). She is a principal investigator of the Title II Technology and Urban Teaching Grant at the University of Wisconsin-Milwaukee. In February 1998, Dr. Pugach received the Margaret Lindsey Award from the American Association of Colleges for Teacher Education for her contributions to research in teacher education.

Herbert J. Rieth, is Professor of Special Education and the Audrey Rogers Myers Professor in Education at the University of Texas, Austin. He received his EdD in Special Education from the University of Kansas. His research interests include analysis of the following: the impact of technology on the classroom ecology, the use of multimedia and anchored instruction on the instruction provided to students with disabilities, the adoption and diffusion of innovating, and the role and impact of technology in teacher education training programs.

Barbara J. Terry has been with the Juniper Gardens Children's Project for more than 20 years, working on many of the educational research grants in researching, developing, and evaluating programs that enhance the educational achievement of young children and students at risk. As a former elementary school teacher, Dr. Terry has always liked the area of teacher training and staff development as it relates to implementing techniques and programs that have been researched and shown to be effective. She travels the country training teachers and administrators how to implement research verified effective programs developed at JGCP.

Bonnie Todis is a Research Associate in the department of Special Education, College of Education, University of Oregon. Her area of expertise is brain injury and individuals with physical disabilities. She has conducted extensive qualitatve research in the area of augmentative technologies.

Cynthia L. Warger is principle of Warger, Eavy & Associates, a communications firm in Reston, VA, which specializes in education print and media. Dr. Warger received her Ph.D. in educational psychology from the University of Michigan. She also holds a master's degree in special education. She has taught in the public schools, directed teacher education programs at the university level, and served as an education association executive. While editor of *Teaching Exceptional Children,* she won national EdPress awards for excellence. She edits the *TAM Connector,* the newsletter of the Technology and Media Division of the Council for Exceptional Children.

Yong Zhao is Assistant Professor of Technology in Teaching and Learning at Michigan State University. His interests include design, development, and dissemination of technological innovations in educational contexts.

Judith M. Zorfass is Senior Director of Strategic Planning within Education Development Center's Center for Family, School, and Community. Since joining EDC in 1986, she has served as the project director, principal investigator, and/or technical monitor for six OSEP-funded projects focused on integrating technology into the curriculum to benefit students with disabilities. These projects have involved carrying out research, providing technical assistance, and developing online and offline products for dissemination. She is the lead author of *Make It Happen!,* a professional development approach for supporting middle school students with disabilities in technology-rich, inquiry-based learning. In addition to *Teaching Middle School Students to Be Active Researchers* (ASCD, 1998), she is the author of numerous book chapters and journal articles. She is a frequent presenter at national conferences. Her doctorate from the Harvard Graduate School of Education is in reading and language development.

Dedicated to:
David Malouf,
U.S. Department of Education,
Office of Special Education Programs
Ellen Schiller, ABT Associates

Introduction

Special Education Technology and the Field of Dreams

DAVID B. MALOUF
U.S. Department of Education,
Office of Special Education Programs

Educational researchers, innovators, and reformers tend to suffer from excessive levels of optimism. They often feel that their findings or ideas are so self-evidently beneficial that they will propel themselves into widespread and effective use in the schools, requiring only moderate levels of dissemination in practitioner-friendly formats. In a sense, this is a "Field of Dreams" view of educational change: "Produce it and they will implement."

Technology is particularly problematic in this regard because it is so compelling and has advanced so dramatically and has become such an essential component of modern life. Introducing technology into education gives the impression of innovation and effective-ness for no reason other than that technology is involved. Attention tends to be focused on the technology itself, and important aspects of appropriate implementation and proof of effectiveness are often overlooked. Furthermore, the allure of technology is unlikely to diminish anytime soon. Instead, it seems to be renewed with each new technological advancement.

Given the high expectations people have for technology, it is not surprising that millions of dollars have been spent for the acquisition and implementation of technology in schools. For students with disabilities, federal laws such as the Technology-Related Assistance for Individuals with Disabilities Act of 1988 and the 1997 Amendments to the Individuals with Disabilities Education Act (IDEA) have attempted to ensure that these students have full access to instructional and assistive technologies. For example, the 1997 amendments to IDEA introduced a provision that all teams developing individualized education programs for students with disabilities must consider whether the child requires assistive technology devices and services.

Substantial amounts of money and effort have been spent on research and development related to the use of technology with students with disabilities. In some cases, these efforts have developed and tested new products, such as assistive devices or instructional software. In other cases, these efforts have developed and tested new approaches for using existing technologies, such as word processors, multimedia, or the Internet. These efforts often have demonstrated improved educational outcomes for a sample of students and thus offer meaningful and productive ways to use technologies with these students. Disappointingly, however, there is little evidence that these efforts have engendered broad or sustained improvements for a substantial number of students or schools. Technological innovations often are abandoned as soon as the project that introduced them exits the school, and there are very few instances in which such innovations have been widely adopted or have become common practice.

Clearly, if we intend to continue exploring better ways for using technology with students with disabilities, we must be concerned not only with the effectiveness of innovations but also with their adoption and implementation. In this book, accomplished researchers in special education and technology discuss various facets of this issue. Cuban's chapter examines a number of recurrent and popular explanations for why technology is underused in education. His observations set the stage for many of the themes that appear in subsequent chapters. Woodward, Gallagher, and Rieth review the research on technology in special education and discuss the problem of studying implementation and how it might be addressed through alternative research strategies. MacArthur and Todis describe two naturalistic studies with some surprising findings about how technology is actually implemented with students with disabilities. Blackhurst discusses the key factor of professional development, and Greenwood et al. describe a classroom intervention that has evolved to incorporate technology in a meaningful way. Okolo and Ferretti, Zorfass, Englert and Zhao, and Halpern and Benz reflect on their current and past work, focusing particularly on the implementation and sustainability of their innovations. Finally, Pugach and Warger's chapter aptly summarizes the main points from each of the book's contributors and puts these points in the broader context of curricular and technological reform for students with disabilities.

There are two primary audiences for this book. One comprises persons involved in the implementation of technology with students with disabilities, including teachers, administrators, and policymakers. For this audience, the book highlights some important considerations for making technology implementation meaningful and enduring. A second audience includes researchers and developers working in the area of technology for students with disabilities. For this audience, the book suggests important design considerations and provides ideas for giving research a more powerful voice by expanding its vocabulary of real-world implementation.

Special education technology will never be a field of dreams in which innovations can be cast to the winds to find widespread and meaningful implementation. Scaling up and sustaining these innovations always will be a challenging job, but one that also promises possibilities.

ONE

No Easy Answer

The Instructional Effectiveness of Technology for Students With Disabilities

JOHN WOODWARD
University of Puget Sound

DEBORAH GALLAGHER
University of Northern Iowa

HERBERT RIETH
University of Texas at Austin

A natural starting point for thinking about the use of technology in special education settings—or, for that matter, in all educational settings—is its impact on student learning. There are, after all, other significant ways in which technology is used in special education, from routine administrative tasks and individualized education plan (IEP) management to novel attempts to use expert systems for diagnosis and qualification for services (Cuban, 1993; Hofmeister, 1986; Hofmeister & Ferrara, 1986). However, finding ways to improve learning for students is the predominant focus for most educators.

One key reason for this focus on student learning has to do with the way some technologists conceptualized the use of microcomputers when they first appeared on a large scale in the early 1980s. Bork (1981), Papert (1980), and others offered dramatic visions of how microcomputers could change education and move students toward much deeper levels of critical and creative thinking than what traditional instruction typically provided. A similar level of enthusiasm for microcomputer-based education was apparent in the special education literature at the time (e.g., Hofmeister, 1984). Microworld simulations, LOGO, and the initial promise of artificial intelligence all fueled the hope that the microcomputer and other technologies would transform learning for all students. This kind of hopeful thinking about technology-based instruction persists today in some quarters, due in large measure to the increasing availability and power of microcomputers and other technological devices, as well as to the growing influence of constructivist theories of learning and instruction (e.g., Cognition and Technology Group at Vanderbilt University, 1997; Jonassen, 1999).

Virtually anyone remotely familiar with the evolution of microcomputer use in education over the past 20 years is aware of the fact that these lofty visions have not been met. At the same time, the actual uses of technology are much more varied than originally anticipated. Cuban (1993) characterized the kind of thinking during the early 1980s as a "technophile's" vision of education. He argues that radical, transformative attempts to break outside of traditionally inflexible patterns of teaching are unlikely given the way schools have been structured historically. Factors such as age-graded classrooms, the segmentation of knowledge into skills and specific content areas, and deep-seated assumptions about the educational process (e.g., teaching is telling, learning is listening) greatly inhibit innovation in schools.

Most certainly, there is an enormous gulf between the possibilities for how computers could be used to advance learning and the mundane ways in which they have been used by students in schools over the past 20 years. This is a legitimate topic of concern and criticism in its own right, and Cuban, among others, has addressed this issue in critical and thoughtful ways over the past 15 years. More germane to the intent of this book, however, are the surprisingly varied ways in which spe-

cial educators actually have researched the instructional uses of technology. Some of their efforts have been predictable and in keeping with mainstream instructional uses of computers (e.g., computer-assisted instruction, or CAI). Other efforts, such as the use of expert systems for ongoing assessment, have been novel.

The purpose of this chapter is to describe thematically—and, to some extent, historically—research into the instructional uses of technology in special education over the past 20 years. We draw on a wide range of professional literature to make more coherent and comprehensible what initially may appear to be splintered visions of instructional technology research in special education. In the first section of this chapter, we review the complex ways in which technology has been used for teaching basic skills. The educational technology literature often refers to this as using the computer as a "tutor," and CAI is the most common type of software employed for this purpose.

In the second section of this chapter, we continue our review of the instructional uses of computers with special education students, but with a focus on assessment. In particular, we describe attempts to develop computer-based diagnostic systems to help teachers assess student performance in an ongoing fashion. These efforts generally have been ignored in previous summaries of the research literature on special education technology because they fall outside the tutoring conception of computer use. This point becomes apparent shortly in our discussion of past reviews of special education technology research.

The third section describes sobering findings from naturalistic research on how practitioners and students have used computers for instructional purposes. These findings are important for many reasons, not the least of which is the reminder that there is often a significant gap between the researchers' intentions and intuitions of how technology should be used and those of practitioners and students. These findings have implications for a range of technology uses, from augmentative devices, as described by Bonnie Todis (Chapter 2, this volume), to assessment and instruction.

The final section of the chapter builds, in part, on the third section and describes the importance of conducting research in a way that is more sensitive to the world of the practitioner. This kind of research requires a broader vision of technology (e.g., a less dominant role for computers, the additional need for innovative curriculum and pedagogy) and, in many cases, a different disposition toward research itself; that is, investigators often need to go beyond the traditional, experimental approach to research to capture the subtle ways in which innovative methods and materials affect a classroom environment. We argue that changes in methodology are an important step in understanding how technology and innovative methods (curriculum and/or pedagogy) can improve instruction for students with disabilities.

Past Reviews of Technology Research in Special Education

Attempts to summarize the effectiveness of technology in special education have appeared periodically over the past 15 years. This review of technology research differs from those of the past because it takes a broader view of what instructional use of technology means. For the most part, the studies included in past reviews involve the assumption that technology's primary use was to teach content material or basic skills; that is, in those studies, technology was used as an electronic tutor, and the software was best categorized as CAI. Furthermore, past research reviews have used either meta-analytic techniques or broad, thematic approaches to the literature on technology use for students with disabilities.

For example, Schmidt, Weinstein, Niemic, and Walberg (1985) cited a number of problems with the extant CAI research (e.g., anecdotal or poorly written results, use of single-subject as well as group designs); nonetheless, they conducted a meta-analysis of a subset of that literature. Their meta-analysis, which generally supported CAI as a means of increasing academic performance for students with disabilities, was based on global comparisons of CAI and traditional forms of instruction. McDermid (1989) presented a similar analysis of the literature and also highlighted the substandard nature of many research reports of the time.

Ellis and Sabornie (1986) employed another method of research synthesis, one that has continued until today. They organized their synthesis of the technology literature thematically. Specifically, they delineated a series of "promises" that reflected hypotheses or expectations for CAI that either were explicit in individual studies or were widely held beliefs about the potential benefits of technology use in special education. More recently, Shiah, Mastropieri, and Scruggs (1995) used content areas as a framework for reviewing CAI studies. They examined the impact of CAI on mathematics, spelling, reading, and other subject areas. The findings, although mixed, generally supported the potential of CAI for raising academic achievement. Fitzgerald and Koury (1996) offered a similar review of the literature on students with mild and moderate disabilities.

Although these research syntheses may help illuminate the extent to which CAI is effective, they also reflect three fundamental problems. First, as Okolo, Bahr, and Rieth (1993) noted, many meta-analyses and research syntheses (e.g., McDermid, 1989; Schmidt et al., 1985) offer comparisons that are too global in scope. There is a confound between medium and instructional principles, one that Clark (1983) described in a widely cited critique of media research. This problem is apparent in many of the early CAI studies (e.g., McDermott & Watkins, 1983) in which researchers implied that the medium alone can produce significant instructional or cognitive benefits. This issue is compounded further in studies in which the technology incorporates multiple curriculum design variables that, in turn, are contrasted with traditional instructional methods (e.g., Horton, Lovitt, & Slocum, 1988; Kelly, Gersten, & Carnine, 1990; Moore & Carnine, 1989). As Clark argues, it is not the medium but the curriculum design principles embedded in the software that are more likely to contribute to any academic outcomes that favor technology use. Past literature syntheses generally have not explored this confound.

A second and more subtle problem involves the underlying hypothesis in most studies that CAI should lead to cognitive gains that are superior to traditional instructional methods. This is particularly apparent in the thematic treatments of the technology literature. Yet research, particularly when it is conducted under somewhat naturalistic conditions, may result in nonsignificant findings for a variety of reasons, from the fidelity of implementation to weak research designs. In addition, other explanations—not substantively explored in previous research syntheses—may pertain.

Okolo et al. (1993) offer a concise rebuttal to the assumption that there should be superior cognitive gains as a result of technology-based instruction: "Because students with disabilities can be expected to learn at slower rates, have longer histories of academic failure, and need more intensive instruction than their non-disabled peers, short-term interventions hardly can be expected to produce significant changes" (p. 4). The expectation, then, of significant changes in academic performance may not be well founded given that many students with disabilities by definition exhibit profound learning difficulties and that their progress over time is highly irregular. Systematically examining the literature for "box score" gains may overestimate implicitly the potential effects of CAI for this population of students. Furthermore, such analyses unintentionally may ignore other benefits to CAI for students with disabilities (e.g., improved motivation).

Finally, most reviews of technology research in special education ignore research in

which the technology is used in assessment, rather than instruction; that is, there have been studies in which traditional teaching comprised the experimental intervention, but a computer diagnostic system was used to help teachers make instructional decisions (e.g., stay with the program, change instructional approaches).

For all of these reasons, we have opted to use broader parameters in our review of the instructional uses of technology. The following section reviews instructional effectiveness research in special education technology in a historical manner. We trace the evolution of technology research from studies that contrasted CAI with traditional, teacher-directed instruction to studies with more discrete focuses. The latter research generally examines the effects of specific instructional variables embedded in CAI programs, such as feedback, explicit strategies, and motivation (e.g., the role of games). This section concludes with a discussion of attempts to use technology more comprehensively for whole-class instruction.

Technology as Tutor

Comparisons to Traditional Instruction

It can be argued that much of the early CAI research in special education was guided by a common logic: Machines have an immense potential for providing the extensive and highly individualized practice that students with disabilities need to learn basic skills. After all, the remedial and special education literature abounds with a number of effective interventions, such as direct instruction (Becker, 1977; Englert, 1984), peer tutoring (Delquadri, Greenwood, Whorton, Carta, & Hall, 1986; Fuchs, Fuchs, Bentz, Phillips, & Hamlett, 1994), and cooperative learning (Johnson & Johnson, 1986; Stevens & Slavin, 1991). Yet each of these methods tends to be labor-intensive and requires added teacher training. When microcomputers were introduced in the late 1970s, CAI held the promise of providing the intensive, individualized remediation for students with disabilities and to be less demanding of teachers' time and training.

Many studies conducted throughout the 1980s attempted to determine whether CAI was a complete or "stand-alone" instructional delivery system, or if some form of explicit teacher guidance, supervision, or direct instruction was also needed. This was seen as a particularly important issue if CAI was to do more than drill students on low-level skills such as math facts or spelling words. Empirical support for computer programs that could tutor students with disabilities successfully in areas ranging from logic to geography or health education was critical, given the range of academic subjects special education teachers are expected to teach and the typically limited content preparation these individuals receive in their preservice education (see Cawley, 1994).

The study by McDermott and Watkins (1983) of commercial CAI math and spelling programs typifies the early comparisons between CAI on microcomputers and traditional textbook instruction. In that yearlong study, 205 elementary school students with learning disabilities were taught with CAI spelling, CAI math, or conventional methods. Results on two norm-referenced measures indicated no significant effects for CAI, perhaps due to the overall quality of the software programs.

Contrasts between technology and traditional teaching persisted into the 1990s. In particular, Higgins and Boone (1990) looked at how hypermedia, a new form of software, could be used as an integral part of content area instruction. They reported successful results for hypermedia study guides in a comparison of lecture, lecture and hypertext study guide, and hypertext study guide alone conditions. The hypertext study guide that accompanied the Washington State history text incorporated typical branching methods (e.g., buttons linked to graphic displays, vocabulary terms defined on a separate window). The authors have employed hypermedia as a supplement to reading texts in two other studies (Boone & Higgins, 1993; Higgins & Boone, 1991) in which traditional norm-referenced measures were used as key dependent measures. In each case, results generally supported the use of hypermedia as an instructional aide.

Although other broad comparisons of CAI and conventional instruction for students with disabilities have been done since the early 1980s (e.g., Lally, 1981; Podell, Tournaki-Rein, & Lin, 1992; Van Laarhoven, 1996; Watkins, 1989), their numbers have diminished, in part because of Clark's (1983) critique of media research. In some of the studies (e.g., McDermott & Watkins, 1983), the impact of the media may have been overestimated, hence Clark's observation that media are only delivery systems pertains. In other studies, where researchers were more explicitly concerned with instructional design variables, it also has been suggested that the medium (e.g., CAI, hypertext) contributed to outcomes that generally favored technology-based instruction. Consequently, there has been a substantial confound between the reputed benefits of the media and format or instructional design features that also have varied across experimental and comparison conditions. These problems typically have been overlooked in previous research syntheses on special education technology.

A further problem with traditional comparisons between CAI and conventional instruction concerns the quality of the software used in the research. Special education technologists (e.g., Hofmeister, 1984) at the time criticized the low quality of early commercial CAI programs, citing their lack of attention to such important instructional design variables as the careful selection of examples, the quantity and type of feedback, and the use of cumulative review procedures. Special education curriculum designers felt that these variables could affect positively academic outcomes for students with disabilities. Subsequent studies comparing CAI and traditional instruction have examined more thoroughly the specific instructional design variables used in software programs (e.g., Kelly, Gersten, & Carnine, 1990; Moore & Carnine, 1989). Even though these studies do little to transcend the confound between technology and curriculum, they do exemplify the move in the research toward a closer examination of curriculum design variables and their impact on learning.

Curriculum Design and
Its Impact on Learning

By the mid-1980s, the dissatisfaction of special education researchers with the limited range of software and its overall quality was apparent. Consequently, many researchers turned to a well-articulated body of process-product and instructional design principles that they then used in CAI development and research. In many instances, researchers applied principles that typically were used in highly behavioral, task-analytic approaches to instruction (Engelmann & Carnine, 1982; Gagné, Briggs, & Wager, 1988; Woodward et al., 1986).

Other researchers approached the design of technology-based instruction from an information processing framework. Explicit techniques for controlled practice and feedback on basic skills were viewed as helping to develop automaticity, which in turn allows students to devote more cognitive resources to comprehension or problem solving (Goldman & Pellegrino, 1987; Hasselbring, Goin, & Bransford, 1988; Lesgold & Resnick, 1982).

Thus research from the mid-1980s through the early 1990s examined the impact of discrete variables, such as feedback, massed and distributed practice, and explicit cognitive strategies. In a wider sense, the research also examined motivation because of its direct relation to drill and practice programs. CAI programs allowed researchers to explore these variables, often under highly controlled conditions in which students in the experimental and comparison conditions used modified versions of the same CAI program. Special education technology researchers (e.g.,

Carnine, 1989) noted that in instances in which the medium did vary, it was the specific instructional design principles rather than the medium (i.e., not the CAI or the textbook) that contributed to any significant differences in outcomes. These studies clearly attempted to address Clark's (1983) observations regarding media as a confounding variable in instructional technology research.

This focus on instructional design variables was an important phase in special education technology research. Identifying the impact of critical instructional variables had potentially significant implications because these features could be added to or subtracted from CAI programs for students with disabilities. At the very least, many at the time thought that the features could comprise important criteria for judging the overall quality of a software program and that these criteria, in turn, could influence the design of commercial software for students with disabilities.

Feedback

Nontechnology-based research in special education long has pointed to various forms of feedback as a critical instructional design variable for students with disabilities. *Feedback* has connoted either redundant information (e.g., visual prompts, verbal cuing) or immediate corrective feedback (e.g., "correct/incorrect," "right/try again"). Research syntheses by Bangert-Drowns, Kulik, Kulik, and Morgan (1991) and Lysakowski and Walberg (1982) supported the use of even more detailed forms of feedback. For example, these researchers argued that strategic feedback—briefly reviewing the steps or strategies for answering a question or completing an algorithm—was a more effective way of reducing errors and helping students master skills than was merely telling students the correct answer.

Feedback as Redundant Information. Torgesen and his colleagues (Torgesen, Waters, Cohen, & Torgesen, 1988) conducted a series of studies on the effects of speech synthesis as a form of feedback. They were particularly interested in the different informational attributes of microcomputers (i.e., graphics, sound, and text) and their effects on the beginning decoding process in reading.

Torgesen et al. (1988) found that students taught decoding with three different computer presentations—visual only (pictorial representation of the word and word), audiovisual (pictorial representation, synthesized pronunciation of the word, and word), and audio only (synthesized pronunciation of the word and word)—showed comparable improvements in levels of speed and accuracy, at least when contrasted with a no-treatment condition. Moreover, the number of sessions required to achieve word mastery was similar. Other reading studies (e.g., Jones, Torgesen, & Sexton, 1987; Wise & Olson, 1994) generally have supported the view that synthesized speech can help students learn how to segment words.

These studies have implications for hypertext and multimedia. Although added sources of information (e.g., graphics, definitions, background text on separate windows) through dynamic links may be available to students, there is no reason to believe that these options will be employed consistently, if at all. How students actually use hypermedia is an underinvestigated research topic in special education.

Simple Feedback. Using the computer for simple corrective feedback also has produced mixed results. For low-level skills such as memorizing spelling words, research (MacArthur, Haynes, Harris, & Owings, 1990) has shown that immediate "correct-incorrect" feedback is more effective than if students receive delayed feedback either at the end of the lesson or the next day. In these studies, CAI also led to higher rates of on-task or student engagement. Other studies (e.g., Howell, Sidorenko, & Jurica, 1987; Lin, Podell, & Rein, 1991) contradict the reputed value of computer-based feedback, suggesting that for simple declarative knowledge tasks such as

memorizing vocabulary words or math facts, human tutors are more sensitive to individual needs. In these CAI studies, tutors were able to offer more precise, task-specific feedback and were capable of maintaining higher levels of engagement during drill and practice sessions.

Complex Feedback. The extent to which computers can be an effective mechanism for providing more complex forms of feedback is equally mixed and appears to be contingent on the nature of the task. For simple tasks, attempts to increase efficacy and self-esteem through positive attributions (e.g., "You are really trying hard," "You really know these") may be undercut by instruction that is initially or even progressively tailored to a student's level of competence.

Collins, Carnine, and Gersten (1987), on the other hand, found complex or strategic feedback to be highly effective in teaching secondary students with learning disabilities how to draw conclusions from two statements of evidence and how to determine whether a three-statement syllogism was logically correct or incorrect. In that case, the researchers modified the type of feedback and kept all other instructional features the same. Elaborate feedback for errors (i.e., feedback that gave the correct answer and reminded of the reason or strategy for determining that answer) was much more effective than simple, "right-wrong" feedback. For a challenging, if not artificial, task like syllogistic logic, complex feedback may be an effective variable for increasing student achievement.

Massed and Distributed Practice

Another instructional design variable directly related to systematic basic skills practice has to do with the quantity and distribution of new information. As cognitive psychologists and educators (Anderson, 1983; Pellegrino & Goldman, 1987) have argued, automaticity in basic skills allows limited cognitive resources to be devoted to other, more complex tasks. Hasselbring et al.'s (1988) CAI addition fact program exemplifies how computers can be used to regulate the structure of basic skills practice.

In Hasselbring et al.'s (1988) program, the student is first pretested on the range of math facts. Once the unknown pool of facts is established, the program gradually introduces more difficult facts as determined by the size of the addends. The amount of practice on new facts is carefully controlled—no more than two new facts and their reversals at any one time. Finally, practice is systematic, with new or target facts interspersed with known facts. Research using commercial software in which these features are missing suggests that students are more likely to retain alternative, inefficient strategies such as counting rather than direct retrieval of math facts (Bahr & Rieth, 1989).

Similar studies involving researcher-developed CAI programs in which the material is systematically reviewed over time have been conducted in vocabulary (Johnson, Gersten, & Carnine, 1987), social studies (Gleason, Carnine, & Vala, 1991), and spelling (Stevens, Blackhurst, & Slator, 1991). Results strongly support the use of both massed and distributed practice.

Explicit Strategies

When students engage in tasks beyond the rote drill and practice level, it is essential that they use some form of metacognitive planning, evaluation, and monitoring. Unfortunately, these are distinct areas of weakness for students with learning disabilities (Pressley, Goodchild, Fleet, Zajchowski, & Evans, 1989; Swanson, 1989; Wong, 1993). A general inability to mediate instruction has led special educators to advocate a variety of strategy instruction techniques, from broadly applicable metacognitive strategies to strategies that are highly content-specific. Despite the diverse interpretations of strategy instruction in the literature, special educators generally agree that strategies need to be taught

explicitly, and that successful instruction requires focused practice and long-term follow-up. Explicit strategy instruction has characterized a portion of the special education technology research, and, like the broader debate in the field, the studies cover the range of strategy orientations, from highly task-specific to more generalized approaches.

Woodward and his colleagues (Hollingsworth & Woodward, 1993; Woodward, Carnine, & Gersten, 1988) examined the extent to which more generalized metacognitive strategies for monitoring and planning could be linked to health education using a computer simulation. In both studies, the researchers taught students a set of strategies so that they could succeed at an array of health simulation games. The games required a mix of general "management" strategies (e.g., control stress while changing a habit such as diet or alcohol consumption) and the application of relevant declarative knowledge (e.g., lower cholesterol by reducing your intake of dairy products). In pilot tests, the researchers found that without the guiding strategies, the games were too difficult for secondary students with learning disabilities. However, in both studies, students were able to apply their problem-solving strategies to exercises (videotape vignettes in one case) that were related closely to what they were taught during the interventions.

Explicit strategy instruction for reading and writing requires even broader, more flexible strategies than those described previously. In reading, particularly in content area materials, students are taught a variety of comprehension monitoring strategies that include note taking, generating and/or answering text-embedded questions, and using glossaries and dictionaries. MacArthur and Haynes (1995) designed a software system that contained all of these features and others (e.g., speech synthesis). Separate windows contained text outlines, pictures, and a mini word processor for note taking. They found that students rated the highlighting of main ideas and questions linked to the text as the most helpful features of the program, whereas speech synthesis was viewed as only moderately helpful. Research on this system to date has been limited, and their work does not fully reflect the program's possible integration with teacher-directed instruction in these reading strategies.

Motivation

Although students with learning disabilities are generally acknowledged to have significant deficits in basic skills, special educators (Deci & Chandler, 1986; Okolo, 1992) also note that motivation is a key factor that influences their performance. Ensuring that students will benefit from the discrete instructional design variables mentioned previously and attain high levels of proficiency in a CAI environment, then, is contingent on their active engagement, which becomes even more important in computer lab settings, where it is difficult for a teacher to monitor individual students successfully (Rieth, Bahr, Okolo, Polsgrove, & Eckert, 1988). Thus there have been a series of studies exploring the motivational effects of arcade-like games on the acquisition of math facts and vocabulary words.

Christensen and Gerber (1990) compared a popular math CAI drill-and-practice arcade program with an experimenter-developed, nonarcade program containing addition math facts and, like its commercial counterpart, simple corrective feedback. Although all students showed considerable gains over the course of the study, those students who used the nonarcade program showed the greatest gains. Researchers also found that students in the experimental group practiced significantly more problems than did the arcade group.

These results are consistent with other studies (Axelrod, McGregor, Sherman, & Hamlet, 1987; Chiang, 1986) that have indicated that arcade games create extraneous distractions and that such entertaining learning environments come at the expense of potential increases in learning. Bahr and Rieth (1989), in a study of multiplication drill-and-practice arcade games, also found that games had little effect, in part because they were not incorporated into regular classroom instruction. These studies suggest that arcade games compete for time and attention in the context of drill and practice. Under carefully supervised conditions, arcade games seem to detract from the high amounts of practice required of students with disabilities to master target skills.

Technology for Whole-Class Instruction

A logical culmination of the work on curriculum design principles was its incorporation into videodisc programs that could be used with an entire classroom of students. After all, the microcomputers of the 1980s through the mid-1990s were much less powerful than those today, and there was no World Wide Web to extend their capacities. Orchestrating classroom instruction around a relatively scarce number of microcomputers, even if there was appropriate software, was logistically difficult.

With their rich graphic and storage capabilities, videodiscs offered a dramatic alternative to microcomputers. One videodisc could store approximately one half hour of continuous video or 54,000 still frames per side and provide programs that could be used with an entire group of students in a classroom. This storage and presentational capacity well exceeded anything that could have been done on a typical microcomputer at the time. Furthermore, the opportunity to use a videodisc player and large-screen monitor with an entire classroom of students helped solve the logistical and supervisory problems commonly associated with computer labs.

In the late 1980s, a small group of research and curriculum developers (Hofmeister, Engelmann, & Carnine, 1989; Hofmeister & Thorkildsen, 1989) created a series of commercial videodisc programs in the areas of math and science known as the *Core Concepts* programs (Systems Impact, 1985, 1987a,

1987b). The developers encoded into their programs those instructional design variables investigated in previous CAI research (e.g., simple and strategic feedback, massed and distributed practice, explicit strategies) as well as an array of additional behavioral instructional design variables (e.g., hierarchical task analysis of concepts, a careful selection of examples for teaching a concept, graphical cues that highlighted relevant properties of the stimulus). This resulted in complete instructional programs in traditional secondary topics in mathematics (e.g., fractions, decimals, ratios, algebraic equations), earth science, and chemistry.

Experimental research on these videodisc programs with secondary students with learning disabilities generally supported the "packaging" of the instructional design features incorporated into the programs. Manufacturing costs, among other reasons, did not permit researchers to modify the videodisc programs so that just a single variable could be studied, as had been done in earlier microcomputer research. However, the studies on students with disabilities also typically involved media contrasts (e.g., videodisc vs. textbook instruction) and a focus on different instructional design variables. For example, in studies of secondary and adult students with learning disabilities (Kelly et al., 1990; Kitz & Thorpe, 1992; Moore & Carnine, 1989), videodisc math programs were compared to traditional texts that often were modified to provide additional computation or word problems. Results on dependent measures, ones that were closely aligned to the videodisc curricula, generally supported the instructional design features of the various programs. In the end, however, the increased complexity of the medium and its "fixed format" resulted in many studies that had the same problematic contrasts between traditional print and technology-based approaches that Clark (1983) noted.

Taken as a whole, these videodisc programs and the related research represented the culmination of almost two decades of work in developing highly prescriptive print

and computer-based curricula. Developers directed not only the content of the courseware but also the sequence of the topics and the pedagogical strategies. Research studies that began in the Direct Instruction Model in Project Follow Through (Becker, 1977) finally were distilled in a series of videodisc programs. Moreover, these highly detailed, step-by-step approaches to skill development epitomized traditional instructional methods in remedial and special education.

Technology-Based Assessment

A central feature of the special educator's job in instruction is to ensure student progress toward specific instructional goals or objectives. Ultimately, this involves goals that are stated in IEPs. Over the past 15 years, a variety of technology-based programs have been developed to help teachers assess students more frequently and, at times, to probe student understanding in highly sophisticated ways. Typically, these efforts have been excluded from syntheses of technology research in special education. In all likelihood, this is due to the fact that the computer was not used directly as a tutor.

The main rationale for technology-based assessment was similar to the one used for the computer as an electronic tutor. Researchers argued that technology was the perfect vehicle for orchestrating reliable, high-quality assessment and that it would reduce dramatically the amount of time required to manage the assessment process (Greenwood & Rieth, 1994).

Ongoing Assessment

Through rapid developments in hardware and software, particularly expert systems, special education technologists also have developed ongoing assessment systems that track student progress on a daily basis. More recent systems have attempted to model student understanding, a long-standing concern of artificial intelligence research in education (Wenger, 1987).

Curriculum-Based Measurement. Researchers have used computers as a means for frequently assessing skills and transforming data into a detailed picture of student progress. Curriculum-based measurement (CBM) (Deno, 1985; Fuchs, Fuchs, & Hamlett, 1993) offers a dramatic alternative to traditional conceptions of instructional technology in special education. Rather than encode instructional design variables into CAI or videodisc programs, CBM attempts to help teachers modify day-to-day instruction based on the results of systematic assessment procedures. Teachers administer skills tests or probes, ones that sample student performance from a domain of items reflecting the student's academic program for the year, on a frequent basis. CBM computer programs present these tests on the computer (or print them on paper), analyze the results, graphically depict progress, and advise teachers when and how to modify instruction to meet individual needs (Fuchs et al., 1993).

CBM is based on a task-analytic, behavioral model of learning. Computer displays present an upward sloping growth line that projects the course of student progress on probes over time. If the computer detects a plateau or significant trend that departs from this line of progress, the program alerts the teacher and, in more recent versions, suggests instructional remedies.

Current computerized versions of CBM reflect a history of effort by a select group of special education researchers who generally have been dissatisfied with traditional diagnostic testing for placement in special education and with the tendency to continue current instruction regardless of the ongoing success level of the student (Deno, 1990; Fuchs & Fuchs, 1984, 1986). In terms of instructional interventions, CBM researchers have argued that because a student's academic history involves so much failure, teachers should be cautious in using only one approach or pro-

gram, even if it is empirically validated. Again, this view is in marked contrast to the CAI and videodisc technology efforts described previously.

Computer-based versions of CBM were developed because attempts at encouraging teachers to use some form of frequent, systematic measurement were deemed too labor-intensive (Wesson, Fuchs, Tindal, Mirkin, & Deno, 1986). The earliest computer versions of CBM simply stored, graphed, and analyzed data that had been entered by each teacher after formative measures had been prepared, administered, and scored. Even though research on these systems (Fuchs, Fuchs, Hamlett, & Hasselbring, 1987) suggested that there was little to no time savings over doing this work by hand, teachers generally preferred the computer version of CBM. Enhanced versions of these CBM systems virtually eliminated teacher administration or scoring of student performance data. Students took the tests at the computer (Fuchs, Hamlett, Fuchs, Stecker, & Ferguson, 1987), and the program performed the analyses automatically.

Even more recent versions of computerized CBM have added detailed skills analyses and instructional recommendations for teachers. This was done largely because teachers were still unable to translate frequent assessment results into effective instructional programs (Fuchs et al., 1993). In current programs, skill performance in a particular domain (e.g., math facts, concepts, procedures) is broken down and rated across five categories from *mastered* to *not attempted*. Each probe updates a student's profile and adjusts the rating (e.g., improvement in borrowing may change from *partially mastered* to *probably mastered*) (Fuchs, Fuchs, & Hamlett, 1989; Fuchs, Fuchs, Hamlett, & Stecker, 1990).

Expert systems have enabled CBM researchers (Fuchs, Fuchs, Hamlett, & Ferguson, 1992; Fuchs, Fuchs, Hamlett, & Stecker, 1991) to specify in detail instructional remediation procedures. Previous research (Fuchs, Fuchs, Bishop, & Simmons, 1992) indicated that teachers generally reteach skills using the same instructional method and are unable to present content using different methods that may be more beneficial to individual students. Thus, expert system programs in reading, math, and spelling offered teachers detailed prescriptions. Academic gains, at least measured by CBM probes, supported the computerized prescriptions in most academic areas (Fuchs et al., 1993).

The most recent use of computerized CBM is to monitor entire group performance, with close attention to the lowest 25th percentile group. This form of CBM was devised to manage whole-class instruction, particularly in mainstreamed settings. The CBM program suggests a range of instructional remediation strategies, from CAI to peer tutoring for specific skill development (Fuchs et al., 1993).

Modeling Student Understanding. In contrast to the CBM approach, other researchers working in the area of computer-based assessment have developed interactive programs using a cognitive framework. Rather than survey and track competence on a range of skills, these programs are designed to probe systematically more deeply into one domain. They developed around the assumption that students often exhibit persistent errors because of subtle misconceptions, and that progress through a curriculum does not follow a linear pattern.

Gerber, Semmel, and Semmel's (1994) DynaMath program, which is rooted in dynamic assessment techniques, probes student competence in multiplication through a graduated series of prompts. The program audibly alerts the student to discrete errors, graphically noting the position of the error. At the highest level of prompting, the solution steps in a procedure or subprocedure are modeled in an animated sequence. Over time, student responses are profiled in a database, which in turn affects the generation of new problems. Case study research suggests that the program carefully controls for difficulty, at least as it is measured by procedural complexity. Gerber et al.'s system offers teachers an in-depth analysis of student performance

(e.g., a detailed sensitivity to multiplication problems that are closest to the student's zone of proximal development) as well as specific instructional objectives.

Woodward and Howard's (1994) TORUS program followed a more traditional model based on the artificial intelligence research of Brown and Burton (1978) and Van Lehn (1990). Although TORUS emulated many of the features in Brown and Burton's Buggy system (e.g., student answers are compared to computer analyses of missed problems, a database of errors or bugs is accessed to determine diagnoses), the core of the program was based on a commercial expert system. As with other uses of expert systems in special education, the developers were able to modify and tailor their system to empirical conditions (e.g., the bugs as they are documented through human analyses) and the needs of teachers (e.g., reports that contain certain kinds of information). Field research (Woodward, 1992) indicated TORUS reliably detects misconceptions and identifies difficulties undetected by other computer-based diagnostic programs such as CBM programs.

Although many of these assessment programs were prototypic in nature, they reflected an unexpected evolution in the thinking of how computers could be used to enhance instruction. And even though they may not exemplify the kind of transformative use of computers that the enthusiasts of the early 1980s envisioned, they are clearly novel departures from the tutoring model of computer use. Yet as both the tutoring and assessment dimensions of technology research advanced in the 1990s, naturalistic research began to call into question whether any of these programs would be used in the way researchers designed them.

Naturalistic Research

As we intimated at the beginning of this chapter, the lofty visions of how technology could be used in education as tools for fostering more critical and creative thinking have not been met. One simple but profound way of validating this point can be found in the survey research conducted in the 1980s. In an era when visionaries were prescribing the use of microworlds and problem-solving software, surveys consistently indicated that students with disabilities spent a considerable amount of time merely working on drill-and-practice programs (Christensen & Cosden, 1986; Cosden, Gerber, Goldman, Semmel, & Semmel, 1986; Cosden, Gerber, Semmel, Goldman, & Semmel, 1987; Cosden & Lieber, 1986).

A large-scale study of elementary school students with mild disabilities conducted in 52 Southern California districts using stratified random sampling suggested that students in pullout or special day classes tended to work on computers in their special education classrooms rather than in mainstreamed settings or school labs (Christensen & Cosden, 1986; Cosden et al., 1986; Cosden & Lieber, 1986; Cosden et al., 1987). Unlike mainstreamed students with learning disabilities, these students tended to work on computers by themselves rather than in small groups.

Regardless of setting, however, students with mild disabilities tended to spend much more time working on drill-and-practice programs than did their nondisabled peers. The data also suggested a discontinuity between the CAI software and the content being studied away from the computers (Cosden & Abernathy, 1990). In other words, what teachers taught students using traditional methods bore little relation to the content in the students' CAI programs. In a longitudinal study conducted with many of the same schools that participated in the original study, these patterns persisted over time (Cosden & Semmel, 1987).

A survey of special educators (Cosden, 1988) revealed that teachers generally felt that students showed increases in basic skills when using commercial programs. This was true even though the teachers had a difficult time judging that students benefited the most from these activities—largely due to their inability to measure the benefits of CAI, as well as their unfamiliarity with relatively new software programs. It should be noted that the teachers also expressed frustration with the quality of available software. Nonetheless, these teachers not only rated the drill and practice to be effective, but they also felt that microcomputer use had a considerable and positive effect on student motivation and self-esteem.

Neuman (1991) offered a deeper, if not more disquieting, analysis of how students interact with computers in her qualitative account of computer use at a middle school for students with learning disabilities. Over the course of 6 months, Neuman found an alarming number of barriers faced by students when using commercial software programs, from not understanding teacher directions for gaining access to courseware to an inability to read information on the computer displays. In fact, students generally disliked reading from the screen and deduced other ways to accomplish what the program required. It was common for students to approach even the most routine drill-and-practice programs in a competitive fashion, a disposition presumably based on their wider experience with computer games. Students challenged others, gave themselves pep talks, introduced artificial time constraints, and figured out ways to reset programs to avoid penalties that resulted in lower scores.

Neuman's research highlights the erratic ways that students with learning disabilities employ metacognition. As has been noted in other qualitative research (Rueda & Mehan, 1986), students with disabilities appear more than capable of "working around" barriers or natural constraints and, at times, of effectively subverting the direct intentions of a curriculum.

In another study of computer use (MacArthur & Malouf, 1991), the gap between what special education technology researchers advocate and what teachers do (and believe) in their day-to-day practice was equally revealing. In three case studies, these researchers found that teachers used computers largely for motivation and to improve student self-esteem, not necessarily to raise academic achievement. Because these teachers generally used an extensive amount of individualized, independent seatwork in their everyday classroom routines, it was natural for them to fit computer use into an individualized format. But the teachers also were casual in the way they assigned drill-and-practice activities on the computer, leaving students, at times, to work on inappropriate content. In part, this was due to the logistical problems of reviewing software. Teachers consistently found it much easier to skim a workbook and determine whether the skills were appropriate than to review software programs. Thus, teachers rationalized computer work largely around its potential benefits for motivation and self-esteem.

Despite specific technology training, teachers still tend to exhibit uneven patterns of use. Bahr, Kinzer, and Rieth (1991) found in a reading comprehension study that even after explicit training, teachers found it difficult to integrate prequestion strategies for passages displayed on a computer screen. Woodward's (1993) analysis of the *Core Concepts* videodisc research indicated that teachers varied widely in how they used the programs once the formal studies ended. In one naturalistic study (Woodward & Gersten, 1992) in which eight teachers enthusiastically responded to the program, only one requested to use it the following year. In other studies (Kelly et al., 1990; Woodward, 1994), teachers either were erratic in the way they used the program on a day-to-day basis or only interested in using brief segments of the program intermittently.

Current Approaches to Technology Research: A Shift in Thinking

The marked differences between the researcher's carefully articulated design and use of computers and how they are actually used by practitioners or students has become a source of deep concern for many in the field. Two interrelated themes emerge from contemporary special education technology research: (a) the role of the practitioner's perspective in educational reform and (b) the importance of alternative methodologies for studying technology use in classrooms.

The Practitioner's Perspective

Many researchers have come to believe that technology will reform education incrementally, not in the fundamental way that was envisioned in the early 1980s (for an extended discussion of fundamental and incremental reform, see Tyack & Cuban, 1995). Undoubtedly, there are—and will continue to be—pockets of highly visible change and classrooms where teachers use computers in innovative ways. But many researchers have realized that trying to make broad, substantive changes all at once is naive. Reform on a smaller scale and, at times, with fewer teachers is more likely to lead to more sustained results (Elmore, 1996; Stigler & Hiebert, 1999).

Woodward (1993), for example, described the source of the schism between researchers and practitioners mentioned in the last section of this chapter as a clash in basic perspectives on reform, that is, technologists tend to work from what House (1981) describes as a "research-development-dissemination" (RDD) perspective, whereas practitioners are steeped in a cultural perspective. The RDD approach assumes that outsiders can craft research-based, high-quality programs and then disseminate them directly to practitioners. All that is left is some kind of inservice training for practitioners on how to use the technology. Practitioners, in contrast, accommodate new instructional methods in a far less linear manner. They are also constrained by a host of day-to-day variables rarely ever considered by many technologists.

Cuban (1993) extends this analysis by noting that typical claims for why technology is underused in schools (e.g., logistical difficulties, a lack of funds) are only partial explanations of a deeper problem. Instead, many visions of how technology should be used in the classroom that stem from the research community have been at cross-purposes with core visions of what goes on in classrooms. Teaching is still conceptualized as telling, and many teachers deeply value the emotional connections that they build with their students. Cuban is wary of "high-tech" efforts such as instructional learning systems that are designed to replace these relationships with what some might consider to be more efficient modes of instruction.

Finally, Huberman (1993) offers one of the strongest criticisms of the RDD perspective by claiming that the majority of teachers may not even look at their day-to-day practice through the lens of "interventions." His insightful essay on teachers as independent artisans presents a compelling synthesis of research that suggests teachers are more preoccupied with the minute and fast-moving decisions that need to be made about students than in implementing interventions. Huberman bases his analysis on the teacher thinking and school change literature, and he calls into question the very assumption that naturalistic practice can come anywhere close to the kind of engineering assumed by researchers who want their well-designed and validated interventions to be implemented with high levels of fidelity. Thus, comprehensive approaches to instruction, such as those that attempt to encode direct instruction techniques within tamper-proof software (e.g., Johnson et al., 1987) or videodisc programs (e.g., Kelly et al., 1990), conflict with the more informal and spontaneous instructional decision making that occurs in a classroom.

Alternative Methods for Studying Technology Use

In addition to a growing attempt to understand the nature of educational reform and how teachers accommodate innovations, assumptions about how technology should be used in classrooms have changed. Many special education technologists have moved from the "tutor" to the "tool" metaphor for computer use. Thus, word processors, spreadsheets, multimedia hardware, and software are all part of a complex instructional environment that is likely to include innovative curricula and pedagogy. Technology is not conceptualized to be the sole factor that makes an educational difference. Moreover, how technology is used as a tool has an immense level of variability associated with it. In that regard, it is a better fit with a teacher's spontaneous and informal decision making and far less of an "intervention" that leads causally to increased learning.

As researchers have reflected on these changes in how technology is used, a number of them also have broadened their research methods. Many have become disenchanted with the traditional, quantitative orientation toward research. Although much has been made of the importance of rigorous, "high-quality" research in special education—a methodological perspective that is almost entirely quantitative—the arguments for this perspective are at best circular (for a delineation of one view of high-quality research, see Gersten, Lloyd, & Baker, 2000).

The problems with traditional, quantitative methods are well established and well beyond the scope of this chapter (for a substantive critique of the empiricist approach to special education research, see Woodward & Gallagher, 2000). Generally, researchers find these methods to be logistically impractical, at a great distance from the naturalistic conditions of classrooms and the way teachers think about instruction, and philosophically ill-suited to the kind of in-depth investigations that help researchers better understand the details of an educational reform like technology.

Most important, naturalistic conditions do not reflect the kind of causal and probabilistic logic that pervades traditional experimental research studies. Labaree (1998) captured the issue best when he remarked, "The impact of curriculum on teaching or teaching on learning is radically indirect because it relies on the cooperation of teachers and students whose individual goals, urges, and capacities play a large and indeterminate role in shaping the outcome" (p. 5). How interventions evolve over time, what teachers think about them, and the quality of student contributions— academically, socially, and emotionally— warrant methods that can capture the nuances of a situation (Ball & Lampert, 1999; Heshusius, 1989). Thus, alternative methods such as the qualitative research perspective are important frameworks for conducting research.

What follows are some examples of contemporary special education technology efforts that are guided by more in-depth approaches to research. In some cases, quantitative methods comprise a part of the research, and, in that respect, researchers are not theoretical purists. However, one consistent theme is the sensitivity to the varied and nonlinear ways teachers implement innovative technological, curricular, and/or pedagogical methods. Another clear theme is an openness to other interpretations of the intervention, even as it is being conducted. Jackson (1990) underscored the importance of this disposition when he advocates that researchers move from the tunnel vision of looking for the effects of specific previously identified variables to looking at events in classrooms that may appear incidental at first but that extend, over time, into important patterns.

Contemporary Examples

Chapter 2 in this volume is an excellent example of clashes in perspective. It is easy to imagine how engineers, using an RDD perspective, might have first envisioned natural, simple uses for the augmentative device that Todis describes. Nowhere in this thinking does one find the interplay and confusion of multiple practitioners, not to mention the voices of parents and students. Her chapter reminds us that the magical thinking around

the transformative powers of technology is just that. Rarely are the implementations of technology linear and straightforward. Todis also shows us the value of qualitative methods as a means of understanding the various problems associated with technology use.

Zorfass's work, described in Chapter 5 in this volume, reflects a fundamentally different kind of relationship with practitioners than what was typical of the special education technology research of the 1980s through the mid-1990s. Her work is consistent with qualitative or interpretive perspectives insofar as teachers are viewed as a source of knowledge about an intervention and that they convey their knowledge through any one of a variety of collaborative relations. In fact, the Zorfass and Englert and Zhao chapters in this volume attest to a range of collaborative working relationships. What is apparent from Zorfass's description of the *Make It Happen!* project is that what the intervention looked like in its initial presentation transformed over time as teachers became more comfortable with thematic projects and met new challenges. Zorfass readily acknowledges the iterative nature of the learning process and that teachers "construct and reconstruct" interventions like the I-Search method as they put it into practice.

A clear example of this is in her description of the repair strategies that teachers used when they found that their students did not have sufficient library access and note-taking skills. The teachers created mini-direct teaching lessons on the specific skills as a response to this unanticipated problem. Furthermore, it was clear that a broader based implementation of *Make It Happen!* depended on a sensitive but dynamic facilitator. This facilitator did not act like a supervisor or coach seeking a high fidelity of implementation. Rather, the individual helped settle political problems as they arose in context and, along with the principal, encouraged continued risk taking and collaboration among the participating teachers.

Chapter 9 by Englert and Zhao is another example of both the influence of qualitative methods and the need to ground interventions in the teacher's perspective on reform. They offer a rich picture of the implementation process in a community of practice, and their efforts are predicated upon high levels of teacher input and adaptation. In contrast to technical assistance schemes that come with a predetermined agenda, Englert and Zhao continually encouraged the teachers to participate actively in the construction or implementation of the innovation. The details of their 3-year project offer a compelling and realistic picture of teachers trying out, modifying, and continually refining an intervention for students with mild disabilities. Their efforts also result in a narrative that communicates the complexities of changing practice. All of this reflects Englert's shift over time from complex, quantitative research studies in reading and writing to interpretive research on communities of practice.

Chapter 3 by Okolo and Ferretti exemplifies how technology is embedded within a complex instructional environment. Unlike past special education research in social studies (e.g., Gleason et al., 1991; Kinder & Brusuck, 1993; Lenz, Bulgren, & Hudson, 1990), which focused on the acquisition of declarative knowledge and textbook adaptations, their work demonstrates a complex set of considerations and intervention strategies (Ferretti & Okolo, 1996). It also shows the direct influence of other important work in anchored instruction by the Cognition and Technology Group at Vanderbilt University (1990). First, they work closely with teachers to determine topics that will be sufficiently rich and engaging to students for an extended period of time. Second, they narrow the range of topics based on material that can be used to compensate for complex reading demands (e.g., traditional social studies texts, original documents in foreign languages, 18th-century English). Third, they choose topics that are controversial, thus enabling students to develop different points of view and so that ultimately they can write persuasive essays. This aspect is most apparent in their recent work, which involves the dilemmas of westward expansion in the United States. Fourth,

students complete their projects, which typically appear as multimedia presentations, in cooperative learning groups.

The instructional style in these project-based settings is a mix of teacher-directed teaching as well as dialogue and scaffolding. At times, the teacher models for students how to read source materials, take notes, select visual material for the multimedia presentations, and use the technology for their presentations. On other occasions, a modified form of reciprocal teaching is used to assist students in reading relevant materials. Finally, the researchers work closely with their cooperating teachers in the design and implementation of the projects. This working relationship often entails significant adjustments in the class periods so that students have a sufficient amount of time to complete their projects. It also means researchers collaborate with teachers in the selection of topics as well as the best way to teach the skills related to the project. Working with teachers on complex interventions reflects a different stance for contemporary researchers than does the traditional distance typically associated with quantitative research methods.

The complexity of this research also means that it requires much more than one or two dependent measures of declarative knowledge that typified earlier CAI research in special education. In addition to academic outcomes, Okolo and Ferretti document changes in student attitudes and in classroom organization, and they audiotape and analyze student discourse. Although quantitative methods are brought to bear on a number of these measures, Okolo and Ferretti (this volume) clearly see the limits of experimental and quasi-experimental methods as those methods can be applied to their social studies work. Instead, they elect to follow a form of research that is closer to Brown's (1992) design experiments, as well as case study methods, wherein different components of their approach are systematically varied across classrooms and/or students to provide better information on the differential effects of their intervention.

A final example of the value of qualitative research methods for understanding how teachers accommodate technology comes from Woodward and Baxter's (1999) recently completed 2-year study of middle school special education mathematics classrooms. In the year prior to the study, the researchers observed remedial and special education middle school mathematics classes and piloted reform curriculum as well as the use of various technologies such as calculators and spreadsheets.

In their first year of the study, they found two common patterns of instruction depending on the setting. Teachers in remedial classrooms attempted to move their students (including mainstreamed students with learning disabilities) through the pre-algebra classes far too quickly. The special education students, and most of their peers in the class, were quickly lost and unresponsive to the instruction. A second type of teaching generally occurred in special education classrooms. In this case, students worked monotonously on drill-and-practice worksheets, reviewing basic operations or what seemed to be endless attempts to perform basic operations on fractions. Observations and interviews with the students and teachers suggested that student motivation was a significant problem. In both types of classrooms, students rarely completed their assigned homework.

The researchers' hypothesis was that students with learning disabilities and their peers in the remedial classrooms would be much more engaged by materials that were appropriately paced and conceptually oriented than by drill-and-practice exercises. They also felt that the students would benefit from marked changes in routine throughout the class period (e.g., classroom discussions, partner work, use of the computer lab for anchored instruction problems).

As the researchers observed in classrooms over the 2 years in which the teachers and students engaged in innovative mathematical practices, the early signs were encouraging. Students persisted longer on practice work in the classroom, they were willing to participate in mathematical discussion, and many even turned in homework by the middle of the year. Yet what appeared to be an attributional problem during seatwork eventually suggested something else.

When the teachers gave students challenging problems to solve at the beginning of class as warm-up exercises, some students quickly gave up after their first attempt, occasionally uttering something to the effect of "This is dumb." The more the researchers watched events such as these, and, more important, listened to the informal student conversations before, during, and after class, the more the issue of attribution and tracking became important themes in understanding the lives of these students in school. In effect, the researchers found that remedial mathematics was a defining class for many of the students. As the clearest instance of tracking at the middle school level, the remedial math class helped form or solidify a student's self-definition of academic ability, and it also offered an important context for developing friendships.

Interviews with the general and special education teachers further amplified this theme. The teachers reported that many of their students had very troubling home lives, which unavoidably spilled over into school. Other students had given up on subjects like mathematics, either because they knew that they were in the low-track class and were doing "baby work" or because challenging work was frustrating and only confirmed that they were dumb. As one teacher put, "Most of these students would rather fail than risk making the effort on challenging assignments."

The emergence of this broader attributional and self-concept theme reshaped the second year of the research. The researchers collected a variety of data to explore this issue further (e.g., demographic, attitudinal, self-concept), and the findings—in conjunction with extensive classroom observations and interviews—yielded a much richer and more accurate account of how the mathematics intervention affected the students (Woodward, 1999). Their research is consonant with both Jackson's (1990) sense of looking at events to find and document unanticipated patterns and Labaree's (1998) observation that the effects of curriculum and teaching on learning in naturalistic settings are indirect because teachers and students have disparate goals, inclinations, and capacities.

Conclusion

The history of technology-based research in special education suggests that simple answers to the question of instructional effectiveness are not easy to achieve. Early research was confounded by media (e.g., textbooks vs. microcomputers). The brief interlude of curriculum design research resolved this confound somewhat by investigating the differential effect of specific curriculum design variables on learning. It is not clear, however, whether this research ever had a substantive impact on commercial software for students or whether these variables were ever used as strict criteria for selecting software.

Assessment projects have been the source of some of the most innovative uses of technology in special education research. Developers often have brought a considerable research base to their work, as is apparent in the curriculum-based measurement studies. The application of expert systems to assessment as a way to enhance feedback and teacher decision making also has been one of the more advanced efforts to apply "state-of-the-art" technologies to special education problems.

Unfortunately, a pervasive theme in CAI and assessment research is the mismatch in perspectives between technology developer-researchers and practitioners. Naturalistic research, as well as a growing number of commentaries on how teachers adopt innovations like technology, suggests that simply because a program or approach has been validated by research does not necessarily mean it will be used as intended in practice. The realization has led some in the field to examine carefully the complex and nonlinear pat-terns of technology adoption in the classroom. The issue is further complicated by the move of technology as tutor to technology as tool. Undoubtedly more research needs to be done on the variations in how teachers adopt technology and associated innovations (e.g., curriculum, pedagogy). There is also a need to research the fine-grained effects of different forms of information (e.g., text vs. image or video, variations in graphic presentations) as multimedia is used for learning.

On a larger scale, there is a sense in which many of the researcher-practitioner issues are bracketed by a wider set of considerations. Elmore (1996) reminds us that school innovations are "nested" within factors that extend well beyond much of the professional development and "research to practice" thinking, particularly as it has appeared in special education. Technology adoption is far from equal in schools in the United States, and it is evident that some schools and even districts have positioned its use along with other innovative practices at the center of their school or district mission. As leaders, these institutions may offer valuable accounts of how technology, even as it is embedded in other innovative practices, can be brought to bear on the question that began this chapter: What is the impact of technology on learning? It is unlikely that these accounts will look like the empirical studies of the curriculum design and assessment era. However, this kind of research could provide important insights for special education teachers and administrators who are only beginning to ask how technology can help students with disabilities in their learning. It also can help articulate the nested variables that facilitate or impede its effective use for students with disabilities.

References

Anderson, J. (1983). *The architecture of cognition.* Cambridge, MA: Harvard University Press.

Axelrod, S., McGregor, G., Sherman, J., & Hamlet, C. (1987). Effects of video games as reinforcers for computerized addition performance. *Journal of Special Education Technology, 9*(1), 1-8.

Bahr, C., Kinzer, C., & Rieth, H. (1991). An analysis of the effects of teacher training and student grouping on reading comprehension skills among mildly handicapped high school students using computer-assisted instruction. *Journal of Special Education Technology, 11*(3), 136-154.

Bahr, C., & Rieth, H. (1989). The effects of instructional computer games and drill and practice software on learning disabled students' mathematics achievement. *Computers in the Schools, 6*(3/4), 87-101.

Ball, D., & Lampert, M. (1999). Multiples of evidence, time, and perspective: Revisiting the study of teaching and learning. In E. Lagemann & L. Shulman (Eds.), *Issues in education research* (pp. 371-398). San Francisco: Jossey-Bass.

Bangert-Drowns, R., Kulik, C., Kulik, J., & Morgan, M. (1991). The instructional effect of feedback in test-like events. *Review of Educational Research, 61,* 213-238.

Becker, W. (1977). Teaching reading and writing to the disadvantaged—What we have learned from field research. *Harvard Educational Review, 47,* 506-521.

Boone, R., & Higgins, K. (1993). Hypermedia basal readers: Three years of school-based research. *Journal of Special Education Technology, 12*(2), 86-106.

Bork, A. (1981). Educational technology and the future. *Journal of Educational Technology Systems, 10*(1), 3-19.

Brown, A. (1992). Design experiments: Theoretical and methodological challenges in creating complex interventions in classroom settings. *Journal of the Learning Sciences, 2*(2), 141-178.

Brown, J., & Burton, R. (1978). Diagnostic models for procedural bugs in basic mathematics skills. *Cognitive Science, 2,* 155-168.

Carnine, D. (1989). Teaching complex content to learning disabled students: The role of technology. *Exceptional Children, 55,* 524-533.

Cawley, J. (1994). Science for students with disabilities. *Remedial and Special Education, 15*(2), 67-71.

Chiang, B. (1986). Initial learning and transfer effects of microcomputer drills on LD students' multiplication skills. *Learning Disability Quarterly, 9*(2), 118-123.

Christensen, C., & Cosden, M. (1986). The relationship between special education placement and instruction in computer literacy skills. *Journal of Educational Computing Research, 2,* 299-306.

Christensen, C., & Gerber, M. (1990). Effectiveness of computerized drill and practice games on teaching basic math facts. *Exceptionality, 1,* 149-165.

Clark, R. E. (1983). Reconsidering research on learning from media. *Review of Educational Research, 53,* 445-459.

Cognition and Technology Group at Vanderbilt University. (1990). Anchored instruction and its relation-ship to situated cognition. *Educational Researcher, 19*(6), 2-10.

Cognition and Technology Group at Vanderbilt University. (1997). *The Jasper Project: Lessons in curriculum, instruction, assessment and professional development.* Mahwah, NJ: Lawrence Erlbaum.

Collins, M., Carnine, D., & Gersten, R. (1987). Elaborated corrective feedback and the acquisition of reasoning skills: A study of computer-assisted instruction. *Exceptional Children, 54,* 254-262.

Cosden, M. (1988). Microcomputer instruction and perceptions of effectiveness by special and regular education elementary school teachers. *Journal of Special Education, 22*(2), 242-253.

Cosden, M., & Abernathy, T. (1990). Microcomputer use in the schools: Teacher roles and instructional options. *Remedial and Special Education, 11*(5), 31-38.

Cosden, M., Gerber, M., Goldman, S., Semmel, D., & Semmel, M. (1986). Survey of microcomputer access and use by mildly handicapped students in Southern California. *Journal of Special Education Technology, 7*(4), 5-13.

Cosden, M. A., Gerber, M. M., Semmel, D. S., Goldman, S. R., & Semmel, M. I. (1987). Microcomputer use within micro-educational environments. *Exceptional Children, 53,* 399-409.

Cosden, M., & Lieber, J. (1986). Grouping students on the microcomputer. *Academic Therapy, 22*(2), 165-172.

Cosden, M., & Semmel, M. (1987). Developmental changes in micro-educational environments for learning handicapped and non-learning handicapped elementary school students. *Journal of Special Education Technology, 8*(4), 1-13.

Cuban, L. (1993). Computer meets classroom: Classroom wins. *Teachers College Record, 95,* 185-209.

Deci, E., & Chandler, C. (1986). The importance of motivation for the future of the LD field. *Journal of Learning Disabilities, 19,* 587-594.

Delquadri, J., Greenwood, C., Whorton, D., Carta, J., & Hall, R. (1986). Classwide peer tutoring. *Exceptional Children, 52,* 535-542.

Deno, S. L. (1985). Curriculum-based measurement: The emerging alternative. *Exceptional Children, 52,* 219-232.

Deno, S. (1990). Individual differences and individual difference: The essential difference of special education. *Journal of Special Education, 24*(2), 160-173.

Ellis, E. S., & Sabornie, E. J. (1986). Effective instruction with microcomputers: Promises, practices, and preliminary findings. *Focus on Exceptional Children, 19*(4), 1-16.

Elmore, R. (1996). Getting to scale with good educational practice. *Harvard Educational Review, 66,* 1-26.

Engelmann, S., & Carnine, D. (1982). *Theory of instruction: Principles and applications.* New York: Irvington.

Englert, C. (1984). Effective direct instruction practice in special education settings. *Remedial and Special Education, 5*(2), 38-47.

Ferretti, R., & Okolo, C. (1996). Authenticity in learning: Multimedia design projects in the social studies for students with disabilities. *Journal of Learning Disabilities, 29,* 450-460.

Fitzgerald, G., & Koury, K. (1996). Empirical advances in technology-assisted instruction for students with mild and moderate disabilities. *Journal of Research on Computing in Education, 28,* 526-553.

Fuchs, D., & Fuchs, L. (1996). Consultation as technology and the politics of school reform. *Remedial and Special Education, 17,* 386-392.

Fuchs, L., & Fuchs, D. (1986). Effects of systematic formative evaluation: A meta-analysis. *Exceptional Children, 53*(3), 199-208.

Fuchs, L., Fuchs, D., Bentz, J., Phillips, N., & Hamlett, C. (1994). The nature of student interactions during peer tutoring with and without prior training and experience. *American Educational Research Journal, 31,* 75-103.

Fuchs, L., Fuchs, D., Bishop, N., & Simmons, D. (1992). Teacher planning for students with learning disabilities: Differences between general and special educators. *Learning Disabilities Research and Practice, 7,* 120-129.

Fuchs, L., Fuchs, D., & Hamlett, C. (1989). Monitoring reading growth using student recalls: Effects of two teacher feedback systems. *Journal of Educational Research, 83,* 103-111.

Fuchs, L., Fuchs, D., & Hamlett, C. (1993). Technological advances linking the assessment of students' academic proficiency to instructional planning. *Journal of Special Education Technology, 12*(1), 49-62.

Fuchs, L., Fuchs, D., Hamlett, C., & Ferguson, C. (1992). Effects of expert system consultation within curriculum-based measurement, using a reading maze task. *Exceptional Children, 58,* 436-450.

Fuchs, L. S., Fuchs, D., Hamlett, C. L., & Hasselbring, T. S. (1987). Using computers with curriculum-based monitoring: Effects on teacher efficiency and satisfaction. *Journal of Special Education Technology, 8*(4), 14-27.

Fuchs, L., Fuchs, D., Hamlett, C., & Stecker, P. (1990). The role of skills analysis in curriculum-based measurement in math. *School Psychology Review, 19,* 6-22.

Fuchs, L., Fuchs, D., Hamlett, C., & Stecker, P. (1991). Effects of curriculum-based measurement and consultation on teacher planning and student achievement in mathematics operations. *American Educational Research Journal, 28,* 617-641.

Fuchs, L., Hamlett, C., Fuchs, D., Stecker, P., & Ferguson, C. (1987). Conducting curriculum-based measurement with computerized data collection: Effects on efficiency and teacher satisfaction. *Journal of Special Education Technology, 9*(2), 73-86.

Gagné, R., Briggs, L., & Wager, W. (1988). *Principles of instructional design* (3rd ed.). New York: Holt, Rinehart & Winston.

Gerber, M., Semmel, D., & Semmel, M. (1994). Computer-based dynamic assessment of multidigit multiplication. *Exceptional Children, 61*(2), 114-125.

Gersten, R., Lloyd, J., & Baker, S. (2000). Designing high quality research in special education: Group design experiments. *Journal of Special Education, 34,* 218-237.

Gleason, M., Carnine, D., & Vala, N. (1991). Cumulative versus rapid introduction of new information. *Exceptional Children, 57,* 353-358.

Goldman, S., & Pellegrino, J. (1987). Information processing and educational microcomputer technology: Where do we go from here? *Journal of Learning Disabilities, 20*(3), 144-154.

Greenwood, C., & Rieth, H. (1994). Current dimensions of technology-based assessment in special education. *Exceptional Children, 61,* 105-113.

Hasselbring, T. S., Goin, L. I., & Bransford, J. D. (1988). Developing math automaticity in learning handicapped children: The role of computerized drill and practice. *Focus on Exceptional Children, 20*(6), 1-7.

Heshusius, L. (1989). The Newtonian mechanistic paradigm, special education, and contours of alternatives: An overview. *Journal of Learning Disabilities, 22,* 403-415.

Higgins, K., & Boone, K. (1990). Hypertext computer study guides and the social studies achievement of students with learning disabilities, remedial students, and regular education students. *Journal of Learning Disabilities, 23,* 529-540.

Higgins, K., & Boone, R. (1991). Hypermedia CAI: A supplement to an elementary school basal reader program. *Journal of Special Education Technology, 11*(1), 1-15.

Hofmeister, A. (1984). Special education in the information age. *Peabody Journal of Education, 62*(1), 5-22.

Hofmeister, A. (1986). Formative evaluation in the development and validation of expert systems in education. *Computational Intelligence, 24*(2), 150-159.

Hofmeister, A., Engelmann, S., & Carnine, D. (1989). Developing and validating science education videodiscs. *Journal of Research in Science Education, 26,* 665-677.

Hofmeister, A. M., & Ferrara, J. M. (1986). Expert systems and special education. *Exceptional Children, 53,* 235-239.

Hofmeister, A., & Thorkildsen, R. (1989). Videodisc levels: A case study in hardware obsession. *Journal of Special Education Technology, 10*(2), 73-79.

Hollingsworth, M., & Woodward, J. (1993). Integrated learning: Explicit strategies and their role in problem solving instruction for students with learning disabilities. *Exceptional Children, 59,* 444-455.

Horton, S., Lovitt, T., & Slocum, T. (1988). Teaching geography to high school students with academic deficits: Effects of computerized map tutorial. *Learning Disabilities Quarterly, 22,* 102-107.

House, E. (1981). Three perspectives on innovation: Technological, political, and cultural. In R. Lehming & M. Kane (Eds), *Improving schools: Using what we know* (pp. 42-58). Beverly Hills, CA: Sage.

Howell, R., Sidorenko, E., & Jurica, J. (1987). The effects of computer use on the acquisition of multiplication facts by a student with learning disabilities. *Journal of Learning Disabilities, 20,* 336-341.

Huberman, M. (1993). The model of the independent artisan in teachers' professional relations. In J. Little & M. McLaughlin (Eds.), *Teachers' work* (pp. 11-50). New York: Teachers College Press.

Jackson, P. (1990). Looking for trouble: On the place of the ordinary in educational studies. In E. Eisner & A. Peskin (Eds.), *Qualitative inquiry in education: The continuing debate* (pp. 153-166). New York: Teachers College Press.

Johnson, D., & Johnson, R. (1986). Mainstreaming and cooperative learning strategies. *Exceptional Children, 53,* 454-461.

Johnson, G., Gersten, R., & Carnine, D. (1987). Effects of instructional design variables on vocabulary acquisition of LD students: A study of computer-assisted instruction. *Journal of Learning Disabilities, 20,* 206-213.

Jonassen, D. (1999). *Computers as mindtools for schools: Engaging critical thinking* (2nd ed.). Englewood Cliffs, NJ: Prentice Hall.

Jones, K. M., Torgesen, J. K., & Sexton, M. A. (1987). Using computer guided practice to increase decoding fluency in learning disabled children: A study using the Hint and Hunt I program. *Journal of Learning Disabilities, 20*(2), 122-128.

Kelly, B., Gersten, R., & Carnine, D. (1990). Student error patterns as a function of curriculum design: Teaching fractions to remedial high school students and high school students with learning disabilities. *Journal of Learning Disabilities, 23,* 23-29.

Kinder, D., & Brusuck, W. (1993). The search for a unified social studies curriculum: Does history really repeat itself? *Journal of Learning Disabilities, 24,* 270-277.

Kitz, W., & Thorpe, H. (1992). *The effectiveness of videodisc and traditional algebra instruction with college-aged remedial students.* Unpublished manuscript.

Labaree, D. (1998). Educational researchers: Living with a lesser form of knowledge. *Educational Researcher, 27*(8), 4-12.

Lally, M. (1981). Computer-assisted teaching of sight-word recognition for mentally retarded school children. *American Journal of Mental Deficiency, 85,* 383-388.

Lenz, K., Bulgren, J., & Hudson, P. (1990). Content enhancement: A model for promoting the acquisition of content by individuals with learning disabilities. In T. Scruggs & B. Wong (Eds.), Intervention research in learning disabilities (pp. 122-165). New York: Springer-Verlag.

Lesgold, A., & Resnick, L. (1982). How reading difficulties develop: Perspectives from a longitudinal study. In J. Das, R. Mulcahy, & A. Wall (Eds.), *Theory and research in learning disabilities* (pp. 155-188). New York: Plenum.

Lin, A., Podell, D., & Rein, N. (1991). The effects of CAI on word recognition in mildly handicapped and nonhandicapped learners. *Journal of Special Education Technology, 11*(1), 16-25.

Lysakowski, R., & Walberg, H. (1982). Instructional effects of causes, participation and corrective feedback: A quantitative synthesis. *American Educational Research Journal, 19,* 559-578.

MacArthur, C., & Haynes, J. (1995). Student assistant for learning from text (SALT): A hypermedia reading aid. *Journal of Learning Disabilities, 28*(3), 150-159.

MacArthur, C., Haynes, J., Harris, K., & Owings, M. (1990). Computer assisted instruction with learning disabled students: Achievement, engagement, and other factors that influence achievement. *Journal of Educational Computing Research, 6,* 311-328.

MacArthur, C., & Malouf, D. (1991). Teachers' beliefs, plans, and decisions about computer-based instruction. *Journal of Special Education, 25*(5), 44-72.

McDermid, R. (1989). *A quantitative analysis of the literature on computer-assisted instruction with the learning disabled and educably mentally retarded.* Unpublished doctoral dissertation, University of Kansas, Lawrence.

McDermott, P., & Watkins, M. (1983). Computerized vs. conventional remedial instruction for learning-disabled pupils. *Journal of Special Education, 17*(1), 81-88.

Moore, L., & Carnine, D. (1989). A comparison of two approaches to teaching ratios and proportions to remedial and learning disabled students: Active teaching with either basal or empirically validated curriculum design material. *Remedial and Special Education, 10,* 28-37.

Neuman, D. (1991). Learning disabled students' interactions with commercial courseware: A naturalistic study. *Educational Technology, Research and Development, 39*(1), 31-49.

Okolo, C. (1992). The effects of computer-based attribution retraining on the attributions, persistence, and mathematics computation of students with learning disabilities. *Journal of Learning Disabilities, 25,* 327-334.

Okolo, C., Bahr, C., & Rieth, H. (1993). A retrospective of computer-based instruction. *Journal of Special Education Technology, 12*(1), 1-27.

Papert, S. (1980). *Mindstorms.* New York: Basic Books.

Pellegrino, J. W., & Goldman, S. J. (1987). Information processing and elementary mathematics. *Journal of Learning Disabilities, 20,* 23-32.

Podell, D., Tournaki-Rein, N., & Lin, A. (1992). Automatization of mathematics skills via computer-assisted instruction among students with mild-moderate handicaps. *Education and Training in Mental Retardation, 27*(3), 200-206.

Pressley, M., Goodchild, F., Fleet, J., Zajchowski, R., & Evans, E. (1989). The challenges of classroom strategy instruction. *Elementary School Journal, 89,* 301-342.

Rieth, H., Bahr, C., Okolo, C., Polsgrove, L., & Eckert, R. (1988). An analysis of the impact of microcomputers on the secondary special education classroom ecology. *Journal of Educational Computing Research, 4,* 425-441.

Rueda, R., & Mehan, H. (1986). Metacognition and passing: Strategic interactions in the lives of students with learning disabilities. *Anthropology and Education Quarterly, 17*(3), 146-165.

Schmidt, M., Weinstein, T., Niemic, R., & Walberg, H. (1985). Computer-assisted instruction with exceptional children. *Journal of Special Education, 19,* 493-501.

Shiah, R., Mastropieri, M., & Scruggs, T. (1995). Computer-assisted instruction and students with learning disabilities: Does research support the rhetoric? In M. Mastropieri & T. Scruggs (Eds.), *Advances in learning and behavioral disabilities* (pp. 162-192). Greenwich, CT: JAI.

Stevens, K., Blackhurst, A., & Slator, D. (1991). Teaching memorized spelling with a microcomputer: Time delay and computer-assisted instruction. *Journal of Applied Behavior Analysis, 24,* 153-160.

Stevens, R., & Slavin, R. (1991). When cooperative learning improves the achievement of students with mild disabilities: A response to Tateyama-Sniezek. *Exceptional Children, 57,* 276-280.

Stigler, J., & Hiebert, J. (1999). *The teaching gap: Best ideas from the world's teachers for improving education in the classroom.* New York: Free Press.

Swanson, L. (1989). Strategy instruction: Overview of principles and procedures for effective use. *Learning Disabilities Quarterly, 12,* 3-14.

Systems Impact. (1985). *Mastering fractions* [Videodisc program]. Washington, DC: Author.

Systems Impact. (1987a). *Earth science* [Videodisc program]. Washington, DC: Author.

Systems Impact. (1987b). *Mastering ratios* [Videodisc program]. Washington, DC: Author.

Torgesen, J., Waters, M., Cohen, A., & Torgesen, J. (1988). Improving sight-word recognition skills in LD children: An evaluation of three computer program variations. *Learning Disability Quarterly, 11,* 125-132.

Tyack, D., & Cuban, L. (1995). *Tinkering toward utopia: A century of public school reform.* Cambridge, MA: Harvard University Press.

Van Laarhoven, T. (1996). *A comparison of the effectiveness of teacher-delivered and computer-assisted instruction on the generalization of sight word vocabulary to classroom and community environments.* Unpublished doctoral dissertation, Northern Illinois University, DeKalb.

Van Lehn, K. (1990). *Mind bugs.* Cambridge, MA: MIT Press.

Watkins, M. (1989). Computerized drill-and-practice and academic attitudes of learning disabled students. *Journal of Special Education Technology, 9,* 167-192.

Wenger, E. (1987). *Artificial intelligence and tutoring systems.* New York: Morgan Kaufmann.

Wesson, C., Fuchs, L. S., Tindal, G., Mirkin, P., & Deno, S. (1986). Facilitating the efficiency of ongoing curriculum-based measurement. *Teacher Education and Special Education, 9,* 166-172.

Wise, B., & Olson, R. (1994). Computer speech and the remediation of reading and spelling problems. *Journal of Special Education Technology, 12*(3), 207-220.

Wong, B. (1993). Pursuing an elusive goal: Molding strategic teachers and learners. *Journal of Learning Disabilities, 26,* 354-357.

Woodward, J. (1992, April). *Student misconceptions in arithmetic: Preliminary findings.* Paper presented at the annual meeting of the Council for Exceptional Children, Baltimore.

Woodward, J. (1993). The technology of technology-based instruction: Comments on the research, development, and dissemination perspective of educational innovation. *Education and Treatment of Children, 16,* 345-360.

Woodward, J. (1994). Causal organization and its effect on recall and understanding in secondary science. *Elementary School Journal, 94,* 299-314.

Woodward, J. (1999, February). *Self-concept, self-esteem, and attribution in secondary math classrooms.* Paper presented at the Pacific Coast Research Conference, La Jolla, CA.

Woodward, J., & Baxter, J. (1999). *The workplace literacy project: Final report.* Tacoma, WA: University of Puget Sound.

Woodward, J., Carnine, D., & Gersten, R. (1988). Teaching problem solving through computer simulations. *American Educational Research Journal, 25,* 72-86.

Woodward, J., Carnine, D., Gersten, R., Gleason, M., Johnson, G., & Collins, M. (1986). Applying instructional design principles to CAI for mildly handicapped students: Four recently conducted studies. *Journal of Special Education Technology, 8*(1), 13-26.

Woodward, J., & Gallagher, D. (2000). *From empiricism to interpretation: The changing nature of intervention research in special education* (RN-3). Tacoma, WA: University of Puget Sound.

Woodward, J., & Gersten, R. (1992). Innovative technology for secondary learning disabled students: A multi-faceted study of implementation. *Exceptional Children, 58,* 407-422.

Woodward, J., & Howard, L. (1994). The misconceptions of youth: Errors and their mathematical meaning. *Exceptional Children, 61*(2), 126-136.

CHAPTER TWO

It Can't Hurt

Implementing AAC Technology in the Classroom for Students With Severe and Multiple Disabilities

University of Oregon

Most of the research and development of technology in special education has focused on the needs of students with mild cognitive disabilities or those with sensory impairments. However, the increasing presence of technology in society, and in schools in particular, also has sparked interest in finding technological solutions to the environmental access and communication needs of students with a variety of severe physical and cognitive disabilities. It is reasonable to assume that motorized wheelchairs, personal computers (PCs), environmental control devices, and alternative and augmentative communication (AAC) devices would promote independence, academic and vocational success, and social inclusion for these students, just as they do for many adults with disabilities.

In fact, some of these devices have made a successful transition to classroom settings (Todis & Walker, 1993). For example, there is little controversy about the use of motorized wheelchairs by elementary and secondary students. Although their presence in schools is not completely free of hassles (they are big and heavy, they have to be kept charged, children tend to outgrow them faster than insurance companies are willing to replace them, and sometimes students have chairs that are too powerful or complicated for them to manage), school personnel are usually willing and able to make accommodations for this type of technology. The purpose and operation of wheelchairs, even the high-tech ones, are easily understood by everyone—the student user, teachers, and other students. Training is usually relatively straightforward, and it is clear immediately to everyone whether the student is using the chair successfully and whether the student likes the chair.

Incorporating other assistive technologies into the classroom has not been as uncomplicated or as free of controversy. AAC, for example, although one of the most compelling types of assistive technology (AT) in terms of potential benefits for students, is one of the most difficult to implement well.

Alternative and Augmentative Communication

AAC includes low-tech approaches such as signs and gestures, picture wallets, and communication books. For students who are unable to point or otherwise directly select a word, picture, icon, or object from such a system, other means of access have been developed. Some students who have adequate head control can use eye gaze to select communication choices mounted on a transparent board. For other students, technology can be added to these communication systems to improve access. For example, head-mounted light pointers or light scanning devices might allow some students with severe physical disabilities to make selections from an array of communication choices. As computer technology became more available, variations of these systems were put in electronic formats that deliver the message via voice output. Some devices allow the user to type in lengthy messages and then to play them back by activating a switch. However, devices recommended for students usually are preprogrammed with a number of utterances, ranging from fewer than 10 to more than 100, depending on the size and complexity of the device. Each key or button on the device has a corresponding prerecorded or computer-generated spoken message. Most produce single-word or short-phrase utterances, but some AAC devices can be programmed on different levels that, used in combination, produce more complex messages.

AAC devices originally were developed for previously nondisabled adults who, due to illness or injury, had lost the ability to speak but could either type in a message or remember the location of a particular prerecorded message and then access a button or switch to activate the device to deliver the message auditorily. For those individuals, AAC provided an alternative to sign, written messages, and other types of silent communication, giving them a wider range of communication partners. Naturally, success with these users led developers and practitioners to think of ways to adapt the technology for a wider array of potential users, including those who have never used verbal communication, those with physical disabilities that interfered with access, and those with severe or undetermined degrees of cognitive disability that may impede training. Many students with severe and multiple disabilities match all three of these descriptions.

Access Issues

For most students, access issues are relatively easy to work out. For users who cannot reliably activate a message directly by touching a particular key, a larger, more accessible remote switch is positioned to take advantage of the student's most reliable motor response. Switches might be positioned to use head, foot, knee, and even eye-blink movements. The remote switch activates a light scanning process. In some scanning systems, the student moves through the array by hitting the switch until the desired item is illuminated. In others, the student starts the scanning process by hitting the switch, waits until the right message is highlighted, and then hits the switch again to activate the voice output message. The scanning process can be speeded up by arranging the items in a matrix and then identifying the row or column containing the desired item, rather than scanning through all items in a linear fashion (for a description of AAC devices, scanning procedures, and other adaptations to address access issues, see Tanchak & Sawyer, 1995).

Cognitive and
Communication Issues

Questions related to the cognitive and communicative functioning of AAC users are more difficult to identify and address. Because of the difficulty of assessing cognitive ability in individuals who do not communicate verbally, it is often unclear whether communication difficulties are related to impaired cognitive functioning or to physical issues that have delayed language development or that simply interfere with expressive language. For the latter group of students, AAC holds the promise of unlocking a communicative and cognitive potential that otherwise would be inaccessible. One would expect that once interface problems are addressed, such users would "take off" with an AAC device and use it to access communication opportunities that were not previously available. However, some students with severe physical disabilities appear uninterested in either low-tech or high-tech communication systems. Others use only one or a few of the selections available on the device. Practitioners are left wondering what factor or combination of factors needs to be addressed. Is the device too simple, too complex, too slow, too hard to access, or objectionable to the user for some other reason? Is the problem motivational, cognitive, physical, or a combination of these factors? If physical barriers can be addressed, can cognitive and motivational issues also be overcome with training and reinforcement? With the right device and training, will a potential user suddenly "get it" and begin communicating not just requests and responses but also insights and jokes? For young children, will introduction of an AAC device stimulate communication, interfere with potential development of verbal language, or neither?

These questions illustrate the ambiguity inherent in working with individuals with severe disabilities who do not communicate verbally, particularly children whose linguistic and cognitive potential might be enhanced with the right combination of interventions at the right stages of development. Given the difficulty of assessing a student's abilities and the potential benefits of AAC, many special educators and AAC specialists take the approach that giving AAC a good try "can't hurt." Therefore AAC technology often is recommended for preschool children who do not use speech and for students whose ability to access and use the devices purposefully and independently has not been determined. The immediate and long-term effects of this approach on student AAC users and on professionals, parents, and peers seldom is systematically assessed.

This chapter describes the effects of such recommendations on 5 students. The themes illustrated by these five case studies have been noted in a wider range of students who use AAC in school settings (Todis, 1996; Todis & Walker, 1993).

Project Description
and Methods

The findings presented in this chapter are based on a 2-year qualitative study of 13 students, ranging in age from 4 to 20. These students experienced a variety of physical disabilities and exhibited a range of cognitive abilities. They attended schools in urban and rural settings in the Pacific Northwest and used an array of assistive devices. The most common devices included motorized and nonmotorized wheelchairs, PCs, and dedicated AAC devices with voice output. Many students also used a number of "low-tech" positioning, mobility, and communication devices. Although a few of the students had some degree of visual impairment, none was classified as blind or hearing impaired.

In this study, each student was assigned a field researcher who conducted a weekly participant observation over a 12-month period. These usually occurred at school but occasionally took place in the student's home or in other community settings. During 2- to 4-hour observations, the field researcher observed events and interactions in the setting and doc-umented them in detailed field notes after each session. Field researchers also con-ducted interviews with parents, teachers, and other educators. The interviews were open-ended and unstructured, so the interviewees could raise topics that they considered impor-tant. The field researchers asked questions and checked their perceptions about proce-dures and interactions they observed. They learned each student's history of technology use, including how his or her equipment was acquired and how training was conducted. The interviews also provided an opportunity for teachers and specialists to relate their broader experience over the course of their careers with other students who used AT.

Data for this project were in the form of interview transcripts and field notes. All data were entered into a computer and coded by topic area, using a text data sorting program. Case studies of all students were prepared and presented to a diverse group of profes-sionals including a pediatrician, a child psy-chologist, a physical therapist, two mobility training specialists, a speech pathologist, an AAC specialist, and an occupational thera-pist; all were highly experienced in assessing and training children with disabilities to use AT. These professionals provided perspec-tives on how the sample students' experi-ences compared with those of other children who use assistive devices. They also sug-gested questions to explore through further observation and interviews.

As data were collected and coded, themes were identified and compared within and across cases, and as additional information was collected, it was examined for new themes. As theories emerged about the issues surrounding AT use, the data were searched again for evidence that either supported or refuted tentative theories. Themes were veri-fied and theories were further tested by ask-ing the students and other interviewees to comment on their validity. In the second year, new students were added to the sample to investigate aspects of some themes that were inaccessible in the original group of students.

This chapter examines themes that emerged in the case studies of the students who used or had access to AAC devices. These included 3 preschool students, 1 ele-mentary school student, and 2 high school students. They are described subsequently as they were at the time the study was conducted.

Becky is a 6-year-old with rolandic epi-lepsy. As the result of seizures at the age of 1, Becky has significant receptive and expres-sive language delays. Although she has mild gross motor dysfunction, she is ambulatory. She attended a regular kindergarten for 1 year and then was placed in a self-contained pri-mary program. Becky got her AAC while she was in kindergarten. Her mother attended training on augmentative communication and became committed to saturating Becky's en-vironment with picture symbols so the AAC would become an integral part of Becky's communication system. Although Becky re-ceives training from two private speech thera-pists as well as from a full-time assistant at school, she uses the device only with heavy prompting, and her responses are not always appropriate, leading her teachers to wonder whether she understands the purpose of the device and, if she does, whether she likes it as a means of communication.

Christine is a 5-year-old who attends a preschool early intervention program. She has severe cerebral palsy and is nonambu-latory with limited control of her upper body. Christine is very social: She smiles and vocal-izes when people come near and protests by vocalizing or crying when they leave or turn away. Her motorized wheelchair is used mostly for transporting her to and from the school bus and going out for recess. She does not drive the chair independently. She also has had an AAC device since she was 3, but, because of a number of concerns of both par-ents and teachers, she does not currently use it at home or at school.

Eric, also 5, has blond hair, blue eyes, and an engaging smile. He has a developmental disability similar to cerebral palsy but caused by a brain malformation rather than perinatal brain damage. He has some upper-body control and is able to feed himself with adapted equipment. He is described by his parents and most professionals who work with him as very bright. He has a motorized wheelchair and was trained to use it before he was 3. He has also had an AAC device since he was 2½. Although both AT devices had been used at previous preschools, Eric seldom uses either device at home or at his current preschool, a regular preschool where his teachers receive support from early intervention specialists to help them work with Eric and several other students with disabilities.

Dawn is a 7-year-old elementary school student whose disabilities have never been clearly defined. She has a form of cerebral palsy that has resulted in some physical disabilities. Dawn learned to walk at age 3 and can feed herself and help with other age-appropriate self-care tasks. She also has an undetermined degree of cognitive impairment and autistic characteristics that have decreased somewhat since early childhood. She attends a primary grade program for students with severe disabilities and is integrated for recess, music, and special events with students from the regular school program. Dawn was first introduced to an AAC device during her participation in this project.

Bill, a 17-year-old sophomore in an urban high school, has severe cerebral palsy. He has been using a motorized wheelchair since he was 10 and an AAC device since he was 14. At school, Bill appears uninterested in the AAC device, but school staff are under the impression he uses it frequently at home. His mother reports that he does not use the device much at home because his family understands his nonverbal speech and his vocalizations, but she wants him to use the device more at school. Bill spends nearly all of his school day in a self-contained classroom, mostly in the company of his teacher and teaching assistant. He requires frequent rest periods as part of his recovery from surgery to correct a curvature of his spine.

Sara is a 15-year-old freshman in a rural high school. She was diagnosed with cerebral palsy at 8 months of age. It is hard to determine what Sara's cognitive abilities are. Her mother reports that Sara has no mental retardation and that she "has always been *too* socially aware, *too* smart." Sara's special education teacher described her as both the most physically disabled student the school had ever served and the brightest student in the self-contained classroom. Sara has a motorized wheelchair, which she operates with a joystick. Her AAC device, mounted on the wheelchair, is operated with a head switch, also attached to the wheelchair. She also uses the head switch to access a PC for word processing. Sara seldom used her motorized wheelchair or the AAC device during our observations. The chair was difficult for her to control, and she had to be prompted repeatedly to use the AAC device. She seemed to prefer to use eye gaze, vocalization, and facial and head gestures to communicate. Most of Sara's time at school was spent with teaching assistants in a classroom for students with severe disabilities. She was "mainstreamed" for one class period in a language arts class for students with learning disabilities, where she used her PC.

Themes

An overarching theme across all cases in the study, but especially for students with AAC, was the tendency for technology applied to the needs of students with severe disabilities to become regarded as a treatment rather than an accommodation. Subthemes that illustrate the origins, outcomes, and long-term impact of this phenomenon are described in the next section.

Making the Decision: You Just Never Know

Patterns in the decision making around the purchase of AAC contribute to the phenomenon of technology being regarded as treatment that will improve the student's overall functioning or reveal the student's true capabilities. The notion of their child communicating with an electronic voice output device is initially disturbing to many parents. They may interpret the suggestion as an indication that professionals are giving up on the idea that the child eventually will use speech, as noted by one of Christine's speech therapists:

> It is really hard when you have parents in this situation [who] are trying to deal with this really devastating event. . . . There was still a lot of anger around [the circumstances of Christine's birth] and then there were these [professionals] saying, "Let's have her point to these things," and it was like . . . from Mom's perspective, "I know what she likes and what she doesn't like so what is the big deal?" And almost like, "Why don't they believe me?"

In part to steer away from these sensitive issues, professionals focus on other advantages of AAC besides augmenting and assisting the child's current communication modalities. These include fostering independence, reducing learned helplessness, reducing or preventing problem behaviors caused by frustration, and reducing the discrepancy between receptive and expressive language. In an effort to allay parents' fears that AAC will impede natural communication development, professionals may focus their presentation of the benefits of technology primarily on how use of AAC will actually foster development in this area.

For older students who already may be exhibiting acting-out or stereotypic behavior, lack of motivation, and learned helplessness, AAC represents a possible solution. It may eliminate frustration, thereby reducing problem behaviors, and allow the child to reveal his or her thoughts and feelings. Thus, from the beginning, the role of AAC in increasing opportunities and simplifying communication with adults and peers may be a secondary consideration, with child-centered concerns

of language development and self-determination being the primary focus.

Once these benefits are outlined, parents and professionals may feel a sense of urgency about making the device available, because not providing the device could be regarded as withholding treatment that will both build skills and prevent acquired secondary disabilities. Also, it is often assumed that children who have acquired AAC in elementary school or later and who experience difficulty learning to use the device could have avoided this frustration by being introduced to the device at a younger age. As one of Eric's speech therapists said, "It is assumed that if you want this later down the road that you got to get going on this right now."

This sense of urgency is one reason, but not the only reason, that the decision to try the device is often made in spite of lack of data on whether it has been successful with other students with similar disabilities. Other factors that make it difficult to base AAC acquisition on data rather than emotional considerations and hope are (1) the difficulty of assessing students, especially very young ones, who have multiple disabilities; (2) the sense that AAC is worth a try, even if it has not been successful for other students with similar disabilities, because (a) each child's constellation of abilities and disabilities is unique; and (b) there are probably no other communication alternatives that promise to engage the student to such a degree.

> We don't do any formal cognitive testing, because they can't be tested. We just have to go with what kind of behaviors we do see and make an estimate. Each device requires different levels of cognitive skills. It used to be that in the early 80s people were coming out with matrices, decision-making matrices for AAC. It was great because you say yes or no and it would take you over to this part and yes or no. We found out most kids are not yes or no kids. If you say no, you really should have something else to do. (Clinic-based AAC specialist)

I think it is kinda exciting to give it a try with some of the children you are not real sure if they are going to be able to handle something like that, but the voice-output can make such a difference. That's why it is hard to make a decision about an AAC strategy just on the basis of cognitive level. Because it may open a door that nothing else would. (School-based AAC specialist)

Most parents, once presented with the potential benefits of AAC, are open to the suggestion. Even parents who feel they communicate naturally and well with their child through a variety of means often wish others could see beyond the disability and get to know the child as they do. Dawn's mother, a speech therapist who taught Dawn some simple signs, was ambivalent about the trade-off between continuing with sign and shifting to AAC:

I always feel like signing can just be more, so much more spontaneous, more coming out of her own heart, what she wants to say, than things like [the device]. . . . It's not the best thing, but that's what we have to have, and it's something that other people can understand . . . like her grandparents would be happy if she would use it, or something like that, to talk with them.

Given the potential benefits, especially for students who have mild cognitive impairments or whose cognitive abilities have not been assessed, some professionals and many parents feel that it would be irresponsible not to try AAC, as Sara's special education teacher said:

She's an involved kid. She really is. Got a lot of needs and a lot of potential. It's kind of frightening, you know? You could make her or break her, it feels like. . . . You don't know for sure, the sky is the limit. I mean, you could push and push and push and that person could really come out of your program with tremendous skills and a normal life. I mean you just don't know, so that is kind of scary. And therein lies the challenge of Sara.

Once the decision is made, professionals and families often work together to fund the purchase of the device. A logical approach would be to buy a simple device that the student can use with minimal training. However, financial considerations introduce one of several trade-offs that parents and professionals face when dealing with AAC. Because devices are expensive, and funders are likely to pay for only one during the student's school career, many families decide to get a complex device that the child can "grow into." It is, after all, going to be the child's main means of communication, his or her voice. Therefore raising the funds for the device can become a district/family/community project during which the potential cognitive and developmental benefits are continually repeated and magnified, especially for the family. By the time the device is finally purchased, parents may believe that the device will reveal that the student is not cognitively impaired or is less impaired than professionals have assumed. Training the student to use the device therefore becomes critically important to family and school: The decision to purchase, in spite of the expense and emotional ambivalence involved, has to be "worth it."

Barriers to Communication: If Only . . .

The focus of many students' AAC training turns quickly to treatment rather than to communication goals in part because, for most students with severe and multiple disabilities, the device does not immediately serve a communicative function. Much to the disappointment of parents, most students with severe disabilities do not immediately begin using their AAC devices to communicate with family, teachers, and peers. Barriers to "real" communication with the device seem to emerge one by one, leaving parents and educators with a sense that if only each individual obstacle could be overcome, the device could fulfill its intended function. However, the reasons that AAC devices do not promote communication for this group of students are numerous, complex, interrelated, and extremely difficult to address. Furthermore, they are quite predictable, given the needs of the student and the limitations of the devices. It is not unusual for children to experience all of the problems with device use described subsequently.

Engineering and Design Issues. Developers of AAC strive to make devices adaptable for a wide range of users. Keys are adjustable to respond to varying degrees of touch. Some devices can be programmed with a few simple items but will accommodate or produce more complex messages so they can to some extent grow with the user. Portability, durability, ease of programming, and naturalness of voice output are all addressed in the design of AAC and in the variety of devices available. However, AAC devices are not usually custom-made for individual users. The cost of this approach would put AAC out of reach of most individuals with disabilities. Furthermore, AAC devices are designed to address communication needs, not developmental needs or severe physical access issues. The decision to acquire AAC for these potential benefits, in spite of design features that present barriers to students' independent use of the device, introduces a series of complex trade-offs and dilemmas that must be addressed before the device can be used for communication.

Access and Speed. For children with physical disabilities, there are likely to be several access issues: If the student is not in a wheelchair, how will the device be transported? (More than one speech therapist in the study commented that it was "too bad" that a student was not using a wheelchair because this would have solved a primary access prob-

lem.) How will the student indicate his or her selection on the device if striking the key with a finger is not a reliable motor skill? As outlined in the introduction, a variety of switches are available that can be operated with virtually any reliable motor response. However, most of these require scanning through the available selections and timing the activation of the switch to get the right response. For students with severe physical disabilities, as well as for communication partners, the process can be agonizing:

> One thing that describes Christine is that she seems to be a kid that can really be easily overwhelmed by all the demands on her in terms of the motoric demands—to try and organize her body. The sensory demands of trying to figure out what in the environment she really needs to attend to is a big part of her and how she functions and how she is able to interact in her world. . . . It's hard for me now to think about [Christine] having to get her hand out there to stop something to communicate, with kids' minds changing quickly and a lot of distractions, and she really had to work, to be positioned right and to concentrate and do that and stuff, and it took a lot of time. (Early intervention speech therapist)

Even when the student can access the device directly, the motoric demands can be exhausting:

> The response [on the AAC] costs a lot for him, physically. When he was saying "Hi" to me the other day, even his legs got tense. His feet were moving up on his footrest a little bit. It involves his whole body just to hit "Hi," and so in physical terms, it's expensive for him to respond like that. (Bill's special education teacher)

This process can be challenging for the communication partner as well, as Sara's teacher describes. Sara accessed her device with a head switch:

> It's very laborious to have to sit there to watch her scan a message if she wants to say something spontaneous. I mean just a simple question like, "Hi, Sara, how are you doing?" It's happened so many times, she doesn't respond. She just sits there. Then you prompt her to use her system, and then it's finally scan, scan, scan, scan, scan, "Fine thank you," or "Fine, how are you?" Well, by then the [other students] are down the hallway. (Sara's special education teacher)

Addressing the access issues for some users of AAC may distort the communicative function of the device to a degree that makes it a barrier rather than a facilitator of interpersonal interaction.

Voice Output. The objective of AAC is to permit students who do not speak to communicate by surrogate voice, ostensibly a more natural communication mode than others available to them. However, the two options available for the voice of an AAC are digitized speech or recorded human voices. Although digitized speech is improving, even the best examples are difficult for new communication partners to understand, and, even for experienced listeners, they sound distorted compared with natural speech. (Steven Hawking, an AAC user, describes the digitized voice of his device as "English with a sort of Swedish accent.") Some AAC companies make available different voices for the commonly used items that might be programmed on a device. Users can select a voice that corresponds by gender and age to what their own voices might sound like. However, to be useful, an AAC device must be constantly reprogrammed and personalized with idiosyncratic messages. In practice, the voice on the AAC device is usually that of the student's mother or AAC support person. Some educators question whether it is more

"natural" for a student's AAC to generate computer-generated speech or an adult, usually female, voice. The answer depends on the age and gender of the student and may change as the student gets older. Unfortunately, for most students, the decision has to be made at the time of purchase. In our study, only Becky sometimes had a child's voice— her sister's—on her device. Bill, a 16-year-old high school student, had his mother's voice on his device because she was the only person who could program it. The appropriateness of this from a peer's point of view was not considered.

Setting Issues. For young children, and those who are ambulatory and do not have their devices mounted on a wheelchair, teachers may struggle to make the device fit into the setting. Preschool teachers in particular worry about the safety of such an expensive device that might be dropped, played with by other children, or spilled on. To overcome these concerns, changes are made in the setting that actually impede access to communication partners:

> If you wanted to put your child in his wheelchair and have his AAC device put on the wheelchair and say OK this kid is going to stay in the wheelchair all the time, then his device is always available to him. But if you want your child on the same level with the other little children and sitting at the table with them or sitting on the floor or sitting in the story corner with them or whatever, then you have to choose which is more important. And I think that, at this point anyway, it is physically [more] important for him to be with the kids than for him to push a button and for him to say some word or phrase or something. (Eric's mother)

Concerns about device safety sometimes lead to a decision to use the device exclusively for communication practice in a nonclassroom setting with an adult, underlining its treatment function. The plan may be to introduce the device in regular classroom activities when the student is using it proficiently. However, because training is often protracted, students learn to communicate with their devices in a one-to-one setting with an adult and in other ways with their peers, making generalization to the classroom setting increasingly difficult. Furthermore, when the AAC device is introduced into the classroom, adults are likely to feel they still need to monitor its use to prevent damage and to support communication with peers.

Communicative Function. Beyond the setting considerations, for younger children, the communication function of the device sometimes is not apparent either to the student user or to peers. The complexity of access issues can challenge engineering and design of devices to the point that the communicative function is impaired or destroyed. However, some preschool teachers and speech/language therapists interviewed for this study questioned whether AAC devices, even if they could be used without access adaptations, were regarded by young children as anything other than a novel toy, as noted by an early intervention preschool teacher:

I think that part of the problem is that when educators try to find something that works they try to get kids ready for that situation so they keep moving that skill downward and downward to a point where it really isn't workable. I think even the concept "communication" is too abstract for children under 3. I am not sure when it is going to work for them. But communicating by pictures means they have to keep some kind of abstract thought in their head and mentally represent something that is not there. That I think they are just beginning to do if it is in the here and now. But I think having a thought and translating that into a picture is not something that [most] children at that age are developmentally ready to do.

The problem of the AAC device not being viewed as a means of communication was not limited to the preschool setting. Parents and teachers of older students described how voice output of the device was disregarded by listeners. A speech therapist described how she programmed an elementary student's device to say "[Speech Therapist] says 'Keep your hands off.'" The student delivered this message at show and tell. The students' response was to grab the device and frantically press the buttons. The therapist resorted to saying, "When I said, 'Hold it! What did Sammy just say?' they had no idea. The attention goes to the technology not the kid."

Bill's aide describes Bill's reaction when peer tutors and adults in the classroom at his high school fail to respond: "A lot of times he might say something and doesn't get a response, and maybe he feels stupid because nobody is paying attention, just because it is not him that is speaking. It's something else."

Programming Dilemmas. Professionals or parents programming an AAC for a child face the difficult task of what to include in the limited number of selections that are available. For beginning AAC users with a limited repertoire of communications conveyed through eye gaze, vocalization, gesture, or sign, those few things probably will be included to test and verify that the child understands that the device is another way of communicating those messages. However, the student may appear confused, annoyed, or even angry that he is now required to use the device to "say" these things, when the other communication method may be preferred. Dawn, the student in the following example, requests snacks at home by signing "cracker," "juice," "cookie," and so forth.

Dawn is working in a group of three students with the special education teacher. The teacher shows a pack of crackers to Dawn and asks, "Are these crackers? Yes or no?" indicating that she should press the correct response on her AAC device. [Dawn sometimes indicates "No" through gesture or on her AAC device but never uses "Yes" without heavy prompting.] Dawn presses a key at random. The teacher says, "Oops, looks like you're saying 'No,' " and moves to the next student who indicates "Yes" and gets a cracker. Dawn touches the teacher and signs "cracker," but Jean is questioning the third student who signs "cracker" and gets a cracker. (Field notes)

Programmers also will include other things the student cannot easily convey through other communication modes, such as statements describing emotions or references to objects or people who are out of view. These can provide an opening for communication, but programming beyond the initial statement can be challenging. Teachers and parents are sensitive to these limitations and the effect they have on the AAC user:

> She cannot be conversational with the devices that she has set up, which is real unfortunate because she is a girl that loves to participate and be right there involved with everyone and she is limited to just, you know, what we are able to give her in messages. (Sara's special education teacher)

> We were not getting much communication at all. It is impossible to get much from what is on the device. There is not enough places and it takes too long to activate it. I probably wouldn't use it either. (Christine's preschool teacher)

To provide more response options, the parent or professional responsible for programming may expand the number and complexity of messages available on the AAC device. However, this creates ambiguity about why the student does not use most of the messages available: Is it because they are low-frequency comments? Because the student does not know where they are located? Because the programmer has overestimated the student's communication abilities?

Sara uses almost the same eight squares all the time on that dumb thing even though it's probably got 40, you know. It's just, she's very limited in the ones she'll use, so I don't know why that is. There's a lot of variety on there, but it must not be useful to her or she doesn't know what they say or doesn't see the application for it. (Special education teacher)

> I think it's too much. I think it makes him use it less. I think that he can't remember what he needs to set off different themes, and his limitations of vision and coordination to get into pushing two different things. He has to push three or four different things, he has to turn it on, he has to push symbol theme, has to push the symbol he wants to get at it, then he has to push. . . . I think it is too complicated. The only thing he does consistently is ask for his Dire Straits tape. (Bill's teaching assistant)

Bill's mother says he does not need to use his AAC at home because the family understands his other communication. She thinks that the reason he does not use his AAC at school is "probably just his shyness. His awareness of who he is, and that he is different. He's just a real shy guy until you get to know him."

In spite of the observed barriers to communicative use, parents and teachers seldom "give up on the device." It may be put away, as in Eric's case, until the student is in a different school setting. More often, however, mindful of the powerful developmental and treatment potential of the device and the difficulty in obtaining it, AAC specialists are called in to analyze the problem and design solutions.

Problem Solving:
What to Fix First

It is relatively easy to identify the barriers to student use of their AAC devices but harder to develop strategies to address them.

Identifying the primary problem may be difficult: Perhaps the student needs to achieve a minimal level of speed and accuracy in accessing messages to appreciate the communicative function of the device. Maybe the purpose of the device will be clearer to the student if it is the only communication strategy permitted in a particular setting. Or maybe, until motivational factors that are intrinsic to the communication process take over, additional social reinforcement should be provided when the student uses the device.

Implementing any of these strategies requires intensive training, radical changes to the setting in which the device is used, or, usually, both. These measures are intended to be temporary—not needed once the student understands and appreciates the power of the device. However, because of the difficulty of assessing the student, the unpredictability of communication opportunities, and a number of problems related to training, it is very hard to predict how long the strategies will need to be in place. In this study, none of the students used his or her device consistently except during intensive training in specially adapted settings. Furthermore, the "temporary" intensive strategies adopted to awaken students to the communicative potential of their AAC devices sometimes required sacrificing other goals students and their parents have identified. Ironically, these are often social, academic, or developmental goals that the AAC was supposed to help address.

Saturating the Setting. Some AAC proponents advocate "engineering the environment" for AAC training so that all students and adults in the setting consistently use the same picture of an icon-based communication system (Goosens & Crain, 1986; Goosens, Crain, & Elder, 1991). Teacher and parent proponents of this approach reason that if the student has the messages available and is stimulated by activities in the environment to use them, device use will become habitual. Although none of the AAC users in this study were taught in an engineered classroom, Becky's mother had attempted to have one of her daughter's previous classrooms adapted in this way. When this met with resistance, Becky's mother took it on herself to provide the materials to support AAC use throughout the school day.

Convinced that to learn to use her AAC device Becky needs consistent, intensive training, Becky's mother has responded by buying a photocopier for her home so she can make overlays for the AAC for every occasion. She communicates daily with Becky's teachers to find out what activities they will be doing so Becky will have vocabulary available to participate. However, it is not possible for staff to reprogram the device every time they need a new overlay, so the overlays are used as picture boards. [Becky is supposed to point to the appropriate picture, but the voice output is switched off.] There is also general agreement that Becky's vocalizations decrease when she is dealing with pictures without voice output. Although everyone agrees that Becky responds positively to voice output, this has been sacrificed, perhaps temporarily, to provide adequate vocabulary to allow Becky to participate in more classroom activities.

Although the intent of saturating Becky's environment with pictures is to improve her ability to communicate independently, she requires a full-time one-to-one aide to change the overlays and to prompt her to use the system. According to her speech therapist: "She really needs to have an adult with her. She doesn't take the system over and interact with another child. She kind of needs someone right there and will request or point if encouraged, but she doesn't sit and just interact with a child and the board. . . . She needs a lot of cuing to use the system." (Memo based on field notes)

Improving Fluency. Once the best means of interface with the device are identified, the task of the student is to operate the switch as quickly and consistently as possible. Because this is the basis of successful AAC use, recommendations often are made to focus intensively on speed and accuracy of use during early stages of training. However, a criterion for these training recommendations may not be specified; the goal is simply to use the device more easily and faster. An aide or series of instructional assistants may be assigned to work individually with the student to practice access skills in isolation. Student progress on improving access may be slow or may reach a plateau, but the aides, who have no specified criteria to work toward—and in any case who probably are not taking data on student progress or communicating with each other or the teacher—continue doing their job as they understand it:

> Sara uses a typing program accessed by a head switch on a personal computer in her mainstream Language Arts class. She averages about 5 letters per minute with this scanning program. One day the class was given a multiple-choice test pertaining to a novel the teacher had read to them. The other students circled the letter of the correct response. Sara was instructed to copy the question and all the answers to each question, then go back and put an *X* by the correct answers. The aides explained that she needs to "get her speed and accuracy up." At the end of the class Sara was less than half way through the assignment, which the other students completed in about 10 minutes. (Memo based on field notes)

Motivational Barriers and Dilemmas. When access and speed issues have been addressed as well as possible and student device use is still disappointing, attention may turn to motivational barriers. Because of the difficulty of communicating directly with the student users, parents and educators try to guess what the problem might be:

> He didn't like [the device]. He likes the way he talks [referring to vocalizations

Eric uses as one of his communication modes]. (Eric's mother)

> Eric rejected it. He wouldn't use it and he would push it away when they brought it out. He would just kind of reject it. Then it was taken away to be reprogrammed. It has never come back. (Preschool teacher)

> With little kids, kids zero to 3 I think [Eric] was 2 at the time, communication is so much weighted toward social interaction and not toward words anyway. There are some 2-year-olds that are linguistically competent but most of them communicate by looks and glances and body posture. So that is one of the things I discovered about this little boy that he was a very competent nonverbal communicator. In fact, he got pretty much specific ideas across, not just "I am not happy" but "I want that particular red truck that is sitting across the room" without using a word. (Speech therapist)

Sometimes it is difficult for observers to interpret the student's response to the device.

> When Bill was asked by his mother to use the AAC device, he modified the signal he uses when the charge on his chair is low, indicating that he couldn't use the AAC because the charge was low: Touching the chair twice, touching the [AAC] twice. Knowing that the battery of the device was fully charged, his mother treated this as a joke, "Don't try to fool me!" (Memo based on field notes)

Even if there is agreement that the student is not motivated to use the device, that is seldom the end of it. The response is usually to intensify positive and negative reinforcement to bring the student to a communicative level with device use, at which point reinforcement intrinsic to interpersonal communication should take over. Once the student discovers the power of the device, it is reasoned, motivation will no longer be an issue.

> I told [the school staff] "Don't take his coat off if he doesn't ask you to take his coat off [with the AAC]. If he doesn't say, "Please, will you help me take off my coat?" then don't take it off and let him sit there in it all day. It's up to him." (Bill's mother)

In contrast to the approach of punishing failure to use the device, some educators advocate adding extrinsic reinforcement to encourage device use. Training often takes place during snack or lunch time, in spite of the potential for damage to the device, to reinforce device use with food. Sometimes the reinforcers are social, as Becky's speech therapist describes:

> Making a big deal about it. Being encouraging—rubbing her on the back—"You did that!" or you know really showing them that it was meaningful versus a child pointing and pointing and not getting that feedback that they need. Becky needs a lot of feedback. She needs feedback all the time. She won't be OK just sitting in a classroom on her own. She does best one-on-one.

Because this type of feedback is not available from interactions with peers, it is difficult to project how device use will be generalized to natural communication settings when treatment is completed. In the meantime, for Becky, the immediate effect of saturating her environment and providing intensified reinforcement through a full-time assistant is to decrease contact with other children and limit communication opportunities:

> During transitions from one instructional group to the next, students touch each other, smile, vocalize. Becky's assistant takes the AAC device in one hand and Becky's hand in the other and

leads her to the next group. She sits with the same girl she was with before. They have not looked at each other all morning. (Field notes)

Training: Gearing Up and Dropping Back

In the effort both to find out how well the student understands the function of the AAC device and to make device use habitual, training becomes—temporarily it is assumed—an extremely important focus. Intensification of training often includes encouraging or requiring the student to use the device rather than other forms of communication and increasing the amount of one-to-one training time. However, following unsuccessful intensive training there is often a reevaluation of the role of AAC for the student and an attempt to simplify training and scale back expectations for the AAC.

Assistants for Assistive Technology. Given that training must be intensive, consistent, and available throughout the school day, almost all students who have AAC devices have assistants to help support the technology. Besides training on the device, aides may be needed to help transport a device for a student who is ambulatory. For a student in a wheelchair, an aide may be needed to mount and dismount the device if it is not compatible with wheelchair use or other activities. Aides also perform maintenance and prompt the student to use the device. If it is determined that the device does not fit the classroom setting, as in the case of a preschooler, training may be conducted in another setting, one-to-one between adult and child. Once the decision is made that assistants are needed to provide the intensity of training required and to promote device use throughout the day, aides are likely to be assigned full responsibility for the student, with little training and little supervision. Because the aide is with the student anyway to help with the device, he or she may assume other responsibilities for the student's care and instruction. In any instance in which an assistant is "paired" with a student, there is a danger that the adult will create an additional barrier to peer-to-peer interaction and independence. A speech therapist who had worked with Eric described the progress of another child with whom she worked:

> My observation last week was that the student was pretty independent in pointing to a picture without any cues. Except for the fact that the teacher was sitting right across from her and the student was turned away from the other peers at the table. (Becky's speech therapist)

Another problem with aides assuming most of the responsibility for AAC devices is their lack of training and supervision in providing training and evaluating student progress. The AT or AAC specialist may model a training session with the aide and special education teacher but may not be available for follow-up or to answer questions, as Sara's special education teacher complained:

> With some specialists, you have to practically wrestle them down to the ground to get them to give you exactly what you want. And it's not because they don't want to give it to you, it's because they are so busy, overloaded, and they assume too much. They make the assumptions that it will be just like it was for someone else you had who is like Sara: "Do the same types of things, oh, you are doing great. Just keep doing that." Well we need something a lot more specific, and it is finally come around to where we . . . say, "Write it down. I want pictures, I want directions, and I want like one-on-one training."

With so little support available for aides, "training" may come to mean a period of time that has to be filled somehow with practice using the device. Unless this time is well de-signed, it can be not just wasted but also counterproductive and even punishing for the student.

> Joe, the aide, asked Dawn to indicate with the AAC whether she wanted to listen to music or look at pictures. She indicated pictures. He asked, "You want to see your pictures? Show me Yes or No." He guided her hand first to No, then to Yes, and Dawn pressed Yes. He gave her the box of pictures and told her she could look at them. After a few minutes, Joe took the pictures and told Dawn to make another choice. She chose music, so Joe helped her turn on the tape recorder.
> After two minutes Joe turned off the music and asked Dawn to make another choice. She hit "I am mad" three times. Joe asked, "You're mad? Why are you mad? Tell me with your [AAC device.]" [Observer comment: I wondered how she could/would respond to a question like "Why are you mad" when she does not communicate verbally at all, and there was no way to provide an answer to that question on the device.] (Field notes)

An assistant may question whether forcing students to make the same choices day after day is really effective training, but it is what the specialist said to do. The special education teacher will likely be busy with other students, sometimes in another part of the school and unable to observe and provide feedback on how the assistant could modify or improve instruction.

> Sara's assistants were told that it was important not to "put words in her mouth" by supervising her writing too closely. They interpreted this to mean that they should let Sara write her entire assignment, using her head switch/scanning system, then indicate where corrections were needed. From September through April, to make correc-

tions Sara was required to erase back to the site of the first error and re-input the rest of the text because the software didn't have an insert function. At the rate of 5 letters per minute, corrections seldom got made. At a meeting of a multidisciplinary team on technology in April, when project staff suggested getting software with an insert function, the special educator teacher informed the group that the software does have the capability to insert and replace. (Memo based on field notes)

As noted previously, student progress is not systematically tracked; data are seldom taken. In fact, it is somewhat difficult for assistants to tell whether device use is purposeful and the messages conveyed are intentional. Instead, assistants will report any success they see, even if ambiguous. For example, this is how Becky's teacher evaluated Becky's use of her AAC: "I guess Becky does, apparently, in the classroom, go over and get the device. I guess she did that a couple of months ago, one time." These reports become powerful reinforcers for supervisors and parents, making it difficult to give up on or modify that training, which, after all, may be working.

Because they work in isolation, AAC training for the student/assistant pair may become a repetitive drill, the goal of which is no longer clear. In such an arrangement, device use may become stereotypic, leading the assistant to feel ambivalent or negative about the appropriateness of the device for the student:

Becky hit "Please help me" on the device, the only key she had hit during the training session. She was indicating she needed help with a puzzle piece. The aide responded, "You don't need help." [Observer comment: It must be hard for the assistant to reinforce every request when she feels that doing so promotes dependency in Becky.] (Field notes)

Simplifying Training. After months or years of this type of training, intended to be intensive and to overcome barriers to effective, purposeful AAC use, it is frustrating for all concerned when expectations for the device as a facilitator of communication are still not met. Even more disappointing, the student has not reaped the developmental and interpersonal benefits that were anticipated. To resolve the ambiguity surrounding the situation, to determine what "the problem" is, practitioners attempt to simplify the programming of the device, make the training cleaner, and make the device more usable for the student. Several speech therapists and AAC specialists involved in these six cases referred to this as "dropping back." Behind each suggested change is an analysis of where previous training "went wrong," an attempt to improve training by understanding how the student views the device, and a reevaluation of how the device might fit into the student's life.

I don't know who picked [Bill's device] out. . . . I don't know where it came from. I wish that we could set it up so that if he would just press one button instead of these combinations of things that you have to wait for. . . . It makes more physical work for him, more time for somebody else to wait, and more possibilities for error. But what I have tried to talk to [Bill's mother] about doing is backing up and doing it simple like that, and then gradually make it more complicated for him if the simple stuff works. . . . She wants a lot for him, and if we back up he's not getting a lot, you know. It makes sense to me [to drop back] but maybe not to her. (Bill's special education teacher)

I think we screwed up on Becky by the 20,000 language boards that she has. What happens is all our energy goes into making the device and making the language boards. "If we make enough language boards, she can communicate."

Wrong. Let's stop making the flipping language boards. Let's never make another language board for the next 6 years. Stop making them, because we can't make 6 more and make her 6 times smarter. (Becky's speech therapist)

I really do wish, and I am as bad as anybody, that we would drop back to a prompt sequence that would be real careful in our thoughts and give the direction once, and then if she doesn't do it on one level of prompt you drop back and when she doesn't do it on that level of prompt you drop back, so by the third time you physical [sic] assist and get out of there. (Another of Becky's speech therapists)

We assumed that the device was going to be the end-all. It turns out it is not. She is real resistant to using it. . . . We used to use it in the bathroom because "I am all done" is on it. She never used it. . . . We finally got to the point where we said, "Just turn it on, when we hear it beeping, we will come get you off the toilet. Just use it as a signal." She just wasn't even into doing that. We put the loop tape on and it has a young girl's voice saying "I'm all done." She has been using that successfully. . . . What is really interesting is the first method she uses when she is all done in the bathroom is straight yelling at us. She really ends up vocalizing to tell us she is done to get your attention. That is what is effective and useful for her. (Christine's preschool teacher)

This reevaluation of device use has two goals: to assess how well the student uses the device and to determine what role, if any, the device should have in the student's communication system. This is precisely the type of evaluation that one would expect before a child acquires a device. However, because of the promise AAC holds for all types of development, if only a series of challenges can be

worked out, this evaluation may not be conducted until the student, parents, and staff have experienced months or years of failure. One preschool teacher describes her experience with early introduction of AAC:

I saw time and time again . . . when people would force the issue and the kids would feel unsuccessful and it was hell on the parents. It was really, really hard on parents. It made me feel bad as a classroom teacher. (Eric's early intervention teacher)

Different Views: Ambivalence, Ambiguity, Regret

In spite of the disappointment and frustration evident in the comments set out previously, the promise of AAC for the student with severe multiple disabilities continues to exert a powerful influence over both professionals and parents. This is primarily because, even after intensive work, the child's potential for communication and interaction is still not clear. Still not answered are the questions: What are this child's abilities? What should our expectations be? Who is this child?

Usually, but not always, it is the parents who cling to the view that if only training had been better planned and conducted, their child would be able to communicate his or her thoughts and desires. Bill's mother, Nancy, continues to pressure his teachers to "force" him to use the AAC device at school, in spite of the fact that he rarely uses it at home "because the family understands him so well." Bill's special education teacher has given the issue a lot of thought:

I think the [device] is kind of shooting for the moon. Just trying to get the most for him. Well, the most may not be practical. And I think that's really hard, when what's practical may seem limiting. Especially when you've got somebody like Nancy who's saying, "I hope he can do more and more. I want it I want it I want it." And then in five years you say, "It didn't work." I've spent all this money I've spent all this time on this thing that didn't work. We could have been doing other things.

In Bill's case, the view of both parent and teacher is that Bill has lost out. Nancy believes he lost out because training on the AAC was not consistent, in part because staff underestimated Bill's ability to communicate with the device. The teacher's view is that Bill lost out on opportunities to learn other skills because his mother's hopes and expectations were unrealistic. In each of the cases we studied of students with severe disabilities who had AAC devices, this was the fundamental question: Whose view of the student's abilities and potential should determine the school program? This conflict is not limited to the arena of AT. Parents and educators have the same ongoing disagreement about the appropriateness and utility of teaching reading, continuing speech therapy, including the student in mainstream classes, and a host of other issues that arise when students who are difficult to assess are educated in public schools. Sometimes, it is the school staff who complain that the parents' expectations of the student are too low and that they foster learned helplessness by doing too much for their child. Sometimes, it is the parents who complain that with better teaching and an appropriate curriculum their child would be a different person.

In spite of these differences of opinion, none of the cases we learned about was as polarized as one might expect, given the different views of what the school program should look like. This was due primarily to educators' reluctance to say that they had any student all figured out. The ambiguity inherent in interacting with each of these students pervaded teachers' comments about them:

It is easier for peer tutors not to interact with Bill because it really takes time and concentration. And sometimes all that time and concentration is because

you don't know if he really understood what your question was, you don't know if he understood what his answer was. Each person who works with him sees his needs and what he does or doesn't do differently. (Bill's teacher)

Educators and parents alike remained open to the possibility that there might be "something out there" that would hold the key to communicating with these students. They are reluctant to say that the device, though disappointing, was a poor choice as the focus of the student's program:

I thought the [AAC device] would be the answer to all my prayers and it is presented like that. And I don't know if it is presented that way on purpose. I don't think it is meant to hurt anybody when people do present that way, that they are just excited. That is great. I want people to keep up the enthusiasm. But tell [parents] it is not an answer to every problem and everything they get. You can tell us parents, "[AAC] is not the total answer, but we want you to have it anyway." Because I would have gotten it anyway. I would rather have a partial answer than no answer at all. (Christine's mother)

Bill's special education teacher, for all of her dissatisfaction with Bill's AAC device, is reluctant to say that he should not have it:

I don't know if I would have the confidence to say, "I know what's best, and I know that this isn't practical for the long term, so let's give up on it." I don't think I would want to be in the position of being the one to make that decision. It's almost like we've got to—it's like the reading. We've got to focus on it and do it, prove that it is not going to work. And if it works a little bit, then you can go on with it, regardless of what the practical implications are.

Conclusion

After more than a century of breathtaking technological progress, we ask a lot of our technology, and we are accustomed to getting what we ask for. Because of the wondrous advances and unexpected successful applications of technology, we tend to believe "there must be something out there" that would make communication possible for children who have such obvious communication needs. Furthermore, because of our faith in technology, it is often assumed that by applying a technological solution, we are doing the utmost, the best we possibly can. We also know from numerous personal experiences with new technology that there can be a period of time after the technology is introduced when interface issues are frustrating and the user's learning curve is discouragingly flat. Given these assumptions and experiences, it is understandable that well-meaning people would reason that with adaptation and training, lengthy and painful though it may be, current technology could be adapted to open communication opportunities to individuals with severe disabilities.

Unfortunately, AT for individuals with severe disabilities is different in many respects from convenience technology for the general population. Changes in AAC are not driven by market forces, and "improvement" is hard to define: A design change that, for example, makes interface with a particular device possible for one individual may make the device inaccessible for another.

Another difference between technology for the general public and that developed specifically to compensate for disability is the degree to which AAC can become an emotional and philosophical as well as financial investment. Parents of children with severe disabilities and professionals who work with them may be asking the technology to do much more than assist or augment communication. Consciously or unconsciously, they may expect technology to make life not just easier but "normal." For some parents and professionals, AAC is regarded not simply as a way to facilitate communication, but as a way for the child to access his or her true abilities.

This view, once established, is extremely difficult to change, especially because a developmental focus can supercede communication goals quickly if the device initially proves disappointing as a communication aid. Even if the interactive utility of the device is unclear, it is reasoned, "it can't hurt" to invest the student's time and energy in training because the potential for stimulating linguistic and social development is so compelling: "You just never know" what the student might be capable of. So powerful is the promise of AAC for this population that families and professionals accept difficult trade-offs at every stage of their involvement with AAC.

Trade-offs begin with the decision to acquire a device that provides the student a "voice" but tends to focus the attention of the communication partner on the device rather than on the student. Other trade-offs are inherent in device selection: a simple device the student can use now with little training versus a more complex device the child can grow into. The former sacrifices communicative range for ease of use, whereas the latter has the potential to give the student communicative power, but only after extensive training. The dilemmas continue with programming decisions. If messages from the student's current repertoire are included so the student understands the purpose of the device, the student may be discouraged from using other functional modes of communication. However, if the device is programmed only with new or novel items, the student may not understand the purpose of the device or find it useful.

Intensive training requires other trade-offs: "temporarily" restricting the child's other modes of communication, limiting the topics about which the child can communicate, and changing the way others respond to the student. The effort required to make these changes, in addition to the expense of the device and the potential benefits, often results in training to use the device becoming the centerpiece of the child's curriculum and a major focus of classroom staff and resources. To learn to use AAC devices, most students require intensive one-to-one instruction in an isolated setting until the purpose of the device is clear and the speed and accuracy are sufficient to permit natural interaction. Because of the time required to meet training criteria, which are seldom clear, students miss out on other instructional opportunities as well as peer-to-peer social interaction.

These trade-offs should be a red flag, signaling that AAC technology applied to children with severe disabilities may be significantly different from other technological applications with which we are familiar. Technology that is widely adopted meets needs that are well understood and nearly universally agreed on: to make routine tasks easier, faster, more fun, more comfortable. For the students in this study, AAC did none of these things and, in fact, often complicated and impeded whatever communication modes they had used previously. For what other technology would we accept such training contingencies? What other technology users are forced to change and even distort their habitual interactive practices to this degree to demonstrate facility using a machine?

However, the fact that AAC involves complex, difficult trade-offs is not a deterrent to many parents and teachers of students with severe disabilities who are accustomed to having to wait and see whether treatments and accommodations will produce the intended results. Children with undetermined degrees of disability who do not communicate verbally introduce ambiguity into educational settings. This ambiguity presents a series of persistent dilemmas and unattractive choices that parents and educators struggle with throughout the student's school career. Views of what is in the student's best interest and how the student can best spend time in school may become polarized. Enduring battles between school and family over what kinds of treatment and instruction should be included in the daily school schedule are not limited to the area of AT. Well into high school, parents and teachers argue at every individualized education program meeting

whether to continue reading instruction and speech therapy or move on to activities of daily living; whether to include the student in a mainstream biology class to promote social integration or to use the time for a swimming session. Behind each of these arguments are other questions and dilemmas: Whose view of the child's potential should prevail? What is our responsibility to the student: to hold out for continued treatments that may foster "normal" development, or to provide opportunities to find a role in society with whatever capabilities the student presents? The first course may lead to accusations of wasting time and promoting false hopes. The second course may lead to accusations of giving up on or holding out on the student, limiting his or her potential.

Perhaps the most persistent dilemma in this controversial area is how to give the student a "voice" in the debate. When AAC enters the picture, it may be viewed as the key to understanding the student who will be using it. However, as Becky's preschool teacher suggests, AAC, rather than being an aid to understanding, actually may be a distraction: "Sometimes we give ourselves tools to not confront the task a hand. And the task at hand is this internal stuff between human beings."

References

Goosens, C., & Crain, S. (1986). *Augmentative communication: Intervention resource.* Lake Zurich, IL: Don Johnston Developmental Equipment.

Goosens, C., Crain, S., & Elder, P. (1991, March). *Engineering the classroom environment for interactive symbolic communication.* Workshop presentation, Eugene, OR.

Tanchak, T. L., & Sawyer, C. (1995). Augmentative communication. In K. F. Flippo, K. J. Inge, & J. M. Barcus (Eds.), *Assistive technology: A resource for school, work, and community.* Baltimore: Brookes.

Todis, B. (1996). Tools for the task? Perspectives on assistive technology in educational settings. *Journal of Special Education Technology, 13*(2), 49-61.

Todis, B., & Walker, H. (1993). User perspectives on assistive technology in educational settings. *Focus on Exceptional Children, 26*(3), 1-16.

THREE

Preparing Future Citizens

Technology-Supported, Project-Based Learning in the Social Studies

CYNTHIA M. OKOLO
University of Delaware

RALPH P. FERRETTI
University of Delaware

In this chapter, we discuss an ongoing program of research investigating one approach to improving social studies education in the schools. Our research program is predicated on the belief that all students, including those with mild disabilities, should participate in learning experiences that prepare them to think critically about social issues and to play an active citizenship role. We first discuss the merits of technology-supported, project-based learning for achieving some important goals of social studies education and outline features of this approach. Next, we summarize four studies in which we have evaluated the impact of technology-supported, project-based learning on students' knowledge, attitudes, and discourse about controversial topics. Finally, we describe some of the challenges encountered

AUTHORS' NOTE: Address correspondence or requests for reprints to either author at the School of Education, University of Delaware, Newark, DE 19716. The research reported in this chapter was supported by the U.S. Department of Education, Office of Special Education Programs (#H180E30043). We are grateful to the staff and students at Bayard Elementary School in Wilmington, Delaware, and The College School at the University of Delaware for their participation in the studies described in this chapter.

by our participants and by us in implementing project-based learning and speculate about ways to address them.

Our Approach to Social Studies Education

According to Kliebard (1986), the history of the American curriculum is best understood as a competition of ideological positions for the control of the content and processes of American education. Although other accounts of the history are possible (see Lybarger, 1991), there can be no question that there has been and continues to be considerable disagreement about how best to rationalize social education (Stanley, 1985). In the face of these ideological controversies, there is general agreement about the centrality of citizenship education, broadly conceived, to the social studies curriculum (Stanley, 1985). However, there remains a lack of consensus about how best to prepare a productive citizenry. For some, the focus of citizenship education is directed to the acquisition of basic skills and the transmission of core democratic values, for others to a national curriculum or standardized assessment, and for still others to the student's capacity to think critically and analyze information (Barth & Shermis, 1979; Cherryholmes, 1990; Engle, 1990; Epstein & Evans, 1990; Nelson, 1990). In the absence of a well-established consensus about the matter, it is incumbent on us, as authors of this chapter, to articulate our views about the goals of social studies education.

In our judgment, social studies instruction should encourage the dispositions of thoughtfulness and reflection (Dewey, 1916, 1933) because they are fundamental to participation in democratic institutions. We believe that thoughtful and reflective action is possible when students are challenged to use skills and knowledge in the service of solutions to authentic problems. *Authentic problems* are non-algorithmic, complex, amenable to multiple solutions, involve judgment, require the use of multiple evaluative criteria, and involve self-regulation and the imposition of meaning (Wiggins, 1993).

Authentic problems are the kinds of ill-defined problems (Bransford & Stein, 1984; Simon, 1980) that people confront in everyday life. Like everyday problems, social studies problems often have ambiguous or vague goals (Voss, 1991; Voss, Greene, Post, & Penner, 1983; Voss & Post, 1988; Voss, Tyler, & Yengo, 1983). Questions such as "Did the benefits of industrialization outweigh the costs?" or "Should the Spanish have colonized the indigenous people of Mesoamerica?" do not have generally accepted standards against which all proposed solutions can be evaluated. In fact, there may be many different, apparently contradictory solutions to social problems, whose validity can be determined only by considering the interpretive perspective one takes to the question (Bruner, 1996). Ill-defined problems challenge students to define goals and to identify and analyze evidence that can be used to evaluate the plausibility of arguments offered to support alternative positions (Ferretti & Okolo, 1996; Okolo & Ferretti, 1998). In general, these kinds of problems are best resolved in the context of informed public discussion, during which people gather and consider available evidence and weigh the advantages and disadvantages of various actions. These activities are at the core of democratic action.

We also believe that all citizens, including persons with disabilities, should participate in the processes of democratic decision making. In fact, the guarantee of a free, appropriate public education for students with disabilities is largely due to the application of these democratic and political processes in practice (Curtis, 1991). However, surveys of social studies programs in a range of placements show that social studies instruction often is not provided for students with disabilities (e.g., Kinder & Bursuck, 1991; Patton, Polloway, & Cronin, 1987).

Over the course of 4 years, we have worked in inclusive social studies classes with students in Grades 4 through 6. We have examined the impact of technology-supported, project-based learning on students' knowledge of social studies topics, attitudes, and abilities to construct effective arguments. Subsequently, we outline the five core components of our interventions.

Project-Based Learning

We view projects as a viable supplement to the typical textbook-based curricula and activities that comprise social studies instruction (Carnine, Bean, Miller, & Zigmond, 1994). Project-based activities require students' sustained engagement in authentic learning activities and are characterized by five essential features (Krajcik, Blumenfeld, Marx, & Soloway, 1994). First, an authentic question or problem provides a framework for organizing concepts and principles. Second, students engage in investigations that enable them to formulate and refine specific questions, locate data sources or collect original data, analyze and interpret information, and draw conclusions (Blumenfeld et al., 1991). Third, these investigations lead to the development of artifacts that represent students' proposed solutions to problems, reflect their emerging understanding about the domain, and are presented for the critical consideration of their peers. Fourth, students, teachers, and other members of the community of learners (Brown, 1992) collaborate to complete their projects, share expertise and make decisions about the division of labor, and construct a socially mediated understanding of their topic. Finally, cognitive tools, such as multimedia technology, are used to extend and amplify the representational and analytic capacities of students. We believe that project-based activities can link students' activities to an important intellectual purpose that sustains their motivation for learning over time (Hiebert et al., 1996).

Inclusive Classrooms

Three of the four studies we report subsequently were conducted in Team Approach to Mastery (TAM) classrooms in an urban mid-

dle school in the Christina, Delaware, school district. TAM classes (Bear & Proctor, 1990) contain students with mild disabilities, the majority of whom are learning disabled, and students without disabilities in a ratio of approximately 1 to 3. They are team taught by special and general educators. Students in our participating classes engaged in project-based learning activities in heterogeneous, cooperative groups.

Controversial Questions

We framed the problems for students to investigate as *controversial questions,* or questions about which informed people could reasonably hold different opinions. As Johnson and Johnson (1979) explain, the juxtaposition of competing ideas can elicit conceptual conflict, raise uncertainty, and motivate students to search for information to resolve that uncertainty. Over the course of our studies, students investigated the British and American perspectives on events leading up to the American Revolutionary War, the costs and benefits of industrialization, and the motivations and consequences of the Spanish colonization of indigenous peoples in Latin America.

Discussion and Argumentation

Students must be exposed to the multiple perspectives inherent in controversial questions if they are to benefit from them. Thus, we designed lessons that provided extended opportunities for students to discuss various aspects of the topic they were investigating with their peers. Typically, discussions were preceded by an introduction, in which the teacher reviewed or introduced some background information. Students then discussed a question posed by the teacher in their cooperative groups. Finally, students reported their groups' opinions to the whole class. Our analyses of student discourse demonstrated that students often engaged in heated debate about these topics and, in the course of discussion, raised many different ideas and positions (Okolo & Ferretti, 1998).

In Studies 3 and 4 (Ferretti & Okolo, 1997, 2000), we taught students a rudimentary strategy for developing an argument to support an opinion about a controversial topic. Through demonstration, discussion, and practice, students learned to state reasons, explanations, and examples to support their opinions. Students were prompted to include these elements in their oral discussions and in their writing about the topic.

Multimedia Presentations

To demonstrate what they had learned during their investigations, each group created a multimedia presentation. Using multimedia authoring software, students created a report of their findings and conclusions about the topic that incorporated text, scanned pictures, and digitized sounds. We taught students to use the multimedia authoring program, assisted them with scanning pictures and recording sounds, and structured their final products by requiring them to include certain elements in their presentations (e.g., a statement of purpose, a consideration of more than one perspective, a conclusion). We typically scheduled an open house in each classroom during which students presented their projects to peers, teachers, and parents.

The multimedia projects that students developed provided a focus for their investigations and proved highly motivating for both students and teachers. The opportunity to learn more about computers and acquire multimedia equipment provided the impetus for at least some teachers' participation. Students were eager to use computers and to learn about new equipment such as scanners and digital cameras. They seemed to take pride in developing a professional-looking presentation that would be viewed by their peers and parents. The quality of writing and ideas expressed in students' projects was vastly superior to that contained in paper-and-pencil essays we asked them to write.

Summary of Our Research Findings

Study 1

Our first study (Okolo & Ferretti, 1997b) was conducted in a university laboratory school for students with mild disabilities. Students worked with us for 10 one-hour sessions to develop a computer-based project about the American Revolutionary War. Although students' attitudes were not affected by the intervention, we found substantial and significant improvements in students' knowledge of the topic they investigated.

Study 2

Our second study (Okolo & Ferretti, 1997a) was situated in two TAM fourth-grade classrooms in which students investigated the topic of industrialization and created a multimedia project about either its advantages or its disadvantages. This was a more extended intervention, which spanned two to three class sessions per week for 2 months.

Students made significant gains on a test of their knowledge about industrialization, with comparable gains for students with and without disabilities. We also documented significant gains in students' self-efficacy for learning social studies and in their attitudes toward cooperative learning. However, students in one classroom made significantly greater gains on the knowledge test than did those in the other class. When we reviewed videotapes of large-group instruction conducted in each classroom, we found that significantly fewer behavioral disruptions—in which the teacher stopped a lesson to reprimand one or more students—occurred in the classroom with greater achievement gains. Thus, we concluded that the failure to manage problematic behavior can adversely affect the implementation of project-based learning.

We videotaped and analyzed the discourse of a random sample of student groups in each classroom. These data demonstrated that students with and without disabilities had similar patterns of participation in group activities. Furthermore, while working in groups, students were off task for only about 10% of the time, which compares favorably to off-task rates observed in more traditional elementary and secondary classroom instruction (e.g., Fisher et al., 1978; Rieth & Frick, 1983; Rieth, Polsgrove, Okolo, Bahr, & Eckert, 1987). However, the nature of group interaction we observed could be characterized as occurring at a low cognitive level (Cohen, 1994).

Study 3

Our third study (Ferretti & Okolo, 1997) examined the impact of project-based learning in contrast to more typical social studies instruction. Two sixth-grade TAM classes served as the experimental group, with a third sixth-grade classroom serving as a comparison group. Students learned about the Spanish colonization of Latin America in all three classrooms. In the experimental classes, students investigated this topic from the perspectives of the Spaniards and the indigenous peoples and created a multimedia project to present their findings and conclusions. Comparison class instruction was designed to be motivating and effective. It included reading and discussions about the text and other secondary sources, viewing and discussing videos about the indigenous peoples and the Spaniards, worksheet and map activities completed by heterogeneous cooperative groups, and a play about Christopher Columbus's request to Queen Isabella that the students performed during class. Comparison students also developed a multimedia project and thus had comparable exposure to technology and multimedia authoring. However, their projects were unrelated to Spanish colonization.

Students' knowledge of Spanish colonization increased significantly in all three classes,

and gains were comparable for students with and without disabilities. Although one experimental class significantly outperformed the comparison class, the comparison class made gains similar to those of the second experimental class. Consistent with our findings in Study 2, the lower-performing experimental class experienced numerous difficulties with behavior management.

Although not statistically significant, students' intrinsic motivation for social studies was maintained or improved in the experimental classes and declined in the comparison classroom. Students' self-efficacy significantly increased in all three classrooms. Finally, students' attitudes toward cooperative learning stayed constant in the experimental classes but declined in the comparison class.

Study 4

In both Studies 2 and 3, research assistants played a major role in assisting experimental class teachers with implementation of the intervention. In Study 4 (Ferretti & Okolo, 2000), teachers took primary responsibility for all instruction and supervision of group work based on outlines of lessons about Spanish colonization developed in Study 3. Our research team provided technical assistance to teachers and students as they worked on their computer projects. Two sixth-grade TAM classes participated as experimental classrooms. Teachers in a third sixth-grade TAM classroom, which served as a comparison, taught Spanish colonization through textbook-based readings, discussions, and activities. Unlike Study 3, we did not design instruction for the comparison classroom. Although we provided hardware and software to the class so that all classes had access to technology, students did not complete a multimedia project. Thus, the comparison in this study represented an untreated control.

On a knowledge test about Spanish colonization, the two experimental classrooms made significant gains, which were comparable for students with and without disabilities. Furthermore, the experimental classes made significantly greater gains than did the comparison classroom. Students in the experimental classes maintained their academic intrinsic motivation, whereas scores on this measure decreased in the comparison classroom. Students' scores on a self-efficacy measure increased in the two experimental classrooms but decreased in the comparison classroom. In addition, analysis of student discourse demonstrated that experimental class students developed more sophisticated understanding of argumentation and were better able to use facts about colonization to justify their opinions (Okolo & Ferretti, 1998).

Summary

The studies reported previously support our contention that sustained engagement in multimedia-supported, project-based learning can promote gains in students' knowledge and positive attitudes about self and social studies. We found it especially encouraging that students with and without disabilities made similar knowledge gains. Although they did not catch up to their nondisabled peers, who knew more about the topic at the start of each study, students with disabilities benefited to the same degree. Furthermore, discourse data show that students with disabilities were not excluded from group activities but rather participated in a manner similar to their nondisabled peers.

Our findings also demonstrate that project-based learning can have a positive impact on students' feelings of self-efficacy, motivation to engage in social studies learning, and attitudes toward cooperative learning. Previous research has shown that students' attitudes toward school and toward their own academic competence decline between elementary and junior high school (e.g., Eccles & Midgley, 1989). Indeed, decreases on some of the attitude scales were observed in our comparison classrooms. Thus we believe that the maintenance and increase of attitude scores is an important byproduct of students' participation in these studies.

For the most part, teachers believed that participation in these studies had benefited them and their students. In interviews conducted during and after each study, teachers expressed confidence that students had learned more about the topics they investigated, had improved their collaborative skills, and, in the studies in which we taught argumentation, had increased their ability to reason about controversial topics. Teachers reported that students were excited about the opportunity to use technology and that authoring multimedia projects helped to sustain students' interest. Additional evidence for teachers' enthusiasm can be found among the sixth-grade teachers who worked with us in Studies 3 and 4. After 1 year of participation, 4 of the 6 experimental classroom teachers volunteered to work with us in a subsequent and similar study.

Challenges in Implementing Project-Based Learning in Social Studies

Despite generally positive results and teacher satisfaction, we, and the teachers who worked with us, encountered substantial challenges in implementing project-based learning in social studies classes. Furthermore, when our funding concluded and our research team left a particular classroom, the majority of teachers reverted to their traditional methods of social studies instruction. Subsequently, we consider some of the factors that constrain the implementation of project-based learning in the social studies. Rather than concluding that this approach is just too difficult to be used in typical classrooms, however, we offer commentary about aspects of project-based learning that require more attention, factors that can facilitate implementation, and compromises that might be made in our approach. We have the good fortune to continue this work through our involvement in Project REACH

(Morocco et al., 1998), funded by the U.S. Department of Education, Office of Special Education Programs. Thus, some of the subsequent observations and recommendations are based on our current research program and thinking about social studies instruction.

The Press for Curricular Coverage

Our studies show that students with and without disabilities significantly increased their knowledge of specific topics through technology-supported, project-based learning. Furthermore, we have evidence that students learned to support their positions about controversial topics in discussions with their classmates, by drawing on their knowledge, and by stating reasons, explanations, and examples.

Certainly, one explanation for our results is that students investigated a limited number of topics in depth, devoting up to 2 months to research, discussion, and project construction. Students had the opportunity to develop deeper understanding of their topics as a result of repeated and extended exposure to ideas and information through reading, viewing videos, participating in whole-class and group discussions, and constructing multimedia projects.

Although our participating teachers were pleased with what students learned and agreed that in-depth exploration of fewer topics yields greater learning gains than do those accomplished by the brisk pace and multiple topics of textbook-dictated instruction, they remained concerned about how to balance depth and breadth of curricular coverage. In fact, the amount of time devoted to each unit is a key item of negotiation within the cohort of teachers participating in our present work.

Teachers take seriously their responsibilities to cover the content outlined in the districts' curriculum guides for their grade level and are concerned about expectations of curricular coverage imposed by their administrators and students' subsequent teachers. Similarly, teachers in our project are concerned about coverage of district social studies standards. Teachers legitimately ask how they can justify devoting 6 to 8 weeks to a single topic. Meeting demands for content coverage is hindered by the low importance attached to social studies instruction. Our project classrooms were typical of others described by survey research (e.g., Patton et al., 1987) in which social studies competes for time with science instruction and is often forsaken when special events such as drug education or school pep rallies are scheduled.

We find it ironic that despite the long-acknowledged fact that superficial coverage breeds superficial learning, many of the current proposals for social studies reform work to inhibit the depth of coverage necessary to develop students' deep understanding (cf. Brown, 1996). When teachers are compelled by state or national standards and high-stakes assessments to cover a long list of events, dates, and historical figures, they have no choice but to resort to superficial coverage. Furthermore, a focus on dates, events, and characters only reinforces students' all-too-prevalent views that history is a compilation of facts and singular conclusions (Wineburg, 1997).

We have found teachers more willing to work with us when they can justify the time devoted to a project-based unit as an additional avenue for building skills in the language arts. In our current research program, we have packaged our units to meet both social studies and language arts standards and goals, and teachers are devoting time to their implementation during both these classes. We also found that project-based work necessitates longer blocks of time than the typical 30- to 45-minute periods scheduled for middle school and junior high school classes. It is impossible for students to engage in an extended, meaningful analysis and discussion of information from text or videos, or to discuss and design a portion of a multimedia project, in such short blocks of time. We continue to seek the permission of school administrators to implement some form of block scheduling in our participating classrooms, so that teachers can devote at least two back-to-back periods to project-based activities.

However, the demands for curricular coverage have led us to make compromises that are not fully compatible with our ultimate goals of helping all students develop a deeper understanding of social studies topics and promoting their skills in problem solving. In all our work to date, teachers have implemented only one project-based unit per year. We know that providing only one opportunity to analyze complicated issues, to think critically about controversial topics, and to develop skills such as argumentation, persuasive writing, and multimedia project design is hardly sufficient. Rather, all students need multiple opportunities over the course of years to develop the dispositions and skills we hope our intervention can foster. In our current work, we are attempting to address this dilemma by developing complementary units that students can complete at subsequent grade levels; by developing some shorter, mini-units; and by developing analog units about contemporary topics that can be completed in a shorter period of time than the original unit.

Demands on Teachers' Knowledge

As we mentioned at the outset of this chapter, concern about teachers' knowledge was one of the factors that gave impetus to the formalization of the curriculum. Our project-based approach to the social studies often further strains the limits of teachers' knowledge. During the process of investigating a topic and using a variety of resources, it is impossible to predict fully the questions that will occur to students, the turns that their investigations may take, or the conclusions that they may draw. To respond adequately to questions that arise from students' investigations and to challenge and correct misconceptions that inevitably occur, a teacher needs a rich store of subject-matter knowledge about the domain. Furthermore, to enrich and deepen students' understanding, teachers must possess strong pedagogical content knowledge

(Shulman, 1986). They must be sensitive to students' preexisting knowledge and understandings about social studies and inquiry, and they must know how to transform subject-matter information into representations that will be understandable, interesting, and relevant to their students. Although important for all types of instruction, we contend that subject-matter knowledge and pedagogical content knowledge are especially critical for project-based learning, in which teachers and students stray beyond the circumscribed boundaries of textbook-based learning.

Consider one of our teachers, Mr. H., whose classes participated in Studies 3 and 4. Along with a master's degree in cognition and instruction and minors in English and history, Mr. H. had 23 years of teaching experience at a variety of grade levels and settings. He had been employed overseas and spent several years as teacher trainer in a university demonstration project. On numerous occasions, we observed him drawing on his rich store of subject-matter knowledge to embellish on the lessons we had developed. Consider the following example, in which Mr. H opens a discussion after his class has viewed a video about ancient and contemporary society among the Incas in South America:

Mr. H.: As I watched the film, several things came to mind. I thought of Hitler; I thought of the Japanese in World War Two. Hitler led the German people to some of the most atrocious acts that have ever been committed. By the way, ironically, the last of the film showed a royal guard marching in Peru. If you saw them, you saw a particular type of step, and that step goes back to at least World War Two. It's called a goose step (he demonstrates). You may have seen bands, the drum major, use that step. Can you imagine what it's like to see some troops marching, thousands of soldiers, marching down the street with that step? Sometimes they [the invading troops] took over without any bloodshed, it was so awesome.

We also witnessed many examples of Mr. H.'s ability to transform historical information into anecdotes and examples that would capture students' interest and help them understand ideas that would otherwise be incomprehensible or repulsive. On the occasion excerpted subsequently, Mr. H.'s class read a selection about the Maya and their religious practices. Students expressed outrage at the animal and human sacrifices described in the passage and raised the possibility that the Mayan "heathen" religious practices justified the Spaniard's conquest and subsequent attempts to convert them to Christianity. Mr. H. orchestrates a discussion to provide a context for the Maya's religious practices.

Mr. H.: So, what did you observe while you watched this film?

Logan: They threw people into cenotes and they sacrificed animals.

Mr. H.: What was important to these people, animals or blood?

Class responds: Blood!

Shenita: They sacrificed their own children!

Mr. H.: Who did they sacrifice?

Laquisha: Their enemies, orphans.

Mr. H.: How do you feel about this?

Shenita and others call out loudly they feel "angry," "It's wrong," "It's horrible."

Brian: The priests had so much power!

Mr. H.: Think about it this way. Do you know what capital punishment is?

Rosa: It's when the judge says someone should be killed, like hanged or put in the electric chair.

Mr. H.: Right. Capital punishment is part of our justice system. Criminals are tried by a jury of their peers who decides to gas that person or run electric current through their bodies. Why did the Maya sacrifice people?

Andrew: Because they thought the gods wanted blood.

Maleeka: They thought their crops wouldn't grow unless the gods have blood.

Mr. H.: And why does our society use capital punishment? Why do we decide to kill criminals?

Justine: Because they're bad.

Mr. H.: Because they're bad, and because we don't want them back on the street so they can murder someone else. We use capital punishment as a form of social control. It's part of our attempt to control society, to make the world a safer place. Isn't this just what the Maya did? They didn't have the scientific knowledge that we have today to explain natural events like eclipses, storms, and droughts. They thought the gods controlled these things. They sacrificed people because they wanted to please the gods who controlled their world. They wanted their crops to grow, they wanted to avoid a drought, they wanted their world to be a safer place. Do you see the parallel?

As the previous excerpts illustrate, Mr. H.'s subject-matter knowledge and pedagogical content knowledge form a basis for motivating students and securing their comprehension of historical information, which otherwise might seem uninteresting and irrelevant to students' lives (see, e.g., Spoehr & Spoehr, 1994). Mr. H. also promotes his students' historical thinking by discussing past events in light of societal conditions and the motivations of the people involved. His juxtaposition of human sacrifice and capital punishment is an attempt to help students overcome their natural rejection of practices that, by today's standards and mores, are abhorrent. By encouraging them to see both as a form of social control, Mr. H. helps students make sense of an ancient culture and promotes the development of historical empathy (Wineburg & Fournier, 1994).

Perhaps it is not surprising that we obtained the highest achievement and attitude gains in

Mr. H.'s classrooms. Although our studies included teachers with even more teaching experience than that of Mr. H., we did not observe such rich and extended discussions in other classrooms. Rather, teacher-led discussions in most classrooms rarely ventured beyond the material presented in the lessons, videos, and readings. Undoubtedly, Mr. H.'s rich subject-matter and pedagogical content knowledge were major contributors to the success students experienced in his classroom.

Demands on teachers' subject-matter and pedagogical content knowledge pose additional challenges for effective project-based learning in social studies. Elementary and middle school educators, particularly those who are trained as special educators, have little formal training in history, economics, civics, or any of the other disciplines that comprise the social studies (Patton et al., 1987). Thus, staff development to support project-based learning must address not only issues related to effective implementation but also the enhancement of teachers' knowledge.

Like many other educators who have developed interventions to promote higher-order learning in content areas (e.g., Dalton, Morocco, Tivnan, & Mead, 1997; Palincsar, Magnusson, Marano, Ford, & Brown, 1998; Thomas, Wineburg, Grossman, Myhre, & Woolworth, 1998; Zorfass, Chapter 5, this volume), we have concluded that staff development must be systematic and ongoing. In our current work, we meet with teachers in the summer and monthly throughout the school year. In these "community of practice" (Palincsar et al., 1998) meetings, teachers who are currently implementing a project-based unit share experiences and observations with other participating teachers and our research team. Meetings provide a forum for discussing and resolving instructional and subject-matter difficulties, sharing ideas about how to represent information in ways that engage students and deepen their understanding, and developing camaraderie in support of each other's efforts to improve teaching and learning. Thus, the community meetings offer another opportunity for teachers to expand their knowledge.

Effective Classroom Management

Our data suggest that classroom management is a prerequisite condition for effective use of project-based learning. During 2 years in which we observed uneven effects between the experimental classrooms, we found substantial differences in the number of disruptions occurring in each, with results favoring the better-managed classes. Unfortunately, some teachers are not proficient in managing the multiple goals and needs of student groups who are simultaneously pursuing individual learning activities. Our classroom observations confirmed that project-based learning runs the danger of degenerating into chaos unless teachers have well-established routines for eliciting and maintaining positive student behavior.

Although it is obvious that effective classroom management is a precursor to effective teaching and learning, much of teachers' knowledge about it is either anecdotal or warmed-over applied behavior analysis directed at the consequences of misbehavior. There is, fortunately, an empirically validated body of knowledge about effective classroom management practices (e.g., Brophy & McCaslin, 1992; Jones, 1996). This work demonstrates that effective managers create learning environments that encourage students' cooperation and prevent misbehaviors from occurring in the first place (Brophy & Good, 1986; Kounin, 1970). Among other things, effective classroom managers plan rules and procedures in advance, involve students in the process of making classroom rules, minimize disruptions and downtime in the classroom, and use positive language that directs student attention to what needs to be done (see Good & Brophy, 1997).

Although we experimented with several approaches to behavior management over the course of our studies, we found that each of our attempts received mixed reviews from the teachers. Some preferred highly structured systems, in which students earned points toward a reinforcer, whereas others managed behavior by verbal negotiation and social reinforcement. We did not observe changes in teachers' preexisting management styles as a result of implementing project-based learning. However, we did note that teachers seemed to have different visions of their own roles in group interaction. Whereas all teachers circulated around the room during group work, some facilitated students' work by questioning groups about how they planned to complete a task, asking students to defend their conclusions about a topic of discussion, or suggesting alternatives when a group reached an impasse. Other teachers monitored student work at a more global level, circulating around the room and answering questions as they arose, settling disputes, or looking over students' work to correct obvious errors. Our anecdotal observations suggest that student groups were more engaged and productive when teachers facilitated their work through proactive interactions, questions, and suggestions.

Productive Student Collaboration

We also found that positive and productive collaboration among students can be extremely difficult to achieve. The analysis of student discourse, discussed previously, revealed no differences in group participation for students with and without disabilities. We provided students with instruction, practice, and reinforcement for social skills to promote positive group interaction. This included guidelines such as "Listen when someone else is speaking" and "Ask everyone if they agree with a group decision." Despite the fact that we observed few impolite behaviors and noted encouraging rates of on-task behavior during group activities, the nature of group interaction was disappointing. Students were most often observed to be passively listening and watching, rather than engaged in behaviors that advanced the level of thinking and understanding within the group. The degree to which students offer detailed explanations is one of the most consistent predictors of student achievement within cooperative learning groups (Cohen, 1994; Webb, 1983, 1991). Task-related interactions, such as providing

and requesting information, asking clarifying questions, and summarizing, are especially important correlates of achievement when groups are engaged in open-ended, non-routine tasks characteristic of project-based learning (Cohen, 1994).

In our current work, we are focusing more closely on positive and productive group interaction. Because each group develops a single project, we run the risk that, rather than collaborating, students can each complete a component of the project, working as individuals, and then piece together individual efforts for a group product. Thus, we are cognizant of the need to build in both individual accountability, in which all students will be evaluated on their knowledge of the topic studies, and group interdependence, which provides the impetus for group members to work together and contribute equally (Cohen, 1994; Stevens & Slavin, 1995). Our participating teachers assign rotating roles to students during their group work to encourage higher levels of student involvement from all.

Furthermore, we know that students need instruction and guidance if they are to engage in productive group discussions that advance problem-solving, decision-making, and other higher-level cognitive skills. We have developed activities, based on the work of King (1994) and others (e.g., Fuchs, Fuchs, Bentz, Phillips, & Hamlett, 1994; Palincsar, Anderson, & David, 1993; Webb, Troper, & Fall, 1995), in which we teach students the importance of providing explanations and how to construct them, types of questions that advance a discussion and promote learning, and ways to resolve controversy.

Summary and Conclusions

For nearly 100 years, different ideological positions have competed for control of the social studies curriculum (Epstein & Evans, 1990). Yet, despite the dissension (Stanley, 1985), there is considerable consensus about the centrality of citizenship preparation to the purposes of social studies education. In our view, the responsibility to prepare an informed citizenry entails a commitment to foster the dispositions for thoughtful and reflective dialogue about solutions to authentic problems (Wiggins, 1993). Problems such as these require sustained deliberation over time, working with others to come to terms about goals, procedures, and standards of evaluation that might inform consideration of competing points of view (Ferretti & Okolo, 1996; Okolo & Ferretti, 1998).

In our work, students are challenged to work in heterogeneous groups of mixed ability to develop technology-supported projects (Ferretti & Okolo, 1997, 2000; Okolo & Ferretti, 1997a, 1997b) that reflect their collective judgment about the issue under investigation. Project-based activities afford the opportunity to engage in goal-directed inquiry, to formulate goals and opinions, and to analyze and interpret evidence that informs reflective judgment. Multimedia technology is used by students to create project artifacts that can be displayed for public discussion and debate. Students take great pleasure in producing these technological artifacts, which in turn seems to help kindle and sustain students' motivation for learning.

Our findings show that project-based investigations engender gains in students' knowledge about the domain (Ferretti & Okolo, 1997; Okolo & Ferretti, 1997a, 1997b); improve or maintain attitudes about social studies and enhance feelings of self-efficacy, especially when the intervention is sustained over time (see Okolo & Ferretti, 1997a); and promote the use of data-based justifications to support claims about controversial issues (Okolo & Ferretti, 1998). However, these outcomes can be affected by classroom conditions that are antithetical to student progress. Notably, in two of our interventions (Ferretti & Okolo, 1997; Okolo & Ferretti, 1997a), the prevalence of disruptive behavior adversely affected performance in some classrooms. Chronic classroom disruptions are clearly incompatible with sustained intellectual inquiry. Moreover, limitations in teachers' knowledge, incompatible curricular goals, and the press for broad curricular coverage constrain the sustainability of project-based investigations. Student inquiry rarely proceeds in a completely predictable fashion, and this uncertainty challenges teachers to call flexibly on their background knowledge to support student learning. Without rich pedagogical content knowledge, teachers may be unable to advance students' efforts effectively, promote their understanding, and correct their misconceptions. Moreover, teachers are often compelled by higher-level administrative expectations to opt for broad and superficial coverage of the curriculum. In fact, the ideological competition for the curriculum, to which we alluded earlier, further encourages teachers' dependence on the de facto curriculum—the textbook (see Brophy, 1992).

We believe that some of the logistical challenges to the implementation of these ideas can be addressed by creative responses to competing curricular demands. For example, we mentioned earlier that some teachers currently working with us have used technology-supported, project-based learning to meet goals in the social studies and the language arts simultaneously, leading, in our view, to a more coherent instructional experience from the children's perspective. Accommodations such as these are not terribly difficult to make in the elementary years when block scheduling is prevalent. The specialization of the curriculum and teachers' responsibilities in the middle and high school years makes these kinds of accommodations more problematic, especially in an era of increasing educational accountability. Nevertheless, we are sanguine about the future prospects for the work described in this chapter. Perhaps more than anything, we are heartened by the enthusiasm shown by students and the creativity of our colleagues in the schools who share our commitment to prepare these students for the world they will inherit.

References

Barth, J. L., & Shermis, S. S. (1979). Defining the social studies: An exploration of three traditions. *Social Education, 34,* 743-751.

Bear, G. G., & Proctor, W. A. (1990). Impact of a full-time integrated program on the achievement of nonhandicapped and mildly handicapped children. *Exceptionality, 1,* 227-238.

Blumenfeld, P. C., Soloway, E., Marx, R. W., Krajcik, J. S., Guzdial, M., & Palincsar, A. (1991). Motivating project-based learning: Sustaining the doing, supporting the learning. *Educational Psychologist, 26,* 369-398.

Bransford, J. D., & Stein, B. S. (1984). *The IDEAL problem solver.* New York: Freeman.

Brophy, J. (1992). The de facto national curriculum in U.S. elementary social studies: Critique of a representative example. *Journal of Curriculum Studies, 24,* 401-447.

Brophy, J., & Good, T. (1986). Teacher behavior and student achievement. In M. Wittrock (Ed.), *Handbook of research on teaching* (3rd ed., pp. 328-375). New York: Macmillan.

Brophy, J., & McCaslin, M. (1992). Teachers' reports of how they perceive and cope with problem students. *Elementary School Journal, 93,* 3-68.

Brown, A. L. (1992). Design experiments: Theoretical and methodological challenges in creating complex interventions in classroom settings. *Journal of the Learning Sciences, 2,* 141-178.

Brown, R. H. (1996). Learning how to learn: The Amherst project and history education in the schools. *The Social Studies, 87,* 267-273.

Bruner, J. (1996). *The culture of education.* Cambridge, MA: Harvard University Press.

Carnine, D., Bean, R., Miller, S., & Zigmond, N. (1994). Social studies: Educational tools for diverse learners. *School Psychology Review, 23,* 428-441.

Cherryholmes, C. (1990). Social studies for what century? *Social Education, 54,* 438-442.

Cohen, E. (1994). Restructuring the classroom: Conditions for productive small groups. *Review of Educational Research, 64,* 1-35.

Curtis, C. K. (1991). Social studies for students at-risk and with disabilities. In J. P. Shaver (Ed.), *Handbook of research on social studies teaching and learning* (pp. 157-174). New York: Macmillan.

Dalton, B., Morocco, C., Tivnan, T., & Mead, P. L. R. (1997). Supported inquiry science: Teaching for conceptual change in urban and suburban science classrooms. *Journal of Learning Disabilities, 30,* 670-684.

Dewey, J. (1916). *Democracy and education.* New York: Free Press.

Dewey, J. (1933). *How we think.* Lexington, MA: D. C. Heath.

Eccles, J. S., & Midgley, C. (1989). Stage-environment fit: Developmentally appropriate classrooms for young adolescents. In C. Ames & R. Ames (Eds.), *Research on motivation in education: Vol. 3. Goals and cognitions* (pp. 139-186). San Diego, CA: Academic Press.

Engle, S. H. (1990). The commission report and citizenship education. *Social Education, 54,* 431-434.

Epstein, T. L., & Evans, R. W. (1990). Special section: Reactions to Charting a Course: Social studies for the 21st century. *Social Education, 54,* 427-429.

Ferretti, R. P., & Okolo, C. M. (1996). Authenticity in learning: Multimedia design projects in the social studies for students with disabilities. *Journal of Learning Disabilities, 29,* 450-460.

Ferretti, R. P., & Okolo, C. M. (1997, April). *Designing multimedia projects in the social studies: Effects on students' content knowledge and attitudes.* Paper presented at the annual meeting of the American Educational Research Association, Chicago.

Ferretti, R. P., & Okolo, C. M. (2000). Argumentative discourse, controversy, and project-based learning in the social studies.

Fisher, C. W., Berliner, D. C., Filby, N. N., Marliave, R., Cahen, L. S., & Dishaw, M. (1978). *Teaching and learning in the elementary school: A summary of the beginning teacher evaluation study.* San Francisco: Far West Labs.

Fuchs, J. S., Fuchs, D., Bentz, J., Phillips, N., & Hamlett, C. L. (1994). The nature of student interactions during peer tutoring with and without prior training and experience. *American Educational Research Journal, 31,* 75-103.

Good, T. L., & Brophy, J. E. (1997). *Looking in classrooms.* White Plains, NY: Longman.

Hiebert, J., Carpenter, T. P., Fennema, E., Fuson, K., Human, P., Murray, H., Olivier, A., & Wearne, D. (1996). Problem solving as a basis for reform in curriculum and instruction: The case of mathematics. *Educational Researcher, 25*(4), 12-21.

Johnson, D. W., & Johnson, R. (1979). Conflict in the classroom: Controversy and learning. *Review of Educational Research, 49,* 51-70.

Jones, V. (1996). Classroom management. In J. Sikula, T. Buttery, & E. Guyton (Eds.), *Handbook of research on teacher education* (Vol. 2, pp. 503-521). New York: Macmillan.

Kinder, D., & Bursuck, W. (1991). The search for a unified social studies curriculum. Does history repeat itself? *Journal of Learning Disabilities, 24,* 270-275.

King, A. (1994). Guiding knowledge construction in the classroom: Effects of teaching children how to question and how to explain. *American Educational Research Journal, 31,* 338-368.

Kliebard, H. (1986). *The struggle for the American curriculum: 1893-1958.* Boston: Routledge & Kegan Paul.

Kounin, J. (1970). *Discipline and group management in classrooms.* New York: Holt, Rinehart & Winston.

Krajcik, J. S., Blumenfeld, P. C., Marx, R. W., & Soloway, E. (1994). A collaborative model for helping middle school science teachers learn project-based learning. *The Elementary School Journal, 94,* 483-497.

Lybarger, M. B. (1991). The historiography of social studies: Retrospect, circumspect, and prospect. In J. P. Shaver (Ed.), *Handbook of research on social studies teaching and learning* (pp. 3-15). New York: Macmillan.

Morocco, C., Ferretti, R., MacArthur, C., Okolo, C., Palincsar, A., & Woodward, J. (1998). *REACH: Research Institute to Accelerate Content Learning Through High Support for Students With Disabilities.* Newton, MA: Education Development Center, Inc.

Nelson, J. L. (1990). Charting a course backwards: A response to the National Commission's nineteenth century social studies program. *Social Education, 54,* 434-437.

Okolo, C. M., & Ferretti, R. P. (1997a). The impact of multimedia design projects on the knowledge, attitudes, and collaboration of students in inclusive classrooms. *Journal of Computers in Childhood Education, 7,* 223-251.

Okolo, C. M., & Ferretti, R. P. (1997b). Knowledge acquisition and technology-supported projects in the social studies for students with learning disabilities. *Journal of Special Education Technology, 13,* 91-103.

Okolo, C. M., & Ferretti, R. P. (1998). Multimedia design projects in an inclusive social studies classroom: "Sometimes people argue with words instead of fists." *Teaching Exceptional Children, 31,* 50-57.

Palincsar, A. S., Anderson, C., & David, Y. M. (1993). Pursuing scientific literacy in the middle grades through collaborative problem solving. *The Elementary School Journal, 93,* 643-658.

Palincsar, A. S., Magnusson, S. J., Marano, N., Ford, D., & Brown, N. (1998). Designing a community of practice: Principles and practices of the GIsML community. *Teaching and Teacher Education, 14*(1), 5-19.

Patton, J., Polloway, E., & Cronin, M. (1987). Social studies instruction for handicapped students: A review of current practices. *The Social Studies, 78,* 131-135.

Rieth, H. J., & Frick, T. W. (1983). *An analysis of the academic learning time provided to mildly handicapped students in different service delivery systems.* Bloomington, IN: Center for Innovation in Teaching the Handicapped.

Rieth, H., Polsgrove, L., Okolo, C., Bahr, C., & Eckert, R. (1987). An analysis of the secondary special education classroom ecology with implications for teacher training. *Teacher Education and Special Education, 10*(3), 113-119.

Shulman, L. S. (1986). Those who understand: Knowledge growth in teaching. *Educational Researcher, 15*(2), 4-14.

Simon, H. A. (1980). Problem solving and education. In D. T. Tuma & R. Reif (Eds.), *Problem solving and education: Issues in teaching and research* (pp. 81-94). Hillsdale, NJ: Lawrence Erlbaum.

Spoehr, K. T., & Spoehr, L. W. (1994). Learning to think historically. *Educational Psychologist, 29,* 72-77.

Stanley, W. B. (1985). Recent research in the foundation of social education: 1976-1983. In W. B. Stanley (Ed.), *Review of research in social studies education: 1976-1983* (pp. 303-399). Washington, DC: National Council for Social Studies.

Stevens, R. J., & Slavin, R. E. (1995). The cooperative elementary school: Effects on students' achievement, attitudes, and social relations. *American Educational Research Journal, 32,* 321-351.

Thomas, G., Wineburg, S., Grossman, P., Myhre, O., & Woolworth, S. (1998). In the company of colleagues: An interim report on the development of a community of teacher learners. *Teaching and Teacher Education, 14*(1), 21-32.

Voss, J. F. (1991). Informal reasoning and international relations. In J. F. Voss, D. N. Perkins, & J. W. Segal (Eds.), *Informal reasoning and education* (pp. 37-58). Hillsdale, NJ: Erlbaum.

Voss, J. F., Greene, T. R., Post, T. A., & Penner, B. C. (1983). Problem solving skill in the social sciences. In G. H. Bower (Ed.), *The psychology of learning and motivation: Advances in research and theory* (Vol. 17, pp. 165-213). San Diego, CA: Academic Press.

Voss, J. F., & Post, T. A. (1988). On the solving of ill-structured problems. In M. T. H. Chi, R. Glaser, & M. J. Farr (Eds.), *The nature of expertise* (pp. 261-285). Hillsdale, NJ: Lawrence Erlbaum.

Voss, J. F., Tyler, S. W., & Yengo, L. A. (1983). Individual differences in the solving of social science problems. In R. F. Dillon & R. R. Schmeck (Eds.), *Individual differences in cognition* (pp. 205-232). San Diego, CA: Academic Press.

Webb, N. (1983). Predicting learning from student interaction: Defining the interaction variable. *Educational Psychologist, 18,* 33-41.

Webb, N. (1991). Task-related verbal interaction and mathematics learning in small groups. *Journal of Research in Mathematics Education, 22,* 366-389.

Webb, N. M., Troper, J. D., & Fall, R. (1995). Constructive activity and learning in collaborative small groups. *Journal of Educational Psychology, 87,* 406-423.

Wiggins, G. P. (1993). *Assessing student performance.* San Francisco: Jossey-Bass.

Wineburg, S. S. (1997). Beyond "breadth" and "depth": Subject matter knowledge and assessment. *Theory Into Practice, 36,* 255-261.

Wineburg, S. S., & Fournier, J. (1994). Contextualized thinking in history. In M. Carretero & J. F. Voss (Eds.), *Cognitive and instructional processes in history and social sciences* (pp. 285-308). Hillsdale, NJ: Lawrence Erlbaum.

ClassWide Peer Tutoring Program

A Learning Management System

CHARLES R. GREENWOOD

LIANG-SHYE HOU

JOSEPH DELQUADRI

BARBARA J. TERRY

CARMEN ARREAGA-MAYER
Juniper Gardens Children's Project, University of Kansas

Accelerating the academic progress of young children with and without disabilities in the general education classroom, thereby preventing both early and lifelong trajectories of low academic achievement, is increasingly possible through the use of powerful curricular and instructional interventions (Greenwood, 1996, 1997). One such intervention is the ClassWide Peer Tutoring Program (CWPT) (Greenwood, Delquadri, & Carta, 1997).

AUTHORS' NOTE: The work described and preparation of this manuscript were supported by grants (H180G60002 and H029K0068) from the Office of Special Education Programs, U.S. Department of Education. The opinions expressed in this chapter are exclusively those of the authors and in no way reflect those of the funding agency. We acknowledge the sizable contributions of Nallu Reddy and Charles Hsu. Additional thanks to the staff of Scott Computer Magnet School, Topeka, Kansas, and Whittier Elementary School, Kansas City, Kansas, for their participation in various stages of this project.

CWPT research has addressed what works best in accelerating student outcomes and how it can be applied widely by others and sustained over time within local schools. Increasingly, computer technology has played a role in CWPT (Greenwood, Delquadri, & Bulgren, 1993). Some of the potential contributions of computer technology to CWPT programs are enhanced communications, planning, training, program implementation, data entry, data display, progress monitoring, decision making, and expert advice on program improvement.

The net product of CWPT intervention research has been an expanded knowledge base concerning the design and effectiveness of peer-mediated forms of instruction (Arreaga-Mayer, Terry, & Greenwood, 1997; Delquadri, Greenwood, Whorton, Carta, & Hall, 1986; Greenwood, 1996, 1997; Greenwood, Maheady, & Carta, 1991; Utley, Mortweet, & Greenwood, 1997). Supported by more than 35 experimental studies of our own and by those of others (e.g., Harper, Mallette, Maheady, Parkes, & Moore, 1993; Maheady & Harper, 1987; Mathes, Fuchs, Fuchs, Henley, & Sanders, 1994; Mathes, Howard, Allen, & Fuchs, 1998), this body of work has shown that students at risk and with mild disabilities acquire literacy skills at faster rates, retain more of what they learn, and make greater advances in social competence when using CWPT compared to many conventional, teacher-mediated instructional methods.

In this chapter, we reflect on past experiences developing CWPT and the successes and failures that led to the present work linking CWPT to computer and information management technology. This chapter reports an effort to develop instructional intervention components that accelerated student learning and bring these components to scale in school buildings using behavioral and computer technologies. Current work is investigating the benefits of integrating administrative and instructional CWPT components within a Learning Management Software System for schoolwide use on school building intranets (e.g., Greenwood, Arreaga-Mayer, Utley,

Gavin, & Terry, in press). Some of the real and anticipated benefits of linking CWPT to computer technology include improved communication and management of CWPT information through local area networking (LAN); improved teacher training and program implementation through interactive multimedia, rule-based implementation advice; and increased awareness of weekly student outcomes through computerized progress monitoring and program planning/support software for classroom teachers.

The Problem We Sought to Address With CWPT

CWPT is a product of a 34-year collaboration between community leaders of Northeast Kansas City, Kansas; classroom teachers and principals in neighborhood schools; and the faculty of the University of Kansas (Greenwood, 1999), all seeking a better education for area children through research. This collaboration is formally known as the Juniper Gardens Children's Project (JGCP). Because far too many children in the Northeast Kansas City area failed to attain expected levels of literacy, the founding mission of the JGCP has been to conduct research in local schools leading to the improvement of instruction and the academic and social achievements of area children.

Some of the early instructional interventions produced at the JGCP were "Incidental Teaching," a strategy for accelerating spoken vocabulary in young, language learning children (Hart & Risley, 1978), and "Responsive Teaching," a set of behavioral strategies for classroom management (Hall & Copeland, 1972). In the case of CWPT, it developed in response to problems observed in conventional instructional practices in local classrooms. General education teachers were seeking procedures for integrating students with mild learning disabilities (LD) without creating separate "LD" or "EMR" (educable mental retardation) programs in response to the "least restrictive environment" provisions of the Education for All Handicapped Children Act (1975). At the same time, researchers were concerned because too many students with and without disabilities were not highly engaged in active academic responding during instruction (Greenwood, Delquadri, & Hall, 1984). Consequently, Kathleen Stretton, third-grade teacher at Fairfax Elementary School, was seeking a method of integrating these students with her other students, and she and Joe Delquadri, a researcher at Juniper Gardens, collaborated in the development of what became CWPT. Each brought important elements to the process.

Delquadri had completed a dissertation on the effects of one-on-one, pullout tutoring, and he had engaged even the most challenging students successfully with his tutoring format (Delquadri, 1978). He reported that students who failed to achieve in the general education classroom had made substantial progress when tutored one-on-one outside the classroom. Stretton sought a method that would accelerate mastery of the classroom curriculum for all students, accommodate diversity, and enable all students to play roles that would not label or stigmatize. She also had in place a classwide mastery monitoring system that employed a posted wall chart on which she recorded weekly test results that did not require complicated graphing for her to see individual progress.

The CWPT Spelling Game:
An Acceptable and Effective Practice

The CWPT spelling game emerged from their collaboration (Delquadri, Greenwood, Stretton, & Hall, 1983). Its design sought the benefits of one-on-one instruction when applied class-wide, in which all students were involved simultaneously in peer tutoring. The design also included weekly progress mastering the curriculum as reflected by individuals' results on the wall chart. CWPT became a form of intraclass, reciprocal, classwide peer

tutoring. Tutors in this program were only those students normally present in the general education classroom (intraclass peer tutoring); CWPT did not require use of older/upper-grade students. The tutor and tutee roles were reciprocal—each student functioned as the tutor and tutee during each CWPT session, thereby avoiding the stigmatizing effects of always being the tutee and never the tutor. Later studies confirmed that students also learned important social as well as academic skills from being the tutor (e.g., Simmons, Fuchs, Fuchs, Hodge, & Mathes, 1994).

Other components were also important, including the curriculum and motivation strategies. In the CWPT spelling game, the teacher selected the spelling curricula from the reading program. Each week, tutors used a new list of 20 spelling words. Tutors used a scripted teaching strategy because earlier research had demonstrated that better results were obtained by trained rather than untrained peer tutors (Niedermeyer, 1970). Scripting captured an effective teaching strategy and made the strategy easy to teach to all students. In support of motivation, an individual point system with competing teams was used, similar to the game of basketball. Students earned two points for their team for each correctly spelled word. They earned one point for correcting an error after respelling it correctly three times. As in basketball, students' points were summed for a team total, and a winning team was declared after each session and each week.

The results of the CWPT spelling game were a dramatic reduction in spelling errors—often to the point at which students with LD spelled as accurately as did students without LD on Friday tests (Delquadri et al., 1983)—and all students in the classroom were actively engaged in writing and orally spelling words during CWPT sessions. During conventional spelling instruction that typically involved teacher-led chalkboard discussion followed by seatwork using workbooks, students made twice as many errors on average when tested at the end of each week, and many were not highly engaged during this instruction. During CWPT, the teacher was busy supervising the work of the peer tutors, checking that they followed the scripted procedure and providing help when questions arose about the pronunciation of some words or their spelling, rather than lecturing, discussing, or questioning individual students as in her teacher-led instruction. During CWPT, it was observed that tutors tended to present new material as fast as the tutee could respond by writing the word and spelling it aloud, or made necessary corrections. Similarly, if the tutor drifted off-task, tutees quickly prompted them for the next item. High-paced, partner-regulated instructional interactions are the signature characteristic of CWPT.

Some of the unique benefits of peer-mediated CWPT, as compared to conventional teacher-mediated instruction, are one-on-one teacher/pupil ratios during sessions, relatively immediate error correction, fast pacing and multiple opportunities to respond, learning from both teacher and learner roles, multiple learner response formats (written and oral), inclusion of diverse learners, and social and academic goals addressed in the same instructional time. In summary, CWPT core procedures (Delquadri et al., 1986) are

1. The review, activation of prior knowledge, and introduction of new material to be learned

2. Preparation of weekly units/content materials to be tutored (e.g., reading passages, study guides, spelling word lists or math fact lists)

3. New partners each week

4. Partner pairing strategies

5. Reciprocal roles in each session

6. Teams competing for the highest team point total

7. Contingent point earning

8. Tutors providing immediate error correction

9. Public posting of individual and team scores

10. Social reward for the winning team

This restructuring of the teacher-learner relationship in CWPT to teach spelling matured dramatically as it was extended to other subject matter. A challenge faced by CWPT developers then and now was curriculum development and procedures teaching for the peer tutors. Although the curriculum and the scripted peer tutoring procedures changed in these applications, in most cases the CWPT core procedures remained unchanged (e.g., reciprocal tutoring, scripted tutoring strategies, immediate error correction, point system, progress monitoring). For example, when applied to passage reading, tutees read brief passages from texts to their tutor. The tutor provides two points for each correctly read sentence and one point for each correction. Teachers assess the fluency of the students' reading using oral reading rate measures. When applied to reading comprehension, the tutee responds to who, what, when, where, and why questions (or other teacher-developed questions) concerning the passage, provided by the tutor. The tutor corrects tutee responses and provides feedback. When applied to spelling, the tutee writes and spells words orally from a list. The tutor dictates the words to the tutee and corrects performance and awards points (2 = correct, 1 = error correction completed). Teachers assess improvements due to tutoring weekly using pre- and posttests. Somewhat similar variations are applied to vocabulary, mathematics, and silent reading, as well as seatwork, and the program allows for teacher-developed designs and innovations with respect to curriculum used and peer tutoring strategies within core CWPT procedures. When extended to content area instruction, such as social studies or science, study guides are used to direct the teaching and learning of tutor and tutee (Arreaga-Mayer, 1998; Maheady, Sacca, & Harper, 1988). In all cases, students' learning progress in CWPT is evaluated weekly using formative evaluation measures of mastery or fluency.

These and related procedures generally have been sufficient to integrate students with mild disabilities into the general education classroom successfully. However, a challenge faced by CWPT developers is to expand strategies for including students with moderate to severe disabilities (Kamps, Barbetta, Leonard, & Delquadri, 1994).

CWPT restructures instruction in ways that accommodate greater student diversity. It taps the extensive help and influence of the classroom peer group in the one-on-one teaching process. CWPT supports flexible curricular modifications for individuals and groups of students based on short units of material with frequent opportunities to respond, practice, and receive feedback. It combines individual and group-oriented reinforcement contingencies so that an individual's rewards depend on both his or her own and others' performance—their partner and team. The rather unique property of group-oriented contingencies of reinforcement is their promotion of peer teaching, help, and assistance (Greenwood & Hops, 1981). Because learner-teacher roles change in CWPT, it fosters the social skills needed when acting as someone's teacher/mentor. Consequently in CWPT, compared to most forms of teacher-mediated instruction in general education, students become willing and capable of helping classmates having trouble because they have a real stake in how their partner and team performs. For students with moderate to severe disabilities with paraprofessional aides, they have been integrated into CWPT programs in various ways. In cases in which the aide provides a translation role, as in a child with a hearing impairment who communicates using sign language, this student may be peer-tutored with translation provided by the aide. In cases in which the aide provides a physical assistance role, as with a wheelchair-bound student with limited motor control, the student also may be peer-tutored with assistance of the aide (Greenwood, Terry, & Sparks, 1997).

Problems Maintaining Fidelity and Accelerated Student Outcomes

As the CWPT spelling game was replicated and extended to other teachers who applied it

to other subject areas, it became apparent that how well teachers/students conducted CWPT in each session (fidelity), including how often they conducted CWPT sessions (time to learn), moderated the size of students' weekly outcomes (Greenwood, Delquadri, & Hall, 1989; Greenwood et al., in press; Greenwood, Terry, Arreaga-Mayer, & Finney, 1992). Although initially surprised that a practice like CWPT, designed and validated with the input and participation of classroom teachers, would not be fully implemented by other teachers, we learned that fidelity was nearly always influenced by local contexts including motivational factors, those unique to new individuals, and new settings. Thus, fidelity became a critical element in CWPT research, practice, and professionalism. The following are some important factors that made CWPT more or less successful in increasing students' progress in the curriculum.

Students' Weekly Exposure to CWPT and Their Time to Learn. The most obvious problem was reduced time to learn in CWPT (Greenwood et al., 1992). Students who experienced tutoring less than three or four times per week learned less by week's end. Students who had absences from school, students who were pulled out of CWPT sessions for other instruction because of conflicting goals or schedules, or students whose teacher shortened the length of CWPT sessions or who simply did not conduct CWPT sessions in favor of other activities had reduced outcomes when compared to weeks when the recommended time was devoted to CWPT sessions (i.e., four 30-minute sessions per week per subject matter using CWPT). Reduced weekly exposure to CWPT has nearly always had the effect of decreasing some students' gains on weekly mastery/fluency measures (Greenwood et al., 1992).

Tutors' Use of the Scripted Procedures for Evoking Tutees' Response, Correcting Errors, and Awarding Points Earned. In CWPT, scripts are used so that both tutor and tutee are guided and not left entirely alone to mediate their own learning (Cazden, 1992). Thus explicit instructional strategies used in CWPT require tutors to present specific learning trials, check tutee response, and provide differential forms of correction and help depending on the accuracy of response (Delquadri et al., 1983). Having students read aloud passages, answer specific comprehension questions, retell stories read, predict events based on current information, and check the accuracy of their predictions also have been infused into classwide peer tutoring methods (e.g., Mathes et al., 1994).

In cases in which tutors were not initially well trained in the tutoring procedures, their tutees learned less. Initial training of tutors and tutees involves observing a model, demonstrating, and classwide practice (see the teacher's CWPT manual; Greenwood, Delquadri, & Carta, 1997). The teacher and a volunteer student first model the roles of tutor and tutee (model), pairs of students demonstrate the roles to the class (demonstrate), and pairs then practice the roles classwide as the teacher observed, providing group and individual feedback as needed (independent practice). For selected students showing difficulty demonstrating any aspect of the scripted tutor-tutee interaction, individual teacher-student practice sessions are used to improve individual tutoring skills. Case studies of individual students who failed to reach mastery or fluency of the material by the end of the week often indicated that they were slow responders, and efforts to increase their opportunities to practice, the accuracy of error corrections, and the value of points earned helped accelerate their skills as both tutor and tutee.

Challenging Material for All Students. Our experiences with general education teachers indicated repeatedly that they assigned material to be learned that was too easy for the majority of students, limiting acceleration of what students may learn in a week's time. To better select instructional-level materials for CWPT, teachers learned to pretest their students each week to identify material of sufficient difficulty and to individualize. Where

material was too easy, teachers were encouraged to add more challenging material in each week's tutoring program.

Fulfilling the Teacher's Role in CWPT Sessions. Instruction prior to CWPT each week is designed to promote students' background knowledge, review, and introduce new material. Initial teaching of the material was critically important to establishing an acceptable success-to-error ratio in the initial CWPT session that week. Teachers who eliminated this step dramatically increased students' initial error rates.

To maintain the fidelity of peer tutoring, teachers routinely supervise peer tutoring sessions by moving through the room awarding "bonus" points to tutors they observe to be using the correct procedures. These points count the same as points earned by the tutee. Teachers check tutors' use of points and check to make sure that they are correctly applying the error correction procedure. Research has shown that teachers who did not supervise the peer tutoring process in this way lowered the fidelity of peer tutoring and increased the likelihood of lower weekly outcomes for students. They also risked the onset of point cheating when students realized that they are not being monitored as they were originally trained to expect (Greenwood et al., 1992; Harper, Mallette, Maheady, & Clifton, 1990).

Similarly, the selection of the winning team immediately on completing CWPT sessions provides contingent group reinforcement when it is most likely to influence student motivation positively. Teachers who delayed until later or who did not use the point system risked lowering student outcomes and students' satisfaction and interest in CWPT.

Teacher's Use of All CWPT Core Components. Students whose teacher dropped a core component often performed less well. In summary, the five changes teachers most often made to core components were providing students with unchallenging material for tutoring; providing less than the recommended weekly time devoted to CWPT; eliminating or delaying some aspect of the point system; failing to supervise and maintain the fidelity of peer tutoring during CWPT sessions; and failing to review, activate prior knowledge, and introduce new material. In some cases, CWPT programs have suffered from only single variations like these, whereas in other cases, multiple problems were evident (e.g., reduced weekly sessions, unchallenging material for weeks in a row, and uncorrected, low-quality peer tutoring).

Problems Reaching Scale Within and Across School Buildings

Taking CWPT from classroom to schoolwide applications while also sustaining fidelity and use over time became central issues, and a number of new barriers had to be overcome. For example, we had seen an individual teacher's CWPT program, initially approved by the building principal, terminated by an uninformed central administrator over the objections of both the teacher and the principal. The administrator felt that CWPT was not consistent with district curriculum/instruction policies. And, as mentioned, we had seen cases of incomplete implementation after training as well as radical modifications in the program's core procedures by some teachers.

To address these problems, we developed and tested an administrative-adoption model for CWPT (Abbott, Walton, Tapia, & Greenwood, 1999; Delquadri, Flanagan, & Greenwood, 1987). The goal was to establish administrative and professional development contexts that would support CWPT implementation (e.g., Elmore, 1996). The model was designed to prevent program terminations and to maintain the quality of CWPT implementation (Greenwood, Terry, Delquadri, & Elliott, 1995).

The complete model put procedures in place that addressed (a) formal acceptance of

CWPT as a practice appropriate for use within special and general education programs within a district, (b) formal certification of CWPT as an approved procedure for use in students' individualized education programs (IEPs), (c) orientation and training of multiple levels of district and building staff concerning CWPT, (d) identification of persons onsite with sufficient expertise to become local CWPT experts and to address teachers' questions about CWPT implementation, (e) use of a CWPT fidelity checklist by consult trainer or peer partner to assess a teacher's classroom implementation and provide feedback, (f) multiple new sources of teacher contact and positive reinforcement concerning the program and its effects, and (g) administrative as well as classroom-level formative evaluation procedures (e.g., Delquadri, Elliott, Hughes, & Porter, 1990; Delquadri et al., 1987).

We sought to improve and maintain program quality by providing the teacher with weekly feedback and its effects on students' achievement. We did this by creating observer and coaching roles for teacher partners and the building CWPT facilitator (see Table 4.1). A *teacher's partner,* for example, conducts periodic observations of the CWPT implementation of his or her partner using the CWPT implementation checklist and reports results back to the partner. The *building facilitator* provides a similar observation and feedback as part of his or her schoolwide duties. And the *building coordinator* establishes a building-level evaluation plan and schedules data sharing sessions so that all staff may observe, reflect, and improve on current progress implementing the program and thereby increase student outcomes.

In tests of the model, the overall percentage of teachers participating in CWPT actually increased from 78% to 82% between Year 1 and Year 2. Also important, program implementation quality as measured by fidelity checklists increased from 88% to 94% overall between Year 1 and Year 2 with use of the model. Individual schools varied but each maintained very high levels of teacher participation and implementation quality. Other

TABLE 4.1 Administrative Adoption Model Roles

Program consultant

- ◻ Provides orientation and training materials
- ◻ Provides on-site assistance/ongoing consultation
- ◻ Provides data collection and evaluation plan
- ◻ Attends data sharing sessions

Building coordinator (principal)

- ◻ Compiles a schoolwide data/evaluation plan
- ◻ Meets regularly with building representative
- ◻ Monitors and supports classroom teachers
- ◻ Attends staff training sessions
- ◻ Establishes system of positive reinforcement for staff
- ◻ Schedules and participates in data-sharing sessions

Building facilitator (elected faculty member)

- ◻ Trains teachers in CWPT
- ◻ Attends training sessions
- ◻ Provides follow-up training
- ◻ Assists teachers in adjusting implementation
- ◻ Conducts periodic observations and provides implementation feedback
- ◻ Organizes and supports teachers
- ◻ Meets periodically with coordinator to review data and building implementation/outcome progress
- ◻ Maintains communications with CWPT consultant
- ◻ Supports collection of evaluation measures

Teacher partners

- ◻ Prepares CWPT charts and materials
- ◻ Implements CWPT
- ◻ Observes the CWPT implementation of partner
- ◻ Provides implementation feedback to partner
- ◻ Reports periodic outcomes on implementation checklists and curriculum-based measures affected by CWPT

indexes of change indicated improvement in students' academic engagement, reading achievement, and inclusion of special education students using the model (Greenwood, 1994). Data also indicated that the frequencies of contact between and among teachers, teacher partners, building coordinators, and building facilitators increased and were maintained (Delquadri et al., 1990).

The Contribution of Computer and Information Management Technology

Although this work produced a number of effective and useful components for implementing CWPT, challenges reaching scale remained. Developments in computer and information technologies offered some potential solutions (Greenwood, 1998). Most obvious was reducing time devoted to student progress data and instructional decision making. Less obvious, perhaps, was the potential of computerized communications and student progress information that teachers could act on in their weekly planning.

Challenges

A barrier bringing CWPT to scale was the relatively infrequent opportunities for building staff to communicate, share results, and gain direct access to current information on the use of CWPT. Progress information at the student, classroom, and school levels could not previously be accessed and interpreted fast enough for teachers to act on it by adapting CWPT. The advent of intranets and LAN technology within local school buildings represented a new and unique environment suitable for individual and group communications (e-mail and sharing of documents and data). We expected that building intranets could be used to empower each teacher and each principal in ways that would directly increase the number of CWPT programs, their effectiveness, quality, and longevity, and reduce effort and costs. Therefore, a research component is focused on developing and testing a LAN-based learning management system making CWPT components more accessible and usable.

The potential benefits of CWPT were limited because it took too long to chart and interpret weekly progress data for each individual child in a classroom, and teachers often complained that the workload was too high. Teachers also desired to have more sensitive and thoughtful methods for pairing students for tutoring sessions. We thought that by combining program planning, database, data analysis, and data interpretation functions within a single software tool, we could reduce workload and make classwide formative evaluation acceptable. And, with the right software design on the network, we planned

to extend the principle of formative evaluation to unit, grade, and schoolwide levels of display, summary, and analysis within the CWPT administrative-adoption model. We also sought to make individual programs easier to plan and adapt and instructional decisions easier to make.

The potential benefits of CWPT also were limited because teachers often lacked specific, sensitive information about what to do to improve class and individual student outcomes each week. Thus, we sought to improve diagnosis of common implementation problems and provide specific solutions by linking these problems to observed patterns in students' CWPT outcomes. Although others have linked expert system advice to student performance as a means of identifying error patterns (Fuchs, Fuchs, & Hamlett, 1994) or misconceptions (Woodward & Howard, 1994), our approach examined poor student outcomes in terms of CWPT infidelities and recommended steps to correct these program implementation problems with respect to the entire class and specific individuals having the greatest problems.

From prior CWPT research and practice, we knew that students earning too few points during CWPT were experiencing reduced learning trials and a reduction in content coverage in their tutoring. We also knew that reduction in weekly time to learn in CWPT nearly always led to lower weekly outcomes, particularly for lower-skilled students. Our expert system assists teachers in identifying implementation problems of this type when they occurred, explains their potential effects on progress, and recommends improvements that could be made to reduce the impact of these factors on students' learning outcomes (Greenwood, Carta, Delquadri, & Finney, 1989; Greenwood, Finney, et al., 1993).

The potential benefits of CWPT were limited for a number of other reasons, such as the lack of predeveloped materials designed for CWPT and the time required for teachers to develop their own materials. To obviate this, a research component has focused on producing and validating a range of curriculum

FIGURE 4.1. CWPT-LMS Software Design Integrating Teacher Support and the Administrative-Adoption Model Programs on a Building Intranet

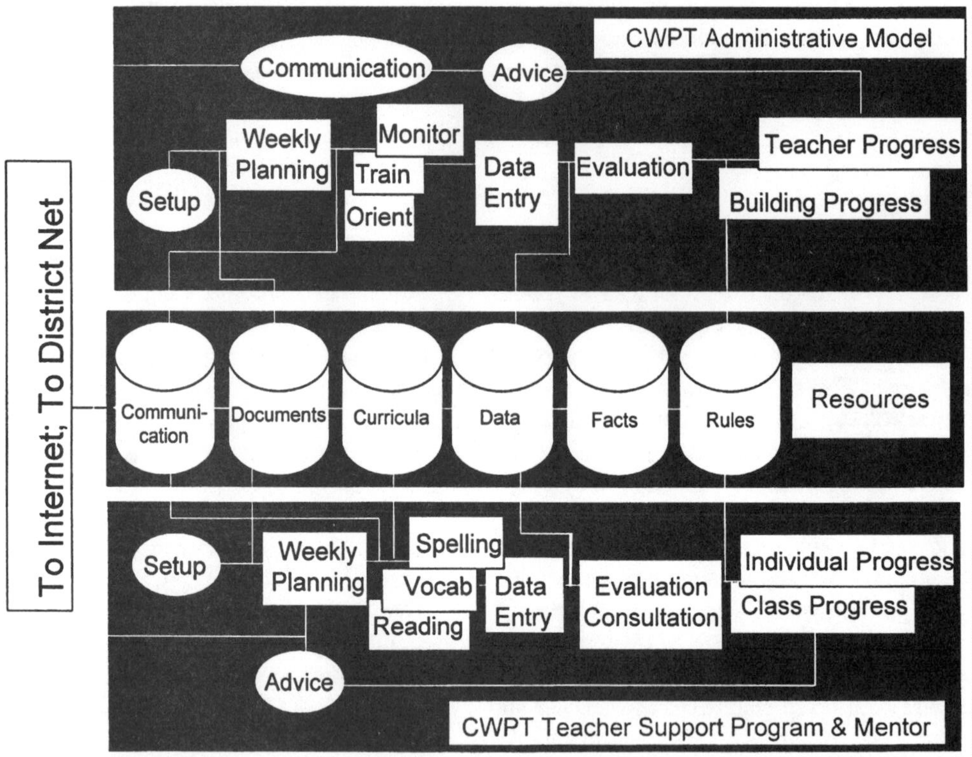

formats and peer tutoring materials for CWPT (Arreaga-Mayer, 1998). The lack of procedures for building- and system-wide implementation and management of the program over time also limited the potential benefits of CWPT. Therefore, another research component has focused on the administrative-adoption model implemented on the building intranet. Yet another limiting factor was the fact that teacher training materials and implementation knowledge were contained only in print-based texts and manuals. Therefore, a research component has focused on improving and expanding this knowledge using interactive CD-ROM and teacher software support programs and other technological forms (e.g., WWW-based, on-line information) so that it may be broadly used.

Current Efforts

The goal of the CWPT-Learning Management System (CWPT-LMS) is to integrate CWPT administrative and instructional functions and make them accessible to building faculty (see Figures 4.1 and 4.2). At the heart of the system is the individual classroom program (see lower panel, Figure 4.1)—at least one CWPT program for each teacher with a workstation on the intranet (see Figure 4.2). Using the teacher support program, teachers set up, plan, implement, evaluate, and consult about one or more CWPT programs they have under way (see Figure 4.3). Through a weekly consultation with the CWPT consultant, each teacher receives suggestions for conducting the next week's program based on an evalua-

FIGURE 4.2. CWPT-LMS Local Area Network Linking Teachers in a Building to Developers at the Juniper Gardens Children's Project

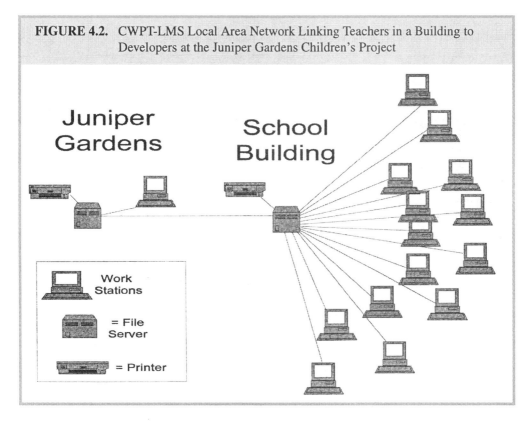

FIGURE 4.3. Teacher at Her Classroom Workstation Using the CWPT-LMS

tion of prior levels of implementation in relation to group and individual student outcomes. Each classroom teacher on the system has access to a range of CWPT-related resources, including manuals and documents, curriculum format models, interactive training and video-based examples, and their own data reflecting all results of weekly formative evaluations. Linked to all individual classroom programs is the CWPT administrative-adoption model and its components (see upper panel, Figure 4.1). This tool is designed for use by the CWPT building coordinator and facilitator in support of orientation, training, and monitoring of progress. It is designed to help establish, maintain, and improve the quality of program implementation of individual teachers. It provides analyses of building-level progress and direct communication between the facilitator and each individual teacher. We now discuss several of the technology tools in the CWPT-LMS in some detail.

Improving Initial Teacher Training: The CWPT Interactive CD

The CWPT Interactive CD is a multimedia teacher's manual containing a wide range of information and media related to the program's use, procedures, and research effectiveness (Greenwood, Delquadri, & Terry, 1998). This interactive technology allows teachers to navigate through the material on their own, exploring according to their interests (see Figure 4.4). Importantly, compared to simple text documents, a range of video and photographic examples are available illustrating specific steps in setting up and running the program. In seconds, one can access what one needs to know about CWPT. With the CD, teachers actually may observe the interactions of tutors and tutees in the program before they attempt to teach their students to carry out these roles. As illustrated in Figure 4.5, the CD's major contents are a Welcome, Implementation of CWPT, CWPT Issues, and a Media Gallery.

The first three sections are organized so that teachers may quickly learn to set up and implement CWPT. The Welcome Section provides an overview of CWPT that is documented by digital video examples illustrating program procedures, interviews with teachers who have used the program, and interviews with students (see Figures 4.6, 4.7, and 4.8). The Implementation of CWPT Section provides a detailed, step-by-step discussion of how to implement the program. The content covered here includes the CWPT Process, CWPT Materials, Spelling and Math CWPT, Reading CWPT, and the Prevention of Problems.

The CWPT Issues Section provides a forum for exploring issues that affect the design and implementation of CWPT. These issues are represented in the following sections: Curriculum, Integrating Students With Disabilities, School-Wide CWPT, and Research Findings. The Media Gallery Section provides a reference and searching environment for accessing various media of interest quickly. Its information is organized alphabetically by topic and is searchable by type of media (e.g., video, graphic). In this section, teachers are able to access a topic of concern or interest quickly.

Supporting Classroom Implementation: Software and Expert System

The CWPT Teacher Support Program and Consultant is a multifeatured software system that supports planning, implementation, evaluation, and program improvement linked to weekly analyses of class and student outcomes (Greenwood, Hou, Terry, & Arreaga-Mayer, 1997). With many of the features of the computerized grade book described by Hayden, Wheeler, and Carnine (1989), it is designed for use by individual teachers.

Program Support. The first step in setting up a CWPT program is to construct the classroom roster and identify the subject matter (e.g., spelling) to be taught. With this infor-

(text continues on page 75)

FIGURE 4.4. CWPT Interactive CD Title Page

FIGURE 4.5. Interactive CD Table of Contents

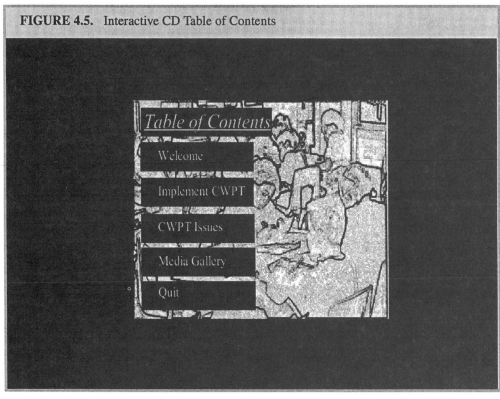

FIGURE 4.6. CD Digital Video Clip Showing Students Engaged in Spelling CWPT

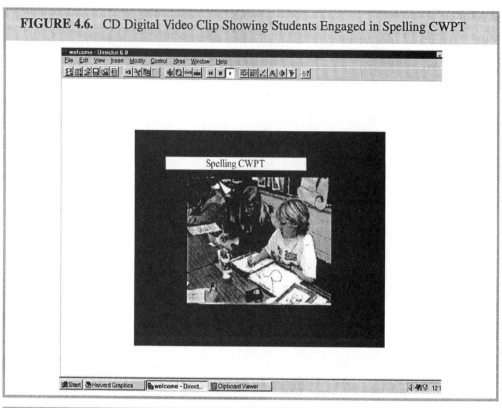

FIGURE 4.7. CD Digital Video Clip Providing a Teacher's Perspective on Her Use of CWPT

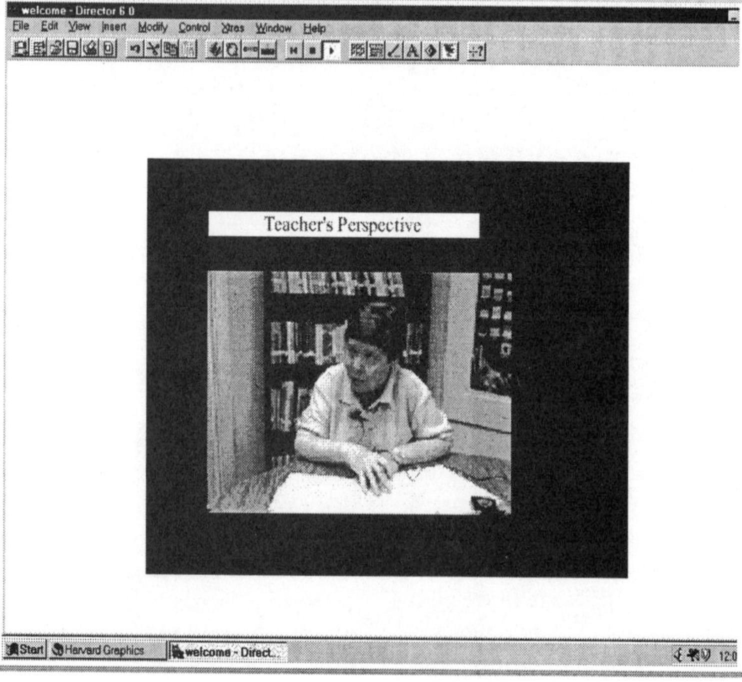

FIGURE 4.8. CD Digital Video Clip Showing a Teacher Recording Students' Points Earned During CWPT

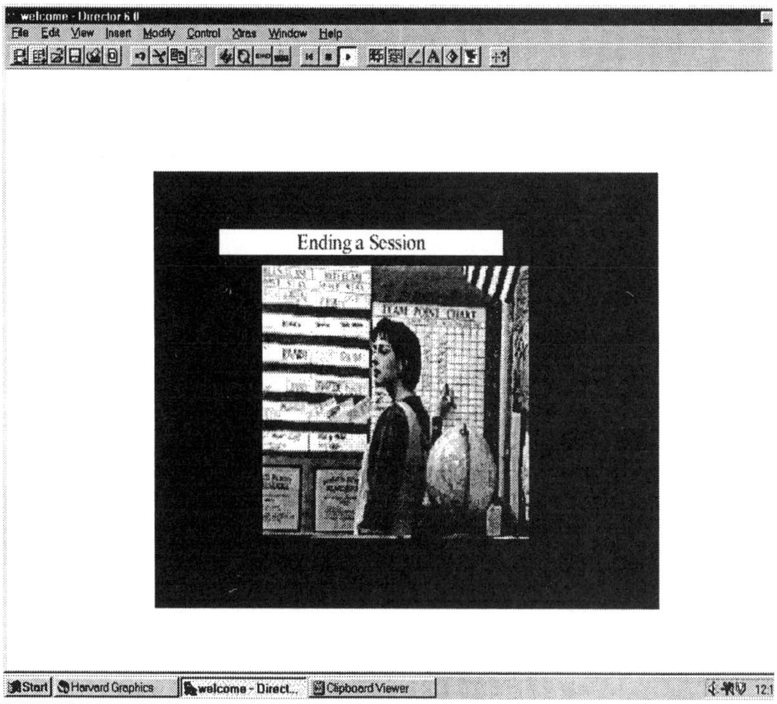

mation, a weekly database is established that anticipates daily data entry reflecting points earned by individual students and test information (e.g., pre- and postpeer tutoring) on the material tutored this week (see Figure 4.9). Using the data typically produced in CWPT, the software automates team point totaling and selection of the winning team. The software also lets the teacher select the length of CWPT sessions, record elapsed time, and signal completion.

Planning for a new week of tutoring includes assigning partners (dyads) and assigning partners to one of two teams (see Figures 4.10, 4.11, and 4.12). The software allows the teacher to select pairs in several ways, including at random, based on best ability match, and teacher (manual) designation. With the exception of the teacher designation option, partner and team assignments are made automatically by the program. The program also provides the teacher tools for removing files,

backing up data to other disks, and restoring data from previous programs.

Progress Monitoring. The program's charting tools let the teacher monitor student and class progress in the curriculum on demand (see Figure 4.12). Charts are available for the class average over all weeks of the program, a selected individual student over all weeks in the program in comparison to the class average (see Figure 4.13), a selected week's display of pretest to posttest progress for all students in the class that week (Figure 4.14), and a display of the proportion of students in the class experiencing a specific progress outcome that week. The first three charts are descriptive indicators of class and individual progress. For example, in Figure 4.13, one can see that the class pretest average ranges between 10% and 30% correct over 12 weeks, whereas after peer tutoring at posttest, the average ranges from a low of 50% to a high of

(text continues on page 78)

FIGURE 4.9. Teacher Support Program: Week 6 Classroom Database in One Teacher's Spelling CWPT Program

Student Name	05/05/97 PreTest Score	05/05/97 Tutoring Day 1 R	Day 1 B	05/06/97 Day 2 R	Day 2 B	05/07/97 Day 3 R	Day 3 B	00/00/00 Day 4 R	Day 4 B	05/12/97 PostTest Score
ADAM	80.00%	23	0	59	0	ABS	ABS			100.00%
ALAN	26.67%	22	0	70	0	32	0			73.33%
AMANDA	66.67%	ABS	ABS	32	0	46	0			100.00%
ASHLEY	53.33%	20	0	ABS	ABS	40	0			100.00%
AUNDREA	66.67%	66	0	39	0	44	0			100.00%
BLAKE	80.00%	75	0	108	0	ABS	ABS			93.33%
BRENDAN	13.33%	7	0	52	0	34	0			86.67%
BRENDON	60.00%	12	0	51	0	38	0			ABS
CHELSEA	46.67%	ABS	ABS	101	0	34	0			80.00%
D'ANDRE	60.00%	0	0	42	0	32	0			86.67%
DUSTIN	46.67%	ABS	ABS	43	0	32	0			73.33%
GALEN	86.67%	30	0	90	0	56	0			100.00%

*** NOTE: Abbreviations are as follows:
Tutoring Days 1 - 4: R = Regular Points
B = Bonus Points

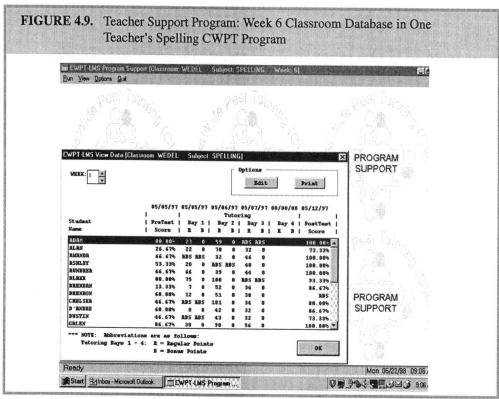

FIGURE 4.10. Teacher Support Program: Menu Sequence for Assigning Students to Partners for Peer Tutoring and Pairs to Competing Teams: Manual, Random, or Skill-Level Methods of Assignment

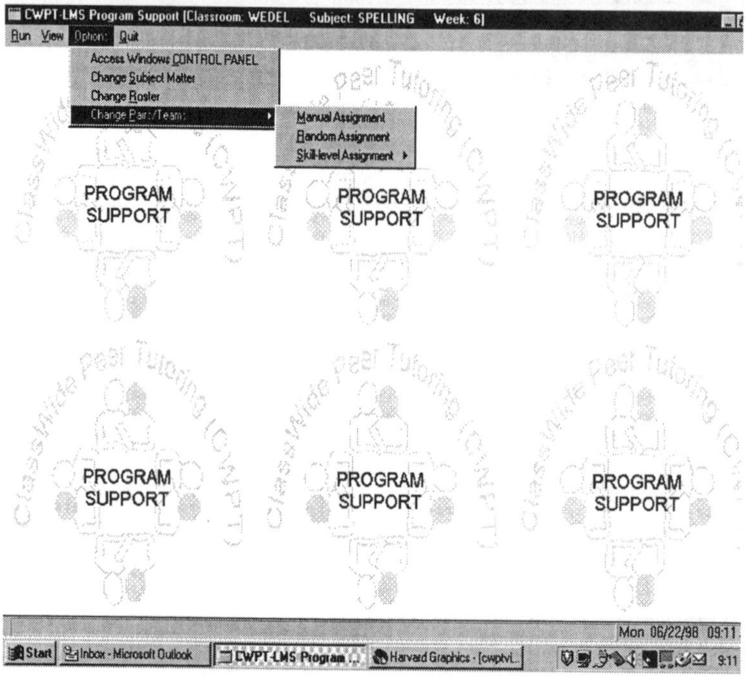

FIGURE 4.11. Resulting Partners and Team Assignments

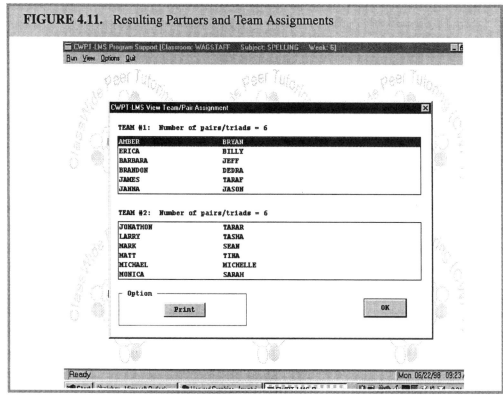

FIGURE 4.12. Teacher Support Program: Menu Sequence for Selecting Data Displays by Classroom, by Week, by Student, and by Outcome Group

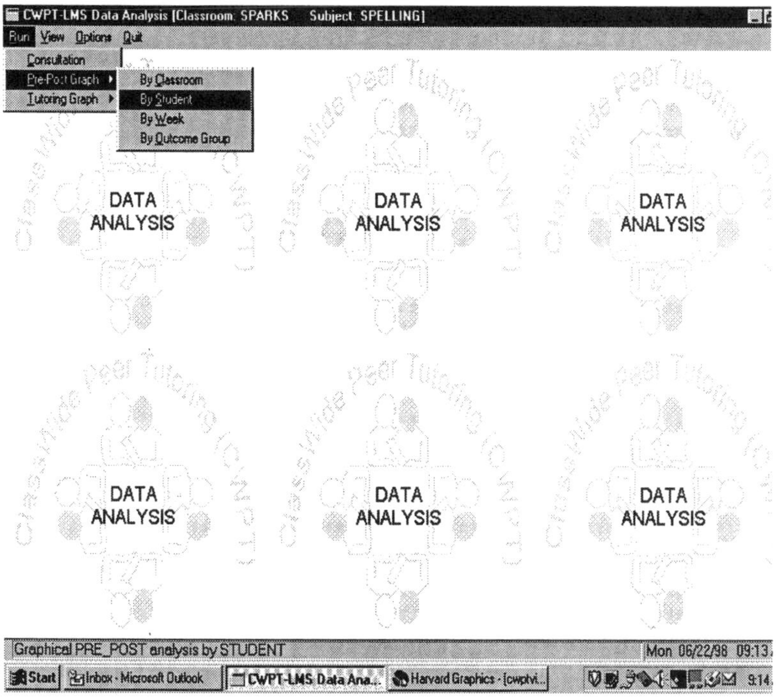

FIGURE 4.13. Teacher Support Program: Pretest-Posttest Data Displayed for One Student With the Class Mean Percentage Correct Over 12 Weeks of Program Use

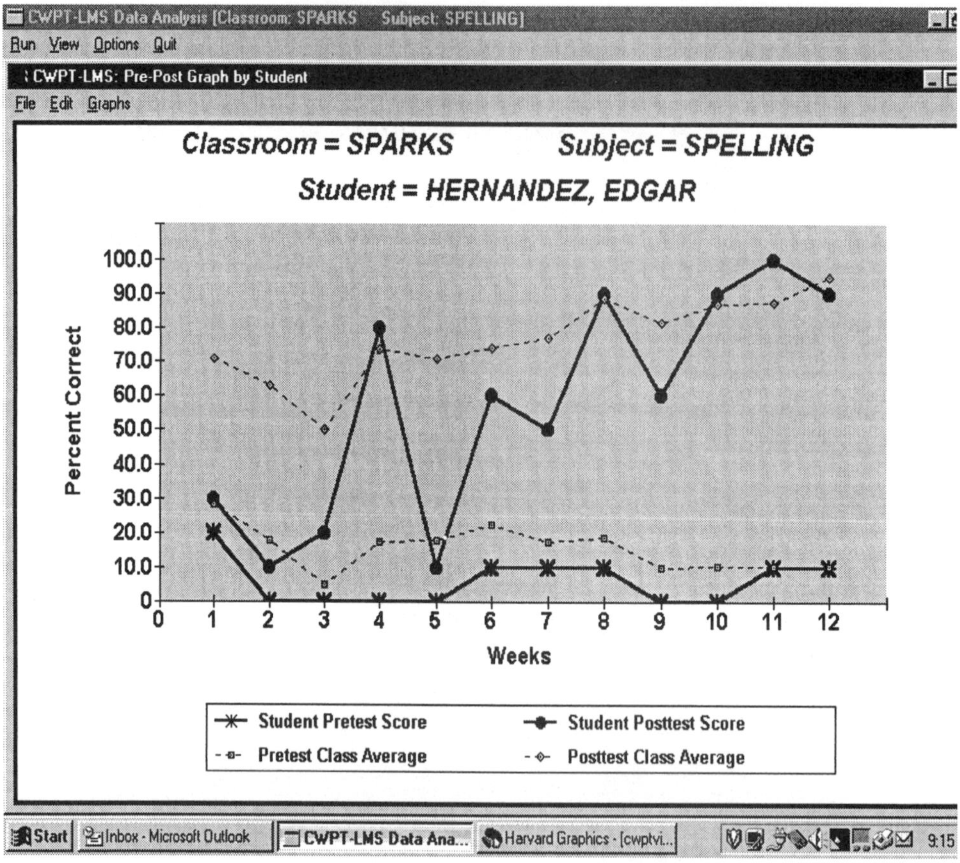

95%. The individual student, Edgar, shows substantial gain in the program in Week 4, with an improving trend over Weeks 6 through 12. His gains after Week 8 are nearly as large as the class average. Similarly, in Figure 4.14, all individual students show dramatic gains after Week 11's peer tutoring.

The fourth chart is diagnostic with respect to student outcomes and implementation concerns. Displayed first in this chart is the proportion of the class for whom tutoring was successful that week. Successful students are those who fell below a criterion level at pretest (40%) and who exceeded a growth criterion level at posttest (80%). Similarly, the proportion of children who were not success-

ful, those who were underchallenged by material too easy for them, or those who did not accelerate their mastery/fluency because of poor quality peer tutoring and/or infrequent tutoring sessions are displayed for teacher review and interpretation. With this information, teachers can reflect on the appropriate strategies needed in the next week to improve class and individual progress.

Interpretation and Advice. These same student outcome data and other program implementation data that week (frequency and time spent in CWPT, points earned by students, individual absences, etc.) are evaluated by the CWPT Consultant software, and advice with

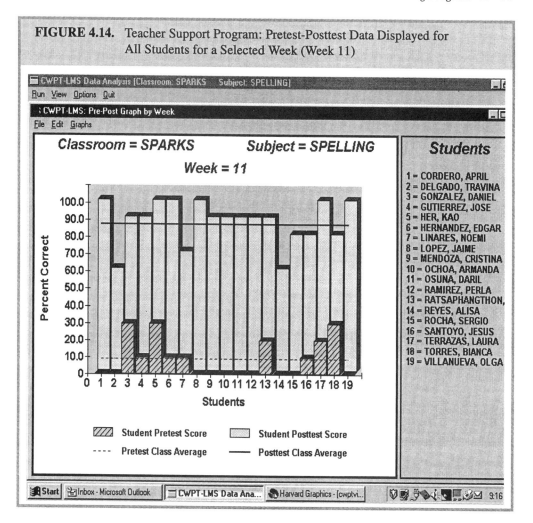

FIGURE 4.14. Teacher Support Program: Pretest-Posttest Data Displayed for All Students for a Selected Week (Week 11)

interpretation/explanation is provided to the teacher at the end of each week. The Consultant provides an evaluation of group and individual progress as well as an evaluation of program implementation (Greenwood, Carta, et al., 1989). Its advice includes focused suggestions for altering the next week's program along with the reasons/rationales for doing so.

The Consultant uses a knowledge base that we developed to evaluate, explain, and advise classroom teachers (Greenwood, Finney, et al., 1993). This knowledge base incorporates lessons learned from a number of previous studies that examined teacher's implementation of CWPT and the adverse effects of some program modifications on student outcomes. The knowledge base also benefits from analy-

ses of children who have failed to reach mastery during a week of CWPT. Using this information applied to the last week's data, the Consultant carries out a dialogue with the teacher as it examines weekly results and explains and expands on issues of importance. From the four examples in Table 4.2, one can sense the flavor of this dialogue. Here we have explanations related to too few successful students that week and the most likely reasons why; teacher's failure to use bonus points and, thus, the concern that the teacher may not be monitoring and acting to improve the quality of the peer tutoring; infrequent CWPT sessions; and content material of correct difficulty for the class. The system contains more than 150 separate messages that

TABLE 4.2 Illustrative Explanations and Advice Contained in the CWPT Consultant's Knowledge Base

---

message(most-important-component) = The number of students within the SUCCESS group this week was not as large as would be hoped. This means that the students were:

1. Underchallenged by the content material because it was too easy for the majority of them this week

2. Underpracticing the material during tutoring such that they did not master the material

3. Experiencing a number of individual problems that compromised the success of the class as a whole.

The most likely cause of small SUCCESS groups is failing to provide enough time to do tutoring. I will now look at the information about tutoring in your class this week to see if a time problem exists.

message(no-bonus points) = I find that you have not been using bonus points with your students. Experience has shown that BONUS POINTS ARE YOUR BEST MEANS of shaping tutor's behaviors and maintaining the quality of tutoring classwide. Bonus points also contribute to maintaining the general enthusiasm of the class for CWPT. You significantly compromise the power of the CWPT technique if you do not circulate through the class, evaluating your students' behavior, and reinforcing good practices throughout each tutoring session as described in the tutoring manual of procedures.

message(no-curriculum-analysis) = No analysis of the appropriateness of curriculum can be completed this week because the average number of days tutored was too low. At such a low frequency of tutoring, it is impossible to discern whether the materials provided students this week were appropriate or not.

message(no-curriculum-problem) = It appears that the difficulty of the tutoring materials was a good match for your students this week. KEEP UP THE GOOD WORK!

---

relate to specific outcomes for the class, individual students, and teacher's implementation of the program.

Supporting School-Wide Implementation: Administrative-Adoption Model Software

The CWPT administrative-adoption model software in development is designed to support use of CWPT at the school building-level. The major functions of the CWPT process at this level are planning, orienting, training, and monitoring progress in specific ways that link the roles of coordinator, facilitator, and teacher partners (see upper panel, Table 4.1). Successful implementation of the model establishes the necessary contexts, systems, training, and supports needed to sustain quality use of the program as previously discussed.

Planning and Orienting. The program provides specific milestones and scheduling tools to help the coordinator and facilitator orient and work effectively with each other and the building faculty (Greenwood, Delquadri, et al., 1993). E-mail and group scheduling will play important roles. For example, an early step in the process is for a building facilitator to be elected and for roles in the model to be discussed and clarified. Another early step is for teachers to begin a baseline assessment of students' weekly progress in the curriculum prior to the implementation of CWPT.

TABLE 4.3 Weekly CWPT Spelling Achievement Summary by Teacher, Week, and Cumulative to Date (% Correct)

	Week	Pre	Post		Week	Pre	Post
Teacher 1	1	63.03	87.08	**Teacher 4**	1	44.64	81.33
	2	75.92	91.42		2	36.00	74.29
	3	37.11	86.32		3	61.90	86.67
	Mean	58.69	88.27		4	55.65	84.06
Teacher 2	1	—	91.59		5	42.03	69.28
	2	79.37	89.7		Mean	48.04	79.13
	3	73.33	89.17	**Teacher 5**	1	33.61	90.00
	4	47.22	92.12		2	40.35	70.48
	5	—	79.68		3	48.57	78.25
	Mean	66.64	88.45		4	41.9	83.98
Teacher 3	1	30.09	87.37		5	48.52	80.00
	2	—	95.15		Mean	42.59	80.54
	3	52.38	92.22	**Teacher 6**	1	84.89	84.94
	Mean	41.24	91.58		2	95.83	64.25
					3	58.33	90.66
					4	55.28	66.67
					5	92.6	48.82
					Mean	77.39	71.07

School Summary for Spelling (*N* = 6 teachers)				
	Minimum	Maximum	Mean	SD
Pre	41.24	77.39	55.77	14.41
Post	71.01	91.58	83.17	7.67

Implementation. The software continues to support the communications and scheduling required to carry out teacher and student training in the CWPT process and thus establish the program in classrooms. In this process, the coordinator and facilitator implement their periodic observations of teachers and provide feedback based on implementation checklists. Teacher partners also begin this process in the first 2 weeks of the full program. The first data-sharing session is conducted. At these meetings, individual teacher and group summary progress data are presented and discussed up to this point in the life of the program (see Table 4.2; Figure 4.13). Focusing on progress data prompts discussion about both success and problems leading to efforts to improve program implementation and increased teacher understanding of the basic procedures and theory behind CWPT (e.g., Greenwood & Maheady, 1997).

From a pilot study, Tables 4.3 and 4.4 provide a building summary of nine separate CWPT programs (6 spelling, 3 math) under way by six teachers in one elementary school using the CWPT Learning Management Software. It is evident that individual teachers have been using CWPT for a relatively short

TABLE 4.4 Weekly CWPT Math Achievement Summary by Teacher, Week, and Cumulative to Date (% Correct)

	Week	Pre	Post		Week	Pre	Post
Teacher 2	1	—	82.99	**Teacher 3**	1	86.67	—
	2	—	92.03		2	60.39	—
	3	40.30	78.08		3	—	84.91
	4	45.30	92.82		4	—	80.84
	5	54.41	76.45		Mean	73.53	82.88
	Mean	46.67	84.47	**Teacher 6**	1	24.06	91.52
					2	81.20	93.96
					3	—	94.49
					4	22.08	95.83
					5	—	95.31
					Mean	42.45	94.22

School Summary for Spelling (*N* = 3 teachers)				
	Minimum	Maximum	Mean	SD
Pre	42.45	73.53	54.22	16.85
Post	82.88	94.22	87.19	6.14

period, ranging from 3 to 5 weeks. The tables contain weekly summaries for each teacher and a summary of all teachers and weeks. Average mastery gains during individual weeks are often dramatic, ranging, for example, from 37% to 86% correct (Teacher 1–Spelling). Over all classrooms, average spelling gains were from 41% to 71% correct, and math gains were from 42% to 83% correct. It is important that variations in some teachers' implementation are clearly evident. For example, Teacher 3–Math shows missing pretest data for Weeks 1 and 2. It would be important to know why these data were not collected or reported. In another case, Teacher 6–Spelling shows negative gain overall, 77.39% at pretest and 71.04% at posttest, with pretest performance on Weeks 2 and 5 higher than posttest. Yet on other weeks, better progress has been made. This clearly indicates one or more problems with this teacher's program, and the data help focus the facilitator's attention on its solution in coming weeks.

Maintenance and Expansion to New Areas. For programs more than 5 weeks long, the maintenance phase reflects the ongoing process of refining implementation quality, problem solving, and monitoring of progress (see Table 4.1). Decision points in individual programs after 5 weeks typically focus on teachers deciding to expand the program to a second or third subject matter area, such as reading and spelling. Also typical is the targeting and development of curriculum for use in the program.

Discussion

In this chapter, we have described the development of CWPT that began as a successful collaboration between a researcher and a classroom teacher and led to other similar collaborations and intervention studies that replicated and expanded CWPT components and applications. Because these intervention studies produced useful outcomes, the work continued, and it has extended beyond the initial developers, and new applications have developed. We described CWPT intervention research in the context of challenges fundamentally involving issues of effectiveness, fidelity, and scale. In addition, we described current work linking computer technology to help overcome these challenges.

By combining CWPT administrative and instructional components in one system supported by computer technology and by making them accessible to building staff in their roles as teachers, facilitators, and coordinators, the potential for scale and sustained use of the program appears radically improved (Gersten, Vaughn, Deshler, & Schiller, 1997). Not only is the individual classroom CWPT program improved with technology, but the larger contexts needed to sustain use and improve quality also are improved and readily accessible. Consequently, the prospects of accelerating the literacy of children with and without disabilities also are improved.

Taking advantage of previously developed and validated components, the CWPT-LMS is designed to support and augment individual classroom applications. Adding technology and information technology to these components, the CWPT-LMS supports building-wide application more than ever before. CWPT-LMS promises benefits of quality and cost savings compared to CWPT without technology and compared to the higher dollar and time costs of human consultants needed to support training and implementation. Thus the CWPT-LMS is an increasingly important and powerful enhancement of CWPT.

As illustrated, the value added to CWPT by computer technology is substantial and important to consider. First, linking the administrative-adoption model to the instructional program through software and LAN technology enables the staff to conduct their particular roles in the program with greater accuracy and support and with less hassle than before. This link adds the very important level of e-mail communication to the use of CWPT for purposes of planning, feedback, scheduling, and sharing progress data. With e-mail, staff exchanges mail, documents, and

procedures with their teacher partners, facilitator, and coordinator. This value should be seen in terms of higher-quality, sustained use of CWPT.

Second, the LMS adds an improved dimension to the accessibility of CWPT information, teacher training, and individual program support. Through access to CWPT information, teachers have quick access to what they need at any time. Through interactive multimedia, teachers have access to a wide range of illustrations not previously available that help them plan and carry out the program. The CWPT support software automates many steps and provides a guide for the conduct of program steps in real time, maintaining quality of implementation with less work. Time-consuming functions like the charting of individual results are automated and extended classwide and not restricted to just those children with IEPs. This enhancement enables use of instructionally relevant measurement for progress monitoring; altering program features when needed; and overall accountability at the student, classroom, and school levels of analysis. For example, teachers can print off the very real progress of each student and give them to parents when they visit. Similarly, the principal can compile an annual summary of progress for use in the building's accountability plan.

Third, the LMS provides teachers with specific information and interpretation fast enough that it can be used to alter CWPT in ways that actually improve student outcomes (Greenwood, Finney, et al., 1993). For example, weekly advice on program improvement provided by expert system software is based on prior research findings in which the effects of particular program features and variations are known in terms of their impact on student outcomes. This information provides for more rapid and successful decisions and uses of the program. In addition, the expert system explanations and rationales continue to improve teachers' understanding of CWPT in ways that extend far beyond the information contained in the manual or the interactive CD.

We believe that the benefits of the LMS for current CWPT users are the improvements in quality and efficiency described and, thus, its greater potential for wide-scale use and benefits to literacy. The research currently under way using the CWPT-LMS is designed to demonstrate these benefits in one school building. The benefits of the LMS to others are the lessons learned concerning the system's development, validation, and utilization. This work provides a needed demonstration of how technology may be linked to existing effective practices (CWPT) in ways that reduce barriers and promote effectiveness, utilization, acceptability, teacher change, and broad impact.

The challenges ahead for the CWPT-LMS are several. The conclusions drawn here are limited by the fact that, to date, the CWPT-LMS has seen application in only one elementary school building, and its generalizability to other school buildings, contexts, and technology platforms remains to be demonstrated in future intervention research. It also remains to be seen how the CWPT-LMS will be used by classroom teachers when removed from the purview of the developer/researcher and outside the research and development context. The extent to which the CWPT-LMS, with its instructional, administrative, and technological components, actually moves to scale in local schools also remains to be seen.

References

Abbott, M., Walton, C., Tapia, Y., & Greenwood, C. R. (1999). Research to practice: A blueprint for closing the gap in local schools. *Exceptional Children, 65,* 339-352.

Arreaga-Mayer, C. (1998). Increasing active student responding and improving academic performance through classwide peer tutoring. *Intervention in School and Clinic, 34*(2), 89-94.

Arreaga-Mayer, C., Terry, B., & Greenwood, C. R. (1997). Class-wide peer tutoring. In K. Topping & S. Ehly (Eds.), *Peer-mediated instruction* (pp. 105-119). Mahwah, NJ: Lawrence Erlbaum.

Cazden, C. B. (1992). *Whole language plus: Essays on literacy in the United States and New Zealand.* New York: Teachers College Press.

Delquadri, J. C. (1978). *An analysis of the generalization effects of four tutoring procedures on oral reading responses of eight learning disability children.* Unpublished doctoral dissertation, University of Kansas, Department of Human Development and Family Life.

Delquadri, J. C., Elliott, M., Hughes, V., & Porter, M. (1990). *The effects of an administrative model for school principals on the effectiveness and maintenance of the reading class-wide peer tutoring program.* Kansas City, KS: Juniper Gardens Children's Project, University of Kansas.

Delquadri, J., Flanagan, P., & Greenwood, C. R. (1987). *The pyramid administrative model for class-wide peer tutoring.* Kansas City, KS: Juniper Gardens Children's Project, University of Kansas.

Delquadri, J., Greenwood, C. R., Stretton, K., & Hall, R. V. (1983). The peer tutoring game: A classroom procedure for increasing opportunity to respond and spelling performance. *Education and Treatment of Children, 6,* 225-239.

Delquadri, J., Greenwood, C. R., Whorton, D., Carta, J. J., & Hall, R. V. (1986). Class-wide peer tutoring. *Exceptional Children, 52,* 535-542.

Education for All Handicapped Children Act, Pub. L. No. 94-142, (November 29, 1975).

Elmore, R. F. (1996). Getting to scale with good educational practice. *Harvard Educational Review, 66,* 1-26.

Fuchs, L. S., Fuchs, D., & Hamlett, C. L. (1994). Strengthening the connection between assessment and instructional planning with expert systems. *Exceptional Children, 61*(2), 138-146.

Gersten, R., Vaughn, S., Deshler, D., & Schiller, E. (1997). What we know about using research findings: Implications for improving special education practice. *Journal of Learning Disabilities, 30,* 466-476.

Greenwood, C. R. (1994, February). ClassWide Peer Tutoring and inclusion. In D. Fuchs (Chair), *Data-based approaches to inclusionary education: Strategies for the policymakers?* Symposium conducted at the second annual meeting of the Pacific Coast Research Conference, La Jolla, CA.

Greenwood, C. R. (1996). Research on the practices and behavior of effective teachers at the Juniper Gardens Children's Project: Implications for diverse learners. In D. L. Speece & B. K. Keogh (Eds.), *Research on classroom ecologies: Implications for inclusion of children with learning disabilities* (pp. 39-68). Mahwah, NJ: Lawrence Erlbaum.

Greenwood, C. R. (1997). ClassWide Peer Tutoring. *Behavior and Social Issues, 7,* 11-18.

Greenwood, C. R. (1998). *Linking technology to the curriculum.* In C. Utley (Chair), *Advances and issues in peer tutoring research.* Symposium conducted at the sixth annual Pacific Coast Research Conference, La Jolla, CA.

Greenwood, C. R. (1999). Reflections on a research career: Perspective on 35 years of research at the Juniper Gardens Children's Project. *Exceptional Children, 66*(1), 7-21.

Greenwood, C. R., Arreaga-Mayer, C., Utley, C., Gavin, K., & Terry, B. (in press). ClassWide Peer Tutoring Learning Management System: Applications with elementary-level English language learners. *Remedial and Special Education.*

Greenwood, C. R., Carta, J. J., Delquadri, J., & Finney, R. (1989). *The class-wide peer tutoring advisor (CWPT:ES): A computerized expert system for teachers and consultants.* Kansas City, KS: Juniper Gardens Children's Project, University of Kansas.

Greenwood, C. R., Delquadri, J., & Bulgren, J. (1993). Current challenges to behavioral technology in the reform of schooling: Large-scale, high-quality implementation and sustained use of effective educational practices. *Education and Treatment of Children, 16,* 401-440.

Greenwood, C. R., Delquadri, J., & Carta, J. J. (1997). *Together we can: ClassWide Peer Tutoring for basic academic skills.* Longmont, CO: Sopris West.

Greenwood, C. R., Delquadri, J., & Hall, R. V. (1984). Opportunity to respond and student academic performance. In W. L. Heward, T. E. Heron, J. Trap-Porter, & D. S. Hill (Eds.), *Focus on behavior analysis in education* (pp. 58-88). Columbus, OH: Merrill.

Greenwood, C. R., Delquadri, J., & Hall, R. V. (1989). The longitudinal effects of class-wide peer tutoring. *Journal of Educational Psychology, 81,* 371-383.

Greenwood, C. R., Delquadri, J., & Terry, B. (1998). *ClassWide Peer Tutoring: CD-Interactive.* Kansas City, KS: Juniper Gardens Children's Project, Schiefelbusch Institute for Life Span Studies, University of Kansas.

Greenwood, C. R., Finney, R., Terry, B., Arreaga-Mayer, C., Carta, J. J., Delquadri, J., Walker, D., Innocenti, M., Lignugaris-Kraft, J., Harper, G. F., & Clifton, R. (1993). Monitoring, improving, and maintaining quality implementation of the Class-Wide Peer Tutoring Program using behavioral and computer technology. *Education and Treatment of Children, 16,* 19-47.

Greenwood, C. R., & Hops, H. (1981). Group contingencies and peer behavior change. In P. Strain (Ed.), *The utilization of classroom peers as behavior change agents* (pp. 189-259). New York: Plenum.

Greenwood, C. R., Hou, S., Terry, B., & Arreaga-Mayer, C. (1997). *The Classwide Peer Tutoring support program* (Version 2.0). Kansas City, KS: Juniper Gardens Children's Project, Bureau of Child Research, University of Kansas.

Greenwood, C. R., & Maheady, L. (1997). Measurable change in student performance: Forgotten standard in teacher preparation? *Teacher Education and Special Education, 20,* 265-275.

Greenwood, C. R., Maheady, L., & Carta, J. J. (1991). Peer tutoring programs in the regular education classroom. In G. Stoner, M. R. Shinn, & H. M. Walker (Eds.), *Interventions for achievement and behavior problems* (pp. 179-200). Washington, DC: National Association for School Psychologists.

Greenwood, C. R., Terry, B., Arreaga-Mayer, C., & Finney, D. (1992). The ClassWide Peer Tutoring Program: Implementation factors that moderate students' achievement. *Journal of Applied Behavior Analysis, 25,* 101-116.

Greenwood, C. R., Terry, B., Delquadri, J., & Elliott, M. (1995). *ClassWide Peer Tutoring: Effective teaching and research review.* Kansas City, KS: Juniper Gardens Children's Project, University of Kansas.

Greenwood, C. R., Terry, B., & Sparks, C. (1997). *Accommodating students with special needs: Classwide Peer Tutoring* [Satellite broadcast and videotape]. Athens, GA: University of Georgia, Interactive Teaching Network.

Hall, R. V., & Copeland, R. E. (1972). The responsive teaching model. In F. W. Clark, D. R. Evans, & L. A. Hammerlynck (Eds.), *Implementing behavioral programs for schools and clinics* (pp. 103-124). Champaign, IL: Research Press.

Harper, G., Mallette, B., Maheady, L., & Clifton, R. (1990). Applications of peer tutoring to arithmetic and spelling. *Direct Instruction News, 9,* 34-38.

Harper, G., Mallette, B., Maheady, L., Parkes, V., & Moore, J. (1993). Retention and generalization of spelling words acquired using a peer-mediated instructional procedure by children with mild handicapping conditions. *Journal of Behavioral Education, 3,* 26-35.

Hart, B., & Risley, T. R. (1978). Promoting productive language through incidental teaching. *Education in Urban Society, 10,* 407-429.

Hayden, M., Wheeler, M. A., & Carnine, D. (1989). The effects of an innovative classroom networking system and an electronic gradebook on time spent scoring and summarizing student performance. *Education and Treatment of Children, 12,* 253-264.

Kamps, D. M., Barbetta, P. M., Leonard, B. R., & Delquadri, J. (1994). ClassWide Peer Tutoring: An integration strategy to improve and promote peer interactions among students with autism and general education peers. *Journal of Applied Behavior Analysis, 27*(1), 49-61.

Maheady, L., & Harper, G. (1987). A classwide peer tutoring program to improve the spelling test performance of low income, third-, and fourth-grade students. *Education and Treatment of Children, 10,* 120-133.

Maheady, L., Sacca, M. K., & Harper, G. F. (1988). Classwide peer tutoring program on the academic performance of mildly handicapped students. *Exceptional Children, 55,* 52-59.

Mathes, P., Fuchs, D., Fuchs, L. S., Henley, A. M., & Sanders, A. (1994). Increasing strategic reading practice with Peabody classwide peer tutoring. *Learning Disabilities Research and Practice, 8,* 233-243.

Mathes, P. G., Howard, J. K., Allen, S. H., & Fuchs, D. (1998). Peer-assisted learning strategies for first-grade readers: Responding to the needs of diverse learners. *Reading Research Quarterly, 33,* 62-94.

Niedermeyer, F. C. (1970). Effects of training on the instructional behaviors of student tutors. *Journal of Educational Research, 64,* 119-123.

Simmons, D. C., Fuchs, D., Fuchs, L. S., Hodge, J. P., & Mathes, P. G. (1994). Importance of instructional complexity and role reciprocity to classwide peer tutoring. *Learning Disabilities Research and Practice, 9*(4), 203-212.

Utley, C. A., Mortweet, S. L., & Greenwood, C. R. (1997). Peer-mediated instruction and interventions. *Focus on Exceptional Children, 29*(5), 1-23.

Woodward, J., & Howard, L. (1994). The misconceptions of youth: Errors and their mathematical meaning. *Exceptional Children, 61*(2), 126-136.

FIVE

Sustaining a Curriculum Innovation

Cases of Make It Happen!

JUDITH M. ZORFASS
Education Development Center, Inc.
Newton, MA

In 1986, the Education Development Center (EDC) received 5 years of funding from the U.S. Department of Education (Office of Special Education Programs [OSEP]) to study the integration of technology into the middle school curriculum to benefit students with and without disabilities. In the first phase of the project (1986-1989), EDC carried out an ethnographic study in four diverse middle schools that focused on classroom-level and organizational-level factors (Morocco & Zorfass, 1988; Zorfass, Morocco, Russell, & Zuman, 1989). In the second phase (1989-1991), EDC developed a model to promote the integration of technology in middle schools based on its research findings (Zorfass, Morocco, & Lory, 1991; Zorfass, Morocco, Tivnan, Persky, & Remz, 1991).

This was an exciting era in which to be conducting middle school research. The confluence of the Carnegie Report (Carnegie Council on Adolescent Development, 1989), *This We Believe* (National Middle School Association, 1982), and publications from the Center for Early Adolescence in North Carolina (Dorman, 1981, 1987) helped to create a top-down and bottom-up groundswell of reform simultaneously. Administrators and teachers alike began to form a vision of how they could reorganize schools and classrooms to meet the needs of young adolescents effectively. Leaders such as Jacobs (1989), Beane (1990), Lipsitz (1984), Slavin (1990), and MacIver and Epstein (1990) were instrumental in calling for the development of a middle school curricula in which

☐ Core content teachers worked together to design and implement interdisciplinary instruction

☐ The curriculum was organized around important themes with rigorous content

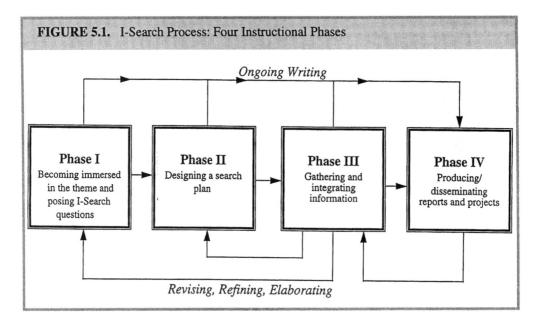

FIGURE 5.1. I-Search Process: Four Instructional Phases

- ◻ Instructional strategies and cooperative learning actively engaged students
- ◻ Technology, media, and materials were integrated into instruction and assessment
- ◻ Teachers designed alternative assessments embedded within the curriculum

The model EDC developed to integrate technology into the curriculum during its second phase of work (1989-1991) resonated with these curriculum recommendations. Based on the work of Ken Macrorie (1988), EDC shaped an I-Search Curriculum Unit that was interdisciplinary, thematic, and inquiry-based. Predating the concept of universal design (Center for Applied Special Technology, 1998; Vanderheiden & Kaine-Krolak, 1995), we conceived of a unit that would be accessible to all students.

The I-Search Unit has four phases of instruction, as shown in Figure 5.1. In Phase I, students pose a question that they care about after becoming immersed in the unit's interdisciplinary theme and overarching concepts. The teachers across disciplines carry out a coordinated set of diverse activities to elicit students' prior knowledge, expand their back-

ground knowledge, encourage reflection, and, finally, guide students to pose personally meaningful I-Search questions. In Phase II, students develop a search plan to guide their future exploration. The plan identifies what they will read (e.g., books, magazines, newspapers, Web-based resources) and watch (e.g., videos, slides, TV documentaries), as well as to whom they will talk (e.g., conducting interviews and surveys and conversing on the Internet) and what they will do (e.g., carry out an experiment, work with a computer simulation, go on a field trip). In Phase III, students gather information, revise their search plans as new routes of exploration appear, and analyze data to make sense of what they are learning. Finally, in Phase IV, students convey what they have learned in a final report and/or exhibition that can involve writing, drama, art, and/or multimedia. Regardless of the medium, students describe their research question (what it is, where their search started, and why they were motivated), their search process, what they learned, and what this knowledge means to them. They also include references.

The I-Search Unit is a natural context for using a wide variety of technology applications to help students—especially those with disabilities—access information, manipulate and process information, and represent their knowledge. For example, CD-ROMs, videos, the Internet, and simulations can provide students with information related to their questions. Spreadsheets, databases, and software for creating semantic maps (e.g., Inspiration software; Helfgott, Helfgott, & Hoof, 1994) can help students process and manipulate information. Students can use multimedia programs, word processing, and graphics programs to create reports and exhibitions. In addition, EDC's (1996) own *Search Organizer* software was explicitly developed with funding from OSEP to guide students, with and without disabilities, through the four phases of inquiry.

The desired student outcomes in the I-Search fall within three domains. By carrying out a rigorous search for information, students construct knowledge related to the interdisciplinary theme of the unit. They develop the kinds of big ideas found in the social studies, mathematics, and science national standards. At the same time, they acquire and apply inquiry skills and processes (e.g., posing a question to research, identifying relevant resources, note taking, and analyzing data). As one student with learning disabilities from an inner-city school explained, "Finally I learned that taking notes isn't as hard as it looks. . . . I used to hate to take notes. Now I kind of like it. This is a good study skill when it comes to doing projects."

Finally, in the psychosocial domain, students learn how to work collaboratively with peers, persevere on tasks, and develop positive self-esteem that is genuinely based on work well done. All these outcomes—academic, inquiry, and habits of mind—reflect recommendations from the National Center of Educational Outcomes (Elliot, Ysseldyke, Thurlow, & Erickson, 1988).

As we built this curriculum model, we wanted to ensure that when schools implemented the I-Search, it would not be a one-round endeavor as so often happens in schools. We saw firsthand during our 3 years of qualitative research that new initiatives quickly come and go, often having little staying power. As one teacher summed it up, "This year it's critical thinking, last year it was cooperative learning. I've stopped listening to the superintendent's annual back-to-school message." The negative effect of rapid-fire initiatives is that change shows up as a tiny blip on the reform radar screen, not a steady upward slope showing how curriculum, instruction, and assessment become stronger over time. In contrast, our goal was sustainability—for the I-Search Unit to take hold, go deeper, and expand in many ways through successive rounds of implementation. Although continuing an innovation is necessary for sustainability, it is not sufficient. The goal is to improve and expand the curriculum over time so that more students with and without disabilities succeed more of the time. Within this definition, we imagined various routes to sustainability, as seen in the following examples:

◻ As each participating interdisciplinary team of teachers carried out the I-Search Unit over several years, they gradually would strengthen the unit by deepening the content so it becomes more rigorous, integrating technology in more effective ways; becoming clearer about assessment criteria; and revising instructional activities.

◻ If the innovation began with one or a few interdisciplinary teams within a school, it would expand to other teams within that school.

◻ If the innovation included teams from one school, it would spread to other schools within a district.

To ensure that this kind of sustainability would, in fact, happen, we surrounded the curriculum with a carefully constructed implementation process called Make It Happen! (Zorfass, 1991). This broader implementation model drew on the Phase I research findings on organizational support in addition to the literature on institutionalization, scale-up, and school reform (e.g., Berman & McLaughlin, 1976; Elmore, 1990; Fullan, 1990; Smith & O'Day, 1991). There are three key components of the Make It Happen! approach:

- ◻ *Professional Development*—With support, teachers design, implement, and reflect on the I-Search Unit to directly link ongoing professional development to strengthening curriculum, instruction, and assessment.
- ◻ *Leadership*—Local facilitators, who serve as change agents, work closely with principals to guide and support each team's endeavors at curriculum innovation.
- ◻ *Scale-Up*—An explicit process for *scaling-up* includes holding Showcase Conferences in which current implementers of I-Search Units disseminate their work to potential implementers.

The purpose of this chapter is to show how the components built into Make It Happen! contributed to sustainability in the three ways described previously. The majority of the chapter is devoted to presenting reflections on three case studies. These cases can be characterized as more informal, distilled summaries than as in-depth single-case studies (Yin, 1994).

The first case focuses on ongoing professional development, showing how one interdisciplinary team of teachers in Indianapolis worked together collaboratively over 4 years to deepen curriculum, instruction, and assessment. Drawn from EDC's Make It Happen! Impact Study (1992-1995), we documented the team's work as we guided the teachers to design, implement, and reflect on their curriculum (Morocco & Zorfass, 1996; Zorfass, 1994; Zorfass & Copel, 1998). The second case concentrates on leadership, illustrating how a local facilitator and the middle school principal in Lawrence, New York, employed a variety of strategies to expand the I-Search from one seventh-grade team to all three seventh-grade teams over a 5-year period.

This case is drawn from the second phase (1998-1991) of EDC's 5-year technology integration project, when we piloted the Make It Happen! model. In addition to providing technical assistance to the facilitator, principal, and the team, we also documented the process (Zorfass & Copel, 1995, 1998). The third case focuses on scale-up, describing how the Make It Happen! implementation process motivated the spread of the innovation across nine middle schools in Lowell, Massachusetts, a middle-sized urban school district. In this case, drawing from our work as consultants to school districts, we served as external change agents responsible for launching and growing the innovation (Zorfass & Copel, 1998; Zorfass & Donahue, 1996).

Each case begins with an introduction describing the relevant component in Make It Happen! It then relates a story, describes the roots and route toward sustainability, and ends with an analysis. The chapter concludes with the discussion of a powerful constellation of crosscutting factors that affirms recommendations by Elmore (1996) to promote sustainability.

Ongoing Professional Development

Introduction

Ongoing professional development creates opportunities for adult learning that are integral to the change process (Darling-Hammond & McLaughlin, 1996; Darling-Hammond & Sykes, 1999; Hawley & Valli, 1996; Lewis, 1997; Lord, 1994; McLaughlin & Oberman, 1996; Miller, 1995). In Make It Happen! teachers on an interdisciplinary team engage in collaborative, sustained discourse to design, implement, and reflect on the I-Search Curriculum Unit. Through this ongoing process, they construct and reconstruct their *worldview* (Eylon & Linn, 1988; Poplin, 1988) as they learn from each other, distribute knowledge, and share expertise (Kinnaman, 1990). This iterative learning process, highly dependent on teacher discourse, meshes with

Kegan's (1995) conceptualization of ongoing professional development as a transformative experience.

Collaboration around curriculum design is a pivotal component. Teachers thoughtfully plan the four phases of the I-Search Unit as they make explicit their philosophies of learning and teaching, identify students' learning outcomes, take responsibility for conducting instructional activities, design assessments, establish performance criteria, and accept a shared responsibility for students with disabilities. During implementation, as teachers carry out these plans, they gather evidence about student learning by reviewing portfolios, observing students in action, listening to their conversations, and even interviewing students individually. Analyzing these data, teachers reflect on how to improve student learning. After the unit ends, the team further reflects on the impact of the unit on themselves, their team, and especially on the students with and without disabilities. They make recommendations about how to strengthen the unit during the next round of implementation, which is the goal of this iterative process. In the Indiana case subsequently discussed, we see how this process played itself out across 4 years.

Toward Sustainability

Named for the first African American to die in the American Revolution, the Crispus Attucks Middle School in the heart of Indianapolis has a long and proud history. Although generations ago it was an all African American school, by 1992 Crispus Attucks was a magnet school with a diverse student body. The school's decision to participate in the Make It Happen! Impact Study in 1992 motivated staff to accelerate their efforts to recruit students with disabilities to be included in the general education program. The handpicked, tightly knit group of teachers shared an attraction to the I-Search Unit because they felt it would introduce them to inquiry-based instruction, promote inclusionary practices, and increase computer use.

Year 1. In 1991-1992 (1 year before the Make It Happen! Impact Study began), the seventh-grade team—comprised of the language arts, social studies, science, mathematics, and Spanish teachers—jumped on the I-Search bandwagon. As participants in the Middle Grades Improvement Project (funded by the Lilly Endowment), they worked with EDC researchers to design and implement two I-Search Units: "The Past, Present, and Future of Indianapolis" and "Natural Disasters: Causes, Impact, and Prevention." In combination, these units gave the team their first foray into inquiry-based learning. Not only would students pose their own search questions (e.g., What effect do the many universities in Indianapolis have on the cultural and economic life of the city? How did the Mt. Vesuvius eruption affect Pompeii?), but they would be gathering information through varied materials and resources. As the team opened the door to the possibilities of field trips and speakers, they, too, were caught up in the spirit of inquiry, as the social studies teacher explained:

> The I-Search Unit . . . forced me, along with all of the other teachers, to go out and learn a lot of new things myself. We've been making a lot of trips to libraries and we've been going around town trying to figure out where we want to take field trips—visiting the war memorials and talking to people at the Chamber of Commerce. These kinds of things get you very excited as a teacher.

The use of varied technologies such as video, computer simulations, databases, and spreadsheets in the disasters unit set a precedent that would extend to future years. Teachers found that videos and computer simulations were particularly useful in helping students build background knowledge and elicit prior knowledge. Both strategies aided reading comprehension of books, articles, and related reference materials.

Year 2. Given this team's expressed enthusiasm for the I-Search, EDC invited the teachers to participate in the impact study. With the blessing of the principal and central office administrators, the team agreed to join the research project. This necessitated adding a special education teacher to the team and including students with disabilities, which they did willingly. In January 1993, several months after the project started, the team came to Boston to be part of a 5-day Curriculum Design Institute. At the institute, they had intensive support from EDC staff; collaborated with a team from a Boston-area school also participating in the project; and had access to project advisors with expertise in science and assessment. Using this assistance, the team designed a unit on water ecology, conservation, and pollution to be carried out in the spring. This new unit became the catalyst for changing instructional practices and assessment techniques to meet the needs of students with and without disabilities. Subsequently, we describe how teachers incorporated cooperative group work, created coaching groups, employed scaffolding strategies, and delved more deeply into assessment.

First, in terms of cooperative group work, teachers organized students into We-Search groups, in which each group included one or two students with disabilities. The teachers expected each group to agree on a multifaceted We-Search question; each student would then take responsibility for a particular aspect of the question. Students would work together to gather and synthesize information, which would culminate in a final We-Search Report. The group work was intended to be a boon for students with disabilities. Not only would they have a boost from peers in locating and relating information, but they would also work with others more able to draft, revise, and edit the report.

Second, based on a recommendation from the special education teacher, each teacher took responsibility for six to eight of the We-Search groups who were investigating questions related to the same overarching concept. They called this larger consortium a *coaching group.* The teachers reasoned that if they were

each responsible for a specific number of groups, they could better track the progress of individuals, especially students with disabilities, through the four phases of the I-Search process, thus preventing any student from "falling through the cracks."

Third, with this added sense of accountability for every student's success, the teachers consciously built scaffolding strategies into their classroom activities. For example, in Phase I of the water unit, teachers distributed a worksheet to scaffold discussions within the cooperative groups. As students expressed and recorded emerging ideas and issues within their groups at the computer, teachers asked clarifying questions to probe deeper and to model conversations that built understanding. As cooperative groups reported on what they were learning and thinking, teachers kept a running record of "What are we learning?" and "What more do we want to know?" on large chart paper for all to see and review periodically. Students filed their processing worksheets in the group's three-ring binder notebook used as a portfolio. During team meetings, teachers reviewed the portfolio to develop a shared understanding of students' growth and needs and, based on this, formulated strategies aimed at helping students make meaning. Teachers found that this strategy helped them focus on the thinking processes of students with disabilities. If teachers discovered misconceptions, faulty reasoning, or lack of understanding, they were better able to work closely with the student. Often a teacher and a student with a disability could be found at the computer, generating and organizing ideas into meaning frames.

Fourth, with input from EDC staff and advisors, the teachers identified criteria, not only for what was expected in the final We-Search paper, but also for carrying out the inquiry process within each phase of the I-Search. Figure 5.2 provides an example of criteria for Phase I that teachers distributed to students. Teachers met with each We-Search group to discuss the students' assessment of how well they thought they were carrying out the process. They often asked students to vali-

FIGURE 5.2. Criteria for Phase I Student Assessment

Phase I: Question

I have participated in the immersion activities by

☐ Appropriately using required knowledge
☐ Participating in class discussions
☐ Doing worksheets, lab sheets, and assignments
☐ Doing my homework

☐ After each activity or after several activities, I have worked with my group to identify between 3 and 6 critical issues.

☐ Our group has elaborated upon each issue we have identified (why, for whom, where, and when, what's known).

☐ Our group has reached consensus in selecting one issue by reviewing all our issues and information.

☐ Our group has justified selecting the issue, explaining how it links to the overarching concepts.

☐ Our group has identified search questions related to the issue.

☐ I have identified what aspect of the questions I would like to pursue.

☐ Our group has explained why these questions are of interest. What was our starting point?

☐ Each student has a copy of the questions.

☐ The search questions have been approved by teachers.

☐ Our group has started to accumulate information for later use in Phase III, based on the immersion activities.

☐ One group has been applying strategies for effective group work.

date their self-evaluations by selecting supporting evidence from individual and group portfolios. The criteria for the final report (see an example in Figure 5.3) guided students when they drafted reports using a word processor, engaged in peer review of drafts, and reviewed drafts with teachers. They also became the basis for the final evaluation.

When EDC engaged teachers in reflection at the end of Year 2, they agreed on several areas that needed to be improved for the next round of implementation. First, they found that the theme of the water unit was too abstract, making it difficult for the students to find their way to personally meaningful questions. Second, the We-Search paradigm was problematic; the expectation that young adolescents could jointly synthesize information and prepare one final report was too ambitious. Third, when the teachers realized that all students, and especially those with learning disabilities, needed more research skills prior to beginning the search process, they developed a plan of action that had the potential to help every student acquire skills.

Year 3. Based on their Year 2 findings, the teachers, with guidance and support from EDC, made several critical changes. First, they designed and implemented a mini I-Search Unit

---

FIGURE 5.3. Specific Criteria for a Written or Multimedia Report

My question

◆ Have a strong lead or good opening. Draw the reader into the topic with a good lead. For example, a story, quote, questions, startling statement.

◆ State your research question as clearly as possible. Show how it relates to the theme and overarching concepts of the unit.

◆ Explain your personal interest or connection with the question. Why did you care about the question?

◆ Tell what you already knew about the topic when you began the search.

The search process

◆ Describe the sequence of steps you followed in your search—what sources you started with and what other sources these led you to.

◆ Describe the materials and resources you used. Which were the best sources of information? Why?

◆ Describe any problems you encountered in locating information and how you solved them.

◆ Explain how the questions changed, expanded, or were revised over time.

◆ Share any breakthroughs: Tell when it really got interesting.

◆ Tell about how people contributed to helping you do your search.

What I learned

◆ Provide basic information to set the context.

◆ Present three or four major findings, conclusions, or big ideas. In doing so, integrate information from your various sources. Support these main ideas with examples, details, stories, and arguments.

◆ Connect this information with the original question.

◆ Show the products of any analysis you have done. Present tables, charts, graphs, timelines, maps, etc., that helped you make sense of information. Explain your analysis and draw conclusions.

---

early in the school year to introduce students to research skills. Here, teachers required students to pose a question based on a newspaper article, develop a research plan that included four different ways to gather information (i.e., reading, watching, asking, and doing), carry out the plan, and prepare an oral presentation for the class using the following prompts:

◧ My question was . . .

◧ I was interested in this question because . . .

◧ To gather information, I . . .

◧ In relation to my question, I found out that . . .

◧ I learned that as a researcher, I could . . .

For this mini-unit, the teachers took students to a nearby university library where, by prearrangement, the librarians taught students about the library's resources, especially how to do computer-based searches to locate information. Before and after the library visit, teachers provided students with direct instruction to build research and note-taking skills. The teachers and students found that this mini-unit paid off, as evidenced by the

---

FIGURE 5.3. Continued

What this means to me

◆ Explain how your knowledge has grown since your starting point.

◆ Explain what you learned that means most to you, and explain why this is significant.

◆ Explain how this knowledge will affect what you think, believe, and know.

◆ Present any conclusions, recommendations, predictions, etc.

◆ Present next questions that you would be interested in exploring.

How I have grown as a researcher

◆ Explain how you developed as a researcher: What skills or abilities did you develop?

◆ Tell how you appreciate yourself as a researcher, writer, presenter.

◆ Comment on what things you did well and the things that were difficult.

◆ Set some new goals for inquiry.

◆ Identify ways in which you helped or were helped by classmates and teachers.

◆ Talk about what you would change or do differently if you were doing another I-Search unit.

References

◆ All references are in alphabetical order.

◆ I have used the correct format.

Appendixes

◆ Each appendix is identified and lettered.

---

following remark made by a student with a learning disability:

> I learned how to use microfilms. Microfilms are films of newspapers and magazines. I learned how to find exactly what you're looking for using Infotrac. Infotrac is a computer that you can draw on to find what you're looking for.

The team made other needed changes as well. With input from EDC, they changed the unit's theme to "A River Runs Through It," which compared Indianapolis's White River to rivers around the world. Wanting to retain the collaborative group work, the teachers created an I/We-Search compromise. Instead of the entire final report being a We-Search, they had each student prepare a separate I-Search paper and then combine efforts for a cumulative final report and exhibition. This gave students a balance between working individually and with peers and still provided support for students with disabilities.

Year 4. In Year 4, the last year of the EDC project, the teachers continued with the mini-unit, as well as with their two full-blown units on disasters and rivers. They were working more on their own, with less direct input from EDC. Now that they had defined the basic shape of these units, the teachers focused on making the units as strong as possible by using two strategies to link teaching and learning. The first strategy they developed was to address instructional problems as they emerged, before they could become barriers to student success. For example, in the first days of the unit on rivers, one EDC researcher informally shared her observation with the language arts teacher that students seemed confused about expectations. At their very next team meeting, the language arts teacher, who served as the team facilitator, brought the problem to the table:

> Remember when we planned the unit, we never got around to deciding on the specifics about how to introduce the unit. Even though each teacher took responsibility for saying something to the students on Day 1, we were not sure of exactly what each one of us planned to say. Now we're here on the second day and students are hearing different messages. They are already confused about what is expected of them.

To reduce student confusion, the teachers listed the essential facts that they wanted to share with students. As each teacher offered another item, one teacher made a list on the board. Then they went back to their classrooms, and each one reiterated the main points. They met again at the end of the day for an update and to figure out how the next day needed to be modified based on student feedback.

The second strategy was to develop rubrics with guidance from EDC. Past years revealed the value of having a set of criteria. Now they wanted to go further to identify what constituted a range of inquiry-based performance from *excellent* to *having difficulty*. As inquirers themselves and with support from EDC, they consulted articles, conferred with the research project staff, and gathered materials at conferences. Figure 5.4 presents an example of an emerging rubric related to the first section of a We-Search paper. As the teachers continued to revise their rubrics, they began to examine their practice. This level of deeper reflection invigorated them and sustained curriculum innovation.

Analysis

Annual repetition of a curriculum innovation can go in three directions: The innovation can reach a plateau, it can become weaker by regressing toward the mean, or it can become stronger and more powerful as teams delve more deeply into teaching and learning and create their own process for ongoing learning. The unequivocal goal for sustainability of a curriculum innovation is for it to become more powerful each year, with more students successfully participating and learning. This was the case in Indianapolis, as teachers engaged in ongoing professional development by designing, implementing, and reflecting on their I-Search Units as recommended in Make It Happen!

With each successive year, the Indiana team of teachers focused on different elements of teaching, learning, and assessment within an inquiry-based curriculum. In the first year, when the teachers departed from their traditional curriculum, they became excited about the possibilities of inquiry for their students. They recognized the power of having students pose their own questions, explore these questions using varied resources, and represent their knowledge in creative ways. In Year 2, they willingly included students with disabilities in this inquiry-based approach. As they became more comfortable with the inquiry-based paradigm, they began to question the kinds of strategies they were using to ensure success for every student, especially after having accepted responsibility for students with disabilities. They were able to ask themselves harder questions as they became clearer about what students do as inquirers and what role teachers play in guiding the inquiry process. This pushed

FIGURE 5.4. Rubric for Evaluating Report: My Search Questions

My Search Question

	4	3	2	1
Strong lead	Arouses reader interest; draws reader into the topic using a captivating lead	Awareness of audience; uses some enticing ways to engage audience	Provides matter of fact introduction; little awareness of audience	No lead
Question stated	Question is clearly stated and makes strong link to overarching concepts as appropriate	Question is clearly stated; mention is made of overarching concepts, but link is tenuous	Question is poorly stated; weak link to overarching concepts	No question and/or no connection to overarching concepts
Personal connection	Detailed explanation of why question is motivating	Some explanation of why question is motivating	Unclear explanation of personal connection	No explanation of personal connection
Starting point	Detailed description of starting point	Some information provided	Unclear or sketchy information provided	No description of starting point

them to take greater responsibility for scaffolding student learning. The teachers' increasing focus on student achievement gradually led them to make a stronger link between their goals, criteria for success, their teaching strategies, and assessment. They later became intrigued with rubrics to evaluate student performance.

The iterative process of designing, implementing, and reflecting had a powerful impact on this team, which contributed to their sustaining the I-Search Unit. Three factors helped them to deepen and improve instruction each year. The first factor is that the team never lost sight of the ultimate goal—to improve student learning for students with and without disabilities. This objective became a beacon to guide their evaluation of new information, decide what to try in the classroom, and reflect on their practices after they tried them out. For example, when they evaluated the We-Search tactic, they asked themselves the following key questions: Did every student participate? Did the cooperative group work mask specific students' weaknesses? Did we give every child the kind of support needed to be a functioning group member? Did we make sure students with disabilities had the support they needed? Did we use technology effectively? What other technology tools would be useful? Did every student learn about the content and the inquiry process? If they were dissatisfied with their answers, they found a way to retain what was strong but also to make improvements.

The second factor is that they set annual goals for improvement that provided a context for ferreting out valuable information. For example, when they were ready to concentrate on criteria and rubrics, they made excellent use of the models in the Make It Happen! materials, the articles distributed by EDC, examples from other teams, and the consultant EDC brought to the Curriculum Design Institute.

The third factor is that the teachers were willing to reflect on their practice and engage in self-evaluation. These teachers were not afraid to be self-critical or critical friends to uncover areas of weakness. They realized that if something was going awry, it could affect their students in a negative way. They took an approach that said, "Fix problems before it's too late." For example, when they found that students were confused at the outset of the rivers unit, they immediately met to rectify the problem. When they found that students needed to be comfortable with the card catalog, library search skills, and note taking, they created a mini-unit with directed mini-lessons.

The same principles of professional development that were in operation in Indianapolis have been put forth by the U.S. Department of Education (National Partnership for Excellence and Accountability in Teaching, 2000). Doing what others have recommended to promote professional growth, these teachers saw themselves as being central to student learning; they focused on outcomes for students with and without disabilities, valued their collegial working relationship, and developed expertise in teaching strategies and uses of technology in context. The ways in which they worked toward continuous inquiry and improvement were embedded in their daily lives as teachers.

Leadership

Introduction

Effective leaders create and support a culture for change by building a learning community that places a high value on collaboration (Klein, Medrick, Perez-Fierero, & MPR Associates, Inc., 1996; Lee, 1993; Mizell, 1994; Patterson 1993; Whitaker, 1997). As change agents, the goal is for leaders to encourage teachers to develop a deep-felt obligation to expand their content knowledge and pedagogy, take responsibility for self-managing their learning, and become sensitive and productive colleagues (Lord, 1994; Sergiovanni, 1992). Patterson (1993) asserts that leaders must encourage participation in decision making, value diversity of perspectives, openly deal with conflict in a safe environment, encourage reflection of practice within a nurturing environment that suspends premature judgments, and allow people to view mistakes as one more way to learn. At the same time, leaders articulate a vision, set and stay a course for change, coordinate overlapping initiatives, ensure access to resources, and deal with the daily logistics of scheduling.

Make It Happen! draws on these principles of effective leadership in guiding two critical change agents—a local facilitator and a middle school principal, working in tandem. The on-the-ground facilitator, drawn from the ranks of the school, could be, in reality, a lead teacher, assistant principal, media specialist, or a curriculum coordinator. The actual school title is less important than his or her grasp of inquiry-based learning and the I-Search process, understanding of adult development and learning, and ability to foster productive discourse within teams. The facilitator needs to be someone with a flexible schedule that allows for convening meetings of the interdisciplinary team and gathering resources.

The facilitator shoulders the responsibility for guiding teams through curriculum design, implementation, and reflection. The facilitator simultaneously serves as a liaison to the principal. The facilitator must hold tightly to the value of full participation of all team members, valuing diverse opinions, resolving conflict, encouraging reflection, and emphasizing to everyone that they are learning from their experience through mistakes as well as successes. But Make It Happen! recognizes that the facilitator cannot work alone; rather, it is critical to have the buy-in, support, and ear of the principal. Many issues related to logistics, assessment, change of schedules, release time, and budgeting emerge that need to be handled in collaboration with the principal.

The Make It Happen! guidelines are written for facilitators—giving them concrete agendas; handouts to promote collaboration and reflection; and suggestions about when, why, and how to connect to principals. The materials embed leadership development in an ongoing curriculum process. Subsequently we see how Harriet, as the facilitator, worked with Al, the principal, over the course of 5 years to ultimately support all three seventh-grade teams.

Toward Sustainability[1]

Lawrence is a middle-class suburb located on Long Island, about 10 miles east of New York's Kennedy Airport. Lawrence has one middle school with Grades 6 to 8 that houses approximately 900 students. With recent population shifts and busing from other districts, the school's student population has become more diversified with the addition of African American, Hispanic, and Asian students. In 1990, the superintendent, middle school principal, and one team of seventh-grade teachers agreed to participate in the evaluation of the Make It Happen! materials. Having recently made the transformation from a junior high school to a middle school, they hoped the approach would help them move away from the current departmentalized system and include students with disabilities in general education classes. They also wanted to use available resources in this technology-rich district.

The subsequent story shows a school traveling for 5 years along the road to sustainability. During the first leg of their journey (Years 1-2), one seventh-grade team piloted the approach, helping the school build a model for implementation. In that first year, they worked closely with EDC; after that, they continued on their own. The third year— characterized as the *second leg*—was a time for expansion to two seventh-grade teams. During the last leg of the trip (Years 4-5), the innovation finally spread to all three teams. Throughout, the facilitator and principal faced and handled an evolving set of key leadership challenges.

Years 1 and 2: One Team Begins the Journey. For the first 2 years of implementation, one seventh-grade team served as the first-round pioneers. The team consisted of the language arts teacher, the social studies teacher, the science teacher, the special education teacher, and the library/media specialists. The mathematics teacher had no interest in participating because she saw her discipline as being tangential.

Harriet, the district's technology coordinator, began serving as the official facilitator during the summer of 1990 when the first I-Search Curriculum Design Workshop was held. Representing EDC, I also attended this summer curriculum institute, serving as a cofacilitator to model the curriculum design process and mentor Harriet. The week got off to a rocky start when the social studies teacher, an untenured teacher, had a change of heart about the Civil War theme the team had decided on earlier in the spring. She feared that by straying from her department's requirements, her students would do poorly on departmental exams; this, in turn, would reflect badly on her. Even though the principal had given the Civil War I-Search Unit his blessing, the teacher could not be swayed from her position. After considerable debate, the team agreed on a new theme—the human body—with a science rather than a social studies orientation. The curriculum issues Harriet faced this first week would continue to crop up in subsequent years.

After reaching consensus on a new theme, Harriet and I guided the teachers through the steps of curriculum design following the Make It Happen! guidelines. This included identifying the overarching concepts, setting goals, designing activities, creating assessments, creating a "To Do" list, and so forth. Given the school's desire to integrate technology, Harriet and the media specialist demonstrated simulations, databases, and graphing programs. They also set up word processors for teachers to write out their activity plans. However, against this backdrop of seeming productivity, Harriet found herself needing to moderate heated debates as questions such as the following arose: How long should the unit run? Who will be responsible for each activity? How can we intersperse the "real curriculum" into the time set aside for the unit? What

should the role be for the special education teacher in the classroom?

Harriet revealed her mastery of negotiation by finding a widely acceptable solution to each major issue. When necessary and without hesitation, Harriet consulted with the principal and kept him informed. For example, she helped the team develop a plan to carry out their unit for 12 weeks (about 50% longer than is typical) and to insert the regular curriculum every couple of weeks. Given that students with disabilities would be part of the unit, the special education teacher would work in the general education classroom, providing support to students with disabilities as well as to other students. The team agreed to begin the unit immediately after the December vacation, allowing them to use the fall to further refine their plans. As it turned out, this timing worked well. It offered the library/media specialists time during the fall to continue to gather materials and resources, the computer teacher time to sharpen students' keyboarding and word processing skills, and the special education teacher a chance to bond with the team. The special education teacher had never before been included in team meetings; but now, after Harriet had worked closely with the principal to rearrange the schedule, she was free during team planning time.

Harriet became the sole facilitator during implementation. I continued to provide technical assistance by phone (in the pre-email era) and when I visited the school every other month. Taking responsibility, Harriet met with the team regularly to troubleshoot and help them stay on track. As issues arose (e.g., access to the library/media center and the computer lab; finding ways to eke out additional planning time; curriculum coverage; and follow-through on planning), Harriet conferred with the principal on a regular basis. She also invited him to visit with teachers frequently, both individually and as a group, to assuage their concerns. Issue by issue, they found solutions and learned how to reach consensus.

When the unit ended that first year, the teachers met with Harriet, the principal, and me to reflect on student accomplishments, teacher professional growth, and the I-Search process. In terms of the students, the teachers discovered that more students than ever before completed the required assigned project (94 out of 95 submitted an I-Search paper). This included students with disabilities, who, until now, would have been pulled out to go to the resource room during social studies. The team reviewed their use of varied resources, including technology tools such as human body simulations and graphing software. They felt that the technology applications, in conjunction with other media and materials, helped students, with and without disabilities, develop concepts about body systems, causes of diseases, and ways to prevent health problems. In discussing their own personal growth, the teachers were proud of themselves for trying new instructional materials, especially the technology simulations. The final conclusion about the I-Search was that this inquiry-based unit was worthwhile and should be continued. Also, they would continue to include students with disabilities. Following their own recommendations, the team implemented the unit in much the same way in Year 2. From Year 2 on, EDC was not involved, except that, as friends and writing colleagues, Harriet and I stayed in touch by phone, visits, and (finally) e-mail.

The consensus after the second year of implementation echoed the previous findings—the unit worked well for students with and without disabilities and should be continued. With growing comfort around technology, teachers found more ways to integrate simulations, spreadsheets, and graphing programs. Even the mathematics teacher, who had joined the team in Year 2 after being pressured by the principal, reported that the unit gave her a genuine way to teach spreadsheets.

Year 3: More Travelers on the Road. A second team joined the effort as a result of the principal's ongoing lobbying. Since the end of Year 1, he campaigned steadily to bring all seventh-grade teams on board. When he encountered negativism or resistance, the prin-

cipal reminded everyone that they had contributed to a schoolwide vision that featured interdisciplinary instruction, the inclusion of students with disabilities, and the integration of technology. At the end of the second year, he stopped cajoling and issued a mandate—every seventh-grade team was required to implement an interdisciplinary project of its choice or do an I-Search Unit within the next 2 years. Harriet and the principal did not deviate from this requirement.

Around this time, Harriet was promoted to assistant principal at the middle school. In this capacity, she served as the facilitator for this new team as well as for the pioneer team. She found a way to give the new team a chance to design their curriculum during the school day instead of during the summer. At team meetings, Harriet would get them started on a specific task and then turn responsibility over to the teachers to carry out a clearly defined next step. Checking back periodically, she made sure that they were paying attention to students with disabilities and thinking about how to use technology. For example, she suggested that they create templates on the word processor to give students a format for taking notes.

During this period of expansion, a question about the teachers' technology expertise arose. Several teachers, from both the new and pioneer teams, wanted to sharpen their technology skills. Given her past role as technology coordinator, Harriet was well aware of how a lack of comfort could stymie efforts at integrating technology into the curriculum. For example, it took a certain level of proficiency to turn Harriet's idea about the templates into practice. To deal with the problem, Harriet arranged for the teachers to have extra support to expand their skills. This kind of technical assistance helped teachers over the technology hurdle.

But then another issue arose for Harriet and the principal to address. Some teachers complained about having too many team meetings during the school day. They were accustomed to using their planning time for their own preparation. Joining Harriet to deal with this real problem, the principal talked openly and often about how he wanted teamwork, sharing, joint decision making, consulting, and so forth, to become a valued aspect of the school's culture. He talked about it, tried to model it, and acknowledged it when it occurred. At the same time, Harriet made sure the meetings were businesslike and focused on substantive issues, such as how students with disabilities were progressing. The powerful combination of having the principal articulate the value of the meetings and having Harriet actually make them a worthwhile experience convinced the teachers that collaboration did have its merits.

As the school year ended, the principal did not retreat from his mandate. For the next school year, he made strategic staff changes and reissued his dictum that all seventh-grade teams were expected to do an I-Search or another interdisciplinary unit of their choice, include students with disabilities, and integrate technology.

Years 4 and 5: Travelers All. Still confronting some resistance, the principal decided that an appropriate course of action would be to take his case to the Principal Advisory Cabinet (a building-level union and administration forum for complaints). He knew that he still had the backing of a majority of staff members who supported the innovation, which served to offset the resistance. When this group lent their voices, a compromise was forthcoming. The interim decision was to go forward with three teams and to evaluate the projects at the end of Year 4.

To ensure success, the principal reconstituted the teams by moving teachers around and hiring new teachers who were excited about the innovation. He also insisted that mathematics teachers become involved and asked the participating mathematics teachers to share lessons learned, especially about using spreadsheets. He and Harriet also were able to install a new Macintosh computer lab for the seventh-grade teams in anticipation of heavier demand for technology access. Harriet, in her role as assistant principal,

became the designated supervisor for all seventh-grade teams. In addition to meeting separately with each team, she also brought the entire seventh grade together for biweekly grade-level meetings. At these meetings, she worked hard to ensure that the conversation would focus on instruction and assessment because her goal was to push teachers to think beyond the ken of their specific curriculum and existing practices. For example, the social studies and language arts teachers shared their holistic scoring methods with mathematics and science teachers, who previously had graded on a 100-point system. They talked about whether to modify requirements for students with disabilities. The answer was "No" to requirements but "Yes" to providing them extra support in the classroom.

After all three teams had completed their units, Harriet convened a debriefing meeting. She asked teachers to reflect on student outcomes, individual professional growth, and collaboration. There was a strong positive feeling on the part of teachers to continue implementation. Taking the next step, Harriet also asked a key question: What resources and organizational support did the teachers and specialists need from Harriet and the principal? What needed to be improved? This last question raised several critical issues that needed to be addressed.

One issue was the use of the library and computer labs. The spread of the innovation had significantly increased the workload of the library/media specialists and the technology teachers. Without question, these specialists were cheerleaders of the I-Search process; they welcomed the project's use of the library and varied technologies. But at the same time, they found that trying to meet the needs of the more than 90 students on three teams, in addition to the needs of teachers, was a formidable task. After considerable conversation, everyone agreed on a solution. Each team would implement their unit during a different semester. This would reduce the competition for resources, namely, the computer lab and media center.

Again, the issue of curriculum coverage surfaced. Teachers voiced concern about abandoning the required curriculum for their discipline. But a new policy within the district, lobbied for by Harriet and the principal, created a context for changing the science curriculum. Science teachers now had permission to spend 3 weeks on an I-Search Unit and to focus on whatever science content was needed to support the interdisciplinary theme. This policy change alleviated teachers' ongoing worries that the I-Search stole time from the "regular" curriculum. Given these policy changes, the original pioneer team expressed an interest in finding another science-based theme related to physical science. To channel their motivation, Harriet found a way to give them release time for another round of curriculum design.

Harriet and the principal tried hard to respond to the teachers' need for organizational support. They knew that if they hesitated in any way, they could hinder sustainability of the innovation. Having come so far, they did not want to take that chance.

Analysis

Harriet and Al, the principal, were both willing to devote time, energy, and attention to the implementation of Make It Happen! in Lawrence. Sharing the same goals, they wanted all seventh-grade teams to function as interdisciplinary teams who carried out inquiry-based, project-based learning. They also wanted students with disabilities to be included on these teams and for technology to be effectively used by all students. Both leaders also shared another characteristic; they were both wise enough to listen to teachers' stated needs and concerns. They knew that to bring about these kinds of changes in a school that still tentatively embraced the middle school model, they would have to deal with the following:

- Changing teachers' attitudes and belief structures—that is, collaboration is bet-

ter than isolation, inquiry is a valuable way for students to develop concepts, students with disabilities can be included in the general education class and participate in inquiry, technology has a role to play in the curriculum, students should be evaluated on process as well as product

- Changing the existing curriculum, departmental approach, and testing procedures—What had to be covered within each discipline? What was the role of department tests? What was the acceptable level of performance for students with disabilities?

- Making logistical changes—making modifications in students' schedules, modifications in teachers' schedules, arranging for teacher planning time, changing the schedule for the resource room teacher so she could be in the general education classroom

- Providing access to materials, equipment, resources, and technology

- Providing training and technical assistance by technology teachers and media specialists

These are the kinds of leadership issues that administrators in middle schools across the country constantly face when they are trying to translate the basic tenets of middle school reform into reality (Ames & Miller, 1994; George & Shewey, 1994; Lee & Smith, 1993; Lipsitz, Mizell, Jackson, & Austin, 1997; Williamson & Johnston, 1996). These are also the kinds of problems that, if not dealt with effectively, can create barriers that impede, or even halt, sustainability.

Harriet and the principal shared attributes as leaders that allowed them to deal with their emerging challenges in an ongoing way. First, as described previously, they were closely aligned in their vision of what they wanted to accomplish. Second, they did not shy away from problems and challenges. Not only were they proactive in anticipating problems, they also reacted quickly, trying to keep problems from escalating. For example, they knew that if they did not address the issue of allocation of resources, they would have certainly lost the critical support of the library and media specialists. Third, they developed a broad repertoire of strategies for problem solving that included mandating change, setting an expectation and applying pressure, taking responsibility for changing an existing structure, negotiating, inculcating values into the culture, modeling the kinds of behaviors they desired, facilitating and supporting, providing technical assistance on an as-needed basis, and acknowledging good work. Figure 5.5 lists each of these strategies and shows how Harriet and the principal translated them into practice.

Effective leaders, like Harriet and Al, need to rely on a variety of strategies (Smith & Andrews, 1989). Although some of these might be more directive, others might be facilitative and supportive. However, it is unwise for a leader to rely on single doses of one kind of strategy. Rather, the power comes from using varied strategies that complement each other. Another important point is that it took both Harriet and the principal, working in tandem, to carry out these leadership strategies. It was the marriage of their individual leadership efforts that brought about the kinds of changes they both wanted across all three teams.

Scaling Up

Introduction

District-level scale-up means having greater numbers of practitioners participate in an innovation over time. Berman and McLaughlin (1978), Hord, Rutherford, Huling-Austin, and Hall (1987), and Fullan and Miles (1992) agree that the driving force behind scale-up is a clear vision, anchored by a well-articulated set of student outcomes (as we saw previously in Indianapolis). But this is not all. Leaders need to respect the evolving implementation process. In a typical sce-

nario, potential implementers become aware of the innovation, early self-selected innovators begin implementation, others learn about the innovation by finding out how it played out in practice, and more practitioners join the ranks as implementers (Huberman & Miles, 1984). One aspect of the subsequent case focuses on using the Make It Happen! showcase strategy to recruit new rounds of teams.

The Lawrence case illustrated the need for facilitation, especially as Harriet carried out that role. As more seventh-grade teams came on board, there was an increasing demand for Harriet's time and attention. But what if a district seeks to expand further than across one grade in one school? What if the goal is to reach as many teams as possible in as many schools as possible across the district? Then there needs to be a well-defined strategy for preparing more facilitators. This is the crux of the Lowell story.

Toward Sustainability[2]

Lowell, located about 30 miles northwest of Boston, is an urban district with a diverse population of more than 15,000 students, including many linguistic-minority students with Southeast Asian and Hispanic backgrounds. In 1992, the district opened its doors to nine new magnet middle schools, each outfitted with technology labs and computers in the classrooms. Although district administrators and building principals were united about their vision for middle grade reform, they were hesitant about what steps to take to achieve a rich and rigorous middle school curriculum for all students across all schools. They sought a curriculum that was powerful enough to meet the diverse developmental needs of the city's student body, including students with disabilities, and compelling enough to take hold and spread across all schools to reach all students.

Francene, one of five desegregation facilitators housed at the central office, was the local champion who introduced Make It Happen! to district administrators after finding

FIGURE 5.5. Leadership Strategies in Lawrence	
Strategy for Addressing Problems	*Examples From Case Study*
Setting expectations	The principal set the expectation that all seventh-grade teams, within 2 years, would do an I-Search Unit or another similar type of unit.
Taking responsibility for changing an existing structure	• The principal reconstituted the teams by moving teachers around. • The principal changed the special education teachers' schedules so that they could be included in team meetings. • Harriet instituted bimonthly grade-level meetings for all the seventh-grade teams, whereas before teachers attended either departmental meetings or team meetings. • Harriet and the principal were able to allocate resources to create a new computer lab.
Negotiating	• The principal negotiated with the union to institute his expectation for more teams to join the effort. • The principal gave teams a 2-year window in which to join the effort. • In working with teams, Harriet had the teachers determine the length of unit and when during the school year they want to implement the unit. • Harriet and the principal guided the teams and the media specialists to develop a strategy for accessing resources. • Harriet and the principal found a way to include students with disabilities in the classroom and change the schedule for the resource room teacher.
Inculcating	• Harriet and the principal frequently reiterated the value of collaboration. • They repeatedly talked about the value of inquiry, not only for students who were typical learners, but also for students with disabilities.

(continued)

FIGURE 5.5. Continued

Modeling	• Harriet and the principal modeled problem solving and collaboration.
	• Harriet tried out many technology applications.
Facilitating collaboration	• Harriet facilitated the collaborative curriculum design process.
	• Harriet facilitated the reflection process during and after the unit.
	• Harriet convened and facilitated team meetings so teachers could share ideas.
Mandating	The principal mandated that all math teachers must be participating members of the interdisciplinary teams when they carry out I-Search Units.
Acknowledging	Harriet and the principal found ways to praise the teachers, as well as the students, for their efforts to carry out inquiry.
Providing technical assistance on an as-needed basis	Harriet made sure that the teachers had technology training.

out about the approach through her networking at the state level. She was diligent in laying the kind of groundwork that resulted in organizational support and financial backing from the superintendent, her supervisor (the desegregation project director), and the middle school principals. These administrators agreed that I-Search Units could be a way to engage general education, special education, and/or bilingual students in a strong curriculum; use the technology in the schools; and foster collaboration among members of newly minted interdisciplinary teams. Over time, the goal was for interdisciplinary teams in all nine middle schools to implement I-Search Units.

Lowell contracted with EDC for 2 years to provide technical assistance around starting up and scaling up the innovation. EDC's responsibility in the first year was to present at the first Awareness Conference, run the first Curriculum Design Institute, provide technical assistance for implementation by the first round of implementers, and help organize the first Showcase Conference to recruit new teams. In the second year, EDC continued to support these activities to a lesser degree, paving the way for the district to continue to scale up through its own internal power. Throughout, EDC mentored a cadre of local facilitators. The designated facilitators were Francene's colleagues, the other desegregation facilitators. They met many of the prerequisites: They were assigned to the middle schools; they had flexible schedules; they understood curriculum, instruction, and assessment; and they were committed to the effective inclusion of all students.

Initiating the Implementation Process

In the spring of 1993, Francene and I planned the first Awareness Session for all classroom teachers in Grades 5 through 8, special education teachers, bilingual teachers, computer and media specialists, and school administrators. The session began with the superintendent and the desegregation facilitator setting the context by offering inspirational messages about the school's responsibility to every child, regardless of strengths, needs, disabilities, or language spoken. As the guest speaker, I then introduced the I-Search Unit, using overheads, video snips, and an interactive simulation. I asked participants to discuss in small groups desired outcomes for students, the teaching and learning process, the role of technology, and assessment.

Before the session ended, we asked the audience to determine if they were interested in proceeding with the I-Search and, if so, which teams wanted to nominate themselves as the first-round pioneers. Breaking out into small groups by teams, they asked themselves: In what ways does the I-Search Unit meet the needs of our students? In what ways does it meet our needs for professional development? What kind of organizational support would we need? Afterward, 14 teams came forward to submit application forms that resembled miniproposals.

During that first summer's Curriculum Design Institute, I led a team of five EDC consultants who worked directly with the 14 participating teams to guide their design of I-Search Units. At the same time, through modeling and discussion, we began to build capacity in the designated local facilitators. At the end of each day, the EDC consultants, Francene, and the local facilitators met to debrief. Together, we made explicit the steps of the curriculum design process, candidly discussed the issues that had arisen, and dissected how we had handled them and what we could have done better. This served as a powerful introduction to the role and responsibilities of the facilitator around curriculum design.

During the 1993-1994 academic year, Francene and I arranged to meet twice with each of the 14 teams—once before they began implementing their I-Search Units and then again while the unit was in progress. Francene invited the relevant local facilitator to shadow us, to see firsthand what ongoing technical support looked like in practice, particularly

how I asked prompting questions to uncover problems, encourage teacher collaboration, and generate next steps to solve problems.

In the spring of 1994, after the 14 pioneer teams finished implementing their units, it was time for them to present the first Showcase Conference to recruit a new generation of innovators. Hundreds of teachers and other staff from all of Lowell's middle schools attended. The conference was held in the cafeteria of one middle school, and the superintendent and the desegregation facilitator welcomed everyone, reiterated the goals for the middle school, acknowledged the hard work and excellent results of the first-round teams, reemphasized their "every child counts" philosophy, and strongly encouraged more teachers to become involved in this districtwide initiative. Then they invited everyone to walk around at their leisure to see what the pioneer teams had accomplished. Each of the 14 teams had set up a display that included, for example, posters listing their theme and overarching concepts, artifacts from activities, short videos of classroom practice, and students' final I-Search papers. What "hooked" many of the guests was seeing and hearing that students with disabilities and bilingual students had successfully carried out sustained research that culminated in a project.

Building Capacity. The teacher-to-teacher contact provided by the Showcase Conference proved to be a fruitful strategy. Immediately afterward, 23 teams signed up for the summer of 1994's Curriculum Design Institute by filling out application forms. As in the previous summer, Lowell's two goals for this summer's institute were for EDC to guide these teams to design their I-Search Units and to simultaneously guide the local facilitators to take responsibility for their teams. Given the large number of participants, I enlisted two EDC colleagues.

We carefully planned each day of the institute to continue to build local capacity. Early each morning, we met with the local facilitators to review the day's tasks. Then the local facilitators took responsibility for working with their assigned teams. At lunchtime, everyone met again to discuss emerging issues. Finally, at the end of the day, everyone met to debrief. Throughout the day, my colleagues and I circulated from team to team to review guidelines, demonstrate facilitation strategies, serve as critical friends, and support the local facilitator's efforts to guide their teams. We noted with interest that with the desegregation facilitators involved, many teams were designing units to include bilingual students. Special education teachers were also playing an important role in shaping the instructional practices to ensure that students with disabilities would fully participate. Similarly, with the library/media specialists involved, the units were rich in technology use (e.g., word processing, videos, simulations, CD-ROMs, databases, books on tape).

During the following school year, as local facilitators took on a stronger role with their teams, we became minimally involved, according to the original plan. With a critical mass of teachers implementing I-Search Units, Lowell continued to maintain its commitment to keeping the process going by holding another Showcase Conference to recruit a third round of implementers. As a result, 122 new teachers on 18 teams came forward to apply for the next summer of curriculum design.

Further Expansion. Further expansion depended on the growing abilities of Lowell facilitators, because EDC was no longer involved as an external consultant. For the third summer of curriculum design, the local facilitators, now on their own, relied on the support materials they developed during the previous summers as well as on strategies modeled by EDC. Of their own devices, they also developed guidelines to help new teams plan and implement I-Search Units. The guidelines included suggestions for modifying the units for students with disabilities and second language learners. These materials became a valuable asset, helping to bring clarity to the curriculum design process. In addition, the facilitators prepared I-Search Unit formats for each of the 18 teams, to ensure uniformity in the structure of the four phases. The goal

was eventually to create a clearinghouse to share copies of the implemented units among all teams, thereby building a rich resource of successful units. As a follow-up to the summer Curriculum Design Workshop, the local facilitators met with the teams during curriculum implementation to troubleshoot and help teachers problem-solve. The local facilitators had personalized the approach and took ownership for its successful continuation.

The third Showcase Conference, planned to recruit a next round of teachers in 1996, became a more elaborate affair than ever before. Lowell invited educational publishers to attend so that they could display wares related to the themes of the I-Search Units. In addition to hosting display tables as in the past, selected teams volunteered to make presentations to the entire assembly. One team talked about how they had developed rubrics for evaluation that especially helped students with disabilities; another talked about how they had included bilingual students; a third team demonstrated with a slide show how they had incorporated art and drama into students' exhibitions; and a fourth team talked about how the media specialist helped them use technology. Finally, a fifth team talked about how it took "a whole school" to do an I-Search, describing the role of the principal, custodian, and families. By 1996, two thirds of the teaching force and almost 5,000 students were involved in I-Search Units. As one teacher said, the I-Search had become "Lowellized" and, as such, was a recognized and natural part of the middle school reform initiative, owned by teachers, administrators, and students.

Analysis

One reason Lowell was attracted to Make It Happen! was because the approach laid out a process for implementation that could be replicated from year to year. This process allowed the district to start small, with a self-selected cohort who expressed interest in the innovation after the first Awareness Session, and to expand gradually to additional cohorts in subsequent years using the Showcase Conference strategy. This approach to sustainability has its merits: It allows a district to pilot the approach with the most motivated teachers, prepares for the allocation of resources over time, and fosters a continuous improvement model (Schmoker, 1996). However, at the same time, there are two inherent challenges in this approach. One challenge is that after the first wave of pioneers comes on board, the district needs a strategy to ensure that they repeatedly solicit buy-in and recruit new teams in subsequent years. Frequently, an innovation fails to be sustained if it cannot motivate additional teachers to take a risk. A second challenge is identifying potential facilitators early on and developing their capacity. Subsequently, we discuss how Lowell dealt with these two challenges.

Buy-In and Recruitment. Lowell made maximum use of the annual Showcase Conference to solicit buy-in and recruit new teachers. On the surface, the Showcase Conference might seem like a straightforward "show-and-tell" event that involves having the current implementers provide demonstrations or make presentations for a wide audience. In fact, a Showcase Conference is a much more complex affair that embeds a subtle set of strategies aimed at instructing, motivating, exciting, clarifying, inspiring, activating, and spurring teachers on. Figure 5.6 lists the strategies used by Lowell and shows what they were able to accomplish. In summary, the Showcase Conference was able to provide prospective participants with the following:

◻ A clear understanding of what the innovation entailed for teachers and students

◻ A belief that the innovation can make a difference to students with a range of abilities and needs based on the actual experience of other teachers who have students with similar backgrounds

◻ An image of the innovation as being malleable, able to be shaped to meet teacher and student needs

◻ Confidence that administrators support risk taking and provide resources

Held annually, Lowell's Showcase Conference became an anticipated public event. It helped to mark the I-Search Unit as a curriculum innovation that had its own identity and momentum. Practitioners felt that by joining the endeavor, they were joining something important that had a culture and heritage of its own within the district. This created a positive emotional climate that contributed to soliciting buy-in and made it easier to recruit new teachers.

Building Capacity in Local Facilitators. From the outset, administrators in Lowell identified a pool of potential facilitators—the desegregation facilitators and the media specialists. These practitioners met the criteria for a facilitator: They had roles and responsibilities related to improving curriculum for students with diverse needs, they had some flexibility in their daily schedules, and they had access to both teachers and administrators so that they could play the liaison role. Lowell also thought ahead about how to work with EDC as outside consultants to build capacity. In planning sessions between EDC and Lowell, they discussed the kind of effective training-of-trainers strategies that could be used with Lowell's staff. These included shadowing, demonstrating, modeling, mentoring, coaching, and debriefing (Miller, Lord, & Dorney, 1994). After weaning itself from external consultants, Lowell also found a way for the local facilitators to become a small working self-help group. Through their collaboration—which involved planning together, helping each other carry out work, and reflecting—they continued to strengthen their skills.

Conclusion: A Powerful Constellation of Factors

The Indianapolis case provided a close-up view of the inner workings of an interdisci-

FIGURE 5.6. Strategies Used in the Showcase Conferences

Strategies Embedded in the Showcase Conference	What the Strategy Could Accomplish
Having the superintendent and desegregation project director set the context by reiterating the middle school mission, praising the teachers, and encouraging participation.	• Administrators make it clear that this innovation is recognized and valued by the district.
Having consistency among the showcases—each display table included the name of the unit and the overarching concepts; the goals for students; the activities for Phases I, II, III, and IV of an I-Search; and examples of student work.	• Teachers make the key elements of the curriculum innovation explicit. • Teachers in the audience see how others applied their own creativity to the design of the units. • Teachers have confidence that an I-Search Unit works for all students because they listen to testimonials by colleagues and see evidence of student success.
Having selected teachers make presentations to everyone about a specific aspect of the innovation.	• Shows how teachers integrated new learnings into the unit. • Shows how teachers expanded the innovation.
Bringing in publishers to show wares related to the units.	• Teachers can review a variety of relevant instructional materials. • Shows that there is organizational support for identifying, purchasing, and utilizing new instructional materials.
Asking teams to fill out an application form.	• Administrators ask teachers to make a commitment.

plinary team that included content teachers, special educators, and technology specialists. Together, they designed curriculum, instruction, and assessment; took responsibility for carrying out their shared plans in their classrooms; met to debrief and problem-solve to ensure that every student succeeded; and refined their work over time, based on reflec-

tion. The other two cases also focused on the work of teams, but from the perspective of recruiting members and facilitating their ongoing work. In Lawrence, we saw what it took for the principal to create a schoolwide culture for collaborative teamwork around interdisciplinary instruction, and for Harriet, the facilitator, to guide the team through the curriculum process. In Lowell, we took another step back. We saw how the administrators relied on the Showcase Conference to recruit new teams and how they supported these additional teams by readying local facilitators.

Emerging from our reflections on these three case summaries is a powerful constellation of three factors that go directly to the heart of sustainability. These factors include having a small group of practitioners collaborate, over time, to focus on changing practice around the integration of technology to benefit students with and without disabilities. This constellation of factors resonates with Elmore's (1996) recommendations in his article "Getting to Scale With Good Educational Practice." He calls for schools to "develop organizational structures that intensify and focus, rather than dissipate and scatter, intrinsic motivation to engage in challenging practice" (p. 19). Interdisciplinary teams are small enough so that members develop a sense of mutual commitment and exercise real influence over each other's core practices. These core practices focus on

> how knowledge is defined, how teachers relate to students around knowledge, how teachers relate to other teachers in the course of their daily work, how students are grouped for purposes of instruction, how content is allocated to time, and how students' work is assessed. (Elmore, 1996, p. 7)

To implement Make It Happen! administrators seek to recruit interdisciplinary teams, not single teachers. As the Lawrence case shows, and as I have seen from my work with teams across the country, rarely does every teacher on the team begin as a motivated, true believer. In reality, teams are frequently a mix of willing and unwilling participants. Those who are willing are usually motivated by intrinsic rewards, stemming from a deep desire to improve teaching and learning. In contrast, those who are skeptical, timid, or not ready for change would be happy to forgo the entire enterprise. But I have seen time and again that

there is power in the team process. Over time, as they repeat the curriculum cycle, teams do develop a sense of mutual commitment and a shared willingness to focus on good practice. The Lawrence story provided an example of teams rallying to improve teaching and learning. But it is the "over time" variable that is critical—and this brings us to the next of Elmore's (1996) recommendations.

Elmore (1996) proposes that schools create structures that promote learning of new practices and incentive systems that support them:

> Teachers are more likely to learn from direct observation of practice and trial and error in their own classrooms than they are from abstract descriptions of new teaching; changing teaching practice, even for committed teachers, takes a long time, and several cycles of trial and error; teachers have to feel that there is some compelling reason for them to practice differently, with the best direct evidence being that students learn better; and teachers need feedback from sources they trust about whether students are actually learning what they are taught. (p. 24)

This chapter reflected on cases that showed how teachers were codesigners of their own curriculum; how, instead of going "solo," they had support for trying new practices from their colleagues; and how they discussed, in an ongoing forum, the impact their practices had on students. But this did not happen as a result of one cycle of curriculum design, implementation, and reflection; rather, it happened because of the repeated cycles, by a team, over time. Teachers incorporated lessons learned in one cycle into their next round of planning and implementation.

The major advantages of interdisciplinary teamwork are that, together, teachers construct knowledge, support each other in translating knowledge into practice, and reflect individually and as a group. At the same time, there are obvious challenges to this kind of collaborative work. It is a challenge to recruit teams, year after year, in which everyone on the team is willing to engage in interdisciplinary instruction, devote planning time to team meetings, and give up the same week over the summer for curriculum design. It is a challenge to identify potential facilitators for these teams, develop their leadership skills over time, and to free them from other responsibilities so that they are consistently available to their teams. It is a challenge for facilitators to create a culture of respect and productivity, mediate differences that naturally arise, make sure that everyone is contributing and learning, document the team's thinking, prompt reflection, and turn to the principal as needed. When a model of change depends on teaming, it must find ways to deal with these challenges to reap the benefits.

We have had the opportunity at EDC to continue to develop and study models of curriculum integration for students with disabilities in two other OSEP-funded projects: Pathways for Learning (1994-1997) and Project ASSIST (1996-1999). Carrying forth our findings from Make It Happen! the centerpiece of the models for these two projects remains having teachers work in teams. In the Pathways for Learning Project, the teams included general education teachers from across several grade levels, special educators, technology specialists, and other specialists (e.g., physical education, music, and health). The goal is to create a seamless pathway of instruction that benefits students with disabilities (Shure, Morocco, DiGisi, & Yenkin, 1999). Findings from this project reveal that teams moved through a developmental progression of struggles that they needed to resolve to move to a new level in their discourse and actions: multiple versus individual perspectives, deprivatized versus isolated practice, learning versus behavior goals, distributed versus individual expertise, reflective discourse versus routine practice (DiGisi, Morocco, & Shure, 1998). In Project ASSIST (1996-1999), the goal is to include students with disabilities in standards-based science and to integrate a range of low- to high-technology tools into inquiry-based science units. Here, the teams include general classroom teachers, the science specialist, the special educator, and the media specialist (DiGisi, Nix, Daniels, Kramer, & Cyr, 1999; Miller, 1999). These two models also have paid careful attention to the role of facilitators; the organizational support needed to create the time and space for team work; the role of the principal; and the role of district leaders in curriculum, special education, and technology. My colleagues and I are committed to studying the factors that promote sustainability, reporting findings, and building on the accumulated knowledge of researchers and practitioners in our future work. We hope that the ultimate beneficiaries of this endeavor will be students with disabilities.

Notes

1. This case is drawn from an unpublished case study coauthored by Judith Zorfass and Harriet Copel (1994).

2. This case is drawn from a case study coauthored by Judith Zorfass and Francene Donahue. The case is available on the Make It Happen! Web site (http://www.edc.org/FSC/MIH/).

References

Ames, N., & Miller, E. (1994). *Changing middle schools: How to make schools work for young adolescents.* San Francisco: Jossey-Bass.

Beane, J. (1990). *A middle school curriculum: From rhetoric to reality.* Columbus, OH: National Middle School Association.

Berman, P., & McLaughlin, M. W. (1976). *Federal programs supporting education change: Implementing and sustaining Title VII bilingual projects* (Vol. 6). Santa Monica, CA: RAND.

Berman, P., & McLaughlin, M. W. (1978). *Federal programs supporting education change: Implementing and sustaining innovations* (Vol. 8). Santa Monica, CA: RAND.

Carnegie Council on Adolescent Development. (1989). *Turning points: Preparing American youth for the 21st century.* New York: Carnegie Corporation.

Center for Applied Special Technology. (1998). *Concepts and issues: Summary of universal design con-*

cepts. Retrieved May 2000, from the World Wide Web: http://www.cast.org/concepts

Darling-Hammond, L., & McLaughlin, M. (1996). Policies that support professional development in an era of reform. In M. McLaughlin & I. Oberman (Eds.), *Teacher learning: New policies, new practices* (pp. 202-218). New York: Teachers College Press.

Darling-Hammond, L., & Sykes, G. (Eds.). (1999). *Teaching as the learning profession: Handbook of policy and practice.* San Francisco: Jossey-Bass.

DiGisi, L. L., Morocco, C., & Shure, A. (1998, July). *A framework of stages to understand the development of teams into a school-wide community of practice.* Paper presented at the 1998 OSEP Research Project Directors' Conference, Washington, DC.

DiGisi, L. L., Nix, A., Daniels, K., Kramer, L., & Cyr, S. (1999). Embracing the complexity of inclusive science classrooms: Professional development through collaboration. *Research in Science, 29,* 247-268.

Dorman, G. (1981). *Improving middle schools: A framework for action.* Carrboro, NC: Center for Early Adolescence.

Dorman, G. (1987). *Middle grades assessment program.* Carrboro, NC: Center for Early Adolescence.

Education Development Center, Inc. (1996). *Search organizer.* Newton, MA: Author.

Elliot, J., Ysseldyke, J., Thurlow, M., & Erickson, R. (1988). What about assessment and accountability? Practical implications for educators. *Teaching, 31*(1), 20-27.

Elmore, R. (Ed.). (1990). *Restructuring schools: The next generation of educational reform.* San Francisco: Jossey-Bass.

Elmore, R. (1996). Getting to scale with good educational practice. *Harvard Educational Review. 66*(1), 1-26.

Eylon, B., & Linn, M. C. (1988). Leaning and instruction: An examination of four research perspectives in science education. *Review of Educational Research, 58,* 251-301.

Fullan, M. (1990). Staff development, innovation, and institutional development. In B. Joyce (Ed.), *Changing school culture through staff development* (pp. 3-25). Alexandria, VA: Association for Supervision and Curriculum Development.

Fullan, M. G., & Miles, M. B. (1992, June). Getting reform right: What works and what doesn't. *Phi Delta Kappan,* 745-752.

George, P. S., & Shewey, K. (1994). *New evidence for the middle school.* Columbus, OH: National Middle School Association.

Hawley, W. D., & Valli, L. (1996, Fall). The essentials of effective professional development: A new consensus. *ASCD Professional Development Newsletter,* 1, 2, 8.

Helfgott, D., Helfgott, M., & Hoof, B. (1994). Inspiration [Computer software]. Portland, OR: Inspiration Software.

Hord, S. M., Rutherford, W. L., Huling-Austin, L., & Hall, G. E. (1987). *Taking charge of change.* Alexandria, VA: ASCD.

Huberman, A. M., & Miles, M. (1984). *Innovation up close: How school improvement works.* New York: Plenum.

Jacobs, H. H. (Ed.). (1989). *Interdisciplinary curriculum: Design and implementation.* Alexandria, VA: ASCD.

Kegan, J. (1995). Giving voice to our hidden commitments and fears: A conversation with Robert Kegan. *Harvard Education Letter, 11*(1), 3-5.

Kinnaman, D. (1990). Staff development: How to build your winning team. *Technology and Learning, 11*(2), 4-30.

Klein, S., Medrick, E., Perez-Fierero, V., & MPR Associates, Inc. (1996). *Fitting the pieces: Studies of education reform.* Washington, DC: U.S. Department of Education, Office of Education Research and Improvement, and Office of Reform Assistance and Dissemination.

Lee, G. V. (1993). New images of school leadership: Implications for professional development. *Journal of Staff Development, 14*(1), 2-5.

Lee, G. V., & Smith, J. B. (1993). Effects of school restructuring on the achievement and engagement of middle-grade students. *Sociology of Education, 66*(3), 164-187.

Lewis, A. (1997). A new consensus emerges on the characteristics of good professional development. *Harvard Education Letter, 13*(3), 1-4.

Lipsitz, J. (1984). *Successful schools for young adolescents.* New Brunswick, NJ: Transaction Publishing.

Lipsitz, J., Mizell, H., Jackson, A., & Austin, L. M. (1997). Speaking with one voice: A manifesto for middle-grades reform. *Phi Delta Kappan, 78,* 533-540.

Lord, B. (1994). Teachers' professional development: Critical colleagueship and the role of professional communities. In N. Cobb (Ed.), *The future of education perspectives on national standards in America* (pp. 175-204). New York: College Board Publications.

MacIver, D. J., & Epstein, J. (1990). *Responsive education in the middle grades: Teacher teams, advisory groups, remedial instruction, school transition programs, and report card entries* (Rep. No. 46). Baltimore: Johns Hopkins University, Center for Research on Elementary and Middle Schools.

Macrorie, K. (1988). *The I-Search paper.* Portsmouth, NH: Boynton/Cook.

McLaughlin, M. W., & Oberman, I. (Eds.). (1996). *Teacher learning: New policies, new practices.* New York: Teachers College Press.

Miller, B., Lord, B., & Dorney, J. (1994). *Staff development for teachers.* Newton, MA: Education Development Center, Inc.

Miller, C. (1999). Teachers and technology specialists team up to improve science education. *What's Working in Special Education, 1*(5), 1, 4.

Miller, E. (1995). The old model of staff development survives in a world where everything else has changed. *Harvard Education Letter, 11*(1), 1-3.

Mizell, M. H. (1994). *The new principal: Risk, reform, and the quest for hard-core learning.* New York: Edna McConnell Clark Foundation.

Morocco, C. C., & Zorfass, J. (1988). Technology and transformation: A naturalistic study of special students and computers in the middle school. *Journal of Special Education Technology, 9*(2), 88-97.

Morocco, C. C., & Zorfass, J. (1996). Unpacking scaffolding. In C. Warger & M. Pugach (Eds.), *Curriculum trends, special education, and reform* (pp. 164-178). New York: Teachers College Press.

National Middle School Association. (1982). *This we believe.* Columbus, OH: Author.

National Partnership for Excellence and Accountability in Teaching. (2000). *Revisioning professional development.* Oxford, OH: National Staff Development Council.

Patterson, J. (1993). *Leadership for tomorrow's schools.* Alexandria, VA: ASCD.

Poplin, M. S. (1988). Holistic/constructionist principles of teaching/learning process: Implications for the field of learning disabilities. *Journal of Learning Disabilities, 21,* 401-416.

Schmoker, M. (1996). *Results: The key to continuous school improvement.* Alexandria, VA: ASCD.

Sergiovanni, T. J. (1992). *Moral leadership: Getting to the heart of school improvement.* San Francisco: Jossey-Bass.

Shure, A., Morocco, C. C., DiGisi, L. L., & Yenkin, L. (1999, September/October). Pathways to planning: Improving student achievement in inclusive classrooms. *Teaching Exceptional Children, 32*(1), 48-54.

Slavin, R. E. (1990). *Cooperative learning: Theory, research, and practice.* Englewood Cliffs, NJ: Prentice Hall.

Smith, M. S., & O'Day, J. (1991). Systemic school reform. In S. H. Fuhman & B. Malen (Eds.), *The politics of curriculum and testing* (pp. 233-267). London: Falmer.

Smith, W., & Andrews, R. (1989). *Instructional leadership: How principals make a difference.* Alexandria, VA: ASCD.

Vanderheiden, G. C., & Kaine-Krolak, M. (1995). *Access to current and next-generation information systems by people with disabilities.* Madison: University of Wisconsin-Madison, Trace Research and Development Center.

Whitaker, B. (1997, January/February). Instructional leadership and principal visibility. *Clearing House,* 155-156.

Williamson, R. D., & Johnston, H. J. (1996). *Through the looking glass: The future of middle level education.* Reston, VA: National Association of Secondary School Principals.

Yin, R. K. (1994). *Case study research: Design and methods* (2nd ed.). Thousand Oaks, CA: Sage.

Zorfass, J. (1991). *Make It Happen! Inquiry and technology in the middle school curriculum.* Newton, MA: Education Development Center, Inc.

Zorfass, J. (1994). Supporting students with learning disabilities: Integrating technology into an I-Search Unit. *Technology and Disability, 3*(2), 129-136.

Zorfass, J., & Copel, H. (1994). *Supporting and expanding the work of interdisciplinary teams: A case study.* Unpublished manuscript, Education Development Center, Inc., Newton, MA.

Zorfass, J., & Copel, H. (1995). The I-Search: Guiding students toward relevant research. *Educational Leadership, 53*(1), 48-51.

Zorfass, J., & Copel, H. (1998). *Teaching middle school students to be active researchers.* Alexandria, VA: ASCD.

Zorfass, J., & Donahue, F. (1996). *Initiating, sustaining, and expanding a middle school initiative.* Unpublished manuscript, Education Development Center, Inc., Newton, MA.

Zorfass, J., Morocco, C. C., & Lory, N. (1991). A school-based approach to technology integration. In J. O'Neil (Ed.), *ASCD Curriculum Handbook* (pp. 11.B.51-11.B.95). Alexandria, VA: ASCD.

Zorfass, J., Morocco, C. C., Russell, S. J., & Zuman, J. (1989). *Phase I final report: Evaluation of the integration of technology for instructing handicapped children (middle school level).* Newton, MA: Education Development Center, Inc.

Zorfass, J., Morocco, C. C., Tivnan, T., Persky, S., & Remz, A. (1991). *Phase II final report: Evaluation of the integration of technology for instructing handicapped children (middle school level).* Newton, MA: Education Development Center, Inc.

CHAPTER SIX

Technology Implementation in Special Education

Understanding Teachers' Beliefs, Plans, and Decisions

CHARLES A. MacARTHUR
University of Delaware

As reflected in the organization of this volume, a full understanding of technology as an educational innovation requires explanation of changes at multiple levels—the students; the teacher or classroom; the organizational levels of school, district, and state; and the larger societal context. This chapter focuses on teachers, viewing them as professionals who make critical decisions about whether and when to use technology and how to integrate it with their instructional programs. Rather than review the literature more broadly, this chapter concentrates primarily on three research projects directed by my colleagues and me.

When innovations fail, teachers often receive a share of the blame for being resistant to change. But resistance to change is a simplistic notion that does little to explain why teachers (and schools) do not embrace new technologies and what needs to be done to support change. In the studies described in this chapter, my colleagues and I chose to view teachers as rational decision makers working in situations that require complex decisions under constraints of resources, expertise, and instructional and planning time. When we began this line of research in the 1980s, studies indicated that teachers had substantial discretion about how to use computers in instruction and whether to use them at all (MacArthur et al., 1985; Sheingold, Kane, & Endreweit, 1983). Though more curriculum support is available now, the extent and nature of computer use in classrooms are still often determined by individual teacher decisions.

Following a preliminary survey of special education teachers' use of computers (MacArthur et al., 1985), my colleagues and I conducted intensive case studies of 4 teachers (MacArthur & Malouf, 1991). Making a virtue of necessity, we chose to study teachers who were early and enthusiastic adopters of technology. Although the results might not generalize to typical teachers, we reasoned that understanding these teachers' motivations and their successes and difficulties in using technology would help us understand why more teachers had not adopted technology and what kinds of organizational, curricular, and professional development support were needed to facilitate effective technology use.

This study was conducted more than 10 years ago, when the latest technology available in the classes studied was an Apple IIgs computer with two floppy drives and a dot-matrix printer—no CD-ROM drives, limited graphics and sound capabilities, cumbersome access to e-mail, and no World Wide Web. Furthermore, access to technology was in general more limited than it is today. Nonetheless, claims about the potential impact of technology on education were similar to today's claims: Computers would motivate students to learn; make instruction in basic skills more efficient; and encourage student-centered, problem-solving approaches to learning—if only teachers would use them effectively. Thus, despite substantial changes in the hardware and software available to teachers, the findings of these case studies remain relevant and revealing of the issues faced by teachers in deciding how to integrate technology with the curriculum.

The theoretical framework for the study was drawn from the literature on teacher thought processes, including their theories and beliefs, planning processes, and decision making (Clark & Peterson, 1986). Thus, we explored how teachers' pedagogical beliefs and goals, beliefs about computers, instructional planning processes, overall classroom organization, and curriculum influenced their decisions about how to use computers. Particular attention was given to ways in which computers were integrated with teachers' overall classroom practices and to the unique issues and problems that computers presented.

Several conclusions emerged from the cross-case analysis. First, as anticipated, teachers made technology fit not only with their educational goals and beliefs but also with their instructional practices and classroom organization. Many of the computer activities we observed were analogs of non-computer activities. A teacher who emphasized the value of social interaction and writing incorporated word processing into his journal writing and writing workshop with little modification. A resource room teacher with a theory about multisensory repetition used computers for a book publishing project that involved repeated reading and writing, and that was similar to a project she had done the previous year without computers. The teacher with the most highly structured classroom used her sole computer primarily for drill and practice, which was organized in the same way that she used independent work folders. A resource teacher who engaged in tutoring and small-group instruction found it difficult to fit computers into her instruction and ended up using them minimally.

Second, on the other hand, teachers' beliefs about the unique potential of computers to motivate students and enhance their self-esteem also influenced decisions about computer use. Most of the teachers included time in their weekly schedule for free-choice computer activities, and some included time for drill and practice that they regarded as a frill. They justified these decisions as an opportunity to learn to use a computer and as a way to let students have fun while getting some instruction. Their beliefs that students' motivation and self-esteem would be enhanced simply by working with computers, regardless of the application, can be seen as a reflection of their own enthusiasm about computers and the societal value attached to technology. Although this enthusiasm was valuable in motivating these teachers to use technology, it also may have prevented them from critically examining the particular applications they used.

Third, computers presented some unique problems for teachers in planning instructional activities and monitoring student performance. In most of the classrooms, computer-assisted instruction (CAI) activities on the computer were not well integrated with other instruction. Only the most highly structured of the 4 teachers had a well-organized system for making assignments and evaluating performance. In the other classes, students often worked on CAI with inappropriate content. Although these teachers carefully selected paper-and-pencil assignments, monitored students as they worked, and checked work daily, they did not do so with CAI. This finding was surprising given the often cited capability of computers to manage instruction.

The routines that teachers used to plan and monitor traditional seatwork did not work with CAI. Planning and monitoring CAI was more difficult. Teachers had difficulty accessing software for preview, and previewing was time-consuming; it took much longer to preview software than to survey the content of a textbook or workbook. Programs that permitted teachers to individualize content (e.g., for spelling) required additional preparation time. Furthermore, CAI programs often were fragmented rather than composed of a range of difficulty levels and related tasks. Monitoring student performance was also more difficult with CAI than with paper seatwork. A worksheet could be checked with a glance while the student worked or quickly afterward. In contrast, checking CAI required extended watching of the screen, using record-keeping features if present, or training students to self-record. Teachers often were unfamiliar with record-keeping features or found that it was time-consuming to use them.

The use of word processing did not present significant problems in learning about software or monitoring student work. With word processing, teachers and students had only one piece of software to master, which they used throughout the year. The primary planning difficulty with word processing was arranging sufficient access to computers. Access ranged from one computer in the classroom to two or three computers plus weekly access to a computer lab. Teachers made fairly good use of word processing software, but none of the teachers had sufficient access to hardware to permit students to compose on the computer for the majority of their writing. One way to interpret these case studies is as examples of how much enthusiastic, energetic teachers can accomplish with minimal support from established curricular models and professional development. This interpretation has implications for professional development. First, teachers need opportunities to discuss their pedagogical beliefs and their beliefs about technology. Teachers naturally and appropriately modify innovations to fit their existing beliefs and practices. However, global beliefs about the value of technology do not provide much guidance in planning instruction. Discussions can help teachers clarify their own educational goals and develop an understanding of specific ways in which technology can support those goals.

In addition, professional development needs to be long term and provide direct support as teachers implement instruction. Sheingold and Hadley (1990) found that development of mastery in educational use of computers was a gradual process, requiring several years, and that on-site support and collaboration were critical. One way to provide such support is through mentoring (Little, 1990). Subsequent to the case studies described previously, my colleagues and I developed a mentoring model for technology staff development that involved training and supporting experienced computer-using teachers as mentors for their colleagues (MacArthur et al., 1995). The project was a collaborative effort between the university and the local school district.

In the Computer Mentor Program, teachers with experience in using computers in their classes participated in a one-semester course that provided guidance in how to serve as a mentor to other teachers and information on specific technology applications and local resources. These mentor teachers selected as protégés one to five teachers in their schools who were interested in making better use of technology in their teaching. The mentoring relationship was structured through the use of individual plans developed between each mentor and protégé. Mentors and protégés met weekly for workshop sessions. Incentives included inservice credit for both mentors and protégés. Administrative support at the building level was considered critical because one of the project goals was to have an impact at the school level. Principals agreed to provide meeting time and access to computers and were encouraged to participate in planning the goals for staff development at their schools.

Evaluation of the mentoring program indicated that both protégés and mentors increased their knowledge of computer hardware and software and used computers more frequently both with students and for personal and professional purposes. The greatest changes took place in schools where principals adopted an active role in the program. For example, one principal arranged for 5 teachers to mentor 17 other teachers. Together, they created a plan for using computer resources at the school and developed lesson plans for all grade levels. Computer use increased dramatically.

Overall, the mentoring program was a cost-effective way to provide staff development that was sensitive to individual teacher needs and that worked with the existing technology in the schools. It provided basic training and classroom support for teachers new to technology and upgraded the knowledge of more experienced computer-using teachers. Teachers shared the burden of reviewing software and planning lessons using technology. One limitation of the program was, perhaps, that it did not do enough to engage administrators. Schoolwide impact was seen only when principals became actively involved. Another limitation was that the project did little to promote curriculum reform, although we believe that a mentoring model would be

an appropriate way to support teachers in technology projects focused on curriculum innovation.

The results of the case studies (MacArthur & Malouf, 1991) also have implications for curriculum innovation involving technology. Providing teachers with general training on technology (or any other educational program) and expecting them to design curriculum on their own is unlikely to have much effect on classroom instruction except, in some cases, with highly motivated and energetic teachers. The motivated teachers in our case studies struggled to find effective ways to use computers but ended up with little innovation in their teaching practices. However, other studies have found much more success in innovation by teachers pioneering the use of technology. For example, Garner and Gillingham (1996) described innovative curriculum developed by six teachers using the Internet for communication. Nonetheless, it seems clear that most teachers, given the complexities of teaching and of technology use, will not choose to design technology-based curricula without substantial support.

Another way to support implementation is to focus on specific curricular models that incorporate technology as one component rather than on technology itself. Providing curriculum enables teachers to see how new approaches can work and gives them models to follow. There are numerous examples of such approaches, including two presented in this volume. Okolo and Ferretti (Chapter 3, this volume) worked with teachers in inclusive classrooms to implement a model for using multimedia to support project-based learning in the social studies. The Make It Happen! project (Zorfass, Chapter 5, this volume) provided a model for school change as well as staff development; teachers worked collaboratively to implement curricula focused on inquiry learning in social studies. Both these projects actively engaged teachers of special education students in long-term professional development focused on change in their curricula. They provided clear curricular models focused on important academic and cognitive outcomes that were supported by technology.

Another example from my own experience is the Computers in Writing Instruction Project (CWIP) (MacArthur, Graham, & Schwartz, 1993; MacArthur, Graham, Schwartz, & Shafer, 1995). CWIP offered staff development in a comprehensive model for writing instruction for students with learning disabilities that included writing workshop, word processing, and instruction in strategies for planning and revising. For most of the special education teachers in the project, the writing workshop was a new approach, and strategy instruction in writing was new to all of them. Word processing was integrated with the methods and goals of writing workshop and strategy development. For example, a peer revising strategy was included that built on peer revising methods of workshops, added explicit instruction in revising strategies, and took advantage of the editing power of word processing. Teachers participated in summer workshops, received on-site support (both instructional and technical) throughout the year, and met in groups for discussion on a regular basis.

High levels of integration of instruction and technology were achieved in nearly all classrooms. Initial problems with teaching students to use the technology and managing classroom activities were resolved early in the year and did not have to be revisited once a routine was established. Teachers used just a few software programs: word processing; spell checker; typing instruction; and a program to produce book covers, signs, and banners. The program had a substantial impact on students' writing ability.

An interesting contrast is provided by one of our current projects that also involves technology embedded in a larger curriculum. My colleagues and I (Ferretti, MacArthur, & Okolo, 1999) are studying the implementation of inquiry-based curriculum in social studies in inclusive classrooms. The curriculum is being developed collaboratively by the research team and the teachers involved in the project. In the first year of the project, stu-

dents used multimedia to present the results of their group investigations. One purpose of using multimedia was to enable students with learning disabilities to demonstrate their knowledge without relying exclusively on writing. However, the burden of producing multimedia presentations was too much for the four classrooms involved in the project, even though we provided templates that made it relatively easy for students to enter text and pictures. The students and most of the teachers did not learn how to use the multimedia system, and the students' lack of typing skills made text entry very time-consuming. The teachers judged it not worth the class time to teach students to use the technology because they did not intend to use it beyond the unit. In addition, without the extra computers provided by the project, they did not think they had a sufficient number of computers to make continued use feasible. In the second year of the project, we reduced the burden by switching from using multimedia presentations made by students to using multimedia, including the Internet, as a source of information for the inquiry projects. This approach has been more successful.

Recent reports suggest that although more technology is now available in the schools, most teachers have not figured out how to integrate technology in a meaningful way with the curriculum. More than half the nation's classrooms are connected to the Web, and schools have an average of one computer for every 5.7 children ("Technology counts '99," 1999). In addition, via the Internet, there has been a tremendous increase in the amount of educational content available. A recent survey ("Technology counts '99," 1999) found that more than 90% of teachers report using a computer at home or work for personal and professional purposes. However, only 50% to 60% report using software or the Web with their students, and only about one third of students use a computer as often as once a week. The two primary reasons given by teachers for not using more were insufficient numbers of computers in their classroom and lack of time to review software and plan how to use it for instruction. Teachers cited the same reason for not using the Web more: They do not have time to review sites and plan how to use them. Staff development that focused on integrating technology with the curriculum did make a difference; teachers who received such training reported greater confidence and used computers and the Web more extensively with their students.

Staff development in any innovation, including technology, needs to be responsive to the complexities of teachers' professional lives and the constraints they face in resources, expertise, and instructional and planning time. It is unrealistic to expect more than a few exceptional teachers to design curriculum based on general training in technology and exposure to a variety of software. The demands on planning time and expertise are simply too high. If the goal is integration of technology in the curriculum, then staff development should present technology as one component of larger instructional models that meet important educational goals. Curriculum developers, or teams of teachers working during the summer, should do the basic work of developing curriculum that incorporates technology. Teachers will have their hands full adapting the curriculum to their individual classrooms. Furthermore, greater recognition is needed that staff development should be long term and collaborative. Collaborative models of staff development provide teachers the time and support they need to understand the conceptual basis of innovative approaches and to incorporate new ideas with their current beliefs and practices. Making such staff development a reality is a problem not only of understanding how to do it, but also of mustering the political will to change our current system of minimal piecemeal staff development.

References

Clark, C. M., & Peterson, P. L. (1986). Teachers' thought processes. In M. C. Wittrock (Ed.), *Handbook of research on teaching* (3rd ed., pp. 255-296). New York: Macmillan.

Ferretti, R. P., MacArthur, C. A., & Okolo, C. (April, 1999). *Making rigorous curricula accessible to all students: Research in social studies.* Paper presented at the annual meeting of the American Educational Research Association, Montreal, Canada.

Garner, R., & Gillingham, M. G. (1996). *Internet communication in six classrooms: Conversations across time, space, and culture.* Mahwah, NJ: Lawrence Erlbaum.

Little, J. W. (1990). The mentoring phenomenon and the social organization of teaching. *Review of Research in Education, 16,* 297-351.

MacArthur, C. A., Graham, S., & Schwartz, S. S. (1993). Integrating word processing and strategy instruction into a process approach to writing. *School Psychology Review, 22,* 671-681.

MacArthur, C. A., Graham, S., Schwartz, S. S., & Shafer, W. (1995). Evaluation of a writing instruction model that integrated a process approach, strategy instruction, and word processing. *Learning Disabilities Quarterly, 18,* 278-291.

MacArthur, C. A., Haynes, J. A., Malouf, D., Taymans, J., Mattson, B., & Driefuss, S. (1985). *Implementation of microcomputers in educational programs for mildly handicapped students* (Tech. Rep. No. 107). College Park: University of Maryland.

MacArthur, C. A., & Malouf, D. B. (1991). Teacher beliefs, plans and decisions about computer-based instruction. *Journal of Special Education, 25,* 44-72.

MacArthur, C. A., Pilato, V., Kercher, M., Peterson, D., Malouf, D., & Jamison, P. (1995). Mentoring: An approach to technology education for teachers. *Journal of Research on Computing in Education, 28,* 46-62.

Sheingold, K., & Hadley, M. (1990). *Accomplished teachers: Integrating computers into classroom practice.* New York: Bank Street College of Education, Center for Technology in Education.

Sheingold, K., Kane, J. H., & Endreweit, M. E. (1983). Microcomputer use in schools: Developing a research agenda. *Harvard Educational Review, 53,* 412-432.

Technology counts '99: Building the digital curriculum. (1999, September 23). *Education Week* [Special issue].

SEVEN

Why Are Most Teachers Infrequent and Restrained Users of Computers in Their Classrooms?

LARRY CUBAN
Stanford University

Two decades after the introduction of desktop computers into schools, it is easy to find examples of teachers in both general and special education classrooms who vary in their use of information technologies.[1] At one end of the spectrum there are many star performers who began in the early 1980s learning BASIC language on their own and fixing personal computers when they crashed. Such teachers—I call them *serious users*—eventually bought a home computer and, in subsequent years, between home and school prepared classroom materials, compiled grades, used e-mail, and constructed Web sites for their classroom or school. Many of these serious users have incorporated classroom or lab computers, multimedia projects, and other uses of technology into their daily activities. Were computers to disappear, such teachers and their students would be upset because both have incorporated the powerful machines into the very fabric of their lives in and out of school.

Just as easily, I could offer as examples from the middle of the spectrum the many teachers who, after a few years of prodding, took a beginners course in using the computer, even purchased one for home, and, after 3 or 4 years, have found that the computer is a useful addition to their classroom repertoire. Such teachers—I call them *occasional users*—use software for administrative purposes, for example, to prepare grades, attendance reports, and handouts for class. For instruction, these teachers place the computer in the same category as a laser disc player, a videocassette recorder, an overhead projector, or a field trip. Were computers (or videos) to become suddenly unavailable, such teachers would adapt without missing a beat because the technology had been marginal rather than central to their work and life.

And, of course, there are plenty of examples of general and special education teachers at the other end of the spectrum who seldom or never boot up a computer in their classrooms—I call them *nonusers*. Although some of these teachers may have taken beginning computer courses, may even have a computer at home, or possibly use the computer for administrative tasks connected to their teaching, classroom use is minimal to nonexistent. Were computers to disappear from schools, students would note little difference in how and what these teachers taught.

More than a decade ago, I claimed that the vast majority of teachers were nonusers, about 1 in 4 were occasional, and 1 in 10 were serious (Cuban, 1986). Data since then largely have confirmed that claim (Becker, 1985, 1991). One researcher found students reporting that they used computers an average of only 40 minutes a week, or less than 4% of the instructional week (Becker, 1994).[2]

Since the early 1990s, however, there has been a modest shift in the spectrum from nonusers to occasional users and from occasional users to serious ones. Combined student and teacher reports in the mid-1990s suggest that more than half of general elementary and middle school teachers continue to be nonusers of computers for classroom instruction, about one third are occasional users, and about 1 in 10 are serious, that is, they use the technologies daily. In the high school, 2 of 10 teachers use the machines daily, whereas just more than 4 of 10 are occasional users. The rest never use the technologies. So over the past decade, there has been some movement in general education among elementary teachers from nonusers to occasional ones and a modest shift toward occasional and serious use in high schools (Means & Olson, 1995; National Center for Educational Statistics, 1997; National Educational Assessment Program [NEAP], 1994, 1996; Schofield, 1995; "Technology Counts," 1997; U.S. Congress, Office of Technology Assessment [OTA], 1995).

For special education teachers in elementary and secondary school settings, however, technology use appears to be more widespread. Because special education teachers not only have to ensure that students are eligible for services but also must monitor and assess students' academic and behavioral progress toward goals established in their individualized education programs (IEPs)—roles that go well beyond that of the general education teacher—information technologies have been used more than in general education classrooms (Woodward & Reith, 1997).

Asking about the frequency of use fails to look at what activities teachers design for students when they boot up classroom, lab, or media center computers. Both supporters and critics of the uses of technologies in schools (including researchers) have pointed out that powerful software and hardware end up being employed in low-level, unimaginative ways (Hunter & Goldberg, 1995; OTA, 1995; President's Committee of Advisors on Science and Technology [PCAST], 1997).

Uses of computers in classrooms for instruction can be differentiated between those that require less or more teacher direction and those that require less or more student initiative. Computer-assisted instruction (CAI) and computer-managed instruction (CMI), for example, require teachers to have access to machines where students can work, individually or in pairs, with software that largely guides students' responses. Thus, CAI refers to computer programs that provide students with drill-and-practice exercises or tutorial programs. Similarly, CMI refers to programs that evaluate and diagnose students' needs, guide them through the next best step in their learning, and record their progress for teacher use. Both CAI and CMI deemphasize the role of the teacher and heighten the role of the software program in directing students' responses.

Teachers also use computer-enhanced instruction (CEI). CEI differs from the other two forms in that it refers to programs that provide less structured, more open-ended opportunities to support a particular lesson or unit plan. Low-end CEI includes word processing and spreadsheets; high-end CEI includes simulations, creating multimedia projects, graphing, drawing programs, and using the Internet. Teachers in CEI are viewed as essential to the learning process because they plan activities students engage in that require a higher level of cognitive development, such as completing projects or using the Internet as a method of information gathering.

Given these distinctions, general education high school teachers and senior students, for example, report that computers are used mostly for word processing. In eighth-grade math, to cite another example, fewer than half of the teachers reported in 1996 that they used computers. Of those that did, 18% said they had students do drill and practice on the machines (CAI and CMI), 13% had students playing math games, 13% had students do simulations, and 5% used software demonstrating new topics in math (both CEI) (NEAP, 1996; Wenglinsky, 1998).

A similar pattern seems to prevail among special educators (Cosden & Lieber, 1986; Rieth, Bahr, Okolo, Polsgrove, & Eckert, 1988). MacArthur and his colleagues, in a series of studies, found that elementary school special educators' beliefs about the advertised benefits of computers still produced limited classroom uses in word processing; drill and practice; and postacademic task rewards, that is, computers as fun (MacArthur & Malouf, 1991).

I begin with teacher and student use to establish that there have been modest changes in use. There has been, for example, a doubling in serious use by high school general education teachers, from about 10% to 20%. Nonetheless, two decades after the introduction of desktop computers, the pace of adoption and use of information technologies by teachers have been episodic, uneven, and slow. Substantial numbers of teachers, in both elementary and secondary schools, seldom or never use the new machines, even as access to technologies has escalated since the early 1990s.[3]

Why do I begin this chapter by focusing on classroom use? There are several reasons. First, a school's acquisition of wiring, ample hardware and software, sufficient teacher training, release time, and technical support—broad access, in other words, and clearly a necessary condition for classroom use—seldom leads directly to most teachers becoming serious users of new technologies. There are, then, grounds for why so many teachers have been tardy and hesitant in their use. What I call *grounds,* however, promoters of serious computer use would label *barriers (or teacher resistance) to implementation.*

Second, determining the pervasiveness, frequency, and quality of classroom uses of technologies is an essential prior condition to assessing the impact of computers on teaching and learning. Policymakers, researchers, and vendors eager to assess the impact of information technologies on standardized test scores, how students think, how teachers teach, the social organization of the classroom, and other desired outcomes must have reliable data on actual classroom use—not on what occurs in occasional experiments lasting a few weeks or months or what teachers and administrators report.

What these reasons add up to is the crucial nexus between policy and practice. What happens after policymakers decide to wire schools, order deliveries of machines, and see that software is installed? Classroom use is an indirect consequence of policy decisions but a direct result of teacher implementation. After two decades of much policy action and expenditures, a fair statement about implementation of new technologies is that most teachers and students now have more access than they did previously, but classroom use continues to be uneven, slow, and of decidedly mixed variety—CAI and CMI mostly interspersed with CEI. Why is that?

Explaining Variation in Implementation

Of the many explanations for variation in teachers' use and their slow-motion welcome of these new technologies, especially in the face of widespread and swift computerization of the workplace, a familiar one often used in the past when new technologies have been introduced has been largely abandoned: Teachers resist innovations that will change their daily routines or threaten their jobs. During the late 1950s and early 1960s, for example, a tidal wave of passion for instructional television surged over educators. When the passion subsided, there was little evidence of teachers using television programming in their classrooms. Promoters of television explicitly blamed teachers for not using television daily in their classrooms (Cuban, 1986).

Although such noises occasionally have surfaced in the past few years, teacher "resistance" is an unpopular explanation for uneven and tardy use of information technologies in the classroom. A far more fashionable explanation has commanded the attention of top public officials, corporate leaders, school boards, and practitioner organizations.[4]

The popular explanation is that either bureaucratic incompetence or a lack of thoughtful, comprehensive, and systematic implementation plans for using the array of new technologies (or a combination of both) has prevented most teachers from working with computers routinely. The argument is seemingly unassailable: Wiring schools and making machines and appropriate software available has been a costly, time-consuming, and rule-conforming nightmare. Once schools are wired and machines are available, teachers still need adequate time and resources to learn how to use the powerful technologies with their students; they need patient help from experts in learning how to integrate the technologies into their daily classroom activities; they need equipment to be maintained by technical assistants. All these demands require changes in procedures and managerial competency in following through on decisions. If those bureaucratic needs are accommodated, the argument runs, most teachers will go from laggards to champions of classroom technologies. Thus, careful planning, managerial competence, and systematic implementation would erase the major obstacles that historically have blocked teachers from becoming serious users (Baier, March, & Saetren, 1986; Means & Olson, 1995; NEAP, 1996; OTA, 1995; PCAST, 1997).

Explaining the broad variation in teacher use by highlighting inadequate, even flawed, implementation is clearly popular, eminently sensible, but terribly short-sighted.

The theoretical framework for the faulty implementation explanation is a rational model of generic organizational behavior. Within this model, the dominant image is the corporate leader as a problem-solving engineer guiding a bureaucratic organization to achieve its goals. Organizations have top-level decision makers whose job is to make sure that operational tasks are designed and completed in a timely and efficient manner. Completing those tasks requires workers or, in this case, general and special education teachers, to have the necessary tools, time, and resources. When top policymakers design improvements in those tasks, implementing these changes requires providing the time, money, and help to those assigned to do the work.

When implementation is episodic and uneven, proponents of this rational-based explanation point a finger at top school decision makers for failing to have the vision, clear objectives, and organizational savvy to overcome obstacles in achieving their goal (in this instance, increased teacher use of technologies). Once policymakers and administrators get a grip on these organizational strategies to provide teachers with sufficient access to the technologies, prepare them to use the machines and software creatively, and secure technical help to maintain the machines in schools, teachers will do the right thing in the classroom. What is needed, those partial to this explanation say, is an engineering approach to implementation— carefully crafted strategies, thoughtful planning, competent managers, and sufficient resources to carry through a systematic and comprehensive design for using information technologies in schools.

Note that this wisdom *du jour* assumes that the task of implementing any organizational innovation including classroom information technologies is little different from implementing a new reading program, a novel math curriculum, or higher academic standards. Using computers in classrooms to improve teaching and learning, then, is no different from implementing new ideas and procedures in IBM or AT&T. In short, there is nothing inherently unique about putting into classroom practice this technological innovation.

What makes the wisdom of the moment short-sighted is the slighting of other explanations, singly or in combination, that may equally, if not more compellingly, account for the stark variation in teacher use beyond flawed implementation plans. Broadening the search for explanations is important to policymakers, researchers, and practitioners because explanations often contain the very seeds from which solutions to problems (a.k.a. "reforms") are fashioned. Restricting the search for credible explanations limits seriously the directions taken to understand, much less deal with, the implementation of information technologies in schools.

For example, one credible explanation derives from other organizational theories that find teachers' slow embrace of innovations, including machine technologies, connected to schools having competing goals (e.g., socialize children with community values and also make them independent thinkers), structures that drive teaching behavior (e.g., the age-graded school), and powerful norms (e.g., teacher autonomy). These organizational features raise substantial barriers that have hindered teachers from using new technologies (Cohen, 1988; Cuban, 1993).

Another explanation is anchored in the demography of teaching. There are major differences among gender and age groups across levels of schooling. Women and older teachers, for example, are perceived as being less facile with the newer technologies than are men and younger colleagues. Thus, fragmentary data and strong perceptions combine to expect elementary schools with more than 90% female faculties to be the slowest in using computers on a serious basis, whereas male-dominated departments in secondary schools have higher rates of usage (Colley, Gale, & Harris, 1994; Shashaani 1994; Tyack & Hansot, 1990).

A cultural explanation points to how occupational groups (teachers, policymakers, and administrators) who frame problems, define effectiveness, and achieve job satisfaction differ dramatically from each other. For example, teachers' beliefs, values, and norms about the job of teaching and how students best learn are quite different from administrators' and policymakers' beliefs and values. Within the age-graded school, teachers are organizational gatekeepers. They decide what gets into their classrooms and how wide the gate should be open. Yet teachers have diverse beliefs about knowledge, teaching, and learning; exhibit a wide range of familiarity with software; and vary in their motivation to use the novel technology. Thus regardless of how passionate administrators and policymakers may be about the new machines, because of these differences among teachers, they will vary in using the new technologies (Cuban, 1986; Elmore & McLaughlin, 1988; Huberman, 1993; Mehan, 1989; Saye, 1998).

Another explanation suggests that there is a covert power struggle between contending groups over whose ideas and interests will prevail in the classroom. Corporate promoters of information technologies, employers concerned about the next generation of workers, parents worried about the economic future of their children, and teacher unions vie for an edge to secure what each group desires. Coalitions form, negotiate, and struggle for their particular interests (Baier et al., 1986; Wirt & Kirst, 1989).

I could generate even more explanations. None of these, however, is as fashionable among policymakers, practitioners, and researchers as is the rationally based explanation that connects erratic progress in getting teachers to use these machines to the lack of organizational competence in systematically implementing new technologies. I offer these competing explanations because they each or in combination illustrate the limits of attributing infrequent and unimaginative teacher use to ineffectual implementation. These alternatives offer very different strategies for increasing teacher use of information technologies and, even further, question the very worth of an outcome such as more students working with electronic machines.

To elaborate the point that multiple explanations may be fruitful for policymakers, practitioners, and researchers to consider, I will explore one alternative in more detail. In doing so, I am not dismissing totally the common explanation of inadequate administrative control over implementation for limited and infrequent teacher use. After all, one could hardly object to policymakers specifying objectives clearly, providing adequate resources, employing efficient procedures, and smoothing access for teachers who want to use powerful machines in their classrooms. I offer an alternative to underscore how important explanations are in the framing of policy problems. For example, in the past decade, public officials and promoters of spending more to put new technologies in the schools have succeeded at framing the core problem of limited teacher use as, How can we get teachers to increase both the frequency and creativity of their instructional use of computers?

Framing the question in this manner assumes that the problem is inadequate teacher use of computers in schools. In other words, why don't teachers use the new technologies more? Answer: Because teachers lack access and help. Hence the solution is self-evident to promoters: Wire schools. Buy more computers. Provide technical support. Train teachers to use available software. Implement access, and teacher use will both accelerate and become creative.

This commonly accepted definition of the problem and solution excludes questions such as, How effective are the technologies in helping teachers teach and students learn? What are the gains and losses for both teachers and students in increased use of classroom

technologies? Can the money allocated for information technologies be better used in other ways by students and teachers?

Framing the problem and solution in this popular way not only excludes alternative explanations, but it also once again makes teachers vulnerable to blame. What happens, for example, if access and support are amply supplied and still most teachers are occasional users or nonusers and student use of software applications is viewed as pedestrian? The answer becomes self-evident: As in the past, disappointment with limited and uncreative uses of expensive investments will lead to teachers getting bashed. I do not believe that advocates of the flawed-implementation explanation want that to occur. Intentions notwithstanding, inadequate use of previous technological innovations, indeed, has led to strong and unrelenting criticism of teachers—the very people who are drafted to put school reforms into practice, yet who have had little voice in the decisions to buy the technologies or design the implementation strategies. Thus I offer an alternative way of framing the problem of infrequent and limited use of technological innovations. Before moving to that alternative, I suggest some standards by which to judge the adequacy of any explanation for teacher response to this particular technological innovation.

Any explanation accounting for the frequency and quality of teacher uses of information technologies that is compelling to readers would have to accommodate rich data collected over two decades, showing

- ◧ Wide variation in use among general and special educators
- ◧ The slow pace of adoption and use among teachers
- ◧ A majority of general education elementary teachers still being nonusers
- ◧ Evidence of more general and special educators becoming occasional and serious users
- ◧ Low-end uses (e.g., more CAI and CMI than CEI) of these powerful

technologies for teaching and learning among both general and special educators

The rational explanation of inept implementation does tidily explain the two-decade slow pace of most K-12 teachers adopting the new technologies for instruction in their classrooms. Securing more hardware and software, wiring schools, and providing opportunities for teachers to learn and use the technologies are essential prior conditions for classroom use that have required much time and money. For some teachers, greatly increased access to the technology in the past decade has expanded their use. However, those favoring this explanation have difficulty accounting for the sharp variation between elementary and secondary schools in teacher use, the early adoption by special educators of many of the new technologies, and the ways that teachers in both special and general education use the software in their classrooms. Thus, there is need for an alternative explanation.

An Alternative Explanation for Variation in Use

In offering an alternative, I have drawn from my experience as a teacher and administrator, my current research in elementary and secondary schools, and familiarity with research on school reform. From this direct experience and research, I have cobbled together concepts drawn from different theories to create a patchwork explanation that seemingly embraces the contradictions embedded in the evidence set out previously. The components of the explanation are italicized and elaborated on subsequently.

Cultural beliefs about the nature of knowledge, how teaching should occur, how children should learn, and the purposes of schooling are so widespread and deeply embedded that they shape the thinking of policymakers, practitioners, parents, and citi-
zens concerning what ought to happen in schools between teachers and students.

For millennia, deeply rooted Western beliefs about the nature of knowledge (a body of human wisdom accumulated and tempered over time that must be passed on from one generation to another), teaching (the communicating of that wisdom), and learning (the absorption of that wisdom) have marked the earliest efforts to school the young. These folk beliefs unfolded within the family when it acted as the first school for infants and toddlers. Strengthened by formal religions and ethnic cultures as they emerged over the centuries, these cultural beliefs have shaped the character and direction of religious instruction prior to the introduction of tax-supported public schools. With the invention of such schools in the United States, the model of the teacher as the authority who passes on the required knowledge through telling students what they must learn continued as the dominant form of instruction.

Occasional European and American philosophers and educators over the past 500 years objected to these ingrained cultural beliefs and saw the child as central to an education rather than as a receptacle for a body of knowledge accumulated over centuries. Such reformers viewed the teacher's primary role as guiding the unfolding of the child's talents to their fullest and were eager to develop student-centered ways of educating the young. Twentieth-century reformers, for example, introduced into public schooling the kindergarten, small-group learning approaches, the movable desk, and other child-centered practices. These changes have come slowly and often have been reshaped by these traditional and dominant cultural norms.

Thus it should come as no surprise that, in many classrooms, uses of new technologies that challenge these historic traditions would find teachers deeply conflicted over how much of the new to embrace and how much of the old to maintain (Cohen, 1988; Metz, 1990; Meyer & Rowan, 1977).

This strong web of cultural beliefs about knowledge, teaching, and learning suggests

that the purposes and outcomes for public schools in a democratic society mark it as unique, different from other public institutions such as businesses and the military.

Most American social institutions have clearly defined purposes. Few people would dispute that the primary purpose of General Electric or General Motors is to provide dividends to their stockholders. Profit margin is everything. The armed services seek to maintain peace and defend the nation in time of danger. But public schools differ from these institutions in having conflicting purposes that have been (and are) constantly debated and changed. Public schools are unique in this respect.[5]

Parents, for example, expect public schools to provide a safe and healthy place, 8 or more hours a day, for their sons and daughters. Parents want schools to equip their children with the knowledge and skills that will them give an edge in the climb up the socioeconomic ladder to financial and social success. Taxpayers and parents expect students to become literate adults who reason clearly, think independently, and carry out their civic obligations. Both want graduates of schools to meet workplace and university requirements, including technological literacy. Thus, schools are to build citizens, prepare workers for the job market, cultivate children's moral character and potential, and give each child a push up the social ladder.

With such diverse purposes for public schools, conflicts inevitably arise because of limited resources and lack of agreement over which goals should have priority. The history of American public schools is marked by debates over which goals should have primacy and allocations of sufficient resources to achieve the goals of the moment. Constraints continually have forced policymakers, administrators, and teachers to make choices among competing goals. In short, public schools have been wracked by tugs of war over which purposes should have priority in educating the next generation.

Because public school policymakers and administrators are totally dependent on tax-payers and parents for their political and financial legitimacy, when criticism arises over what they should be doing, they often will adopt innovations that opinion setters in the larger society deem appropriate for schools, such as character education programs, different reading methods, and new technologies. Adoption of these innovations is often couched in language that is consistent with the web of social beliefs—for example, the new technologies will help teachers and students do a better job of teaching and learning. Such symbolic embraces of innovation are crucial to maintaining the support of influential constituencies (Goodlad, 1984; Labaree, 1997; Meyer & Rowan, 1978; Tyack & Hansot, 1982).

Within this unique social institution of public schools and the larger framework of cultural beliefs within which it operates, the organizational structures of the district, school, and classroom have shaped, in part, teachers' instructional practices.

District and school organizational structures also have influenced how teachers have taught. *Structures* refer to the way school space is physically arranged, how content and students are organized into grade levels, how time is allotted to tasks, and how organizational rules govern the behavior and performance of both teachers and students. These structures result from the basic imperative of public schooling: to manage large numbers of students with broad variation in abilities and motivation who are required to attend school, absorb certain knowledge, and maintain orderliness. The age-graded school, self-contained classrooms, a curriculum divided into chunks for each level, 50-minute periods, and large classes are structures that have developed over time to meet this basic imperative.

The classroom organization nested within the larger school structure assigns the general education teacher the task of managing 25 to 40 or more students of approximately the same age who involuntarily spend—depending on their age—anywhere from 1 to 5 hours daily in one room. The teacher is expected to maintain control, teach certain subject matter, motivate students to learn, vary levels of instruction according to student differences, and provide evidence that students have performed satisfactorily.

For the special education teacher, the conditions and anxieties are both similar and different. With fewer students, the special education teacher is expected to organize learning for a highly diverse set of individuals; teach differently to each child; assess each student's individual progress; manage the paperwork generated by a host of district, state, and federal regulations; and constantly negotiate with general education teachers who also have their students. And don't forget the constant stream of meetings with students, parents, other teachers, and experts involved in charting and monitoring what happens with each student.

Within these overlapping school and classroom structures, both general and special education teachers have rationed their energy and time. They have coped with conflicting and multiple demands by inventing teaching practices that have emerged as resilient, imaginative, and efficient solutions to dealing with conflicting obligations and managing diverse students in a small space for extended periods of time.

Like policymakers and administrators, teachers are also very concerned about efficiency. Where they differ is that both general and special education teachers have to manage classrooms and create individual personal relationships; they have to cover academic content and cultivate depth of understanding in each student; they have to socialize students to abide by community values and nurture creative and independent thought. These complex classroom tasks, unlike anything policymakers and administrators have to face, require careful expenditure of a teacher's time and energy. So in trying to finesse conflicting goals within an age-graded school organization, teachers use criteria forged out of their experiences to decide which electronic tools they routinely will use.

Teachers ask about new technology, Is it simple enough for me to learn quickly? Can it be used in more than one situation? Is the software program motivating? Does the program contain skills that are connected to what I am expected to teach and know that students need? Is the machine and software reliable, or do they break down often? If they break down, do I have to fix them, or is there someone else who will? How much time and energy do I have to invest in learning to use them versus the potential return in student learning? Will students using the machines weaken my ability to maintain order? For most teachers, an overhead projector, videocassette recorder, copy machine, and textbook—but not necessarily classroom computers—fit these efficiency criteria nicely. In applying these criteria, most teachers end up as occasional users or nonusers of computers. For a small fraction of teachers, however, these efficiency questions are adequately answered by computers.

Thus far, this patchwork quilt of an explanation stresses that the structures of the age-graded school produce regularities in instruction and position the teacher as gatekeeper for innovations. Teachers cope with the dilemmas imposed by these structures, over which they have little control, by inventing creative compromises in their classroom practice (Cuban, 1993; Doyle, 1986; Dreeben, 1973; Dreeben & Barr, 1983; Johnson, 1990; Mehan, 1989; Ponder & Doyle, 1978; Sarason, 1971).

Not only does the web of social beliefs, unique purposes of schooling, and organizational structures influence what teachers think and do, the cultures of teaching that have developed within the occupation tilt toward maintaining regularities in classroom practices.

The occupational ethos of teaching breeds conservatism—a preference for stability and a cautious attitude toward innovation. This conservatism is anchored in the very practice of teaching, the people who enter the profession, how they are informally socialized, and the school culture of which teaching itself is a primary ingredient.

The aim of teaching is to change children into youth viewed as desirable by parents and society. Yet teachers are wholly dependent on their students for producing successful results. Moreover, as yet, there is no firm societal consensus about what the desirable outcomes are for teaching and the entire enterprise of schooling. Understandably, teachers are often reluctant to take risks in modifying practices, particularly to embrace technologies or student-centered instructional reforms that place even more reliance on students for results.

The people who enter the teaching profession also encourage conservatism within the occupation. Often, newcomers seek contact with children, appreciate the flexible work schedule, and, while acknowledging the limited financial rewards, still embrace the service mission built into the occupation. Of the young who enter teaching, women outnumber men. Moreover, men often move out of the classroom in search of recognition, more organizational influence, and higher salaries. Attracted by work schedules that permit flexible arrangements with family obligations and vacations, women and men, for different reasons, have few incentives to alter occupational conditions or seek major improvements.

Furthermore, recruits to the occupation tilt toward continuity because of their prior school experiences. As public school students for 12 years, entering teachers unwittingly served an apprenticeship as they watched their teachers teach.

Thus, classroom practices tend to be stable over time. After all, homework assignments, discussion, seatwork, tests, and an occasional film to interrupt the routine were all methods familiar to teachers in their own schooling and, more often than not, seemed to keep the class moving along. Rather than making fundamental changes—such as teaching in small groups, integrating varied content into units, creating multimedia projects, and letting class members choose what to do—tinkering with methods, polishing up techniques, or introducing variations of existing ones would be consistent with the basic conservatism of the occupation (Cohen, 1988, 1989; Feiman-Nemser & Floden, 1986; Jackson, 1968; Lortie, 1975; Rosenholtz, 1989; Sarason, 1971; Waller, 1965).

The web of cultural beliefs, competing purposes, school structures, and cultures of teaching are components of an explanation that suggests why stability is the norm in teaching practice. But teachers innovate. How to explain both stability and change? What helps to explain both constancy in practice and frequent classroom innovations are two factors: the history of district and school innovation and, second, teacher beliefs, their knowledge of subject matter, and their discretionary authority as gatekeepers for classroom change.

All districts differ in their attitudes toward change. Most districts prize stability; their leaders reward maintaining the status quo. Some districts, however, have a history of embracing innovations, establishing support mechanisms for teachers to grow, and rewarding teachers who are instructionally adventurous. Such districts have leaders who become early adopters of an innovation. Such district leadership encourages individuals and small groups of teachers to visit other schools and adapt changes being undertaken elsewhere. For many teachers in such districts, a culture of innovation pervades schools; they will experiment with new ideas (Fullan, 1991; Hess, 1999).

Although the district's history of leadership in innovating can encourage teachers to be risk takers, what ultimately accounts for teachers deciding to change their routines and import a new practice into their classroom is what they know and what they believe. After all, what teachers know about a subject gets converted into teachable language and activities for children. A social studies teacher, for example, not only has content knowledge of, say, U.S. history, but also knows how to get across to 15-year-olds who are uninterested in academic subjects, or ever going to college, what the Bill of Rights means through concrete (and innovative) case studies drawn from street law. The novel metaphors that a biology teacher uses to illustrate the concept of evolution to sophomores in a college-preparatory class are drawn not from a textbook but from the experience he has had with previous students who got stuck in their understanding of the concept.

If pedagogical content knowledge counts, so do the teacher's professional and personal beliefs about the social role of schooling, authority in a classroom, and how children learn. An elementary school teacher, for example, who believes that children working together in small groups can learn from editing one another's writing will organize classroom furniture, including computers, differently from that of a teacher who views learning as filling up pupils with editing rules. The special education teacher deeply concerned about motivating disengaged high school students who believes in behavioral reinforcement will seek to strengthen conforming behavior by holding out to her unmotivated students the reward of playing computer games for 15 minutes. Knowledge, beliefs, and attitudes shape what teachers let enter, what they adopt, and what they keep out of their classrooms (Clandinin, 1985; Elbaz, 1983; Fenstermacher, 1986; Grossman, 1989; Gudmundsdotter, 1991; Shulman, 1987).

Finally, there is the political power component. Those who have the authority to design and adopt innovations, to decide what gets funded and implemented, also shape how teachers maintain stability and respond to innovations.

Teachers, the foot soldiers of every reform aimed at improving student outcomes, seldom determine which innovations get funded, designed, adopted, and implemented. Such decisions most often fall within the domain of policymakers. Their values and their criteria diverge considerably from what practitioners would prize. Practitioners bring moral and service values inherent to teaching that differ from the technical and scientific values that drive most policymakers. Practitioners accumulate expert knowledge about students and how to teach skills and subject matter that few policymakers plumb. From these values and expertise emerge standards for judging the worth of an innovation that may diverge sharply from those of policymakers. Of course,

teachers seek improvement in students' performance and attitudes, but what teachers count as significant results are seldom test scores but attitudes, values, and actual behavior on academic and nonacademic tasks in and out of the classroom. What becomes especially important to teachers is how they can put their personal signature on the mandated innovation—be it computers or cooperative learning—and make it work for their students and themselves (Berman & McLaughlin, 1978; Cuban, 1993; Elmore & McLaughlin, 1988; Welker, 1992; Wolcott, 1977).

But why are the criteria that practitioners prize seldom invoked by policy entrepreneurs? The question boils down to one of power and status: Whose standards count? When national, state, and district policymakers—holding implicit views of how organizations work, using scientific findings to bolster their decisions, and having access to media—place their weight behind, say, information technologies, legitimacy in making changes rests with those at the top of the organization, not those at the bottom, whose organizational views, expertise, and values might differ. Without the cachet of scientific expertise, access to top officials, or easy entree to reporters, individual teachers are stuck. Collectively, teachers have organized into unions and, more recently, asserted their political clout by taking explicit positions on school reform. Yet in making instructional policy and judging its success, unions play a limited role. Thus, when individual teachers do choose to act as gatekeepers or to adapt innovations, they do so unobtrusively or, in some cases, engage in guerrilla warfare with administrators and policymakers. Organizational legitimacy, use of scientifically derived data, and power often determine whether innovations get adopted, but it is the practitioners who exert their power as gatekeepers and determine, ultimately, what gets past the classroom door.

Note how the components of this alternative explanation include the environment (cultural beliefs and the uniqueness of schools among social institutions), the organization (the structures of schooling), occupational culture (the nature of teaching, who enters the occupation, and the long apprenticeship of observing teachers), the politics of adopting innovations and the power of some over others to make the choices of which innovations should be adopted, and, finally, the individual whose knowledge and beliefs help shape classroom behavior. By constructing a multifaceted explanation that draws from large and small settings, from collectives to individuals, the task becomes to explain three seemingly contrary teaching behaviors: a small minority of teachers eagerly adopting innovations, a larger number of teachers adapting versions of the innovation that fit their purposes and beliefs, but most teachers maintaining familiar routines and largely ignoring the innovation.

Let me now be more explicit in elaborating on the data and applying the criteria that I mentioned previously to illustrate how the alternative explanation can account for these seemingly contrary behaviors among teachers in using computers for instruction.

Explaining the Data

How does the alternative explanation account for

☐ Wide variation in use among general and special educators

☐ The slow pace of adoption and use among most teachers

☐ Majorities of general educators still being nonusers

☐ Low-end uses of technologies

Regardless of greatly increased access to the technologies in schools, the pervasive cultural beliefs in society (in which teachers share), organizational structures, and occupational cultures of teaching would explain the languid pace of using computers in classrooms among general educators. Variation in use—small numbers of serious users, more occasional users, and majorities of nonusers—

also can be attributed to these powerful environmental, organizational, and occupational factors. That few teachers were (or are) consulted prior to decisions by policymakers to buy new technologies only underscored how powerless teachers were (and are) to shape what gets funded and adopted. Such impotence seldom would encourage educators to take initiative in embracing innovations designed by others, thus further accounting for varied use across different levels of schooling.

For that minority of teachers who incorporated the technologies into their daily repertoire, the histories of particular districts in embracing innovations and the diverse beliefs of teachers harnessed to classroom autonomy enhanced by increased availability of computers came into play. These factors also help explain low-end uses, because those teachers who became occasional and serious users were still influenced by the larger cultural beliefs, multiple purposes of schooling, and organizational structures. Let me now explain how increased use of computers for instruction may be linked to CAI and CMI rather than CEI.

For the adventurous technological pioneers in schools, two possible outcomes may occur. Some classroom champions of technology end up folding machines into a repertoire of teaching activities that others may characterize as conventional, even traditional (CAI and CMI); others find that the machines and particular software (CEI) alter the social practices of teaching and learning within the classroom that, over time, create a very different kind of work setting. All of this is plausible for general educators but less so for special educators.

Among special educators, the use of new technologies has been adopted more swiftly, is more pervasive among classrooms, displays less variation in frequency, and illustrates a broad range of applications (Pressman, 1987; Viadero, 1997; Weber & Demchak, 1996). How come?

I turn again to the alternative explanation. Certain key components within the special education setting operate differently from those in general education. Although special educators certainly experience the same social web of public school beliefs and conflicting purposes as general educators do, there are critical differences that may explain the discrepancies in frequency and quality of use. The norms within special education, for example, prize individualization of instruction, materials, and assessment. Credential programs for special educators stress students' different learning styles, developmentally appropriate activities, and multiple methods of instruction. Moreover, the role of the special educator covers multiple tasks of determining eligibility, constructing IEPs, monitoring the progress of the IEPs, and assessing academic and behavioral progress. The eligibility and placement process brings other professionals and parents together with the special educator and offers opportunities for learning a great deal about individual students and their backgrounds. Because class sizes are much smaller than in regular classes, special educators can apply their knowledge, values, and expertise more easily than can their cousins in general education. Because of all these factors, welcoming and adapting innovations, especially technological ones, has found fertile ground among special educators (Woodward & Reith, 1997).

For the sake of argument, let us assume that the alternative argument I offered is credible and explains the wide variation and low-end uses among teachers, slow acceptance of technologies in the classroom, and large majorities of teachers remaining nonusers. So what? Of what practical implication is such an explanation for policymakers, teachers, administrators, and researchers? There are several answers to the question.

So What? Implications of the Alternative Explanation

I offer four implications that could flow from this alternative explanation. First, how a prob-

lem is framed too often points to its solution. The current popular definition of the problem (faulty implementation in securing access to technologies) and solution (more hardware and software; more professional development and technical support) revolves around creating more access and help for both general and special educators. Such a solution is viewed as both necessary and sufficient to create more serious users among teachers. But were the snail's pace of teacher adoption and low-end use of the new technologies among general educators to continue even after major expenditures, teachers who lack input into expenditure decisions, forming policies, and designing implementation plans would be left vulnerable to another round of bashing as unrepentant resisters.

The alternative explanation suggests that any increase in frequency and quality of classroom use of technologies among general and special educators will take decades and will produce a variety of traditional and innovative hybrids of technology use in classrooms. This explanation shrinks expectations for snappy outcomes in a social institution serving multiple purposes (custodial, character-building, preparing workers, and making citizens, etc.) in which teachers must juggle contradictory commands to both socialize and educate the next generation.

The alternative explanation implies that existing expectations, in light of schooling as an institution and the history of previous technological innovations, are inflated and ultimately self-defeating. Why self-defeating? Because inflated expectations often lead to disappointment and, as in the past, another round of finger-pointing at teachers. After almost two decades of unrelenting criticism of public schools and eroding faith in what schools can achieve, another cycle of blame for the very people who are expected to prepare the next generation for the millennium would be even more corrosive of a unique institution expected to achieve so much with so little support in so few years.

Second, for promoters to secure teacher acceptance for information technologies, they will have to go much further than creating access. In light of this alternative explanation, more availability may be a necessary condition, but it is insufficient to convert nonusers into serious ones. Advocates among policymakers and administrators for more information technologies in classrooms will have to accept as worthy the expertise and authority that teachers have accrued over the years; they will have to listen more carefully to the questions that teachers ask about an innovation—questions that differ greatly from those that policymakers or administrators ask; they will need to pay attention to teacher hopes and fears about the craft of teaching, learning, and their students; they will need to respect teachers' skills of adapting innovations to the topography of the classroom. Furthermore, policymakers and administrators will have to share power with teachers in designing and implementing plans for classroom use of technologies. Delivering machines and software to classrooms, providing courses for teachers, and hiring technicians to service machines are necessary but insufficient to convert the majority of nonusers into accomplished, dedicated users. The alternative explanation requires policymakers and administrators to acknowledge and act responsively to teachers' concerns and expertise.

Third, the alternative explanation points to the differences between general and special educators in using information technologies. The experience of broader use of information technologies among special educators suggests that policymakers pursue other strategies if they wish to generate more occasional and serious users among general educators. Preparation of special educators welcomes diverse approaches to reach children with disabilities and cultivates an ethos of individual attention (and IEPs) wedded to class sizes of 10 to 15. These professional beliefs and structures suggest that policymakers pursuing an approach that makes hardware, software, professional development, and technical support available as the primary way to increase use is seriously deficient as a strategy in the way it ignores critical structural and cultural factors that shape the practice of teaching.

Finally, the record of use and nonuse of information technologies among general education teachers in the past two decades strongly suggests that computers have entered classrooms very slowly, with modest to minimal changes in what teachers commonly do. In other words, there have been minor incremental changes in many but not most teachers' repertoires of classroom activities. Computers have prompted some changes, of course. Of equal if not more importance is that the structures and cultures of the school and classroom have altered what teachers do with these machines.

This mutual adaptation of technology and practice in which both changes support the view that technology is more than a machine or piece of software, so making both available will not solve the problems that policymakers frame. To restate the obvious one more time: It is not the machine or software; it is what teachers and students do with both. It is not about technology; it is about teaching and learning. Teacher creation of hybrid uses of technologies points to new technologies spurring revisions in existing social practices within a classroom leading to adaptations in social relationships between the teacher and students and among students. "The crucial ingredient," Hugh Mehan (1989) wrote, "is people's experience with the machine, not its 'inherent' features. It is what people do with the machine, not the machine itself, that makes a difference" (p. 19).

Hence, those who would embrace the alternative explanation I have offered would urge policymakers, administrators, and practitioners to abandon current mainstream wisdom of just making hardware and software accessible and offering a menu of professional development. Those who would accept an alternative explanation would see the slow development of imaginative hybrids among occasional and serious teacher-users as an outcome to cheer rather than to censure.

I end where I began. Technophiles and technophobes have debated often and loudly about the virtues and vices of the new machines. The debates seldom have shed light on the conundrum of teacher use of new technologies after two decades of hype and massive expenditures. Teacher use in general and special education has been uneven, erratic, and, for technophiles, far too slow and unimaginative. I have argued that the historical legacy of technological innovation in schools and how policymakers have framed the uses of technology in classrooms have affected both implementation and classroom use. I have contrasted the present popular explanation for teacher use—framing the problem as flawed implementation and its obvious solution—with an alternative one that points toward very different strategies.

Taking a step back from the squabbles over whether computers should be in classrooms, labs, or media centers to view how historical data about teacher use of technologies is grafted onto a strategy of implementation is helpful in illuminating how a problem is framed and what solutions are chosen. Taking a step back from battles over buying laptops and antipornography filters for Internet-wired machines to analyze variations in use among general and special educators and ask questions that seldom get asked can be helpful in determining what the problems are and what solutions seem most sensible. Such steps backward ultimately can mean steps forward in arriving at workable compromises for managing a stubborn conundrum to better help teachers teach and students learn.

of high access, but inferring high use by teachers and students is a leap of faith, not factual accuracy. Most statistics are derived from surveys of school officials and self-reports from teachers. Although such information is helpful, overestimates of use are common. Combining the few actual classroom studies researchers have done with teacher reports and student reports of computer use offers increased reliability.

3. In using the word *slow,* I mean it as a relative comparison to the computerization of the workplace in manufacturing, business, military, hospitals, and other institutions. See Cuban (1993).

4. *Resistance* is in quotation marks because it is basically language used by policymakers and administrators to characterize motives of teachers who object to a planned change rather than a dispassionate understanding of the teachers' perspective in managing unsolicited innovations that come from outside their classrooms. Of course, there are, indeed, teachers who explicitly fight against and even sabotage innovations that they have little voice in designing or adopting. Such teachers have a point in being excluded from participating in these decisions; they are a decided minority. Most teachers will consider innovations that might benefit their students. These teachers often raise objections if the innovative program or materials are weak or even misguided. After all, just because a new curriculum or program is innovative does not make it automatically worthwhile. They also will raise questions about what they might lose as a consequence of the change they are expected to make and the inadequate help extended to them in making the changes. Often, such legitimate questions and objections are compressed into the favored word of nonteachers: *resistance.*

5. Hospitals are an example of a social institution in which the primary purpose is to restore ill people to health and to relieve suffering. With the onset of managed health care, conflicts over competing purposes of securing adequate profit margins and of helping sick people recover and easing pain have registered noticeably on the public's radar screen.

Notes

1. Definitions of teacher use of computers and other technologies vary. Much depends on the criterion used. I define *serious users* as teachers who routinely use computers as part of their weekly repertoire of activities, that is, at least once a week; an *occasional user* would use them at least once a month. For a discussion of different criteria, see U.S. Congress Office of Technology Assessment (1995, pp. 102-104).

2. Accurately determining teacher use of computers is difficult. Because machines and software are distributed in most schools between labs, libraries, and classrooms, statistics about access or figures showing how many students there are per computer within a school (e.g., 25:1 or 6:1) are misleading estimates of either student or teacher use of the machines. Low ratios of students to computers in a school, say 3 to 1, is evidence

References

Baier, V., March, J., & Saetren, H. (1986). Implementation and ambiguity. *Scandanavian Journal of Management Studies, 2*(3),197-212.

Becker, H. (1985). How schools use microcomputers: Results from a national survey. In M. Chen & W. Paisley (Eds.), *Children and microcomputers* (pp. 87-108). Beverly Hills, CA: Sage.

Becker, H. (1991). How computers are used in U.S. schools: Basic data from the 1989 I.E.A. Computers in Education Survey. *Journal of Educational Computing Research, 7,* 385-407.

Becker, H. (1994, March). *Analysis and trends of school use of new information technologies.* (Contractor rep.). Washington, DC: Office of Technology Assessment.

Berman, P., & McLaughlin, M. (1978). *Federal programs supporting educational change: Vol. VIII. Implementing and sustaining innovation.* Santa Monica, CA: RAND.

Clandinin, J. (1985). Personal practical knowledge: A study of teachers' classroom images. *Curriculum Inquiry, 15,* 361-385.

Cohen, D. (1988). Teaching practice: Plus que ca change. In P. Jackson (Ed.), *Contributions to educational change* (pp. 27-84). Berkeley, CA: McCutchan.

Cohen, D. (1989). Practice and policy: Notes on the history of instruction. In D. Warren (Ed.), *American teachers: Histories of a profession at work* (pp. 393-407). New York: Macmillan.

Colley, A., Gale, M., & Harris, T. (1994). Effects of gender role identity and experience on computer attitude components. *Journal of Educational Computing Research, 10*(2), 129-137.

Cosden, M., & Lieber, J. (1986). Grouping students on the microcomputer. *Academic Therapy, 22*(2), 165-172.

Cuban, L. (1986). *Teachers and machines.* New York: Teachers College Press.

Cuban, L. (1993). *How teachers taught.* New York: Teachers College Press.

Doyle, W. (1986). Classroom organization and management. In M. Wittrock (Ed.), *Third handbook of research on teaching* (pp. 392-431). New York: Macmillan.

Dreeben, R. (1973). The school as a workplace. In R. Traver (Ed.), *Second handbook of research on teaching* (pp. 450-473). Chicago: Rand McNally.

Dreeben, R., & Barr, R. (1983). *How schools work.* Chicago: University of Chicago Press.

Elbaz, F. (1983). *Teacher thinking: A study of practical knowledge.* London: Croom Helm.

Elmore, R., & McLaughlin, M. (1988). *Steady work.* Santa Monica, CA: RAND.

Feiman-Nemser, S., & Floden, R. (1986). The cultures of teaching. In M. Wittrock (Ed.), *Third handbook of research on teaching* (pp. 505-526). New York: Macmillan.

Fenstermacher, G. (1986). Philosophy of research on teaching. In M. Wittrock (Ed.), *Third handbook of research on teaching* (pp. 37-49). New York: Macmillan.

Fullan, M. (1991). *The new meaning of educational change.* New York: Teachers College Press.

Goodlad, J. (1984). *A place called school.* New York: McGraw-Hill.

Grossman, P. (1989). A study of contrast: Sources of pedagogical content knowledge for secondary English. *Journal of Teacher Education, 40*(5), 24-32.

Gudmundsdotter, S. (1991). Values in pedagogical content knowledge. *Journal of Teacher Education, 41*(5), 44-52.

Hess, F. (1999). *Spinning wheels: The politics of urban school reform.* Washington, DC: Brookings Institution.

Huberman, M. (1993). The model of the independent artisan in teachers' professional relations. In J. W. Little & M. W. McLaughlin (Eds.), *Teachers' work: Individuals, colleagues, and contexts* (pp. 11-50). New York: Teachers College Press.

Hunter, B., & Goldberg, B. (1995). Learning and teaching in 2004: The big dig. In U.S. Congress, Office of Technology Assessment (Ed.), *Education and technology: Future visions* (OTA-BP-EHR-169, pp. 157-187). Washington, DC: Government Printing Office.

Jackson, P. (1968). *Life in classrooms.* New York: Holt, Rinehart & Winston.

Johnson, S. (1990). *Teachers at work.* New York: Basic Books.

Labaree, D. (1997). Public goods, private goods: The American struggle over educational goals. *American Educational Research Journal, 34,* 39-81.

Lortie, D. (1975). *Schoolteacher.* Chicago: University of Chicago Press.

MacArthur, C., & Malouf, D. (1991). Teachers' beliefs, plans, and decisions about computer-based instruction. *Journal of Special Education, 25*(5), 44-72.

Means, B., & Olson, K. (1995). *Restructuring schools with technology.* Menlo Park, CA: SRI International.

Mehan, H. (1989). Microcomputers in classrooms: Educational technology or social practice. *Anthropology and Education Quarterly, 20,* 4-22.

Metz, M. (1990). Real school: A universal drama amid disparate experience. In D. Mitchell & M. Goertz (Eds.), *Education politics for the new century* (pp. 75-79). London: Falmer.

Meyer, J., & Rowan, B. (1977). Institutionalized organizations: Formal structure as myth and ceremony. *American Journal of Sociology, 83,* 340-363.

Meyer, J., & Rowan, B. (1978). The structure of educational organizations. In M. Meyer (Ed.), *Environments and organizations* (pp. 78-109). San Francisco: Jossey-Bass.

National Center for Educational Statistics. (1997). *Condition of education, 1997.* Washington, DC: U.S. Department of Education.

National Educational Assessment Program. (1994). *Reading assessment.* Princeton, NJ: Educational Testing Service.

National Educational Assessment Program. (1996). *Math assessment.* Princeton, NJ: Educational Testing Service.

Ponder, G., & Doyle, W. (1978). The practicality ethic in teacher decision making. *Interchange, 8*(3), 1-12.

President's Committee of Advisors on Science and Technology. (1997, March). *Report to the president on the use of technology to strengthen K-12 education in the United States.* Washington, DC: Author.

Pressman, H. (1987). *Making an exceptional difference.* Boston: Exceptional Parent Press.

Reith, H., Bahr, C., Okolo, C., Polsgrove, L., & Eckert, R. (1988). An analysis of the impact of microcomputers on the secondary special education classroom ecology. *Journal of Educational Computing Research, 4,* 425-441.

Rosenholtz, S. (1989). *Teachers' workplace: The social organization of schools.* White Plains, NY: Longman.

Sarason, S. (1971). *The culture of school and the problem of change.* Boston: Allyn & Bacon.

Saye, J. (1998).Technology in the classroom: The role of dispositions in teacher gatekeeping. *Journal of Curriculum and Supervision, 13,* 210-234.

Schofield, J. (1995). *Computers and classroom culture.* Cambridge, UK: Cambridge University Press.

Shashaani, L. (1994). Gender differences in computer experience and its influence on computer attitudes. *Journal of Educational Computing Research, 11,* 347-367.

Shulman, L. (1987). Knowledge and teaching: Foundations of the new reform. *Harvard Educational Review, 57,* 1-22.

Technology counts. (1997, November 10). *Education Week,* 11-17.

Tyack, D., & Hansot, E. (1982). *Managers of virtue.* New York: Basic Books.

Tyack, D., & Hansot, E. (1990). *Learning together.* New Haven, CT: Yale University Press.

U.S. Congress, Office of Technology Assessment. (1995). *Teachers and technology.* Washington, DC: Government Printing Office.

Viadero, D. (1997, November 10). Special assistance. *Education Week,* 14.

Waller, W. (1965). *The sociology of teaching.* New York: John Wiley.

Weber, D., & Demchak, M. (1996). Using assistive technology with individuals with severe disabilities. *Computers in Schools, 12*(3), 43-55.

Welker, R. (1992). *The teacher as expert.* Albany: State University of New York Press.

Wenglinsky, H. (1998). *Does it compute? The relationship between educational technology and student achievement in mathematics.* Princeton, NJ: Educational Testing Service, Policy Information Center, Research Division.

Wirt, F., & Kirst, M. (1989). *Schools in conflict.* Berkeley, CA: McCutchan.

Wolcott, H. (1977). *Teachers and technocrats.* Eugene: University of Oregon, Center for Educational Policy and Management.

Woodward, J., & Reith, H. (1997). A historical review of technology research in special education. *Review of Educational Research, 67,* 503-536.

CHAPTER EIGHT

Designing Technology Professional Development Programs

A. EDWARD BLACKHURST
University of Kentucky

The primary purpose of this chapter is to describe a model that can be used to guide the development and implementation of professional development programs to facilitate the use of technology by special educators and related personnel. A secondary purpose is to provide examples of ways to approach various activities associated with technology professional development and describe how technology can be used in the delivery of professional development programs. Many of the examples and illustrations evolved from col-laborative activities between personnel at institutions of higher education (IHEs) and those in local education agencies (LEAs). The information presented has been synthe-sized from more than 33 years of personnel preparation research, service, demonstration, and instructional projects conducted by the author and his colleagues at the University of Kentucky. Studies have been conducted on the delivery of technology inservice training programs at the local, regional, state, and national levels. Other studies have addressed

AUTHOR'S NOTE: Preparation of this chapter was supported in part by the University of Kentucky and Grant H180U50025 *Examination of the Effectiveness of a Functional Approach to the Delivery of Assistive Technology Services in Schools,* from the Division of Research to Practice, Office of Special Education Programs, U.S. Department of Education. The conclusions drawn do not necessarily represent the official position of the University of Kentucky or the U.S. Department of Education.

comprehensive preservice programs focusing on the use of technology at the undergraduate, master's, educational specialist, doctoral, and postdoctoral levels.

Studies using a variety of research methodologies have generated the information that is presented. Citations of case studies, research and development activities, historical research, experimental and quasi-experimental investigations, evaluation research, survey research, and field tests are provided throughout the chapter to enable readers to access additional information and supporting evidence related to the observations and recommendations reported. In addition, brief vignettes from case studies and excerpts from documents and instructional products are provided to illustrate further the concepts presented in the chapter.

Background

The impetus for the information presented in this chapter began in 1964, when the U.S. Department of Education, through its Bureau of Education for the Handicapped—now called the Office of Special Education Programs (OSEP)—funded the first of what eventually would become a network of 14 regional Special Education Instructional Materials Centers (SEIMCs). A primary goal of the SEIMCs was to provide information, training, and technical assistance about instructional materials to special education teachers. The Educational Resources Information Center (ERIC) Clearinghouse that was operated by the Council for Exceptional Children (CEC) and four Regional Media Centers (RMCs) for the Deaf were added to the network, and a coordinating office was established to facilitate collaboration among the members of the network. (For a comprehensive description of the IMC/RMC Network and its activities, see the December 1968 special issue of *Exceptional Children*.)

The University of Kentucky (UK) operated 1 of the 14 SEIMCs. We had the responsibility of serving special educators in Kentucky, Tennessee, West Virginia, and North Carolina. Our staff operated a mail-order lending library that eventually contained more than 2,000 instructional media and materials suitable for use in special education programs. We also conducted inservice training programs, provided consultation services to teachers, operated an instructional materials locator system, developed instructional materials, worked with State Education Agency (SEA) officials to stimulate the development of local SEIMCs throughout the region, conducted applied research on instructional materials, and collaborated with others in the IMC/RMC Network on projects of mutual interest.

It soon became apparent that the "traveling minstrel" approach to inservice training was inefficient. Subsequently, we began to develop instructional packages in the form of slideshow presentations that could be duplicated and sent to school districts for use at locally delivered inservice programs. We also developed manuals that could be used in "trainer of trainers" programs in an effort to standardize the content of some of our training programs and, at the same time, broaden the impact of our instructional efforts. Many of those early efforts continue to have an impact on the approaches we currently use to design and implement technology professional development programs, as is demonstrated in this chapter.

Although our efforts to provide inservice training to special education teachers were appreciated and well received, we were concerned about two problems that kept reappearing. First, at the inservice level, much of the training that was being requested from school personnel was of the "one-shot" variety. Most of our requests from LEAs were for training about specific instructional materials or processes. In most cases, there did not appear to be a framework for providing professional development to teachers. Training needs assessments were conspicuous by their absence, and little consideration was given to comprehensive or coordinated planning by those in LEAs who were responsible for professional development activities.

A second problem was that instruction about many of the topics we were addressing was not finding its way into the special education personnel preparation preservice programs at IHEs. Our funding agency discouraged us from providing training to students or faculty at IHEs. Because the SEIMCs were located at IHEs, the concern was that our resources would be drained off by our host institutions. Consequently, we were instructed to focus our direct training efforts at the inservice level. However, we were able to provide consultation services to faculty and loan them instructional materials for use in their classes. In many cases, though, we found that many special education faculty at IHEs did not have the knowledge or skills needed to provide instruction about the newer instructional methods and materials to students preparing to be special education teachers. On occasions when we were approached by faculty members for assistance in helping them plan for the integration of content about new materials into their curricula, we often found that their efforts to modify their curricula were sporadic and splintered. Many faculty members encountered difficulty in getting their colleagues to engage in collaborative planning.

The Impact of the Competency-Based Teacher Education Movement

At the time we were wrestling with the problems previously set out, the Competency-Based Teacher Education (CBTE) movement was evolving. CBTE was touted as an effort to improve our nation's schools by improving accountability in teacher preparation programs. A key component of this movement was the identification of competencies that students in teacher education programs should possess upon graduation. (For a comprehensive overview of issues associated with CBTE at that time, see the special issue of *Phi Delta Kappan,* "Competency-Based Teacher Education," 1974.)

Members of the UK special education faculty embraced the concepts associated with CBTE. We saw CBTE as a vehicle that could be used to facilitate revision of both preservice curricula and inservice professional development activities. In sorting through the emerging descriptions of various CBTE programs, we decided that the following principles made the most sense for guiding our efforts to prepare better special education teachers.

Characteristics of Ideal Competency-Based Teacher Education Programs

- Lists of competencies required of students are publicly stated.
- Learner objectives are specified in behavioral terms.
- Criteria for evaluating competencies are specified.
- Alternative instructional activities are made available to students.
- Achievement is a constant, whereas time for students to meet criteria is variable.
- Programs are individualized to accommodate individual differences in prior achievement and ability.
- Both learners and teachers are accountable for program success.

These seven principles were adopted formally by our faculty and were added to the Process Objectives section of our 11-page Mission Statement, which is revisited and revised at least biennially. The most recent major revision was in 1997. At that time, faculty were still in agreement about the importance of those principles. We believe that they are standing the test of time. In one of our revisions, the acronym *CBTE* was changed to *CBPP* (Competency-Based Personnel Preparation) because we use the principles to guide curriculum development efforts for all of our personnel preparation programs—not just those for teachers.

Our faculty acknowledge that these seven principles represent an ideal toward which we should strive. However, reality and experience have shown that there are numerous constraints that make this ideal difficult to attain. For example, it is difficult to hold time variable in a traditional university system that is operated on a semester basis. Likewise, scarce resources create difficulties in providing alternate instructional activities. In addition, traditional three-credit courses frequently mitigate against smaller units of instruction that are often presented in CBPP programs. Furthermore, the state of our knowledge is such that many competencies—or the criteria for evaluating them—have not been validated.

Nevertheless, our faculty endorse the concept of CBPP and view it as a process for improving the quality and relevance of instruction at both the preservice and inservice levels. We further acknowledge, however, that it is necessary to make certain compromises in meeting the theoretical ideals and that our past, current, and future program revisions are viewed as approximations of the principles represented previously. The complete text of our Mission Statement can be found at the department's World Wide Web site (http://serc.gws.uky.edu/www/mission/missmenu.html).

The CBTE (or CBPP) movement has not been without its critics, however. For example, Hirsch (1975) claimed that the accountability associated with its implementation was a danger to humanistic education. Blatt (1976) was critical on several fronts: the difficulty of validating competencies, the potential for graduating teachers who are technicians instead of educators, and infringement of the rights of university scholars to determine the nature of teacher education.

Nevertheless, many elements of the CBTE movement have survived. Those who were uncomfortable with the term *competency* began using terminology such as *knowledge and skills* needed to perform given tasks. Whether one agrees or disagrees with such an "outcomes-based" approach to personnel preparation, the fact of the matter is that accrediting agencies, such as the National Council for the Accreditation of Teacher Education (NCATE), now rely on the professional standards of various specialty organizations when making decisions about whether to accredit teacher education programs at IHEs. The CEC (1998) has established international standards, in the form of required knowledge and skills, for all special education teachers and for the preparation and certification of those who are qualified to teach in different areas of special education. The CEC must verify that IHEs meet those standards before NCATE will accredit a special education teacher preparation program.

We also believe that similar considerations are affecting the professional development of currently employed teachers. This is reflected in documents, such as the Kentucky Performance Standards, that have been developed in Kentucky and are being promulgated by the SEA as a guide for professional development activities and teacher certification programs (http://www.kde.state.ky.us/otec/epsb/standards/default.asp).

Evolution of a Model to Guide Curriculum Development

In response to concerns in the early 1970s about the labeling of special education students, we began to search for alternatives to state teacher certification standards that required us to operate programs according to categories of disability (e.g., educable mentally retarded, learning disabled, emotionally disturbed). We initiated a significant effort that resulted in the development of a "noncategorical" special education teacher preparation program for teachers of students with mild learning and behavioral disabilities.

The curriculum was developed after we identified the knowledge and skills (competencies) needed by special education teachers across disability areas. Commonalities were identified and a common core was developed for the "methods" courses in the special education teacher certification program. Thirteen instructional modules were developed that students in all certification areas were required to take. Class sessions were designed so that the common content areas were delivered in large groups to all students in the various certification areas, with subsequent small-group sessions used to address applications of the content to specific disability groups. We used the principles outlined previously to guide our planning efforts. We also collaborated in developing modules and used team teaching for the delivery of instruction to capitalize on the strengths of the different faculty members who were involved. The results were encouraging, and students reported considerable satisfaction with this approach (Blackhurst, Cross, Nelson, & Tawney, 1973).

In reviewing the procedures that we used in designing our noncategorical methods course, we realized that we approached our task from the perspective of revising existing courses, which is the approach that most university faculty take when pursuing curriculum revisions. After 3 years of experimenting with this approach, we concluded that our efforts were effective but relatively inefficient. We made numerous revisions, many of which would have been unnecessary had we approached our curriculum planning in a more systematic fashion. On further reflection and analysis, we generated a model that could be used to guide future curriculum revision efforts and the development of new curricula. The model identified the various elements associated with curriculum development, their interrelationships, and the sequence that should be followed in its implementation. The application of the model also reflected principles associated with CBTE that were described previously (Blackhurst, 1977).

At this writing, UK faculty have been using the model that emerged from these early efforts for more than 25 years to guide curriculum development activities in preservice special education personnel preparation programs (Blackhurst, 1979, 1981, 1982; Blackhurst, Bott, & Cross, 1987; Blackhurst, McLoughlin, & Price, 1977). Two variants of the model also have been developed. The first variant was conceptualized as a way that special education teachers could design their own continuing education programs (Blackhurst, 1993). The second variant, which is described in the next section of this chapter, provides guidance to those who are designing inservice professional development programs about technology applications in special education.

In 1984, as part of a federal grant program, we developed a formal, 2-year affiliation with Fayette County Public Schools (FCPS), the second-largest school district in Kentucky. A consortium was formed to focus on the implementation of microcomputers in the school district. Many of our efforts were devoted to planning for the use of microcomputers and the preparation of teachers and administrators to use them. We used the curriculum development model that we had been using in our university work to design inservice programs about technology for teachers and administrators. We found that the model could be adapted for such purposes easily and that the resulting inservice training that we offered was effective and well received.

Unfortunately, the consortium project was not highly successful. We were able to increase awareness about technology in teachers and principals, but much of the consortium's work never came to fruition. This was largely due to a lack of vision on the part of top-level administrators in the school district.

Key administrators, starting with the superintendent, did not understand microcomputers, were uncomfortable with them, and failed to see their potential for their students. In addition, they were concerned about the costs that would be required to equip schools with computers and, most important, the costs to provide professional development programs for the teachers.

Against the advice of the consortium leadership (which included LEA representatives), the FCPS administration elected to provide the schools with labs that were equipped with integrated learning systems (ILSs). Contracts for the ILS labs included hardware, software, and staff to operate them. Students were scheduled into the labs on a regular basis, where they received preprogrammed instruction via the ILS. Computers were not made available in classrooms and, consequently, there was no need to train teachers in computer literacy. The result was that personnel in this very large school district did not participate in many of the important developments in technology that occurred in the 1980s and early 1990s.

In 1990, the state legislature passed the Kentucky Education Reform Act (KERA) (1990), which has been categorized as the most sweeping statewide educational reform movement in the nation. Part of that reform effort was the establishment of the Kentucky Educational Technology System (KETS), which provided a $400-million-dollar technology initiative to develop a networked technology system within schools and across school districts. Each school in Kentucky and each school district was required to prepare a technology plan as part of the KERA requirements.

We provided a series of daylong workshops to more than 300 school-based and district-based technology coordinators about how to approach the task of developing technology plans to meet KETS specifications. We also participated in the efforts of FCPS to develop their plans. It was apparent, during that process, that the prior inattention to technology training of FCPS personnel impeded the planning process, because many of the participants were unaware of the potential of technology. Despite this, however, plans were developed for each of the schools and for the district that met the criteria established by KETS.

Concerns about assistive technology (AT) issues resulted in the formation of a second formal collaborative arrangement with FCPS. Beginning in 1995, we have been conducting a project to examine the impact of the use of a functional model (Blackhurst & Lahm, 2000; Blackhurst, Lahm, Harrison, & Chandler, 1999) on the delivery of AT services to students with disabilities in FCPS. A major component of that project was to provide training to key personnel about AT, the functional model, and how to apply it. A second component was to develop policies and guidelines related to planning and implementing technology, in general, and AT, in particular. A major segment of this planning effort related to professional development of FCPS staff. At the time of this writing, these developments are continuing. Time will tell whether they have a lasting impact.

A second project was initiated in late 1999 to implement the use of the AT model in other school districts in Kentucky. In those districts, we formed teams of professionals who are targeted for training in the participating schools. We are working closely to develop collaborative relationships with members of the teams. Those individuals are participating in the planning of the training and providing recommendations about the ongoing relationships with our project staff, including the nature of follow-up support services that will be provided. (The importance of the development of collaborative relationships when implementing change is highlighted in chapters in this volume by Zorfass—Chapter 5— and by Englert and Zhao—Chapter 9.)

The problems that occurred in our prior efforts to stimulate technology training of FCPS staff also have led us to place heavier emphasis on educating top-level administrators about the potential of technology for students with disabilities. We have been working

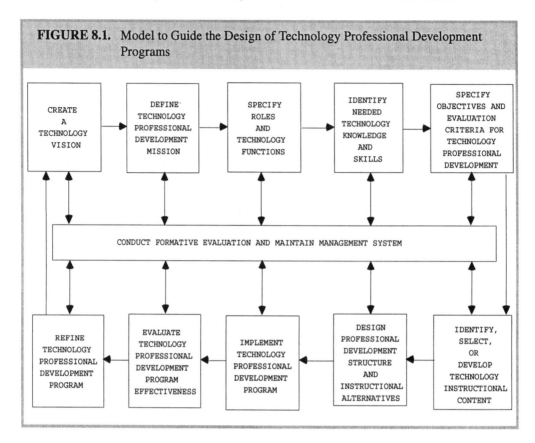

FIGURE 8.1. Model to Guide the Design of Technology Professional Development Programs

to provide those individuals with information designed to increase their awareness. Those activities also have prompted us to modify our technology professional development model. The remainder of this chapter focuses on information about the model, accompanied by suggestions for its implementation and illustrations of its application that have accrued over the years.

A Model to Guide the Design of Technology Professional Development Programs

Originally, the elements in the model in Figure 8.1 were described in generic terms so that they could be applied to any content area. Our current focus on technology has led us to revise the terminology to help users focus on technology professional development. A second change was the addition of the first box (Create a Technology Vision) that highlights

our earlier conclusion about the importance of having a vision of technology to provide a foundation for subsequent activities.

What follows is a description of procedures that we have found to be effective in applying the model. Examples are provided to illustrate how the various steps in the model can be implemented when designing a comprehensive inservice professional development program for special education personnel on uses of technology. Application begins with the element in the upper-left-hand corner of the model in Figure 8.1.

Step 1: Create a Technology Vision

At the time of this writing, we are collaborating in a series of case studies across five federally funded collaborative research projects related to technology applications in special education programs. A preliminary cross-project finding related to technology applications in schools points to a strong need to include special education technology plans in the general technology plans of school districts—as opposed to the development of separate plans for applications of technology in special education. Such inclusion is reflected in the vision statement that follows below.

This vision statement provides the foundation for the development of technology plans

---

Technology Vision

Technology offers a broad range of activities to improve educational opportunities for all students. For example, word processing programs can permit students to write and revise compositions with ease. Students can communicate with experts and other students at remote locations through telecommunication systems. Instructional computer software and interactive multimedia programs can provide personalized instruction and immediate feedback about the correctness of answers. Students can gain immediate access to current information stored on compact disks, electronic databases, and the Internet.

Students who are prepared to deal effectively with the demands of a technological, information-based society also will be able to use computers for personal applications and recognize other potential uses and problems. They will understand what a computer is, how it operates, and what it can and cannot do. They will be able to use the computer as a tool to improve the quality of their lives. They will develop values concerning the computer and its role in society. They also will understand the potential for the abuse of computers, such as violating the privacy of personal information that is stored in data files.

Students with special education needs will be particularly affected by the applications of technology. As assistive devices permit them to gain control of their environment, students with learning and behavioral disabilities, communication disorders, sensory impairments, and physical disabilities will be able to participate more readily in the mainstream of education. Technology can be a valuable tool for those with special needs for repetition, motivation, variety of presentation, individualization, short and concentrated study periods, small incremental steps toward learning, alternative ways to communicate, reduced extraneous input, and one-to-one attention. Computers and their accompanying software programs and related equipment can help a concrete thinker follow and learn abstract concepts at an individualized rate. They can stimulate and immediately reinforce reluctant learners, remove pressures for legible handwriting and accurate spelling from the expression of complex thoughts, and allow minds locked in uncontrollable bodies to communicate.

Teachers will find the computer to be an efficient assistant that can be used to free up more of their time to work directly in educating their students. Record keeping, grading, and report preparation can be greatly facilitated by using computers. Organized, quality instructional programs can be offered to students, and stimulating and reinforcing supplements to regular educational programming can be provided by computer and related technologies. Correspondence with parents and others can be done more efficiently. Individualized education programs (IEPs) also can be developed and managed via computer.

Administrators can be assisted by using technology to maintain centralized and easily retrievable information about students, staff, scheduling, management, maintenance, equipment, and materials. Contact with parents and significant others outside the school can be maintained easily with appropriate computer hardware and software programs. State and federal accountability reports and budget information can be prepared efficiently using electronic databases, spreadsheets, and word processing programs.

Various forms of technology have become an integral part of daily living; and, if educators accept their responsibility, they must prepare students to integrate into a technologically oriented society through responsible, conscientious, and organized preparation and training. This responsibility is particularly critical for those students with special education needs who stand to profit from the use of technology more than many students in our nation's schools.

for all students and includes the acknowledgment that students enrolled in special education programs have unique needs that potentially can be met through technology. This vision statement was developed in consultation with the FCPS representatives involved in our collaborative research project and is being used to guide the activities of our research project. It will be interesting to see whether it is formally adopted by the school district upon completion of the project, whether it will be revised, or whether it will be ignored.

Step 2: Define the Technology Professional Development Mission

Implicit in the vision statement is the necessity to develop an ongoing professional development program to ensure that all personnel in the school district have the knowledge and skills needed to bring the vision to fruition. Subsequently, Step 2 in the process is to define the mission for the technology professional development program. The mission statement serves as (a) the conceptual underpinning for educational activities associated with the professional development program, (b) the basis for decision making with respect to short- and long-range planning and development, and (c) a guide for the role of staff in the implementation of the mission. An example follows. Note how special education needs are integrated into the statement, which addresses district-wide concerns.

Because the program development model is a dynamic one, modifications can be made in the mission statement as feedback is received through implementation of the other elements of the model. In fact, the double-headed arrows in Figure 8.1 indicate that feedback from any element has the potential to affect any other element.

Step 3: Define Technology Roles and Functions

The third step in designing a technology professional development program is to identify the roles to be performed by potential recipients of instruction and then to define the

functions that are associated with the performance of each role. In collaboration with FCPS staff, the role that was identified for special education teachers was to use technology to improve learning, behavior, or motivation of students with disabilities or to teach those students to use technology to enhance their personal productivity.

Nine functions were then defined that were deemed to be important for the successful performance of that role. These statements complete the declarative stem: Upon completion of the technology professional development program, special education teachers should be able to. . . .

- ◨ Demonstrate the acquisition of a body of knowledge about the use of technology in special education
- ◨ Evaluate computer software and related materials for their potential application in special education programs
- ◨ Develop a plan for technology use in a special education program
- ◨ Use technology in special education assessment and planning
- ◨ Use technology to facilitate instruction in special education programs
- ◨ Use technology to compensate for learning barriers that are due to communication disorders, physical disabilities, learning and behavioral disabilities, or visual impairments
- ◨ Use technology to generate teaching aids for the special education classroom
- ◨ Use a computer as an aid to personal productivity
- ◨ Assemble, operate, and maintain the components of technology systems in a special education environment

Step 4: Identify Technology Knowledge and Skills

Once technology functions are defined, the knowledge and skills associated with those functions are identified. A task analysis was performed to identify the knowledge and skills associated with each of the functions

Technology Professional Development Mission

The primary goal of the Technology Professional Development Program is to ensure that all personnel employed by the district have the knowledge and skills necessary to use technology to enable them to accomplish their assigned responsibilities in an effective and efficient manner.

Professional development activities will be provided to meet the following specific goals:

- Students and staff will be able to use technology to enhance their personal productivity.

- Teachers will be able to integrate technology into the school curriculum.

- Students with special education needs will be able to function in the school environment through the use of instructional and assistive technologies.

- Personnel responsible for working with students who have medical needs will be able to operate equipment required to support the existence of such students while they are in school.

- School administrators and associated personnel will be able to use technology to manage school operations.

- School personnel will be able to collect data to evaluate the impact of the use of technology and make revisions in policies and procedures based upon the evaluation data.

Implementation

All staff are required to prepare a Professional Development Plan, which is updated on an annual basis. At the time of initial development, and with each revision, staff will include the technology professional development needed or planned for the ensuing year. Technology Self-Assessments will be made available to different categories of personnel to assist in planning professional development activities.

Central Administration will circulate a needs assessment to determine technology professional development needs and to identify those that are common across categories of personnel. Specific technology professional development programs and support systems will be developed based on the results of the needs assessments. Staff will be able to enroll in professional development programs that fit their individual professional development plans.

Professional development activities will be based on the knowledge and skills needed to become proficient in the use of various technologies. Criteria for evaluating mastery will be included in the design of all professional development programs. Whenever possible, alternative learning activities will be made available. Instruction typically will include a blend of didactic instruction, observation of successful practices, and hands-on experiences.

listed previously. For example, seven competencies were identified that associated with the function on Using Technology to Facilitate Instruction in Special Education Programs:

◻ Use technology to support effective instructional practices

◻ Teach special education students to operate equipment and run computer software

◻ Use tutorial, drill-and-practice, simulation, and problem-solving software programs appropriately

◻ Arrange and manage the classroom environment to facilitate the use of technology

◻ Evaluate the effectiveness of technology applications in the special education curriculum

◻ Maintain a resource file of information about technology applications in special education

◻ Adhere to ethical standards when applying technology in special education

We have found that it is necessary to revisit lists of technology knowledge and skills continually to ensure that they are in line with current trends, legislation, regulations, hardware, and software. Originally, for example, the focus was primarily on microcomputers. With the development of multimedia systems and the Internet, that original focus was broadened considerably. Similarly, with the mandate in the 1997 reauthorization of the Individuals With Disabilities Education Act (1997) (IDEA—Public Law 105-17) that AT must be considered for every student who has an individualized education program, it became necessary to place additional emphasis on the knowledge and skills needed to plan and implement AT services.

Forty-one different technology competencies were originally identified as important for special education teachers (Blackhurst & Cross, 1993). The current list is displayed in the form of a self-assessment instrument, which appears in Appendix A. That self-assessment is being used to help teachers identify their technology professional development needs and to plan the topics for technology professional development programs.

Methods for Identifying Competencies. When designing technology professional development programs (or any professional development programs, for that matter), it is obviously important to obtain a very clear understanding of the topics that should be addressed. This can be done through the development of competency lists that specify the knowledge and skills needed by personnel who are performing various professional roles.

Beginning with our work in the early 1970s, we have explored different ways to identify knowledge and skills. To date, we have identified 10 different methods that can be used:

1. Competency statements can be extracted and translated from the content of existing instructional materials, workshops, formal courses, and related professional development programs.

2. Task analyses can be conducted based on the roles and responsibilities of different professionals.

3. Assessments of the needs of school learners can be conducted, resulting in the identification of competencies required to meet those needs.

4. Assessments of the characteristics and needs of people holding the positions for which instruction will be targeted can be conducted.

5. Theories of learning and instruction can be examined with an eye toward extrapolating competencies that are required to implement them.

6. Methodologies used in research projects that have resulted in positive changes in learners can be identified.

7. Cluster analysis using a statistical approach can be used to define groups of competencies.

8. Direct observation of people performing given jobs can result in the generation of a list of knowledge and skills needed to perform those jobs.

9. Delphi studies can be performed in which experts identify knowledge and skills through a series of iterations designed to refine their professional judgment.

10. Retrospective analysis of job performance can be used to identify observed incidents of effective and ineffective behaviors on the part of target populations.

At one time or another our faculty and advanced graduate students have used each of the procedures set out previously, with the exception of cluster analysis. We have found that ongoing professional development programs or formal coursework provide a good starting point for competency identification, because objectives and content can be extrapolated into competency statements. Interviews with practitioners and direct observation of them performing the targeted functions also are quite useful. Task analysis is the most frequent approach to competency identification. Individuals or committees analyze the tasks needed to perform functions associated with various professional roles (e.g., Kinney & Blackhurst, 1987).

Task analysis and personal interviews, however, seem to be the procedures that are most subject to bias because of their strong reliance on personal opinions. Indeed, Shores, Cegelka, and Nelson (1973) cautioned about the use of such approaches and called for the use of direct observational studies to identify competencies. Attempts to conduct such studies are fraught with their own problems, however. They are very time-consuming and logistically difficult, and they can inject their own forms of bias generated by the presence of data collectors in the natural environment.

In exploring alternative competency identification methods, we have found that the Critical Incident Technique (Flanagan, 1964) has considerable merit for the identification of competencies. This technique uses reports of effective and ineffective behaviors that are obtained from individuals who have been in position to observe members of the target performance. Its value lies in the fact that respondents must include descriptions of antecedent conditions, specific behaviors that occurred, and consequences of the behavior that lead the respondent to conclude that the behavior was either effective or ineffective. Examples of special education application of this technique are available for identifying competencies required of special education professors (Ingram & Blackhurst, 1975) and elementary teachers who are mainstreaming special education students (Redden & Blackhurst, 1978).

At the time that this chapter was being written, critical incident studies to identify instructional and AT competencies for special education teachers were being conducted by the author. Incidents were being collected via the World Wide Web and through conventional print surveys. The following is an example of how a critical incident in the area of AT was collected and how the information was translated into a competency statement.

An Assistive Technology Critical Incident Report

Describe a time that you observed someone (including yourself) provide assistive technology services in an *EFFECTIVE* way to a student with disabilities or to someone who works with that student. The result of such action should have had a *positive* effect on the following general aim: *When providing assistive technology services, the general aim is to enable students with disabilities to improve their ability to function in the environment.*

Approximately how long ago did this incident happen? ___*Approximately 2 months*___

What specific circumstances led up to this incident? *The student had difficulty communicating his needs in class. He was mostly nonverbal and didn't initiate communication.*

(continued)

An Assistive Technology Critical Incident Report (continued)

Exactly what did you, or the person you observed, do?___*A "Speak Easy" communica-*___
*tion device was borrowed on a trial basis and he was taught how to use it.*___

What resulted that made you believe that this was an effective action? ___*The student*___
used the device and became more responsive to both expressive and receptive forms of
*communication in class. The district purchased a device for the student.*___

Competency Identified as a Result of This Incident Report

Special education teachers who work with students who have severe communication problems should be able to integrate the use of augmentative communication aids into the classroom.

Note that critical incident research relies on memory of respondents; consequently, it is subject to all of the errors and biases associated with selective recall. However, because the incidents are reports of observed behavior, they have more validity than those that represent only opinions. In the final analysis, we have found that the most comprehensive approach to competency identification combines elements of as many of the 10 procedures defined previously as possible.

Cautions About Competency Lists. When developing competency lists or using the competency lists of others, designers of professional development programs need to be cautious about accepting the validity of such lists at face value. It is important to realize that most competency lists have not been subject to empirical validation. The fact of the matter is that validation of competency lists is a complex issue requiring research that is logistically difficult and time-consuming to conduct. Rather than wait for the results of such research, however, instructional designers should realize that there is an evolutionary process in the validation of competencies, as illustrated subsequently.

Validating Competency Lists

Phase 1: Task Analysis

Phase 2: Social Validation

Phase 3: Documentation of Effective Practices

Phase 4: Direct Observation

Phase 5: Learner-Referenced Evaluation

Most competency lists currently being circulated are the result of task analyses performed in Phase 1 validation studies. People who are knowledgeable about a particular topic will meet to discuss the tasks needed to perform a particular job. It is important to realize that competency lists produced in Phase 1 are generally the least valid, but at least they are a starting point.

Often, the results of task analyses developed in Phase 1 are submitted to panels of judges who are acknowledged authorities on the topic in Phase 2 social validation studies. Delphi studies and survey research typically are used to generate competency lists that at least have face validity. Respondents are asked to evaluate the importance of each competency statement presented in a questionnaire format. What follows is an example of a response metric that was used in a social validation study that we conducted (Blackhurst, MacArthur, & Byrom, 1988).

Social Validation Study Response Metric

X = Not sure about the importance of this competency

S = Specialty area; of interest to only a few teachers

N = Not useful

U = Useful

E = Extremely useful for improving teaching effectiveness or productivity

---

It is not recommended that Likert-type scales, such as rating the importance of each statement on a scale of 1 to 5, be used as the response mode in social validation studies. Our prior experience with such ratings indicates that judges typically produce mean ratings of 4.4 or greater on all items. Judges apparently find it difficult to discriminate among items that, on the surface, all appear to be valuable. Instead, it is recommended that percentages of respondents be tabulated for each response option. An example of this type of research and analysis can be found in our national study that identified the microcomputing competencies that special education professors should have (Blackhurst et al., 1988). We used the results of that study to generate a technology self-assessment that special education professors could use to identify their professional development needs. This has been very useful in the postdoctoral program on technology applications in special education that we have operated for 14 years (http://serc.gws.uky.edu/www/complists/profassess.html).

In Phase 3 competency validation activities, reports of effective and ineffective practices are collected. Case studies fall into this category. The Critical Incident Technique, the qualitative methodology described previously, is particularly useful for collecting data about such practices.

Phase 4 validation uses direct observation studies that can verify competencies empirically. Both quantitative and qualitative research methodologies can be used for this purpose.

Learner-referenced evaluation is conducted in Phase 5 validation studies. Investigations in this area are based on data collected about the impact of the use of technology with learners. Empirical studies can be performed comparing the differences between instructional applications that use technology and those that do not. In addition, inferences can be drawn about competencies teachers need from the use of intervention studies, as illustrated in the following vignette.

Learner-Referenced Evaluation: An Example

Kay Stevens designed a computer program that used a near-errorless teaching method, called the *constant time delay response prompt fading instructional procedure,* to teach students with learning disabilities to memorize the spellings of words. The students operated the tutorial computer program independently (Stevens, Blackhurst, & Slaton, 1991). Barbara Edwards performed a study using similar procedures to teach adolescents with learning disabilities how to spell abbreviations (Edwards, Blackhurst, & Koorland, 1995). Both researchers used multiple-probe single-subject research designs and found that the computer programs were effective.

Based on those studies, several inferences were drawn about some of the competencies that teachers need to have if they are to use technology in special education. These included the ability to

- Use a computer for instructional purposes
- Set up a speech synthesizer for use with a computer
- Select instructional content in the curriculum that is appropriate for instruction via computer
- Configure computer software to deliver instructional content
- Operate a printer
- Manage the use of computer-assisted instruction in the classroom

---

Because they are based on empirically documented performance of learners in a school environment, considerable faith can be placed in the validity of the competencies identified through such studies.

It is clear that much needs to be done to validate technology competencies (and others related to special education teaching). It is also clear that the process of competency validation is a logistically difficult and time-consuming process. However, it is our belief that professionals should not delay their instructional design efforts until validated competencies become available. It is sufficient to identify competencies that are deemed to be important and make them available for public scrutiny. Furthermore, it is important that users of competency statements be flexible enough to modify their competency lists as evidence about the validity of the competencies becomes available.

Other Uses of Competency Lists. Although the CBTE movement has been focused primarily on preservice teacher preparation programs, concepts associated with that movement have implications for a wide variety of practical applications in schools, the most obvious of which is for designing inservice professional development programs. However, competency lists also have been used to aid in job design by specifying tasks to be accomplished in different roles. We have found that they can be used to assist various teacher selection processes, such as defining responsibilities in recruitment materials, screening of applicants, obtaining reference information, and guiding the interview process. They also can be translated into instruments for evaluation of performance and accountability reviews. Finally, individuals can use them to construct their own professional development plans.

The technology self-assessment in Appendix A is an illustration of one of the ways competency lists can be used. The self-assessment consists of a set of competencies that were deemed to be important for special education teachers who are interested in using technology in their classrooms. After the competency list was developed, a response metric was added to enable special education teachers to identify the extent to which they had knowledge or skills about each topic and whether they were interested in developing additional knowledge or skills about each one. That self-assessment can be used in two different ways. It can be used by special education teachers to identify knowledge and skills that need to be developed as part of their individual professional development plans. It also can be used as a needs assessment by those who are responsible for designing inservice professional development programs.

Step 5: Specify Technology Objectives

Once competencies are specified and the training needs of the targeted teachers are identified, the next step is to write statements of objectives associated with each competency that will be the topic for professional development. Over the years, we have found that a real danger in the design of professional development programs is to develop instruction that focuses only on cognitive and performance objectives. Three other types of objectives also should be considered: *affective,* *experiential,* and *consequence.* Affective objectives relate to attitudes, whereas experiential objectives refer to experiences for which it is almost impossible to predict the outcome (e.g., visit to a home of a child who uses AT or observation of a person teaching in a technology-rich environment). Perhaps the most critical type of objective is the consequence objective. In such cases, the recipients of instruction would have to demonstrate how the application of knowledge or skill effected positive changes in students.

What follows is a vignette about the application of the different types of objectives in a technology professional development to illustrate their use and their interrelationships.

We have found that consideration of the various types of objectives, and designing instructional activities related to each, can

---

A Variety of Objectives

In a professional development program on how to integrate use of the World Wide Web into the curriculum, special education teachers were taught about the various features of the Web (*cognitive*) and then observed how other colleagues were using the Web in their classrooms (*experiential*). The teachers were then required to demonstrate that they could use the Web to locate and obtain information in a simulation that was conducted in a computer lab and then develop a unit for use in their classes (*performance*). As the result of application of the instructional unit, their students were able to locate, retrieve, and use information that was accessed from the Web (*consequence*). During an actual instructional sequence, the teachers demonstrated sensitivity to the needs of their students by adjusting the rate or method of presentation according to the responses of their students (*affective*).

enhance the quality of professional development experiences greatly.

Objectives that relate to skill development often can be formatted as checklists to guide the monitoring and evaluation of people as they progress through their professional development activities. As with the functions and competencies, the objectives are continually monitored and modified, as appropriate.

Step 6: Identify, Select, and/or Develop Content

After competencies and objectives have been identified, consideration is turned to the content of the program. This includes a determination of the instructional materials, activities, resource materials, texts, and audiovisual aids necessary for meeting the objectives. The content is then translated into instructional units, modules, or other types of programs.

Targeting Professional Development to Stages of Learning. Often, teachers and other school personnel voice complaints about the nature of inservice professional development programs they attend. Common complaints include dissatisfaction with "one-shot" inservice training programs, statements that inservice programs often do not match their needs, and claims that they have prior knowledge about the topic being presented.

Although planning professional development programs that can accommodate a variety of individual differences is difficult, one way to address those differences is to design instructional activities that reflect various stages of learning of the participants. This conceptualization was originally proposed by Haring, Lovitt, Eaton, and Hansen (1978), who claimed that such an orientation is appropriate for all subject matter areas and for all learners, regardless of age.

Our faculty have used this orientation in many areas of preservice and inservice personnel preparation programs. We also stress the importance of considering stages of learn-

ing when designing instruction and selecting instructional methods and materials for learners with disabilities. An illustration of how stages of learning can be used to guide teachers in determining the type of software that should be used (e.g., tutorial, drill and practice, simulation, or problem solving) when teaching students can be found elsewhere (Blackhurst & Lahm, 2000). The concept of stages of learning is particularly useful when instruction is focused on skill development. Consideration of stages of learning also affects the selection of procedures to use in delivering professional development programs, because different methods of instruction are appropriate for use in different stages. (Note how this approach could be used to address the problems associated with differing entry points for teachers identified in the TELE-Web project by Englert and Zhao, Chapter 9, this volume.)

Within this conceptualization, five stages of learning are addressed. The initial stage is *acquisition,* in which learners are taught to respond correctly to some form of instruction. Methods of instruction focus primarily on awareness and tutorial procedures in the acquisition stage. After learners acquire the skills, they develop fluency in responding during the *proficiency* stage. Drill-and-practice instructional activities are provided in that stage. In the *maintenance* stage, learners are able to demonstrate what they have learned over time. Additional independent practice exercises are provided in the absence of instruction during the maintenance stage. In the *generalization* stage, learners respond correctly in situations that are different from those in which acquisition, fluency, and maintenance occurred. Simulation activities are used to assist learners in developing generalization skills, with additional opportunities to practice generalization. After learners are able to generalize, they move to the *adaptation* stage, in which they apply what they have learned in circumstances that are different from that in which they were taught. Problem-solving instructional procedures are used to facilitate adaptation and application. At each stage, it may be necessary to return to tutorial and practice activities to provide remediation if a learner encounters difficulty.

Whenever possible, those who plan professional development programs should attempt to identify the stage of learning for potential participants and develop instruction that is compatible with that stage. The type of content that is provided and the instructional procedures that are used are then targeted to that stage, as illustrated in the following example.

Instruction About Using the World Wide Web

A comprehensive professional development program was created to instruct teachers how to use the World Wide Web, develop units of instruction for their students, and integrate instruction about using the Web into the curriculum. Different instructional methods were used, and a range of activities were incorporated into the program. Different teachers participated in different parts of the program, depending on their stage of learning. What follows is an overview of instructional activities that focused on the use of the Web. Teachers entered instruction at the appropriate stage.

Acquisition Stage: Learning How to Access Information on the Web

Teachers who had no prior experience with the Web attended a workshop session that was held in a computer lab. Awareness instruction was provided that included numerous demonstrations of information that could be obtained on the Web. *Tutorial activities* were provided to instruct the teachers about Web browsers and helper applications and how to use them. The teachers actively logged onto the Web and followed the directions provided by the instructor. Teachers were required to demonstrate acquisition of content by completing and submitting a self-assessment that posed questions about the Web and how to use it. They also had to demonstrate their use of a Web browser to the instructor, who completed a competency checklist to ensure that each teacher had acquired the necessary skills.

Proficiency Stage: Learning to Use the Web Accurately and Rapidly

Teachers who had prior experience in using the Web and those who had successfully completed the Acquisition Stage instruction were provided with a series of scenarios that required that they conduct *supervised practice activities* associated with various aspects of using the Web. For example, they had to locate and download three different helper applications that extended the usability of their Web browser (e.g., audio and video players); conduct three searches using Web search engines and different ways to combine descriptors to locate Web sites; locate information on three sites identified in each of the scenarios; navigate through three sites that used frames and three that did not use frames; locate three sites related to the subject matter that they taught; and download files and information from three different types of sites. These activities were conducted in a computer lab under the direction of an instructor who was available to provide assistance, if needed. Each scenario was accompanied by a series of questions, the responses to which were checked by the instructor.

(continued)

Instruction About Using the World Wide Web *(continued)*

Maintenance Stage: Accurate Web Use in the Absence of Instruction

Each teacher was provided with a WebQuest that was to be completed independently after the activities conducted in the proficiency stage (information about designing WebQuests is available online at http://edweb.sdsu.edu/webquest/). They also had to develop a comprehensive list of Web sites that would be appropriate for use with their students. Answers to the WebQuest and an annotated list of Web sites were generated and returned to the instructor for review. These *independent practice activities* were initiated in the computer lab and were assigned as homework assignments in preparation for the following session.

Generalization Stage: Using the Web in New Settings and Situations

An instructional session was provided that focused on methods to teach school-aged students how to use the Web. Lesson plans for teaching students about the Web were distributed and discussed by the teachers. Their use of the lesson plans also was demonstrated. *Simulation activities* were used to enable teachers to develop skills and practice implementing the lesson plans. Teachers then applied the lesson plans in their home schools with their students. Anecdotal records were kept about successes, problems, and adaptations required in those instructional settings. Checklists were compiled to ensure that students could use the Web.

Adaptation Stage: Using the Web for Instructing Students

Guidelines for developing instructional units that required use of the Web in several different content areas were presented to teachers. Several sample lesson plans on the use of the Web were distributed to teachers. Commercially available instructional packages related to the use of the Web for instruction also were demonstrated. Teachers developed lesson plans and engaged in *simulation and problem-solving activities* to develop a unit of instruction that could be used with their students. The teachers then applied the unit in their home school, collecting data about the effectiveness of their units and evaluation forms from their students. Follow-up consultations were given by the instructor to provide any needed remediation or recommendations for modifications in activities.

Clearly, attention to the type of planning illustrated in this example and the logistics involved in providing such an approach to professional development require considerable expenditures of time and effort. However, we have found that attention to such details can pay big dividends in the form of a more proficient teaching staff, greater satisfaction of teachers about professional development programs, and—most important—improved educational opportunities for students.

Using Framed Presentation Outlines. Those involved in providing professional development programs often are faced with a dilemma about the type of handouts to provide people who will be participating in presentations. On the one hand, if complete notes of all points made in the presentation are provided, there is the danger that participants either will not attend to the content or will lose interest. If no notes are provided, there is the danger that the burden of note taking will cause participants to get behind in the

TABLE 8.1 Presentation Outline

Overview of Assistive Technology	*Examples*

Objective 1: The Assistive Technology Continuum

High-tech: Incorporates sophisticated electronics or computers	• Scanner • Speech synthesizer
Medium-tech: Relatively complicated mechanical devices, such as switches and wheelchairs	• Hand-operated bikes
Low-tech: Less sophisticated than medium tech devices and can include items such as adapted spoon handles, nontipping drinking cups, and Velcro fasteners	• Transfer boards
No-tech: Solutions that make use of procedures, services, and existing conditions in the environment without the use of devices or equipment	• Mixing bowl wedged in drawer for person with one arm

Objective 2: Functions Aided by Assistive Technologies

Existence: Devices that provide assistance in the basic functions needed to sustain life	• Retrofit toilet seat
Communication: Devices that facilitate the reception, internalization, and expression of information	• Phone system for deaf
Items that stabilize, support, or protect portions of the body that require them	
Devices that help a person move about horizontally, vertically, or laterally. Items in this category can be used for horizontal travel, lateral transfer, and vertical elevation.	

presentation, become fatigued, lose interest, or leave the presentation without valuable reference materials.

Our faculty have explored a number of strategies for dealing with this problem and have found that a good approach is to use specially designed handouts to facilitate participant note taking. Such handouts are developed in the form of a *framed presentation outline* (see Table 8.1). These handouts contain a list of the objectives for the presentation, printed information, mutilated phrases and sentences, and space for additional notes. The mutilated items typically contain blanks for participants to enter information that is presented in visual displays, such as projected transparencies or

presentation graphics. The following is an example of a partially completed framed presentation outline that was used in a professional development program that introduced information about AT to teachers.

As can be seen from this example, the participant filled in the blanks with important concepts that were presented. That individual also jotted notes (in this case about video examples that were shown of types of ATs). The definitions associated with the terms and concepts already were printed on the outline, relieving the learner of the burden of having to write them.

Long experience with the use of framed presentation outlines has documented their value in professional development programs. Feedback from participants who have used handouts in this format has indicated that the framed outlines typically help them to (a) maintain their attention on the topic being presented, (b) keep them in sequence with the presenter, (c) reduce the frustration of attempting to copy large amounts of important information, (d) reduce writer's cramp, and (e) provide a useful resource they can take with them for future reference (Blackhurst & Morse, 1996).

Step 7: Design Structure

The structure of the professional development programs depends on the nature of the objectives and content that are to be delivered. This will vary from traditional lecture/discussion, simulations, the use of videotapes and other multimedia, computer-assisted instruction, coursework presented via the Web, hands-on contact with technological devices, and practica in the use of technology. Some programs are delivered in large groups, others may be in small-group, independent study, or one-to-one tutorials. The important thing to note is that the structure should be dictated by the competencies, objectives, and content. Too frequently, professional development designers start with a predetermined format and then work backward. Often, that approach does not lend itself to the most effective outcomes.

Technology Options for Delivering Professional Development Programs. Traditionally, group instruction has been employed as the most common vehicle for delivering professional development programs. Such instruction typically has been provided in small-group, large-group, and workshop formats. However, technology is playing an increasingly important role in the delivery of instruction for professional development programs. With the increased sophistication and availability of technology—particularly computers—the array of options for delivering instruction has been expanded greatly.

The array of professional development providers also has broadened considerably. Historically, professional development programs were most often considered to be the responsibility of individual school districts and professional organizations. There is an increasing number of state- and federally funded projects designed to provide professional development on topics that have broad implications across school district lines. Private, for-profit organizations also are providing professional development products and workshops. It is anticipated that there will be a continual increase in the number of instructional delivery options that are available and in the number of organizations that will provide such options.

When planning the use of technology to deliver professional development programs, we have found that a useful perspective is to focus on a continuum of options ranging from *no-tech* to *high-tech.* High-tech options use sophisticated electronic systems such as communication satellites, compressed interactive video, and computer systems that employ the Internet and its components for interactive instruction. Medium-tech systems use computer-assisted instruction programs and multimedia products that can be made available in a variety of delivery modes. Low-tech delivery options include the use of print modules, correspondence courses, videotapes, audiotapes, and related products that can be delivered by instructors or used independently by learners. No-tech options are those that require the face-to-face, personal contact typical of one-to-one tutorials or group presentations.

Decisions about which options should be employed for any given professional development program should be dependent on the location of the proposed participants, the types of objectives that are to be developed, the content that is to be delivered, and the availability of technology resources. Increasingly, combinations of approaches across the technology continuum are being seen. For example, no-tech presentations often are supported by the use of medium-tech, computer-displayed presentation graphics. The remainder of this section is devoted to descriptions of several technologies that we have found to be useful in teaching about technology applications in special education.

Anchored Instruction. An option for providing instruction about technology applications in special education that is showing considerable promise is *anchored instruction.* According to Hasselbring (1994), anchored instruction involves the development and use of shared experiences between the teacher and the learner that can help the learner construct new knowledge and understanding through the development of rich mental models. The rationale for the use of anchored instruction is that instructors face learners with a wide range of dissimilar backgrounds. Consequently, there is often no common reference point (or shared knowledge) between instructors and learners upon which instruction can be based. For example, one can talk about the use of an infrared scanning device to operate a communication aid to assist people who have difficulty speaking, but it is easy to develop misconceptions about such devices unless one experiences them or sees examples of them. To rectify this problem, conceptual anchors, in the form of very brief audio and/or video vignettes that can serve as examples, are integrated into instructional programs to provide a common frame of reference for learners. Once the common frame of reference is established, instruction can proceed in a quicker and more efficient fashion than when traditional verbal examples are provided to learners.

Researchers (e.g., Brown, Collins, & Duiguid, 1989; Cognition and Technology Group at Vanderbilt Learning Technology Center, 1993a, 1993b; Sherwood, Kinzer, Hasselbring, & Bransford, 1987) have been developing multimedia materials that use anchored instruction. Their research has documented the success of this approach across a range of learners.

Multimedia instructional materials incorporate two or more of the following media forms: text, drawings, pictures, animation, sound, computer programs, or moving pictures. For example, an inservice program that uses slides and audiotapes would be considered a multimedia presentation, as would a videodisc program that is controlled by a computer.

In recent years, technological advances have led to the development of *hypermedia instructional materials.* Hypermedia instructional programs use computers to control access to text, graphics, sound, and animated images (Blackhurst & Cross, 1993; Hasselbring, Goin, & Wissick, 1989). Although multimedia instructional programs most frequently present information in a linear fashion, the use of computers to control the display of information provides the ability to access information in nonlinear ways. For example, with appropriately designed hypermedia computer programs, an instructor can click a mouse pointing device on "hot spots" or "buttons" on the computer screen, which provide links to other information (Howell, 1992). Thus, a mouse-click on a word could produce a definition of that word, or a mouse-click on the name of an assistive device could produce an image from a videodisc or CD-ROM that shows a picture of the device and then a brief video illustrating its use.

Although multimedia programs can be developed to present anchored instruction, we have found that hypermedia programs can provide greater flexibility in such instructional programs. Presenters using multimedia programs are most frequently restricted to the presentation of information in the sequence in which the presentation was designed. On the other hand, presenters using well-designed hypermedia programs can modify the sequence of instruction or can provide enrichment or supplementary information based on questions or comments from participants.

We conducted a study to explore the use of anchored instruction to provide instruction about AT to a range of potential special education audiences: undergraduate students, graduate students, and practicing professionals (Blackhurst & Morse, 1996). Forty-nine video vignettes ranging from still photos to videos that lasted up to 3 minutes (most ranged from 15 to 45 seconds) were placed on a videodisc. A presentation graphics program was developed that enabled the instructor to click on hot links at different places in the presentation to display the video images. A framed presentation outline (see Table 8.1) was developed to facilitate note taking.

Three field tests were conducted to obtain reactions from the different target groups. Reactions from all groups were very positive, with the best reactions coming from the practicing professionals. An average rating of 4.8 across 12 variables associated with the presentation was obtained from the professionals, with 100% indicating that they would definitely recommend it to their colleagues. Subsequently, the anchored instruction unit was used in a professional development program to introduce school-based special education consultants to AT terms and concepts. It also was used to provide statewide training to speech/language pathologists and physical therapists via compressed interactive video.

Although there are significant development costs (time, obtaining vignettes, preparing media, and projection equipment) involved in the preparation of programs in anchored instruction format, they appear to be worth the effort. In addition to enhancing learning, the programs, once developed, make it easy to replicate instruction. Additional information about designing such programs is available from the sources cited in this section.

Communication Satellites. The use of communication satellites for professional development of teachers was first explored on a large-scale basis via the Appalachian Educational Satellite Project (AESP), which was conducted by UK in the mid-1970s. Funded by the Appalachian Regional Commission with funds from the National Institute of Education and the National Aeronautics and Space Administration (NASA), the AESP delivered inservice instruction to teachers in the Appalachian region of Alabama, Maryland, New York, Pennsylvania, and Virginia. Live and videotaped instruction and inter-

active seminars related to ways to improve reading instruction and provide career education were the primary topics that were broadcast via the ATS-F experimental satellite that was launched in 1974 by NASA (Bramble & Ausness, 1976).

Typically, instruction delivered via communication satellite involves one-way transmission of audio and video instruction to sites equipped with satellite receiving dishes. Audio transmission from the receiving sites is usually delivered back to the transmitting site via conventional telephone lines, unless the receiving site is also equipped with satellite transmission capabilities. Because transmission sites are very expensive, their locations most often are restricted to agencies and colleges or universities that have the resources to develop and operate them.

The growth of distance education facilities, such as those used for communication satellites, has been nothing short of phenomenal. For example, a technology initiative incorporated into KERA in 1990 served as the stimulus for expanded networking and distance education facilities in Kentucky. By early 1997, 1,750 communication satellite downlinks were in place in that state alone. Every school building in Kentucky is equipped with a satellite receiving dish, as are several hospitals, libraries, colleges and universities, mental health centers, and related agencies. This system enables the transmission of one-way audio and video by satellite and interactive audio via phone lines. The Kentucky system has been switched to a digital one that can accommodate three different channels for simultaneous transmission of audio and video to those download sites.

Special education content is being delivered to teachers and other interested parties via communication satellite in this one-way video and two-way audio format. For example, the University of Georgia has been producing special education training in the form of special topical seminars that have been broadcast nationally (Philip McLaughlin, personal communication, April 1998), and UK has been delivering coursework to special education teachers in rural areas of Kentucky for a number of years (Collins, 1997). Production of training for this medium will continue to be restricted to facilities that have the capability of producing content that can be uploaded to communication satellites and to recipients that have the capability of downloading satellite transmissions. With the advent of small receiving dishes, the potential recipient base will be rapidly expanded. The expense of production and the rental of satellite transponder time for broadcast transmission will continue to be a barrier, however.

Compressed Interactive Video. Video teleconferencing has great potential for the delivery of professional development programs across a wide geographical area. Currently, most video teleconferencing systems for distance education programs are in the form of compressed video, which provides for live, interactive audio and video. Compressed video requires digital telephone lines and the use of devices called *codecs* (compression decoders) at the connected sites. The rates of video transmission are typically in the range of 10 to 15 frames per second (compared to 30 frames per second for commercial television or videotape). This lower rate of transmission results in video that is somewhat "jerky." The compression rate is dependent on the quality of the telephone lines and of the codecs (Moore & Kearsley, 1996).

Compressed video, however, with its two-way, live, face-to-face communication capability, is most like traditional group instruction and is often preferred by learners (in contrast to the one-way video and two-way audio of most instruction via communication satellite). For example, compressed video was the preferred mode of delivery among the 115 special education teachers who had received instruction over a 7-year period at UK, with 67% of them requesting more compressed video programs. When given the opportunity for open comment, the learners listed 31 comments describing the advantages of compressed video delivery of instruction. Advantages that were noted included two-way interaction,

less travel time, available technology, instructor's ability to see and respond to learners, late evening classes available in some cases, serving students simultaneously, convenience, accessibility, availability, same as being physically present, students interacting with other sites, and ability to move around during presentations.

As with communication satellite systems, compressed video systems require special equipment, phone lines, and facilities to transmit and receive presentations, although they are less expensive than satellite transmission systems. The special facility requirements often result in difficulties in scheduling instruction. People providing different distance education programs often find themselves competing for available time slots.

The Internet and Its World Wide Web. In recent years, the development of the Internet telecommunication system has provided a number of options for the delivery of preservice and inservice education that may contribute to the solution of the problem of remote delivery of education. A summary of many of the options is presented in Table 8.2.

Although different components of the Internet have been used for instructional purposes for several years, the World Wide Web, with its graphical user interface and hypertext links for easy access to sites around the world, has evolved as the component that has the greatest implications for instruction. New terminology and concepts, such as *Web-Based Instruction* (WBI), *Web-Based Teaching* (WBT), *Web-Based Performance Support Systems* (WBPSS), and *Virtual Classroom,* have emerged to reflect this growing interest. In addition, numerous Web sites have been developed that focus specifically on the use of the Web for instructional purposes (e.g., Web-Based Training Information Center at http://www.filename.com; Virtual Online University at http://www.juststeve.com/VOU-Home.html).

Many colleges and universities have been experimenting with courses offered via the Internet. For example, the NewPromise.com

TABLE 8.2 Ways the Internet Can Be Used for Professional Development Programs

Type of Communication	*Illustrative Tools*
Transmission of text messages	Electronic mail (e-mail)
Announcements to all participants	Electronic mailing lists (listservs)
Asynchronous topical discussions	Discussion lists; Electronic bulletin boards
Simulations	MOOS and MUDS
Delivery of instructional materials	Telnet, FTP, or Gopher sites, Web pages with download links
Assessment of student performance	Form-based Web pages
Text-based, real-time discussions	Chat rooms
Real-time manipulation of graphic images	Whiteboard video conferencing systems
Submission of assignments	E-mail with attachments
Synchronous audio communication	Internet phone
Asynchronous audio communication	Audio downloads from Web pages; Streaming audio
Face-to-face visual communication	Desktop video conferencing (CU-See Me)
Distribution of motion video	Downloaded digital movies and streaming video (QuickTime); Shockwave videos
Internet access plus wideband audio and video	Internet plus hybrid CD-ROMs
Management of the delivery of instruction	Education Web servers (TopClass)

SOURCE: Adapted from Pernell, 1996.

Web site lists more than 2,400 courses that can be taken via the Internet (http://www.caso.com/index.html). The western states have formed a "Virtual University," called the Western Governors University (http://www.wgu.edu/wgu/index.html). The "World Lecture Hall" at the University of Texas lists hundreds of courses on a variety of topics. Syllabi and related materials for those courses are available at that Web site for perusal by interested parties (http://www.utexas.edu/world/lecture).

The most comprehensive study of the status of distance education programs in IHEs was conducted in 1995 by the National Center for Education Statistics (Lewis, Alexander, & Farris, 1997). A representative sample of 1,276 IHEs provided information about current and projected distance education activities. Projections from that investigation indicated that one third of IHEs in the United States offered distance education courses, and an additional 25% were planning to do so by 1998. The data indicated that WBI would play an increasingly important role in the delivery of distance education. For example, among the IHEs that offered distance education programs, 74% were planning to start or increase their use of computer-based technologies, such as the Internet, for the delivery of distance education programs.

In experimenting with the delivery of WBI for the delivery of both preservice and inservice instruction in special education, our faculty have identified a number of concerns about using WBI. Some of those concerns are related to logistics, such as the type of equipment needed to deliver instruction, the equipment required for students, the computer software that is needed, ways to gain access to the Web, personnel who have the technical skills to develop and implement such instruction, and financial resources that are required. Other concerns are related to instructional content, such as the type of content that is appropriate for delivery via this medium, the formats that should be used for different types of content, and how to incorporate audio and video materials into lessons. Format concerns focus on issues related to the design of screens, the approach used to deliver instruction, and how to arrange for appropriate learner interactions with the content. Still other concerns relate to management of the delivery of WBI, such as how to individualize instruction, how to facilitate interaction among learners and between learners and instructor, how to administer tests, how to ensure that learners do not cheat during test taking, how to provide feedback, and how to manage the potentially large numbers of learners who might enroll for a given instructional program.

Most of these issues revolve around the design of instruction, the content to be delivered, and the measurement of learner progress. These are curriculum issues that can best be solved by subject matter specialists and instructional designers. The management issue, however, is one that potentially can be solved through a combination of computer hardware and software in the form of technology systems that can be used to connect students to instructional programs, present instruction, facilitate student interactions, and manage the technical aspects of instructional delivery.

A new genre of software has emerged that has been designed to manage the delivery of WBI. Examples include *Web Course in a Box* (http://www.wcb.vcu.edu/wcb/menus/start.html), *Learning Organization Information System, Lotus Learning Space, Oracle Learning Architecture, TopClass, Online Learning Infrastructure,* Teamscape's *Learning Junction* (Hall, 1997), *Easy to Use Distance Education System* (http://www.etudes.cc/home.html), and WebCT (http://www.webct.com/). Such software systems make it possible to place instructional content on the Web, post announcements to learners, maintain an internal e-mail messaging system among learners and instructors, conduct threaded discussion groups, provide interactive exercises, and post exams that are corrected either automatically or by the instructor.

We conducted a study to explore the TopClass (WBT Systems, 1997) education server software system for managing the delivery of instruction about special education via the Web (Blackhurst, Hales, & Lahm, 1997). The investigation involved the installation of a computer system that could be used to place content on the Web, development of several units of instruction that could be delivered via the Web, and implementation of a pilot study to deliver and evaluate the instructional units. Students included special education teachers and graduate students who were enrolled in a course titled "Telecommunications in Special Education." The reactions of the learners were very positive. In addition, there was some evidence that learners were able to master content that was presented via TopClass and appeared to be satisfied with the operation of the system and the opportunities that it provided for receiving interactive instruction via the Web. It appears that computer programs, such as the TopClass server software system, have features that will enable instruction about special education topics to be delivered via the Web. Such instruction can be provided for either inservice or preservice programs. Guidelines for the design and development of WBI also were identified as the result of that research.

Additional elaboration and explanation of terms, concepts, and procedures related to

WBI can be obtained elsewhere (e.g., Brooks, 1997; Driscoll, 1998; Hall, 1997; Harrison, 1999; Khan, 1997; Kilby, 1997; McCormack & Jones, 1998; Porter, 1997; Williams, 1995, 1996).

Need for Distance Education Programs. Several of the approaches described previously obviously are used in distance education programs. Clearly, there is a strong need for continuing education and distance education programs among the general public. This need was documented in a national telephone survey of 1,122 adults (Dillman, 1995), the majority of whom verified this need and thought that it was important for state land-grant universities to provide such services. Such opinions cut across all age groups, income levels, and backgrounds. Eighty-one percent of the respondents reported that obtaining additional education and training was necessary for them to be successful at work.

Although this study documented the need for distance education programs in the general population, several studies reflect similar opinions of teachers. For example, Bobbitt and McMillen (1994) and the OSEP (1995) have shown that approximately 10% of the 300,000 people who are teaching in special education programs lack certification in the area in which they are teaching. Conclusions drawn from those studies cited the need to deliver university coursework and inservice instruction to people who are providing services to students enrolled in special education programs.

Such opinions appear to be consistent with those of school officials responsible for administering special education programs. For example, we surveyed 97 directors of special education of school districts in eastern Kentucky (Lahm & Shuping, 1995) to determine the need for AT training. Fifty percent of the respondents reported a great need for AT courses to be offered via distance education, 32.1% reported a moderate need, and 17.9% reported a slight need; none reported no need to deliver AT training via distance education.

The professional literature also provides considerable documentation of the effective-ness of a variety of distance education programs across a number of different populations, such as the certification of teachers of students with moderate and severe disabilities (Collins, 1997), preparation of science teachers (Boone, 1995), mentoring student teachers (McDevitt, 1996), using telecommunication systems for inservice education (Blackhurst, 1978), providing support to beginning teachers (Thomson & Hawk, 1996), use of audiotapes to provide technical assistance to beginning special education teachers (Morsink, Blackhurst, & Williams, 1979), using interactive telecommunications to assist elementary school teachers in identifying students with disabilities (Slaton & Lacefield, 1991), and the use of team teaching and compressed video to provide certification programs for special education teachers who are not fully certified (Collins, Hemmeter, Schuster, & Stevens, 1996).

In an effort to evaluate the effectiveness of distance education for teachers enrolled in special education programs, we surveyed 115 participants in the UK distance education program to prepare teachers of students with moderate and severe disabilities and early childhood special education during the spring 1996 semester. Students who had enrolled in any distance learning course that had been offered via communication satellite transmission (one-way video and two-way audio) or compressed video (two-way video and audio) in the department during the prior 7 years received a survey. Forty-seven of the students responded, for a return rate of 41%. Among the responses, 64% of the students requested that the course offerings be expanded; 30% suggested that the program continue as it is, and none suggested that the courses be reduced or discontinued (6% did not respond). Another study of 262 teachers in predominantly rural West Virginia reacted favorably to the use of telecommunications for continuing education purposes (Howley & Howley, 1995).

Such needs also extend beyond special education teachers to other professionals who work with students in special education programs, such as speech/language pathologists, occupational therapists, and physical therapists (Cross & Collins, 1995, 1996). Many of those individuals are located in rural areas or in locations that make it very difficult for them to travel to IHEs to gain access to coursework needed to complete their professional certification or upgrade their knowledge and skills. In attempting to deal with this problem, significant efforts have been conducted to design and implement distance education programs related to special education (e.g., Bynner, 1986; Cheney, Cummings, & Royce, 1990; Collins, 1992, 1997; Collins et al., 1996; Howard, Ault, Knowlton, & Swall, 1992; Johnson & Amundsen, 1983; Knapczk, 1993; Ludlow, 1994; Royce, Cummings, & Cheney, 1991; Savage, 1991).

The value of telecommunication systems such as compressed video and communication satellites was further demonstrated during the 1999-2000 academic year. We set up a series of live, interactive "guest lectures" by authorities from New York, North Carolina, Oregon, and Iowa. Five nationally recognized authorities each conducted a 2½ hour class on topics related to transdisciplinary services, community-based instruction, technology for communication, and transition services for students with moderate and severe disabilities. These authorities broadcasted from their home locations to teachers and graduate students enrolled in classes on the UK campus and at receiving sites throughout eastern Kentucky. Although evaluations of this activity are ongoing, the reactions to the first of these have been extremely positive. As one teacher from a very rural area put it, "I'm so grateful to have been able to interact with that professor. I've read her work and never thought that I'd have an opportunity to ask her questions on a face-to-face basis. This distance learning stuff is terrific!"

In summary, the emerging body of evidence indicates that there is a need for distance education programs for professional development, that a variety of such programs are effective, and that they are viewed favorably by recipients of such programs. This appears to be the case for people across a wide array of disciplines, including professionals who are providing special education services.

A challenge, however, is to train individuals to design, develop, deliver, and evaluate distance education programs. We currently are offering a doctoral program that is designed to prepare such individuals. A list of functions and competencies guiding the development and implementation of that program is provided in Appendix B. Students in that program are learning how to use compressed video, satellites, and the Web to deliver instruction about special education. It will be interesting to follow the graduates of this program to evaluate its impact.

Step 8: Implementation of the Program

The instructional program is implemented as designed. No additional information about implementation is provided, because logistics will be idiosyncratic to the context in which the professional development will be delivered.

Step 9: Evaluation

The program is evaluated according to the evaluation plan. Formative evaluation and summative evaluation are involved. Formative evaluation is conducted during the development and implementation process. It is reflected in the double-headed arrows in the model in Figure 8.1, which indicate that findings related to any element in the model have the potential to affect any other element. Summative evaluation is done at the completion of the program and after any required follow-up activities.

Of the many evaluation questions that could be asked about technology professional development programs, our faculty have determined that three are particularly critical in determining effectiveness and obtaining data useful for modifying the program:

1. How satisfied were participants with the instructional program?

TABLE 8.3 Database Checklist

A S	1. Design a database to maintain student records.	P	M _____
A S	2. Configure automatic entry of date and standard value fields.	P	M _____
A S	3. Configure the database to perform calculations, such as column totals.	P	M _____
A S	4. Enter student information into the database.	P	M _____
A S	5. Sort records alphabetically and numerically.	P	M _____
A S	6. Retrieve and group records using record selection rules.	P	M _____
A S	7. Print tabular data such as a class roster.	P	M _____
A S	8. Print data in customized format such as emergency information.	P	M _____
A S	9. Print mailing labels for students' parents.	P	M _____
A S	10. Merge database information into word processing documents.	P	M _____
A S	11. Delete records.	P	M _____
A S	12. Develop templates to maintain records of teaching resources.	P	M _____

Note: A = awareness of the item; S = skill is developed; P = additional practice is required; M = item was mastered.

2. Do participants attain competencies that were specified for the instructional programs?

3. Are participants able to apply the knowledge and skills obtained during instruction?

As a result of exploring various approaches to evaluation, we developed a template for a generic evaluation form that can be used to assess participant reactions to answer the first evaluation question (Appendix C). The template can be used for virtually any professional development program and need only be supplemented with questions that are specific to the subject content of the instructional program.

Traditional tests for acquisition of knowledge can be used to answer the second evaluation question. Performance events also can

be designed to determine whether participants have acquired any skills that were taught. Checklists can be used by participants to self-monitor their acquisition of knowledge and skills. They also can be used by instructors as a means of verifying skill acquisition. Table 8.3 is an excerpt from such a checklist that we developed for use in a workshop that taught special education teachers how to develop databases and use them to maintain student records.

This checklist served two purposes, one for participants, the other for instructors. Participants monitored their acquisition of knowledge and skills by circling the *A* to indicate they had developed awareness of the item and *S* to indicate they had developed that particular skill. At appropriate times during the workshop, instructors would visit with the participants to verify mastery of the items. If necessary, they would circle *P* to indicate that additional practice was required and provide corrective feedback or other suggestions. If the item was mastered, the instructor would circle the *M* and initial the blank to verify mastery (see Table 8.3).

The third evaluation question is answered through direct observation of job performance. Examination of any products that illustrate the application of knowledge and skills taught during professional development programs also is a suitable methodology, when applicable. The use of checklists and direct observation instruments is facilitated when competency lists are developed, as described previously. Different response metrics can be used with such lists, depending on whether they are to be used as self-assessments or as evaluation instruments.

Step 10: Refinement and Revision

Revisions are made in the program based on the results of the evaluation. Revision activities are performed through a recycling of the steps in the model. Management of the design process and the delivery of instruction also are evaluated and revised, as necessary.

Technical Assistance, Consultation, and Follow-Up

Although not reflected in the professional development model in Figure 8.1, our faculty have found that it is particularly important that support services be provided to recipients of technology professional development programs. We have found that, when many people attempt to apply technology after they return to their regular work environments, "something that never went wrong before . . . will." Such follow-up support most often is provided face-to-face or via telephone.

The Internet has opened new avenues for providing technical assistance to teachers. Such assistance can be in the form of WBPSS that provide a range of resources, including online reports, "ask the specialist" question-

and-answer e-mail systems, online discussion groups, lists of links to other resources on the Web, and online databases. Some of these are operated by professional organizations such as the CEC, some are operated by IHEs, some are sponsored by commercial vendors, and others are operated by individual school districts. Some of these resources are devoted primarily to technology applications, whereas others focus on special education topics. What follows are some examples:

◻ Access to the ERIC Clearinghouses and useful information about ERIC is available from the ERIC Home Page (http://www.accesseric.org/).

◻ Numerous resources related to the special education profession can be accessed from the CEC Web site (http://www.cec.sped.org/).

◻ Searches of the professional literature can be done online using the ERIC database (http://ericae.net/scripts/ewiz/amain2.asp).

◻ The AskERIC question-and-answer service about educational topics, with an emphasis on technology, is operated by the ERIC Clearinghouse on Information and Technology (http://ericir.syr.edu/). Questions can be posted on the Web site and answers are received via e-mail.

◻ Discussions of a variety of special education topics can be accessed via Internet newsgroups.

◻ The Hyper-ABLEDATA database of thousands of assistive technologies and related information can be searched online (http://www.trace.wisc.edu/tcel/).

◻ The Adaptive Device Locator System, which is a useful adjunct to the Hyper-ABLEDATA assistive technology database, also can be searched online (http://www.acsw.com/adlsweb1.html).

◻ Links to hundreds of special education-related Web pages can be accessed from our UK Web site (http://serc.gws.uky.edu/www/resources/resmenu.html).

Some professional development programs include mentorship or consultation arrangements that occur on a continuing basis. Technology can be used for that purpose as well. For example, one of our master's degree students conducted a qualitative study that explored the use of the Internet to support teachers in the management of students with challenging behaviors (Meers, 1998). In her thesis research, she used a combination of face-to-face meetings, telephone, fax, e-mail, and interactive Web forms to help general education teachers design and implement behavioral management systems with students who were exhibiting disruptive classroom behaviors.

Meers (1998) served as a consultant to three teachers and showed them how to use e-mail and specially designed forms on Web pages to interact with her. Their communications resulted in the identification of targets for behavioral change in a student in each of their classes. The teachers received ongoing advice and instruction about how to observe the targeted behaviors, implement a behavioral management system, and collect data to determine effectiveness of intervention. All students showed significant improvement in targeted behaviors, as measured by a changing criterion research design.

Meers (1998) reported that the teachers liked the system:

> One stated that the system was easy, fun, and less time consuming than traditional methods of getting consultative assistance. Another noted that the program was very helpful and reported sharing information with other teachers and parents. These comments are refreshing because the majority of complaints, in past research, have been the time involved. (p. 79)

She also reported efficiency data that imply considerable savings in time for providing consultation services via the Web.

Technology applications also can have significant implications for following up on instruction. For example, we used a low-tech approach for providing inservice support to beginning teachers of students with learning disabilities (Morsink et al., 1979). We gave each new teacher an audiocassette and indicated that the teachers could record any problems that they were having during their first year of teaching. They could send the tapes to the instructor, who then taped responses that included suggestions for ways to deal with the problems. The teachers reported that they found such information to be quite helpful as they worked their way through their initial year of teaching.

Rule and Stowitschek (1991) showed how high-tech systems also could be used to provide support to special education teachers. They used two-way, full-motion video and interactive audio communication that extended directly into the teachers' classrooms, with positive results.

A Perspective About Technology

Technology professional development programs often trigger negative reactions among potential participants, as reflected by this teacher's comments when informed that her school would be required to develop a technology plan, a component of which would require inservice training for all school personnel:

A Common Attitude

I really hate having to learn how to use a computer. I'm no good with machines and I really don't want to spend the time learning how to use one. I'd rather spend my inservice hours on improving my teaching skills. I don't need to know how to operate a computer to be a good teacher.

Such concerns about the operation of equipment have been observed ever since Pressey developed the first teaching machine in 1926 (Nazzaro, 1977). Too often, technology applications in schools have tended to focus on the operation of equipment such as film projectors, videotape recorders, and computers. In the mid-1960s, however, a trend emerged that has changed the way professionals perceive technology applications in education. At that time, educators began considering the concept of *instructional technology.*

After considerable deliberation, a congressional Commission on Instructional Technology (1970) concluded that technology involved more than just hardware. The Commission concluded that, in addition to the use of devices and equipment, instructional technology also involves a systematic way of designing and delivering instruction. At about the same time, Haring (1970) reached a similar conclusion when he examined the use of instructional technology in special education.

We further defined these distinctions 10 years later in a comprehensive review that concluded that there were two types of technology applications in special education: *media technology* and *systems technology* (Blackhurst & Hofmeister, 1980). The former focused on the use of various devices, whereas the latter focused primarily on systematic approaches to instruction.

With the rapid development of microcomputer technology in the early 1980s, increased research on instructional procedures, and the invention of new devices and equipment to aid those with health problems, physical disabilities, and sensory impairments, the ensuing years have witnessed a very dramatic evolution. As a result of exploring such developments over more than a quarter of a century, we have developed a view of technology that is helping us place the various approaches into perspective. This view is a broad one, in which six types of technology are recognized: the *technology of teaching, instructional technology, assistive technology, medical technology, technology productivity tools,* and *infor-*

mation technology (Blackhurst, 1997; Blackhurst & Edyburn, 2000; Blackhurst & Lahm, 2000).

Technology of Teaching. The technology of teaching refers to instructional approaches that are systematically designed and applied in very precise ways. Such approaches typically include the use of very well-defined objectives, precise instructional procedures based on the tasks that students are required to learn, small units of instruction that are carefully sequenced, a high degree of teacher activity, high levels of student involvement, liberal use of reinforcement, and careful monitoring of student performance. Instructional procedures that embody many of these principles include approaches such as direct instruction (Carnine, Silbert, & Kameenui, 1990), applied behavior analysis (Alberto & Troutman, 1995; Wolery, Bailey, & Sugai, 1988), competency-based instruction (Blackhurst, 1977), learning strategies (Deshler & Schumaker, 1986), adjunct auto-instruction (Renne & Blackhurst, 1977), and response prompting (Wolery, Ault, & Doyle, 1992). Most often, machines and equipment are not involved when implementing various technologies of teaching; however, they can be, as is seen subsequently.

Instructional Technology. Although there are differing opinions about the nature of instructional technology, the Commission on Instructional Technology (1970) provided the following definition:

Instructional technology is a systematic way of designing, carrying out, and evaluating the total process of learning and teaching in terms of specific objectives, based on research in human learning and communication, and employing a combination of human and nonhuman resources to bring about more effective instruction. (p. 199)

Typical applications of instructional technology may use conventional media such as videotapes, computer-assisted instruction, or more complex systems, such as the hypermedia-anchored instruction programs and the use of the Web that were described earlier.

It is important to note the various components of the definition and to realize that technology is really a tool for the delivery of instruction. In this conceptualization, technological devices are considered as means to an end and not an end in themselves. Use of technology cannot compensate for instruction that is poorly designed or implemented.

Assistive Technology. AT employs the use of various types of services and devices designed to help people with disabilities function within the environment. ATs include mechanical, electronic, and microprocessor-based equipment; nonmechanical and non-electronic aids; specialized instructional materials; services; and strategies that people with disabilities can use to (a) assist them in learning, (b) make the environment more accessible, (c) enable them to compete in the workplace, (d) enhance their independence, or (e) otherwise improve their quality of life. These may include commercially available or "homemade" devices that are specially designed to meet the idiosyncratic needs of a particular individual (Blackhurst & Cross, 1993). Examples include communication aids, alternative computer keyboards, adaptive switches, and services such as those that might be provided by speech/language pathologists, physical therapists, and occupational therapists.

Medical Technology. The field of medicine continues to amaze, with the advances constantly being made in medical technology. In addition to seemingly miraculous surgical procedures that are technology-based, many individuals are dependent on medical technology to stay alive or otherwise enable them to function outside of hospitals and other medical settings.

It is not uncommon to see people in their home and community settings who use medi-

cal technology. This also is the case with some students who are in schools. For example, some devices provide respiratory assistance through oxygen supplementation and mechanical ventilation. Others, such as cardio-respiratory monitors and pulse oximeters, are used as surveillance devices that alert an attendant to a potential vitality problem. Nutritive devices can assist in tube feeding or elimination through ostomies. Intravenous therapy can be provided through medication infusion, and kidney function can be assumed by kidney dialysis machines (Batshaw & Perret, 1992). In addition to keeping people alive, technologies such as these can enable people to fully participate in school, community, and work activities.

Technology Productivity Tools. As the name implies, technology productivity tools are computer software, hardware, and related systems that enable people to work more effectively and efficiently. For example, computer software such as database programs can be used to store and rapidly retrieve information; word processing programs can be used to edit text material easily; fax machines can facilitate the transmission of written documents over long distances; expert system computer programs can aid in decision making, such as the educational placement of students with disabilities; and videoconferencing facilities can reduce the need for travel.

Information Technology. Information technologies can provide access to knowledge and resources that can facilitate the use and application of each of the prior types of technology. Notable among the various resources for professionals is the ERIC database, which enables people to search much of the world's literature related to education. The CEC maintains a large database of information related specifically to people with disabilities and those who are gifted. The most predominant of the information technologies is the Internet—particularly, its World Wide Web component. Not only can the Internet supply information to professionals who provide special education services, Web sites can be used by people with disabilities to facilitate learning, productivity, personal enrichment, and the use of leisure time.

An Illustration. Each of the technology types set out previously, used singly, has significant implications for the delivery of special education services. It is important to remember, however, that they also might be used in combination. Take, for example, the case of Carrie, a fifth grader.

Using Multiple Technologies

Carrie had a horseback riding accident that damaged her spinal cord. She has breathing difficulties and is unable to use her hands to operate a computer keyboard. Carrie must use a respirator to help her breathe (*medical technology*). She also uses a voice-operated computer (*assistive technology*) with a software program that was designed to deliver spelling instruction (*instructional technology*) using a constant time delay response prompt fading instructional procedure (*technology of teaching*). Her teacher stores progress reports in an electronic grade book program and uses a word processing program to prepare progress reports for Carrie's parents (*technology productivity tool*). She also uses the Web to conduct ERIC searches related to assistive technology and to obtain information about resources that she can use to improve Carrie's instruction (*information technology*).

Although this example may be somewhat extreme, it serves to place into perspective the various types of technology. In reality, it is more likely that only one or two types of technology would be used simultaneously.

Considerations for Planning. This discussion suggests that technology be viewed in its broadest sense when designing professional development programs. Planning should take all forms of technology into consideration when determining the professional development needs of school personnel. (You might want to refer back to the sample Vision and Mission Statements to see how those reflect the different types of technology that were identified previously.)

Furthermore, although it is important to teach school personnel to operate equipment such as computers or assistive devices, professional development activities should be conducted within the context of providing reasons for doing so. Technology should be viewed as a tool for improving the instruction of students and the efficiency and effectiveness of their teachers. Equipment operation can be an important component of technology professional development programs; but such instruction should be viewed primarily as the development of foundational skills. The productive application of those skills is the ultimate goal.

Concluding Comments

Information presented in this chapter has focused on a model that can be used to guide the design of technology professional development programs. Several planning and instructional methods found to be successful over time also were described. Various approaches to the delivery of instruction also have been described to illustrate the potential that technology has for reaching people who may otherwise find it difficult to participate in traditional professional development programs. Ways that IHEs and LEAs can collaborate in the design and delivery of both inservice and preservice personnel preparation programs also were illustrated.

It is important to realize, however, that there are many unanswered questions about both the role of technology in special education and the use of technology for delivering instruction in professional development programs. It is very easy to become enamored with the many "bells and whistles" associated with different technology applications. There is a need for a research agenda to collect data that can provide definitive answers to questions such as these:

◘ What technology knowledge and skills are needed by the different professionals who provide services to students enrolled in special education programs?

◘ How can characteristics of adult learners be taken into consideration when designing technology professional development programs for special educators?

◘ What involvement should recipients of training have in its planning? How can such involvement be obtained?

◘ What instructional procedures are effective in teaching special educators about technology applications?

◘ What are the pros and cons of various formats for delivering instruction via different distance education systems?

◘ What types of ongoing contact and interaction among recipients of training should be provided?

◘ What are the costs and benefits of different technologies for delivering instruction in professional development programs?

◘ What are the barriers to providing technology professional development programs? How can they be overcome?

◘ How can follow-up services and support best be provided?

◘ What is required to upgrade the skills of those who are responsible for planning and delivering technology professional development programs?

Answers to these and other related questions will help to advance the knowledge base and enable individuals who are responsible for designing and delivering technology professional development programs to make informed decisions based on empirical evidence.

References

Alberto, P. A., & Troutman, A. C. (1995). *Applied behavior analysis for teachers* (4th ed.). Columbus, OH: Merrill.

Batshaw, M. L., & Perret, Y. M. (1992). *Children with disabilities: A medical primer.* Baltimore: Brookes.

Blackhurst, A. E. (1977). Competency-based special education personnel preparation. In R. D. Kneedler & S. G. Tarver (Eds.), *Changing perspectives in special education* (pp. 156-182). Columbus, OH: Merrill.

Blackhurst, A. E. (1978). Using telecommunication systems for delivering in-service training. *Viewpoints in Teaching and Learning, 54,* 27-40.

Blackhurst, A. E. (1979). Curriculum planning as an element of quality control in special education personnel preparation. *Teacher Education and Special Education, 2,* 39-41.

Blackhurst, A. E. (1981). Noncategorical teacher preparation: Problems and promises. *Exceptional Children, 48,* 197-205.

Blackhurst, A. E. (1982). Competencies for teaching mainstreamed students. *Theory Into Practice, 21,* 139-143.

Blackhurst, A. E. (1993). Continuing professional development. In A. E. Blackhurst & W. H. Berdine (Eds.), *An introduction to special education* (3rd ed., pp. 218-233). New York: HarperCollins.

Blackhurst, A. E. (1997). Perspectives on technology in special education. *Teaching Exceptional Children, 29*(5), 41-48.

Blackhurst, A. E., Bott, D. A., & Cross, D. P. (1987). Noncategorical special education personnel preparation. In M. C. Wang, M. C. Reynolds, & H. J. Walberg (Eds.), *The handbook of special education: Research and practice* (Vol. I, pp. 313-329). Elmsford, NY: Pergamon.

Blackhurst, A. E., & Cross, D. P. (1993). Technology in special education. In A. E. Blackhurst & W. H. Berdine (Eds.), *An introduction to special education* (3rd ed., pp. 77-103). New York: HarperCollins.

Blackhurst, A. E., Cross, D. P., Nelson, C. M., & Tawney, J. W. (1973). Approximating non-categorical teacher education. *Exceptional Children, 39,* 284-288.

Blackhurst, A. E., & Edyburn, D. L. (2000). A brief history of special education technology. *Special Education Technology Practice, 2*(1), 21-35.

Blackhurst, A. E., Hales, R. M., & Lahm, E. A. (1997). Using an education server software system to deliver special education coursework via the World Wide

Web. *Journal of Special Education Technology, 13*(4), 78-98.

Blackhurst, A. E., & Hofmeister, A. M. (1980). Technology in special education. In L. Mann & D. Sabatino (Eds.), *Fourth review of special education* (pp. 199-228). New York: Grune & Stratton.

Blackhurst, A. E., & Lahm, E. A. (2000). Foundations of technology and exceptionality. In J. Lindsey (Ed.), *Technology and exceptional individuals* (3rd ed., pp. 3-45). Austin, TX: PRO-ED.

Blackhurst, A. E., Lahm, E. A., Harrison, E. M., & Chandler, W. G. (1999). A framework for aligning technology with transition competencies. *Career Development for Exceptional Individuals, 22*(2), 154-184.

Blackhurst, A. E., MacArthur, C. A., & Byrom, E. (1988). Microcomputing competencies for special education professors. *Teacher Education and Special Education, 10,* 153-160.

Blackhurst, A. E., McLoughlin, J. A., & Price, L. M. (1977). Issues in the development of programs to prepare teachers of children with learning and behavior disorders. *Behavior Disorders, 2,* 157-168.

Blackhurst, A. E., & Morse, T. E. (1996). Using anchored instruction to teach about assistive technology. *Focus on Autism and Other Developmental Disabilities, 11,* 131-141.

Blatt, B. (1976). On competencies and incompetencies, instruction and destruction, individualization and depersonalization: Reflections on the Now-Movement. *Behavioral Disorders, 1,* 35-42.

Bobbitt, S. A., & McMillen, M. M. (1994). *Qualifications of the public school teacher workforce: 1988 and 1991.* Washington, DC: U.S. Department of Education, National Center for Education Statistics.

Boone, W. J. (1995). Science teacher preparation with distance education technology. *Journal of Technology and Teacher Education, 3*(1), 93-104.

Bramble, W. J., & Ausness, C. (1976). Appalachia's on the beam. *American Education, 12*(4), 21-24.

Brooks, D. W. (1997). *Web-teaching: A guide to designing interactive teaching for the World Wide Web.* New York: Plenum.

Brown, J. S., Collins, A., & Duiguid, P. (1989). Situated cognition and the culture of learning. *Educational Researcher, 17,* 32-41.

Bynner, J. (1986). Masters teaching in education by distance methods. *Distance Education, 7,* 23-37.

Carnine, D. W., Silbert, J., & Kameenui, E. J. (1990). *Direct instruction reading* (2nd ed.). Columbus, OH: Merrill.

Cheney, C. O., Cummings, R. W., & Royce, P. P. (1990). Training rural early childhood special educators. *Teacher Education and Special Education, 13,* 210-212.

Cognition and Technology Group at Vanderbilt Learning Technology Center. (1993a). Anchored instruction and situated cognition revisited. *Educational Technology, 33*(3), 52-70.

Cognition and Technology Group at Vanderbilt Learning Technology Center. (1993b). Integrated media: Toward a theoretical framework for utilizing their potential. *Journal of Special Education Technology, 12*(2), 75-89.

Collins, B. C. (1992). Identification of the advantages and disadvantages of special education service delivery in rural Kentucky as a basis for generating solutions to problems. *Rural Special Education Quarterly, 11,* 30-34.

Collins, B. C. (1997). Training rural educators in Kentucky through distance learning: A model with follow-up data. *Teacher Education and Special Education, 20,* 234-248.

Collins, B. C., Hemmeter, M. L., Schuster, J. W., & Stevens, K. B. (1996). Using team teaching to deliver coursework via distance learning technology. *Teacher Education and Special Education, 19,* 49-58.

Commission on Instructional Technology. (1970). *To improve learning: A report to the President and the Congress of the United States.* Washington, DC: Government Printing Office.

Competency-based teacher education. (1974). *Phi Delta Kappan, 55*(5) [Special issue].

Council for Exceptional Children. (1998). *What every special educator must know: The international standards for the preparation and certification of special education teachers* (3rd ed.). Reston, VA: Author.

Cross, D. P., & Collins, B. C. (1995, April). *Status of interdisciplinary preparation for personnel involved in teaching special education students in Kentucky.* Paper presented at the Kentucky Federation Conference of the Council for Exceptional Children, Louisville.

Cross, D. P., & Collins, B. C. (1996, April). *Status of interdisciplinary preparation for personnel involved in teaching special education students.* Paper presented at the annual conference of the Council for Exceptional Children, Washington, DC.

Deshler, D. D., & Schumaker, J. B. (1986). Learning strategies: An instructional alternative for low-achieving adolescents. *Exceptional Children, 52,* 583-590.

Dillman, D. A. (1995). *What the public wants from higher education: Work force implications from a 1995 national survey.* Washington, DC: ERIC. (ERIC Document Reproduction Service No. ED 388 193)

Driscoll, M. (1998). *Web-based training: Using technology to design adult learning experiences.* San Francisco: Jossey-Bass.

Edwards, B. J., Blackhurst, A. E., & Koorland, M. A. (1995). Computer-assisted constant time delay prompting to teach abbreviation spelling to adolescents with mild learning disabilities. *Journal of Special Education Technology, 12,* 301-311.

Flanagan, J. C. (1964). *Measuring human performance.* Pittsburgh, PA: American Institutes for Research.

Hall, B. (1997). *Web-based training cookbook.* New York: John Wiley.

Haring, N. G. (1970). The new curriculum design in special education. *Educational Technology, 10,* 24-31.

Haring, N. G., Lovitt, T. C., Eaton, M. D., & Hansen, C. L. (1978). *The fourth R: Research in the classroom.* Columbus, OH: Merrill.

Harrison, N. (1999). *How to design self-directed and distance learning programs.* New York: McGraw-Hill.

Hasselbring, T. S. (1994, June 1). *Anchored instruction—Why are we here?* Presentation conducted at the Advanced Institute on Anchored MultiMedia for Enhancing Teacher Education, Nashville, TN, Vanderbilt University.

Hasselbring, T. S., Goin, L. I., & Wissick, C. (1989). Making knowledge meaningful: Applications of hypermedia. *Journal of Special Education Technology, 10,* 62-72.

Hirsch, E. S. (1975). Accountability: A danger to humanistic education? *Young Children, 31,* 57-65.

Howard, S. W., Ault, M. M., Knowlton, H. E., & Swall, R. A. (1992). Distance education: Promises and caution for special education. *Teacher Education and Special Education, 15,* 275-283.

Howell, G. T. (1992). *Building hypermedia applications: A software development guide.* New York: McGraw-Hill.

Howley, A. E., & Howley, C. B. (1995). Receptivity to telecommunications among K-12 teachers in a rural state: Results of a West Virginia survey. *Rural Educator, 17*(1), 7-14.

Individuals With Disabilities Education Act Amendments of 1997, Pub. L. No. 105-17. Retrieved August 4, 2000, from the World Wide Web: http://www.ed.gov/offices/OSERS/IDEA/IDEA.pdf

Ingram, C. F., & Blackhurst, A. E. (1975). Teaching and advising competencies of special education professors. *Exceptional Children, 42,* 85-93.

Johnson, M. K., & Amundsen, C. (1983). Distance education: A unique blend of technology and pedagogy to train future special educators. *Journal of Special Education Technology, 6,* 34-45.

Kentucky Education Reform Act of 1990. Kentucky School Laws Annual, Kentucky Revised Statutes 156.160, 160.345 (1990).

Khan, B. H. (Ed.). (1997). *Web-based instruction.* Englewood Cliffs, NJ: Educational Technology Publications.

Kilby, T. (1997). *Web-based performance support systems.* Retrieved August 4, 2000, from the World Wide Web: http://www.filename.com/wbt/pages/whatiswbpss.htm

Kinney, P., & Blackhurst, A. E. (1987). Technology competencies for teachers of young children with severe handicaps. *Topics in Early Childhood Special Education, 7*(3), 105-115.

Knapczk, D. R. (1993). Use of distance education and audiographic technology in preparing practicing teachers in rural communities. *Rural Special Education Quarterly, 12,* 23-27.

Lahm, E. A., & Shuping, M. B. (1995). *Survey of needs for assistive technology distance education in eastern Kentucky.* Lexington: University of Kentucky, Department of Special Education and Rehabilitation Counseling.

Lewis, L., Alexander, D., & Farris, E. (1997). *Distance education in higher education institutions* (Rep. No. NCES 970062). Washington, DC: National Center for Education Statistics.

Ludlow, B. L. (1994). Using distance education to prepare early intervention personnel. *Infants and Young Children, 7,* 51-59.

McCormack, C., & Jones, D. (1998). *Building a Web-based education system.* New York: Wiley Computer Publishing.

McDevitt, M. A. (1996). A virtual view: Classroom observations at a distance. *Journal of Teacher Education, 47,* 191-195.

Meers, D. T. (1998). *Using the Internet to support teachers in the management of students with challenging behaviors.* Unpublished master's thesis, University of Kentucky, Lexington.

Moore, M. G., & Kearsley, G. (1996). *Distance education: A systems view.* Belmont, CA: Wadsworth.

Morsink, C. V., Blackhurst, A. E., & Williams, S. (1979). SOS: Providing in-service support to beginning LD teachers. *Journal of Learning Disabilities, 12,* 150-154.

Nazzaro, J. N. (1977). *Exceptional timetables: Historic events affecting the handicapped and gifted.* Reston, VA: Council for Exceptional Children.

Office of Special Education Programs. (1995). *Seventeenth annual report to Congress on the implementation of the Education of Handicapped Act.* Washington, DC: U.S. Department of Education.

Pernell, R. (1996). *Managing online learning.* Retrieved August 4, 2000, from the World Wide Web: http://www.scu.edu.au/sponsored/ausweb/ausweb96/educn/pennell/paper.html

Porter, L. A. (1997). *Creating the virtual classroom: Distance learning with the Internet.* New York: John Wiley.

Redden, M. R., & Blackhurst, A. E. (1978). Mainstreaming competency specifications for elementary teachers. *Exceptional Children, 44,* 615-617.

Renne, D. J., & Blackhurst, A. E. (1977). The effect of adjunct auto-instruction in an introductory special education course. *Exceptional Children, 43,* 224-225.

Royce, P., Cummings, R., & Cheney, C. (1991). Project NETWORK: a distance learning model in early childhood special education. *Rural Special Education Quarterly, 10,* 2-4.

Rule, S., & Stowitschek, J. J. (1991). Use of telecommunication for inservice support of teachers of students with disabilities. *Journal of Special Education Technology, 11,* 57-63.

Savage, L. B. (1991). Satellite delivery of graduate courses for teachers of gifted students. *Rural Special Education Quarterly, 10,* 29-34.

Sherwood, R. D., Kinzer, C. I., Hasselbring, T. S., & Bransford, J. D. (1987). Macro-context for learning: Initial findings and issues. *Journal of Applied Cognitive Psychology, 1,* 93-108.

Shores, R., Cegelka, P., & Nelson, C. M. (1973). Competencies needed by special education teachers. *Exceptional Children, 40,* 192-197.

Slaton, D. B., & Lacefield, W. E. (1991). Use of an interactive telecommunications network to deliver inservice education. *Journal of Special Education Technology, 11*(2), 64-74.

Stevens, K. B., Blackhurst, A. E., & Slaton, D. B. (1991). Teaching memorized spelling with a microcomputer: Time delay and computer-assisted instruction. *Journal of Applied Behavior Analysis, 24,* 153-160.

Thomson, W. S., & Hawk, P. P. (1996). Project DIST-ED: Teleconferencing as a means of supporting and assisting beginning teachers. *Action in Teacher Education, 27,* 9-17.

WBT Systems. (1997). TopClass [Computer software]. Dublin, Ireland: Author.

Williams, B. (1995). *The Internet for teachers.* Foster City, CA: IDG Books Worldwide.

Williams, B. (1996). *The World Wide Web for teachers.* Foster City, CA: IDG Books Worldwide.

Wolery, M., Ault, M. J., & Doyle, P. M. (1992). *Teaching students with moderate and severe disabilities: Use of response prompting procedures.* White Plains, NY: Longman.

Wolery, M., Bailey, D. B., & Sugai, G. M. (1988). *Effective teaching: Principles of applied behavior analysis with exceptional students.* Boston: Allyn & Bacon.

Appendix 8A

TECHNOLOGY SELF-ASSESSMENT FOR
SPECIAL EDUCATION TEACHERS

A. Edward Blackhurst
Department of Special Education and Rehabilitation Counseling
University of Kentucky
©2000

Directions: For each of the statements listed, indicate your level of knowledge and skills. Circle the letter that best reflects your opinion. Place an asterisk next to the items that would be of highest priority for your professional development. The results of your ratings can be used to establish objectives for the development of a technology professional development program. Use the following key:

N = *No* knowledge or skills in this area.

A = Limited knowledge in this area; Need to increase *awareness*.

S = Have awareness; Need to develop *skills* in this area.

E = Have some skills in this area; Need to refine and *expand* them.

P = Have good knowledge and skills; *Proficient* in application of this topic.

AUTHOR'S NOTE: Permission is granted to duplicate and use this self-assessment for noncommercial purposes.

In order to use technology effectively in special education programs, teachers should be able to . . .

Demonstrate the acquisition of a body of knowledge about the use of technology in special education.

1. Explain historical developments and trends in the application of technology in special education. . . . . N A S E P

2. Define terms, concepts, and issues related to technology applications in special education. . . . . N A S E P

3. Identify ways that computers and related technology, such as interactive video, the Internet, and assistive devices, can be incorporated into the special education curriculum to meet the instructional goals and objectives of students. . . . . N A S E P

4. Read, evaluate, and apply information about technology research and applications in special education that appear in the professional literature and trade magazines. . . . . N A S E P

5. Maintain a professional development program to ensure the acquisition of knowledge and skills about new developments in technology as they become available. . . . . N A S E P

Evaluate computer software and related materials for their potential application in special education programs.

6. Identify the purpose of instructional software programs, their objectives, their validity, and the adequacy of the program documentation. . . . . N A S E P

7. Determine the characteristics of learners for whom a software or related technology program is appropriate. . . . . N A S E P

8. Identify the commands required to use technology materials and the academic and physical demands placed on the student. . . . . N A S E P

9. Identify the options that exist to enable the teacher to modify features of software programs. . . . . N A S E P

Develop a plan for technology use in a special education program.

10. Articulate goals and a philosophy for using technology in special education. . . . . N A S E P

11. Identify elements of the special education curriculum for which technology applications are appropriate and ways they can be implemented. . . . . . . N A S E P

12. Ensure that special education students have equitable access to technology in any plans that are developed. . . . . N A S E P

13. Prepare guidelines and rules for technology use in the special education classroom. . . . . N A S E P

14. Write proposals to obtain funds for technology hardware and software. . . . . N A S E P

Use technology in special education assessment and planning.

15. Identify and use programs for assessing exceptional children and
planning their educational programs. ....N A S E P

16. Use computer software programs to analyze, summarize, and report
student performance data to aid instructional decision-making.........N A S E P

17. Use computers to generate assessment reports......................N A S E P

18. Explain the pros and cons of computerized programs
that generate IEPs...N A S E P

Use technology to facilitate instruction in special education programs.

19. Use technology to support effective instructional practices...........N A S E P

20. Teach special education students to operate equipment and
run computer software. ....N A S E P

21. Use tutorial, drill and practice, simulation, and problem-solving
software programs appropriately.................................N A S E P

22. Arrange and manage the classroom environment to facilitate
the use of technology...N A S E P

23. Maintain a resource file of information about technology
in special education...N A S E P

24. Adhere to ethical standards when applying technology
in special education...N A S E P

25. Evaluate the effectiveness of technology applications in
the special education classroom.................................N A S E P

Use technology to compensate for learning barriers that are due to learning and behavioral disabilities, communication disorders, physical disabilities, or sensory impairments.

26. Determine the assistive technology devices and services needed for
students with learning and behavioral disabilities, communication
disorders, physical disabilities, or sensory impairments. ....N A S E P

27. Connect and use alternate keyboards, other adaptive input and
output devices, and construct materials for their use.................N A S E P

28. Use technology to enable students to control other devices
in their environment. ....N A S E P

29. Work with assistive technology specialists and related personnel
to plan for, and use, assistive technology devices and services
with students who need them. ....N A S E P

Use a computer to generate teaching aids for the special education classroom.

30. Use software programs to produce worksheets, tests, signs,
transparency masters, and other visual aids......................N A S E P

31. Use instructional shell programs and authoring systems to develop computer-assisted instruction lessons.............................N A S E P

Use technology as an aid to personal productivity.

32. Use a word processor to prepare lesson plans, class notes, correspondence, and other written documents.......................N A S E P

33. Use database programs to maintain student records and resource files... N A S E P

34. Use an electronic spreadsheet program to store and report student grades..N A S E P

35. Use the Internet, electronic mail, and other telecommunication systems. ....N A S E P

36. Access information from electronic data bases to support professional activities...................................N A S E P

Assemble, operate, and maintain the components of technology systems in a special education environment.

37. Connect and operate audio and video equipment and input and output devices such as alternate keyboards, printers, monitors, speech synthesizers, video systems, and modems. ....N A S E P

38. Configure software to ensure that all of its features will work properly with the equipment being used.................................N A S E P

39. Demonstrate the proper care of technology systems and related software...N A S E P

40. Use simple diagnostics to determine problems that arise and perform routine maintenance. ....N A S E P

41. Use the operating system software and utility software programs that accompany the computer being used to format disks, load, run, save, and copy programs..N A S E P

Appendix 8B

COMPETENCIES NEEDED TO DEVELOP AND DELIVER
DISTANCE EDUCATION PROGRAMS

A. Edward Blackhurst
Department of Special Education and Rehabilitation Counseling
University of Kentucky
1999

What follows is a list of 10 functions and 97 competencies that need to be performed in order to design, develop, deliver, and evaluate distance education programs. A task analysis, based on more than 30 years of experience with a continuum of distance education programs ranging from *no-tech* to *high-tech* was performed to generate the list.

The distance education functions that need to be performed in order to meet the responsibilities associated with the role of distance education provider are listed in boldface. The competency statements are subsumed under the functions. The functions and competencies complete the following declarative stem:

Professionals who are responsible for the development and delivery of distance education programs should be able to . . .

Assess the needs of potential recipients of distance education programs.

- ▣ Identify the distance education target population and its relevant demographic characteristics.
- ▣ Design instruments and procedures for conducting a distance education needs assessment.
- ▣ Collect needs assessment data.

◧ Analyze data collected from the distance education needs assessment.

◧ Prepare a report summarizing the results of the needs assessment and the implications that the data have for designing and delivering the distance education program.

◧ Develop distance education program goals and objectives that will meet the needs of the target population.

Make decisions about the type of distance education programs that are appropriate for different situations.

◧ Identify the options that are available for meeting the needs of the target population.

◧ Determine the procedures that could be implemented under no-tech options, such as extension courses, in-service training programs, and trainer-of-trainer models.

◧ Determine the procedures that could be implemented under low-tech options, such as correspondence courses, printed instructional modules, audiotapes, videotapes, and teleconferences.

◧ Determine the procedures that could be implemented under medium-tech options, such as computer-assisted instruction programs, multimedia packages, and CD-ROM programs.

◧ Determine the procedures that could be implemented under high-tech options, such as communication satellite delivery, compressed interactive video delivery, or delivery via the Internet.

◧ Determine which of the options would be most viable for meeting the distance education needs of the target population.

◧ Identify existing training materials that are available that could be used in the distance education program.

Design distance education programs.

◧ Prepare instructional design specifications for instructional products to be developed for a distance education program.

◧ Identify the competencies to be developed in the distance education program.

◧ Provide a rationale and justification for each component in the distance education program.

◧ Specify objectives for the instructional products to be developed.

◧ Identify the prerequisite knowledge and skills necessary for successfully completing each component of the distance education program.

◧ Develop evaluation procedures and criteria for determining the attainment of objectives in the distance education program.

◧ Prepare a content outline for each instructional component in the distance education program.

◧ Specify the learning activities and alternatives for each component in the distance education program.

◧ Identify the references and resources that can be used in each instructional component in the distance education program.

◧ Develop a plan for translating the instructional design specifications into instructional products for use in the distance education program.

Develop materials for use in distance education programs.

- ❑ Translate instructional design specifications into products that can be used in the delivery of the distance education program.
- ❑ Use the following hardware to develop components of various instructional products: digital cameras, video camcorders, digital scanners, audio recorders, Internet phones, Internet QuickCams, multimedia computers, slide scanners, copy stands, compressed video transmission systems, audio and video editing equipment, digitizing boards, multimedia computers, Web servers, CD-ROM burners, and other related equipment.
- ❑ Use the following types of computer software to perform the following functions associated with different instructional products: preparing print materials, capturing video and audio, editing video and audio, editing graphics, controlling videodiscs, controlling CD-ROM content, developing computer-assisted instruction, generating pages for the World Wide Web, developing interactive instruction for use on the Web, operating modems, connecting to the Internet, accessing features on the Internet, uploading and downloading files, developing hypermedia programs, developing CD-ROM disks, building and using databases, developing spreadsheets, preparing presentation graphics, and other related functions.
- ❑ Pilot-test instructional products developed for distance education programs.
- ❑ Revise instructional products, based on results of pilot-testing.
- ❑ Produce instructional products, with instructions about how to use them in distance education programs.

Deliver distance education programs.

- ❑ Deliver distance education across a continuum of no-tech to high-tech options.
- ❑ Provide face-to-face instruction.
- ❑ Use the Postal Service to deliver stand-alone instructional products and then monitor their use and evaluate student performance.
- ❑ Use the telephone and audiotapes to provide technical assistance and support to students receiving distance education.
- ❑ Provide instruction via teleconferencing.
- ❑ Provide instruction via electronic mail.
- ❑ Provide instruction via communication satellite.
- ❑ Provide instruction via compressed interactive video.
- ❑ Provide instruction via the World Wide Web.

Evaluate the effectiveness of distance education programs and make program revisions based on evaluation data.

- ❑ Define the scope for a distance education evaluation plan.
- ❑ Identify distance education evaluation concerns and evaluation questions related to those concerns.
- ❑ Define sources of data and criteria for answering distance education evaluation questions.
- ❑ Develop instruments and timelines for collecting distance education evaluation data.
- ❑ Collect data related to the evaluation of distance education programs.
- ❑ Analyze the data collected during distance education evaluations.
- ❑ Interpret the results of distance education evaluations.

▐ Make recommendations for modifications in distance education programs based on evaluation data.

▐ Prepare written reports describing evaluations of distance education programs.

Administer distance education programs.

▐ Develop a vision and mission statement to guide the development of a distance education program.

▐ Develop and implement policies and procedures for recruitment, interview, selection, orientation, placement, monitoring, and evaluation of distance education project staff.

▐ Formulate goals and objectives for a distance education program.

▐ Determine the facility and equipment needs for implementing a distance education program and a plan for using those resources.

▐ Coordinate the development of curricula and materials to be used in a distance education program.

▐ Obtain external agency resources and collaboration necessary for implementation of a distance education project.

▐ Develop a budget and fiscal monitoring procedures for a distance education project.

▐ Develop internal and external communication and public relations systems to explain the purpose and activities of a distance education project.

▐ Use evaluation data to make modifications in a distance education project.

▐ Develop procedures for facilitating professional growth of staff involved in the deliver of distance education.

Interpret and conduct research on distance education procedures and materials.

▐ Locate, read, analyze, and interpret literature on distance education.

▐ Identify and describe distance education problems that need to be solved through research efforts.

▐ Use a variety of research methodologies (e.g., descriptive, correlational, causal-comparative, experimental, qualitative, single-subject, survey) to conduct distance education research.

▐ Describe the dependent variables associated with distance education studies and the independent variables that potentially could affect them.

▐ Generate hypotheses or research questions based on distance education literature.

▐ Identify a research design that is appropriate for answering distance education research questions or hypotheses.

▐ Operationally define appropriate distance education terms and concepts.

▐ Develop procedures for obtaining an appropriate sample of subjects upon which to conduct distance education research.

▐ Select or develop instruments for collecting data for distance education research projects.

▐ Develop procedures and materials that are needed for conducting distance education research projects.

▐ Prepare the appropriate documents to ensure that human rights of subjects are protected during distance education research projects.

▐ Obtain necessary resources and permissions for conducting distance education investigations.

▐ Provide training to those who will assist with distance education research projects.

◻ Implement distance education research projects.

◻ Analyze the data and interpret results obtained from distance education research projects.

◻ Formulate conclusions based on the results of distance education investigations.

◻ Identify the limitations of distance education research projects.

◻ Determine the implications that distance education research has for practitioners and for further research.

◻ Write and disseminate reports that describe distance education investigations and their results.

Provide consultation, training, and technical assistance services to others who are developing distance education programs.

◻ Conduct an assessment of a distance education project in order to define needs for technical assistance.

◻ Develop goals and objectives for technical assistance.

◻ Develop a written technical assistance plan.

◻ Identify the responsibilities for both the technical assistance provider and the technical assistance recipients.

◻ Develop a menu of technical assistance products and services that can be provided.

◻ Deliver technical assistance according to the plan that was developed.

◻ Evaluate the technical assistance that was provided.

Prepare proposals to obtain funding to support distance education programs.

◻ Describe the funding process and preliminary planning activities needed in the development of distance education proposals.

◻ Identify sources of funding for distance education projects.

◻ Identify needs to justify the use of distance education.

◻ Use a variety of approaches for preparing needs justification sections of distance education proposals.

◻ Write goals and objectives for a distance education project.

◻ Develop a work plan for conducting a distance education project and use a project planning computer program.

◻ Prepare a management plan for a distance education project.

◻ Define content for an institutional capability statement.

◻ Describe the potential impact of a distance education project.

◻ Develop an evaluation plan suitable for a distance education project.

◻ Identify the resources needed to conduct a distance education project.

◻ Prepare a budget, budget justification, and cost-benefit analysis for a distance education project.

◻ Develop a distance education project dissemination plan.

◻ Explain the processes used in preparing and submitting proposals, negotiating grant awards, maintaining communication with the fiscal agent, and preparing required project reports.

Appendix 8C

**GENERIC EVALUATION FORM TO
ASSESS PERCEPTIONS OF PARTICIPANTS IN
PROFESSIONAL DEVELOPMENT PROGRAMS**

EVALUATION FORM

Insert Instructional Program Name Here

LOCATION: _____DATE: _____

DIRECTIONS: Circle the item that best represents your opinion about this presentation.
Add comments where appropriate. Use this key:

1 = Strongly Disagree   2 = Disagree   3 = Unsure   4 = Agree   5 = Strongly Agree

1. The objectives were met.	1 2 3 4 5
2. Content presented was relevant to my needs.	1 2 3 4 5
3. The presenter was knowledgeable about the content.	1 2 3 4 5
4. The presenter was well-prepared.	1 2 3 4 5
5. The presentation was well-organized.	1 2 3 4 5
6. The presentation was made in an effective manner.	1 2 3 4 5
7. The quality was appropriate.	1 2 3 4 5
8. The session met the expectations I had for it.	1 2 3 4 5
9. Audiovisual aids were appropriate.	1 2 3 4 5

10. Handouts were appropriate.   1   2   3   4   5

11. The demonstrations (if included) were appropriate.   1   2   3   4   5

12. The activities for participants were helpful.   1   2   3   4   5

13. The presenter was responsive to participants' needs.   1   2   3   4   5

14. The time schedule was appropriate.   1   2   3   4   5

15. How much did you learn? (Circle one)
    Not much   A little   Some   A lot   More than I expected

16. The strongest aspects of the session were: _____

    _____

17. The weakest aspects of the session were: _____

    _____

18. If the session were to be repeated, what changes should be made? _____

    _____

19. To what extent do you believe that you will be better equipped to perform your
    professional responsibilities as a result of participating in this session?
    No Better   Unsure   Somewhat Better   Much Better

20. Would you recommend this session to your colleagues? (Circle one)
    No   Unsure   Perhaps, with changes   Definitely

The Construction of Knowledge in a Collaborative Community

Reflections on Three Projects

CAROL SUE ENGLERT
Michigan State University

YONG ZHAO
Michigan State University

Few research-designed interventions have been designed that consider fully the complexity of teaching practice and that target the classroom teacher as part of the change process. To promote deep changes in teaching practice requires the support of an educational culture that functions as a learning organization—expert at dealing with change as a normal function and part of its work as a way of life (Fullan, 1993). For too long, strong links between professional development, classroom practice, and student progress have not been forged (Greenwood, 1998).

Traditional models of disseminating research information to teachers have been characterized by three shortcomings that could be addressed using alternative staff development models. First, staff development models are often short-term, limited to a few professional training sessions. Complicating this problem is the fact that researchers often present an innovation as though it is uniformly similar in its applications across a variety of settings, subject matter areas, and teachers (Englert, Tarrant, & Rozendal, 1993). Successful implementation requires that innovators not only address the initial beliefs, concerns, attitudes, and local teaching contexts of teachers but that they maintain a long-term presence to adapt the innovation to match the evolving needs and abilities of teachers and students. Second, researchers tend to focus on a predetermined research agenda or the goals of the funding agency, which often means that teachers are instructed to use an innovation in a precise manner dictated by developers who are external to the local school context. However, transmission models have failed to make long-lasting changes in teaching practices (Cohen, 1988; Cuban, 1983), and the provision of teaching prescriptions cannot capture the complexity of responding appropriately on a moment-to-moment or day-to-day basis (Duffy, 1993). To implement an innovation effectively, teachers cannot be simply ordered to make changes, especially when the innovation requires complex changes (Fullan, 1991). Deep changes in instructional practices that underlie sustained use are more likely to result when teachers have been active participants in the construction or implementation of the innovation, which brings them beyond short-term superficial changes and develops greater theoretical knowledge and teaching expertise (Englert et al., 1993). Third, change is a social rather than private process. Teachers need time to reflect and talk about practice as well as to receive the support of a community to achieve successful implementation and evolve as professionals (Fullan, 1991; Talbert & McLaughlin, 1994). To assimilate innovations, teachers should have opportunities to reflect on and reformulate their assumptions about the teaching-learning process. This is most easily accomplished when teachers participate in conversations that promote deeper thinking and provoke questions about their practice that can lead to significant and worthwhile changes in practices.

The problems inherent in the staff development components can be addressed in the implementation and evaluation phases of curriculum development. At Michigan State University, researchers undertook a staff development model that fostered educational change through teacher's participation in the collaborative design and implementation of research-based innovations. In three projects spanning 8 years of collaboration, researchers emphasized the collaborative community in the construction of the interventions, as well as the

epicenter for the professional growth and renewal of all participants.

In this chapter, these projects are reviewed to gain insights into processes that favor long-term professional growth and change. Attention is given to facets that might inform the literature about three professional development issues, especially those that address these issues (Sirtonik, 1990):

- ❏ How can a collaborative culture be created to encourage and support educators as inquirers into what they do and how they might do it better? To what extent do educators consume, critique, and produce knowledge? (Inquiry)

- ❏ How can a collaborative culture promote the engagement of educators in a critical discourse leading to the design and implementation of research-based practices that improve the conditions, activities, and outcomes of schooling? (Competence)

- ❏ How can educators be empowered to participate authentically in pedagogical matters of fundamental importance— problems of teaching practice and how teaching and learning can be aligned to support the learning of all students, but especially students with disabilities and those at risk for school failure? (Social justice)

Case 1:
The Early Literacy Project

In 1990, researchers and four teachers initiated collaboration involving the construction of a literacy curriculum for students with mild disabilities. A small cohort of teachers was invited to collaborate in designing, enacting, and evaluating the curricular approach in the first year, and this set of teachers was expanded to a new cohort of teachers in Years 2 and 3. Thus the collaborative culture was continually expanded to include new members, which presented a unique opportunity to study the ways that the community provided apprenticeships to new members, as well as how teacher change could occur on a long-term basis.

The Collaborative Process

From the start, there were several steps that were taken to ensure a successful collaboration. Researchers recognized that collaboration involved a style of collegial interaction between interdependent and coequal parties who are voluntarily engaged in shared decision making as they work toward a common goal (Friend & Cook, 1996). Three key elements were emphasized when the collaborative project was instituted.

First, teacher participation was strictly voluntary. Teachers were invited to join the community based on a genuine interest in literacy instruction. Later, we added the proviso that teachers needed to have time to participate in after-school meetings. Typically, the only teacher participants who did not return to the collaborative community from one year to the next were teachers who felt pressure (from fellow teachers or administrators) to join the project or teachers who had neither the time nor the particular interest in studying literacy. As Vaughn, Hughes, Schumm, and Klingner (1998) reported, "Determining teacher willingness and interest is more difficult than implementers of professional development programs might think" (p. 70). Teachers who participate in professional development programs because of perceived pressures when their real interest in participation is low do not implement many changes in their teaching routines despite extensive support or demonstration lessons in their classrooms (Vaughn et al., 1998). Thus we attempted to account for this variation in teacher participation by emphasizing the voluntary nature of participation and articulating the program's philosophy so that teachers could preassess their interest and alignment with the basic assumptions about teaching

and learning that would likely inform the curriculum development process.

Second, teachers and researchers were asked to pledge themselves to a mutual goal: the development of a literacy curriculum to accelerate the literacy learning and achievement of students with mild disabilities. To create a collaborative culture in which this goal could be attained, the group needed frequent face-to-face interactions that would be conducive to the exchange of information, resources, practices, and materials. The teachers themselves asked to meet in biweekly, after-school meetings in which they and researchers could come together to share ideas, problems, and questions. This raised the stakes for the researchers to ensure that a vital learning community was created that remained responsive and useful to the teachers.

Third, the group established norms for social interactions that fostered mutual interdependence. In the first year, teachers initially looked to researchers to provide answers, but researchers responded to requests to "tell us what to do" with information from the research literature or questions rather than answers to prompt reflection and inquiry as opposed to the generation of fixed solutions. Gradually, the participants came to understand that each member of the group had information and ideas that were vital to the growth and learning of the other members. Shedding traditional expectations associated with what constituted legitimate authority and expertise, participants experienced greater parity and responsibility for the curriculum development and research process, as well as improved feelings of self-efficacy and self-worth. By establishing a precedent that researchers and teachers worked together to exercise leadership in the curriculum development process, a collaborative culture was created in which the power over the topics and the change agenda were mutually shaped by the teachers' and researchers' concerns, interests, and questions (Anders & Bos, 1991; Englert & Tarrant, 1995).

Fourth, the teachers and researchers created communicative norms and mechanisms for intercommunication. A prototype for meetings evolved that allowed for the critical exchange of ideas and information. Typically, in the biweekly meetings, members focused on a literacy practice or innovation that was brought to the group by a teacher or researcher. The participants then concentrated on the educational opportunities that resided in the practice and applications to other classrooms. The group also focused on particular dilemmas, problems, or questions raised by researchers or teachers.

The commitment to the group deepened as the community performed several functions vital to group cohesion and the professional growth of its members, including conversation (exchange of personal information that builds trust and relationships), instruction (providing information, ideas, resources, and materials), problem solving (collaborative decision making involving problem identification, generation, and implementation of solutions), and inquiry (identification of questions, data collection, and analysis). In essence, the meetings provided a support network for change: Teachers could acquire and exchange ideas and resources that might help them build new literacy practices, they could access the collective mind of the group to problem-solve and work out problems of practice, and they had a group that conveyed the notion that "we sink or swim together." Researchers hoped that teachers would have more ownership in the program and be more likely to implement recommended instructional practices if an atmosphere of mutual respect and shared knowledge could be created (Vaughn et al., 1998).

Simultaneously, recognizing that teachers were often afraid to implement new instructional practices because of a fear of failure (Vaughn et al., 1998), researchers sought to communicate the notion that the community was available to help teachers get an idea accomplished, whether that entailed tracking down materials, engaging in problem solving, or providing feedback and teaching suggestions.

Lessons Learned

As we examined the collaborative process of this first project from different perspectives, there were several findings that emerged related to the collaborative process and the teacher-researcher community. These are enumerated subsequently.

Teacher Change Is Long Term. Our longitudinal examination of the teacher-researcher community showed that teacher change proved to be a long-term process, involving several years of participation in a collaborative community. In the first year, teachers concentrated on implementing particular literacy activities; but in the second and third years, teachers developed a deeper understanding of the principled or theoretical uses of the activities. As reported by Vaughn et al. (1998), we found that teachers learned the general features and parameters of an activity but did not immediately know how to maximize its effectiveness or provide the differentiated instruction to accelerate the learning of all their students. Teachers could make local changes in their implementation of specific activities or materials, but the more significant changes in teachers' theories about teaching or their ability to focus on multiple facets of performance within the activity required time and teacher reflection (Englert, Raphael, & Mariage, 1998).

For example, researchers found that new teachers on the project might emphasize student talk or discourse in the classroom, but they failed to understand fully how to turn over control of the discourse to students or how to assess students' cognitive performance within the discourse (Englert et al., 1998). Like all learners, teachers needed time to learn new processes, and it was not feasible for them to assimilate all the complexities of an innovation immediately. Once teachers developed greater automaticity in implementing an activity, they could shift their attention from their own learning to focus on the learning, discourse, and performance of their students. Implementing innovations in ways that demonstrated deeper conceptual understanding of the principles underlying its effective use took more than 1 year (Vaughn et al., 1998). Yet the deeper conceptual understanding of what, how, and why something should be done was vital for teachers to segue student responses to teaching actions, and to distinguish between the valuable from not-so-valuable learning opportunities that inevitably arose during instruction (Fullan, 1991).

Complex Interventions Require Time to Learn. Teachers' uses of innovations in the second and third years of the project were characterized by more consistent and sustained implementations within and across the domains of the curriculum (Englert et al., 1998). Teachers progressed from a focus on single enactments of particular activities to a broader understanding of how the various activities connected to accelerate achievement. For example, in their first year of participation, teachers often halted their instruction of particular literacy strategies (e.g., expository writing and reading) to introduce a new strategy (e.g., story maps) because they did not see how the components connected. In succeeding years, teachers simply integrated these strategies into thematic units so that their instruction was seamless, consistent, and sustained from the start to the end of the year. Teachers needed to experience a complex process in its entirety before they could understand the connections among the parts; correspondingly, as teachers experienced the parts over a sustained period of time, they came to understand the whole.

Learning Follows Personal Interests. Teachers learned best and demonstrated greater risk taking in the areas in which they perceived the greatest need or in which they had the greatest personal interests. Researchers could not mandate what mattered to teachers: If teachers had greater interests in reading comprehension, they expended more energy to address this area, as opposed to studying writ-

ing. Recursively, by allowing teachers to take leadership in studying particular areas of the curriculum, the community was enriched by the greater diversity of literacy practices that it was afforded by the distributed work of its members. Teachers shaped the agenda with their ideas and interests, giving them an entry point into the change process and granting their ideas, questions, students, and classroom contexts a formative role in the curriculum (Perl, 1994). Over time, the literacy practices that were initiated and studied by individual teachers came to be shared publicly in the biweekly meetings and then borrowed by the other members of the community and co-constructed by the group into a commonly held set of literacy practices that came to be understood by all Early Literacy Project (ELP) teachers (Englert & Tarrant, 1995; Englert et al., 1998). This was not to suggest that the process was perfect in accomplishing teacher change. When suggested practices conflicted with teachers' basic views of literacy instruction or their perceptions of learners, they had difficulty adding new practices. However, the support of the community significantly helped teachers maintain their engagement with a collaborative process that was sometimes uncomfortable and that challenged their teaching assumptions and beliefs (Marks & Gersten, 1998). When teachers finally were persuaded through their participation to try new activities and saw the positive effects on students' motivation or achievement, it was often the first step in provoking deeper changes in their beliefs about teaching and learning. In this respect, the community was a more powerful and dominant entity influencing teacher behavior than individual researchers, and changes in teachers' beliefs often followed changes in teaching behavior.

Theoretical and Practical Knowledge Fuels Learning. Teachers and researchers provided different types of information that informed the community—but both types of information were essential. Teachers' implementation efforts and subsequent descriptions of literacy practices provided concrete ideas that were exportable to other classrooms. Nothing instructed other teachers as well as a story (Perl, 1994), and within teachers' classroom stories, the speaker and other members of the community learned about teaching, learning, students, and themselves. Narrative descriptions of practice, for instance, conveyed abstract knowledge in a language form that could be examined, borrowed, and transformed (Englert & Tarrant, 1995).

Simultaneously, researchers embedded talk about theory within these situated descriptions to concretize the meaning of principles that otherwise would be too abstract or removed from practice to be understood. Like two sides of a coin, the practical and theoretical were interwoven to form a multifaceted discourse about literacy instruction (Englert & Tarrant, 1995). Teachers and researchers were interdependent in the types of knowledge they constructed and negotiated in literacy conversations: Together, their mutual talk about principles and practice formed a tightly woven braid of meaning that came to represent common assumptions about ways-of-doing and ways-of-knowing literacy.

Curriculum Changes Need to Be Calibrated to Students. Teachers had to create new roles for themselves as curriculum authorities and developers. When new teachers joined the community, they looked to other teachers and researchers to be the "experts," until they came to understand that all teachers had to construct and transform literacy practices to suit their local contexts. Teachers' continual referencing of the curriculum to particular students and contexts likewise helped the teacher-researcher community continually calibrate the practices to the students for whom the curriculum was intended.

Student Outcomes Sustain Teachers' Efforts. Teachers' implementation of innovations was sustained by the effects of the curriculum on their students (Englert et al., 1993). Students' excitement and enthusiasm for the curricular activities had a pronounced effect on teachers' enthusiasm for the curriculum. Similarly, teachers' descriptions of the effects of the curriculum on their students motivated and influenced the implementation practices of other teachers. Teachers' narratives about their students and the effects of innovations proved to be extremely powerful in overcoming other teachers' biases and resistance to particular practices. As Gersten and Woodward (1992) note, "Noticeable increases in student performance are often the turning point for many teachers, leading them to a greater investment in the new techniques or innovation" (p. 206). The biweekly meetings provided an occasion in which teachers could share their successes, enhancing their own self-agency and leading other teachers to try promising practices.

Case 2: The Literacy Environments for Accelerated Progress Project

Although the ELP yielded successful student outcomes, there were limitations that warranted deeper explorations of the nature of the teacher-researcher collaborative community and its effects over time. One phenomenon that we observed was that the third and final cohort of teachers who joined the project assumed that the curricular approach was fully formed and completed. Rather than viewing curriculum development as an exploratory, constructive process, these teachers tended to hold more traditional views of their roles as implementers of fixed curricula.

Simultaneously, we observed that there was a parallel tendency on the part of the returning teachers to "display" their knowledge of the curriculum. Instead of focusing on their curricular innovations and risk-taking efforts, these teachers displayed their knowledge through curricular artifacts and resources. As a community, participants believed that they had achieved their goal of developing a successful literacy curriculum, but concurrently, the group had lost the norms and habits associated with *continuous learning*. In arriving at the perceived destination, we had lost the habits of questioning, experimentation, variety, and inquiry—the engine and fuel of vitality and self-renewal (Fullan, 1993).

In the Literacy Environments for Accelerated Progress (LEAP) Project, we sought to determine whether the collaborative and constructive efforts of the group could be sustained over 4 years to address a critical problem: accelerating the literacy performance of "nonreaders" and "nonwriters" in the primary grades. A small group of the original group of ELP teachers, as well as two new teacher members, began a renewed collaboration with researchers in the first year of the project. This group was extended in the second and third years (the current year of the project) to include new members.

There were three important charges that individual members accepted when they joined the project, including (a) a willingness to read or study the practices of other literacy researchers (positive stance to learning); (b) an acceptance of risk taking in borrowing, developing, implementing, evaluating, and reporting on literacy practices (positive stance to risk taking); (c) a willingness to transform one's beliefs, activities, materials, or the social organization of one's classroom (open stance to change); and (d) an acceptance of responsibility in contributing to the knowledge-building and knowledge-transforming properties of community membership.

Collaborative Process

The constructive work of the LEAP community was enhanced through several collaborative mechanisms. Discourse communities are characterized by a common language and participation structure for communication among the members (Englert & Rozendal, 1997; Swales, 1991). Initially, the language or referential system of the LEAP project consisted of the activities and principles that defined the former project, which was embedded in the history of the members associated with the first project. These constituted group-oriented ways of "doing and talking about literacy." Although teachers and researchers were relatively satisfied with many of these literacy practices, we attempted to shift talk away from existing practices in which members might think they had the "facts" or "truths" to refocus attention on new practices that might lead to new interpretations, justifications, and meanings for literacy events (Englert & Rozendal, 1997).

Several types of texts were used to promote cognitive shifts and the formation of new understandings, including newsletters, biweekly discussion groups, research articles, video-texts, and classroom artifacts. In the biweekly meetings, researchers and teachers sought to "seed the environment" with new ideas and practices. Researchers brought in research articles for discussion. However, sensitive to the fact that apprenticeships involve "knowledge-in-action" (Applebee, 1996) and that research articles tend to strip knowledge out of contexts, we shifted to the use of video texts as a mechanism for making visible to participants the ways-of-talking, ways-of-doing, and ways-of-responding in literacy activities. Teachers and researchers made videotapes of innovative practices that were being implemented in the research classrooms and then shared these video texts in meetings. Video texts preserved the view of teaching and learning as a situated activity, enabling teachers and researchers to position their respective points of view, goals, and interpretations for deeper analysis and commentary. Researchers used the video texts to make visible the particular types of social interactions, arrangements, theoretical principles, or teacher and student discourse for the consideration of the group. Teachers used video texts to make public their pioneering efforts as they illustrated the successes or problems they experienced with an innovation, pointed out the "messiness" of teaching, or problem-solved with the group about how an innovation could be implemented or adapted for their own or others' contexts. For all participants, the video texts helped resolve questions about "how to make pedagogic situations (organized to produce deeper understanding)" out of the daily lives of teachers and students (Lave, 1996, p. 162).

What was fascinating was that teachers never watched a videotape in its entirety without conversation—they talked over and interrupted the videotape, repeatedly. Experienced teachers seemed to use the videotape to jumpstart their thinking and then jumped ahead to consider the implications of a particular innovation for their own students and teaching contexts. Teachers presented questions and guided the conversation to negotiate a number of practical implementation issues, such as the value of the innovation, the formation of instructional groups, selection of materials, management of time, effects on students, and so forth. Researchers guided the group to focus on exemplars of specific principles, to illustrate the application of research-based practices in classroom contexts, or to develop the conceptual bases for particular practices. In these conversations, the participants scaffolded and directed the group's attention to various issues of concern or challenged others' assumptions. Challenges and conflict were part of the knowledge construction process, often leading to productive changes in the teaching process or curriculum content. Thus our analyses showed that the unit of meaning making was not the videotape, but the members engaged in discursive and social interactions related to the events depicted on the video texts. Seeing the video texts provided the occasion for deeper conversations related to the potential problems, affordances, adaptations, and the joint meaning of various literacy innovations in situated contexts. In this manner, teaching practices assumed their form and meaning through negotiated discourse and conversation. Correspondingly, curriculum was not delivered to teachers by the researchers or by teachers to students (Richardson & Anders, 1998); curriculum was developed in meaningful conversations and activities through collaboration with others in the professional learning community.

Connecting innovative practices to student outcomes was a simultaneous collaborative effort of the participants on the LEAP project that shaped the curriculum development process and the conversations in the community. As already mentioned, video texts provided an important source of data about student performance, as the group focused on student discourse as a source of information about the development of literacy knowledge in students. Video texts gave teachers firsthand opportunities to observe student behavior and consider instructional factors associated with student performance (Gersten & Brengelman, 1996). This careful attention to student performance during a lesson is a characteristic of skilled teachers (Gersten & Brengelman, 1996, p. 70), but one that is very difficult for teachers to accomplish given the rapid pace of lessons. Video texts provided a lens through which all teachers could be spectators of their own and others' lessons, thereby helping them become more observant and reflective about teachers' and students' performance and deepening their understanding of what effective teachers do and think.

Conversations that focused on the explicit links between changes in student performance and teachers' use of innovations also were triangulated with other information. For example, when writing was the focus of conversation in the teacher-researcher meetings, we collected the journals of two case study students in each classroom and completed a sequential analysis of the types of skills and strategies used by students across the year. When the group was problem solving about reading instruction, we administered a reading test to collect data on the reading achievement of students. These student data were shared with the teacher participants to promote their ownership of the student data and to help them evaluate the efficacy of their instruction. Thus we tried to better coordinate the inquiry-related activities of researchers and teachers by intertwining our implementation and evaluation efforts and by aligning the professional development, classroom practice, and student progress monitoring functions of the project. We recognized that the personal stakes for teachers in implementing new innovations were high (House, 1974) and that teachers needed to have the same access as researchers to data that provided a perspective and basis for assessing the potential value of innovations (Guskey, 1986). Instead of removing classroom data for private analysis at the university, data were shared to promote teachers' joint ownership and control of the project and to improve their sense of influence over student outcomes through timely interventions.

Finally, the researchers published a quarterly publication to conventionalize the project's "best practices," research questions, and outcomes so that the shared knowledge that evolved in meetings would be accessible and known by all members. Newsletters always emanated from the discourse of the biweekly meetings, so they served a note-taking function because they captured the language, practices, and social interactions of the community. Sometimes, newsletters were used to extend the discourse by making transcripts of lessons available so that teachers could reflect on the lesson discourse in closer detail and study the exemplification of an innovation (principles or activities) embedded in the social interactions of teachers and students during literacy events. Generally, the format of the newsletters involved the provision of descriptions of one or more teachers' practice(s) related to a given area of the curriculum, relational statements that linked particular practices to theory or that provided explanations of why particular practices were effective, descriptions of or references to related literacy research, and questions that promoted deeper problem solving related to the implementation of specific practices. Thus newsletters simultaneously formed, conventionalized, and informed the practices of the community. Newsletters enabled individual experiences to be publicized and represented to the group, thereby shaping what came to be known as the *project curriculum* and documenting the historical development of the project.

Lessons Learned

Analyses of the meetings revealed several findings that built on those reported in the first case study (Englert & Rozendal, 1997).

Bidirectional Processes. As observed on the ELP, teachers and researchers worked collaboratively to build situated reasons, interests, goals, or concerns. Teachers helped construct practices from the research literature and theory (ideas that were seeded by researchers), whereas researchers appropriated the resulting innovative literacy practices (ideas that were seeded by teachers) and tied these back to the empirical literature. Together, teachers and researchers planted and harvested interesting ideas that became conventionalized into a set of pragmatic and scientific principles within the discourse of the teacher-researcher meetings. The bidirectional nature of the processes of construction and appropriation enabled both teachers and researchers to sow instructional possibilities within the discourse community and conventionalize what became accepted by others as "legitimate literacy practice." The collaborative discourse of the meetings, therefore, became the critical site in which knowledge was created and professional development activities were centered. Through a recursive process of knowledge appropriation, transformation, publication, and conventionalization, teachers and researchers negotiated a shared understanding of the practices that constituted the LEAP project—what it meant to know, mean, see, talk, and act like a LEAP teacher (Applebee, 1996).

Teacher and Researcher Equality. The gap between research and practice was diminished by the equal positioning of the knowledge and contributions afforded the group by teachers and researchers, as one teacher explained:

> I don't believe there is a gap between research and practice on our project. . . . The researcher and the teacher would need to come together and feel that they

are both very knowledgeable in their specific areas—that one doesn't know more than the other. If I bring up ideas and activities, they wouldn't be shot down, because they may not be research based. But [others would say] "Let's try that" and the researcher would bring the same and say "What about this?" We feel a level of equality—open to feedback and to talk through activities and finding the good in both. [It's okay] that you may or may not like something, but finding out why (is important). (Englert & Rozendal, 1997)

Within the discourse community, teachers and researchers served as apprentices and experts to others, because everyone took responsibility for leading, following, and participating in the culturally organized activities of the project (Rogoff, 1994). What came to constitute the curricular approach could not have happened without the teacher-researcher meetings and the associated conversations about practices. A single researcher designing the curriculum or providing feedback to a single teacher on a one-to-one basis could not have accomplished what the group accomplished with the distributed expertise and cognition afforded the collective by its individual members. Instead, through joint collaborative efforts, teachers and researchers learned to juggle multiple agendas, including those of the researcher and the practitioner to achieve the delicate balance between practice knowledge and research knowledge (Vaughn et al., 1998).

Teacher Knowledge and Actions. Teacher learning and membership on the project became characterized by changing one's participation in the community of practice through the enactment of new practices (Lave & Wenger, 1991). When teachers implemented new literacy practices, they transformed their identity not by what they "knew" about literacy but by their actions and what they "did." Membership in the commu-

nity implied "doing literacy in different ways"—an expectation that prompted teachers to depart from familiar routines as they adopted a learning stance that led to the implementation of new teaching practices and social arrangements in the classroom. Paradoxically, this created a dilemma when new members joined the project because they tended to perform on the peripheral edges of the community as they struggled to internalize the norms, habits, and techniques of the returning teachers and researchers (Lave & Wenger, 1991). Only when new members assumed an inquiry-oriented stance to teaching and learning by implementing new practices that served to "cut new ground" did they come to be viewed as more central and legitimately participating members.

Collaboration and Idea Generation. New and returning teachers on the project were helped continually in transforming their practice to achieve their literacy goals by researchers who visited their classrooms on a weekly basis. Researchers supported learning by asking questions about teaching practice (e.g., "What if?" questions), videotaping lessons, problem solving, and prompting teachers to consider deeper issues related to the curriculum, principles, or individual students. In essence, researchers supported teachers in improving their implementation or evaluation practices and promoted a more reflective, inquiry-oriented stance to teaching and learning. Teachers also participated in the questioning process by pointing out discrepancies between what was intended and what occurred. Collaboratively, teachers and researchers worked out solutions that represented ongoing responses to particular problems or learning contexts. Simultaneously, what researchers and teachers constructed at the local level to suit individual contexts and students also informed the larger community through the participatory mechanisms of the biweekly meetings. Teachers and researchers were coparticipants in a cyclical process of producing and consuming knowledge at the local (classroom) and global (project) level: "Problems, therefore, provided the occasion for change and increased the potential for growth" (Englert et al., 1993, p. 465), thereby setting into motion a chain of problem-solving responses that led to the successive, iterative generations of the curriculum.

Internalized Norms. The most experienced teachers on the project were distinguished by their view of teaching and learning as interactive and messy rather than tidy and finitely sequenced and by the perception of themselves as lifelong learners who will never arrive at a position of total mastery. They had come to internalize norms, habits, and techniques for continuous learning through their participation in the teacher-researcher community. Over a longer period of time, these teachers became change agents in their school or district (Englert et al., 1998; Vaughn et al., 1998) as they sought to extend and create their own learning community by joining forces with other professionals interested in similar questions related to practice. Thus, the community had engendered habits of inquiry, reflection, and lifelong learning as the standard for membership.

Case 3: The TELE-Web Project

The final collaborative project involved the development and evaluation of a Web-based literacy curriculum for elementary students with mild disabilities. The practices and principles of ELP shaped our interpretations of the potential of the Web to support the literacy curriculum. At the same time, the affordances and constraints of the Web also influenced the realization of the curriculum, resulting in a Web-based literacy development environment that was not exactly the same as the original ELP curriculum. The resulting curricular approach, Technology-Enhanced Learning Environments on the Web (TELE-Web) (Zhao & Englert, 1997), was designed to enhance literacy learning for special education students.

The literacy activities and principles of the two former literacy projects served as a basis for designing Web-based environments that incorporated the specific features of the prior projects and that have been found to be effective in general education. Essentially, the technology application was designed to add functions so that the computer could serve as an intellectual partner for teachers and students, stretching cognition between the user and the machine, helping to offload cognitive activity in the face of complexity, and providing strategies and representations to aid writing and reading processes.

TELE-Web consisted of a set of server-side software and client-side plugins that work with a Web server and database applications to offer a suite of multifunctional tools in an integrated fashion for teachers and students to use within a Web browser. It enabled teachers to adopt, develop, manage, and share multimedia literacy materials and to initiate, conduct, and manage collaborative learning projects. In addition, teachers and researchers could archive students' reading and writing responses to observe, monitor, and report students' literacy performance.

There were four central environments that formed the core of TELE-Web: the Writing Room, Reading Room, Library, and Publishing Room. Each of these environments had a teacher and student interface, which allowed teachers and students to create assignments; allowed students to create, revise, and complete assignments; allowed teachers and students to add on or to comment on other students' work; and allowed the students to read other students' stories (Zhao et al., 1998). What was unique in these various environments was the opportunity for students to receive cognitive and social support in each environment, insofar as the cognition and cultural capital and artifacts were distributed across the whole network in TELE-Web (Salomon, 1993). Teachers could develop specific prompts to support individual students based on their reading or writing needs; conversely, students could elect to use teacher prompts, text structure maps, reference notes, or see other students' stories as a basis for gathering information to support writing or reading comprehension.

Collaborative Process

Originally, TELE-Web was developed by using the LEAP curricular approach as a basis for the design of the Internet-based software. Researchers developed and refined the software in the first and second years of the project based on the literacy curriculum associated with the project's predecessors. At the end of the first year of the preliminary development of TELE-Web, some of the project teachers were brought to the university to review the software and consult with researchers about its development. In the second year, three teachers were given computers and invited to explore and implement the TELE-Web software with their students. However, unlike the prior two projects, TELE-Web teachers and researchers did not regularly meet in biweekly meetings, and teachers' implementations of the TELE-Web software remained at the local classroom level. Researchers worked privately with teachers to record their uses of TELE-Web and to solve local problems related to implementation or practice at the classroom level. At the project meetings that teachers attended on a quarterly basis, the focus was on solving technological glitches rather than on developing greater conceptual frameworks for using TELE-Web or for sharing teachers' innovative practices with the other members of the community. Sometimes, the conversations at these meetings tended to be dominated by one of the project teachers with the greatest technological background, and the other two teachers tended to remain on the sidelines as spectators rather than as active players. In these circumstances, it was difficult to ascertain the less-active teachers' beliefs and assumptions about the innovation.

By the end of the second year, only one of the three implementing teachers was fully

implementing the curriculum. The other two teachers were implementing components of the curriculum, but these practices were used episodically, rather than being fully integrated into their literacy curriculum.

Lessons Learned

The TELE-Web project yielded several lessons that complemented the findings of the former projects and that informed the literature about the role of collaboration in the development of innovations that can be implemented and sustained by teachers.

Innovations, Conversation, and Ownership. Community and conversations are an important part of the staff development process. When innovations are transmitted to teachers in "final draft" form, there is no opportunity for teachers to understand or take ownership of the curriculum. Teachers' perceptions that there is genuine room for improvement also influence the degree of collaboration. The fact that TELE-Web was presented to the teacher as a piece of software probably left the teachers with the impression that it was something unalterable or something too expensive to change, like many other computer products they have encountered. In these circumstances, teachers were less likely to feel a sense of their agency in transforming the development process or product. In fact, several of the teachers expressed a general discomfort with new technologies, suggesting a distance between themselves and technological innovations.

Although innovators can design a "finished-looking curriculum" (e.g., Internet-based software), unless teachers use the innovation, it is a pointless effort. Innovations involve substantial changes with respect to the materials, teaching approaches, and beliefs of teachers (Fullan, 1991). Although researchers presented teachers with opportunities to change their literacy materials through TELE-Web, teachers needed additional support to accomplish more complex changes that went below the surface and that altered their fundamental approaches and beliefs about the technological innovation and its place in their literacy instruction. The nature of that support might vary, but we believe that participation in a collaborative community is likely to be vital to help teachers understand the innovation and support their risk-taking efforts. A collaborative community can provide teachers with an authentic audience to sustain their intense participation in the research and implementation activities associated with an innovation. In fact, at the end of the second year of the project, the two teachers who sporadically used the TELE-Web curriculum asked that the project create biweekly meetings using the format of the LEAP project. They explained that they needed deeper conversations situated around their teaching practice to support their understanding of and implementation of the technological innovation. Seeing the finished product did not help teachers gain insight into the "teaching process"—for that, they needed the collaborative community. To assume that the curriculum or innovation could be imparted to others in a transmissible fashion was to fail to understand learning as a social process.

Implementation and Entry Points. For successful implementation, a collaborative community must unfold around the entry-level states and knowledge of teachers. On the TELE-Web project, we made the mistake of failing to create entry points into the curricular innovation for all the teachers. The two former projects allowed teachers to be experts and informants by making public their implementation efforts; we needed to provide the same opportunities for TELE-Web teachers to experiment and participate in a collaborative group to study the innovation, reflect on the nature of the change process in situated contexts, and build curriculum content and process through their own implementation efforts. In other words, we needed to let the curriculum unfold around the teachers' interests and activities rather than expect the project teachers to match arbitrarily the

researchers' notions of what it took to enter the curriculum. For example, one teacher with emergent writers might have explored the spelling environment of TELE-Web and then have shared her findings of the effectiveness of the spelling function at the next meeting. Another teacher who was teaching her students to write expository reports might have been encouraged to explore the mapping tool in TELE-Web as a basis for helping her students plan their expository reports. In both these cases, the teachers' enactment of the TELE-Web curriculum could have been used to teach and lead others to try new practices and simultaneously convey the notion that researchers viewed teachers as active agents and partners in the knowledge-construction process. We needed to capitalize on all of the teachers' talents and interests by creating an authentic learning community that focused on teaching practices in the same way that the former projects built the curriculum around teachers' enactment and risk-taking efforts.

Varying Levels of Discourse Knowledge. Teachers must be participants in a critical discourse that intertwines talk about practice and theory. On the TELE-Web project, we assumed that the incoming teachers possessed the theoretical background for implementing the innovation because of their prior involvement in two research projects. However, our assumption that the teachers needed less support because of their prior background in literacy was incorrect, and the results suggested that a critical discourse must be specifically fashioned around each unique innovation. TELE-Web, in fact, presented the teachers with complex dilemmas as to how they should reconceptualize their teaching roles and conceptualize the role of technology in the teaching-learning process. To assimilate the technological innovation, TELE-Web teachers needed ongoing opportunities to construct new ideas about the teaching-learning process, especially as it related to the potential role of the Internet in expanding the learning community beyond their four classroom walls. To accomplish this goal, teachers and researchers needed to be convened as collaborators in deep conversations that raised new insights, challenged assumptions, and presented examples of alternative uses of the technological innovation so that the members of the community could develop together new ways of knowing and doing literacy, as well as to build bridges between "practice knowledge" and "research knowledge" (Malouf & Schiller, 1995). Professional development opportunities needed to focus on the specific realities of implementing new strategies and the underlying concepts and intent of their effective use (Gersten & Brengelman, 1996).

Simultaneously, the collaborative community needed to be guided by efforts to maintain an even distribution of knowledge and expertise, which is essential for genuine collaboration to take place. In both of the former projects, the teachers and researchers developed a strong sense that every participant had something to contribute to the community, suggesting that there was a great deal of perceived parity among the participants. However, the sense of parity in the TELE-Web project was quite the contrary. Teachers continually deferred to the expertise of the researchers, possibly because the project focused on computers and the Internet, which seemed remote from the teachers' classroom experiences. To the teachers, therefore, the project may have seemed to be more about technology than about literacy. Unfortunately, this created barriers for the two teachers who were literacy experts but who did not feel like they were able to participate in the discourse of the community when the focus was on technology. Conversely, the teacher who entered the project with a great deal of technological experience not only dominated the discourse at the quarterly meetings but made the most requests and suggestions for changes of TELE-Web. Successful innovations somehow must engage teachers at a level at which they feel valued, motivated, connected to the world of research and practice, and simultaneously challenged (rather than overwhelmed) to develop greater exper-

tise and professional competence in the use of the innovation. Researchers, too, must find ways to link the innovation to teachers' prior knowledge and experiences through the formation of communities of practice in which all participants can develop and share their expertise in synergistic ways.

Summary

Different models of staff development can be implemented to maximize teachers' implementation of innovations. Using the criteria of sustained and consistent use of the innovation to evaluate its effectiveness, the staff development model that seemed highly effective in producing long-term change was the collaborative model associated with the ELP and LEAP projects. In both of these projects, teachers continued to use the literacy practices whether the researchers were present or not. In fact, in the 2-year gap between the ELP and LEAP projects, teachers continued to meet with other teacher participants to sustain the learning community that they had helped to start. Furthermore, when researchers approached some of the ELP teachers about joining the LEAP project, the teachers protested that they were not sure that they could incorporate new literacy practices into their teaching repertoire because "ELP was all they had time to do." Clearly, the teachers had developed strong allegiances to the former learning community and the practices that had been constructed within the community. For these teachers, the researchers did not need to be present to sustain the literacy innovation; the teachers had come to own the innovation and were disciple-like in their strong commitment to its continued promotion and use. In this regard, the collaborative community had produced deep and enduring changes in teachers' beliefs and practices.

Nevertheless, when the LEAP community was formed, there were further shifts in the participating teachers' orientation to the collaborative community and the innovation.

The LEAP teachers came to see their role in the community as that of "teaching" and "learning." Instead of perceiving an innovation as static and fully formed, they came to view the innovation as dynamic and continually evolving as a result of their own actions, interactions, and conversations about literacy. They came to see themselves as lifelong learners in a larger topography of professional practice in which teachers rather than researchers were engaged in educational inquiry (e.g., involving habits of questioning, experimentation, and investigation) (Fullan, 1991, 1993).

The third project provided additional confirmation and insight into the role of the community in fostering change. As an outlier in the set of projects, it pointed out the inadequacies of more traditional models of innovation development and dissemination. In moving to a curricular medium involving a technology application, researchers and teachers unwittingly had forsaken the very medium of knowledge construction and change that had been shown to be effective—the establishment of ongoing conversations about theory and practice tied to a particular innovation's development and use. Ultimately, the results suggested that these conversations determined the meaning of the innovation and the participants' deep engagement in its implementation and evaluation. This constructive collaboration in designing and implementing the innovation is being addressed in the final years of the TELE-Web project.

As researchers plan the third year of the TELE-Web project, we will establish ongoing meetings so that educators and researchers can become active participants in consuming, critiquing, and producing knowledge. Within this community, we will use problems of teaching practice to create and transform the innovation. In conversations about the research-based practices associated with TELE-Web, we will seek to integrate research knowledge and practice knowledge and create pedagogic situations out of the daily lives and experiences of teachers and

students (Lave, 1996, p. 162). The features of successful staff development models also will inform the staff development process, including encouraging teachers to modify the innovation to work in specific classrooms and schools, involving teachers in trying the ideas and evaluating effects, fostering risk taking and experimentation, incorporating available knowledge bases, videotaping applications so that teachers can observe each other's practices and analyze teacher-student data, discussing problems of practice and solutions regarding individual students and/or teaching subject matter, presenting examples of the innovation drawn from the project database, reporting on successes or failures to the group, and integrating individual teachers' goals with the project goals (Fullan, 1991; Loucks-Horsley et al., 1987; Stallings, 1989). In this community, we hope that the culture of the school and the culture of the researcher will again begin to overlap in organic ways (Fullan, 1991).

In summary, the case studies suggest that the professional development process is as vital to successful implementation and the achievement of student outcomes as the quality of the innovation itself. Aligning the goals of innovation development, professional development, and student progress monitoring functions can be mutually advantageous for both researchers and teachers, insofar as their complementary efforts can result in the advancement of teaching practice, the improvement of an innovation, and the production of knowledge and dissemination to a broader community of practitioners and researchers (Fullan, 1991).

References

Applebee, A. N. (1996). *Curriculum as conversation.* Chicago: University of Chicago Press.

Cohen, D. K. (1988). Educational technology and school organization. In R. S. Nickerson & P. P. Zodhiates (Eds.), *Technology in education: Looking toward 2020* (pp. 231-264). Hillsdale, NJ: Lawrence Erlbaum.

Cuban, L. (1983). Effective schools: A friendly but cautionary note. *Phi Delta Kappan, 64,* 695-696.

Duffy, G. G. (1993). Rethinking strategy instruction: Four teachers' development and their low achievers' understandings. *Elementary School Journal, 93,* 231-248.

Englert, C. S., Raphael, T. E., & Mariage, T. V. (1998). A multi-year literacy intervention: Transformation and teacher change in the community of the Early Literacy Project. *Teacher Education and Special Education, 21*(4), 255-277.

Englert, C. S., & Rozendal, M. S. (1997, April). *The negotiation of knowledge and practice in the teacher-researcher community.* Paper presented at the annual meeting of the American Educational Research Association, Chicago.

Englert, C. S., & Tarrant, K. L. (1995). Creating collaborative cultures for educational change. *Remedial and Special Education, 16,* 325-336, 353.

Englert, C. S., Tarrant, K. L., & Rozendal, M. S. (1993). Educational innovations: Achieving curricular change through collaboration. *Education and Treatment of Children, 16,* 441-473.

Friend, M., & Cook, L. (1996). *Interactions: Collaboration skills for school professionals.* White Plains, NY: Longman.

Fullan, M. G. (1991). *The new meaning of educational change.* New York: Teachers College Press.

Fullan, M. (1993). *Change forces.* London: Falmer.

Gersten, R., & Brengelman, S. U. (1996). The quest to translate research into classroom practice: The emerging knowledge base. *Remedial and Special Education, 17*(2), 67-74.

Gersten, R. M., & Woodward, J. (1992). The quest to translate research into classroom practice: Strategies for assisting classroom teachers' work with at-risk students and students with disabilities. In D. Carnine & E. J. Kameenui (Eds.), *Higher order thinking: Designing curriculum for mainstream students* (pp. 201-218). Austin, TX: Pro-Ed.

Greenwood, C. R. (1998). Commentary: Align professional development, classroom practice, and student progress in the curriculum and you'll improve general education for all students. *Learning Disability Quarterly, 21*(1), 75-84.

Guskey, T. R. (1986). Staff development and the process of teacher change. *Educational Researcher, 15*(5), 5-12.

House, E. (1974). *The politics of educational innovation.* Berkeley, CA: McCutchan.

Lave, J. (1996). Teaching, as learning, in practice. *Mind, Culture and Activity: An International Journal, 3*(3), 149-164.

Lave, J., & Wenger, E. (1991). *Situated learning: Legitimate peripheral participation.* New York: Cambridge University Press.

Loucks-Horsley, S., Harding, C., Arbuckle, M., Murray, L., Dubea, C., & Williams, M. (1987). *Continuing to learn: A guidebook for teacher development.* Andover, MA: Regional Laboratory for Educational Improvement of the Northeast and Islands and National Staff Development Council.

Malouf, D. B., & Schiller, E. P. (1995). Practice and research in special education, *Exceptional Children, 61,* 414-424.

Marks, S. U., & Gersten, R. (1998). Engagement and disengagement between special and general educators: An application of Miles and Huberman's cross-case analysis. *Learning Disability Quarterly, 21*(1), 34-56.

Perl, S. (1994). Composing texts, composing lives. *Harvard Educational Review, 64,* 427-449.

Richardson, V., & Anders, P. (1998). A view from across the Grand Canyon. *Learning Disability Quarterly, 21*(1), 85-98.

Rogoff, B. (1994). Developing understanding of the idea of communities of learners. *Mind, Culture and Activity: An International Journal, 1*(4), 209-229.

Salomon, G. (1993). No distribution without individuals' cognition: A dynamic interactional view. In G. Salomon (Ed.), *Distributed cognition: Psychological and educational considerations* (pp. 111-138). NY: Cambridge University Press.

Sirtonik, K. (1990). Society, school, teaching, and preparing to teach. In J. Goodlad, R. Soder, & K. Sirotnik (Eds.), *The moral dimensions of teaching* (pp. 296-327). San Francisco: Jossey-Bass.

Stallings, J. A. (1989). *School achievement effects and staff development: What are some critical factors?* Paper presented at the annual meeting of the American Educational Research Association, San Francisco.

Swales, J. M. (1991). *Genre analysis: English in academic and research settings.* New York: Cambridge University Press.

Talbert, J. E., & McLaughlin, M. W. (1994). Teacher professionalism in local school contexts. *American Journal of Education, 102*(2), 123-153.

Vaughn, S., Hughes, M. T., Schumm, J. S., & Klingner, J. (1998). A collaborative effort to enhance reading and writing instruction in inclusion classrooms. *Learning Disability Quarterly, 21*(1), 57-74.

Zhao, Y., & Englert, C. S. (1998). Technology Enhanced Learning Environments: TELE-Web [Internet-based software]. East Lansing, MI: Michigan State University.

Zhao, Y., Englert, C. S., Ferdig, R., Jones, S., Chen, J., & Shah, M. (1998, April). *Supporting writing on the Internet: A dialogue between technology and pedagogy.* Paper presented at the American Educational Research Association, San Diego, CA.

CHAPTER TEN

The Rise and Fall of the Community Transition Team Model

ANDREW S. HALPERN
University of Oregon

MICHAEL R. BENZ
University of Oregon

This chapter is markedly different from the others that are contained in this volume. Unlike these others, which focus on classrooms or schools as the "case" being studied and presented, this chapter describes a system for encouraging and facilitating innovations at the local community level, with support and structure being provided at the state level. Our "case" is best identified as the entire state network that nurtures the activities and accomplishments of the local organizational entities that are responsible for implementing the innovations.

Before embarking on a description and analysis of these innovations, some caveats should be mentioned about their relevance as an example of technology. The program that we present is basically a *systems-change* model, designed to improve the *capacity* of schools and communities to deliver services and provide resources. It is not a service-delivery program per se. Planning and evaluation at the program (not the individual student) level are the focus of attention, and technology is used only as a tool for managing the flow of information that is needed to facilitate the process.

The focus of our innovation has been to help appropriate members of local communities in sharpening their visions, conceptualizing program improvement, obtaining needed resources, improving existing or developing new services, and learning to network effectively with colleagues, all for the purpose of enhancing the transition of students with disabilities from high school as they begin to assume emerging roles as young adults in their communities. The term *transition* refers to this *outcome* of leaving high school successfully; the school-based and community-based *services* that students receive to achieve this outcome; the *planning* that students must do to secure the services that will produce desired outcomes; and the *attitudes* that students, parents, and service providers must all share to regard transition as being worthy of focused and extended effort.

The innovation that we developed is known as the Community Transition Team Model (CTTM). In this chapter, we describe the development of the model, the history of its implementation, our sense of its accomplishments and failures over a decade of use, and the implications of these findings for theories that pertain to the sustained use of innovations. Although the CTTM has been implemented in nine states—Oregon, Washington, Nevada, Idaho, Utah, Kansas, Arizona, Alabama, and New South Wales in Australia—we confine our descriptions and interpretations to the unfolding of the model in Oregon, where our experiences have been the most extensive.

Background for the Model

Since 1984, there has been a growing interest in secondary special education and transition programs, stimulated initially by a federal initiative in this area (Will, 1984). The broad purpose of this initiative has been to ensure that students with disabilities, when they leave school, are prepared to assume their new roles effectively as young adults in their communities. The need for continued attention in this area has been documented by follow-up and follow-along studies of school leavers from special education, which indicate very marginal levels of success in all important areas, including employment, residential adjustment, and personal/social adjustment (Brolin, Durand, Kromer, & Muller, 1975; Edgar, 1987; Fafard & Haubrich, 1981; Fardig,

Algozzine, Schwartz, Hensel, & Westling, 1985; Halpern, 1990; Hasazi, Gordon, & Roe, 1985; Hasazi, Gordon, Roe, Finck, Hull, & Salembier, 1985; Humes & Brammer, 1985; Kregel, Wehman, Seyfarth, & Marshall, 1986; Mithaug, Horiuchi, & Fanning, 1985; O'Brien & Schiller, 1979; Schalock et al., 1986; Zigmond & Thornton, 1985).

Perhaps in response to such findings, the Individuals With Disabilities Education Act of 1990 and the more recent 1997 Amendments to the Act include a number of important initiatives in the area of secondary special education and transition programs. These initiatives focus on transition planning from two important but very different perspectives: (a) improvements in transition planning for individual students through modifications of the individualized education program (IEP) process; and (b) improvements in planning for program capacity to support the service needs that students, families, and teachers identify in individual plans for students. These two types of planning are obviously highly interrelated, in that the plans developed for individual students and their families are inherently dependent on the quality of programs and services that are available to implement any such plan within the school and community where students reside.

In other words, if we are to improve transition outcomes for individuals with disabilities by refocusing the IEP process on such outcomes, we also must improve our capacity to deliver effective programs and services that are needed to produce good outcomes (Heal, Copher, & Rusch, 1990). In the area of secondary special education and transition programs, such capacity building is fairly complex because it involves the school system, the adult service system, the private sector (e.g., employers), and the interactions among all three. A systems-change model is needed to achieve this capacity building. We developed and implemented such a model—the CTTM—over a 9-year period beginning in 1985.

Systems change is a very tricky business, in that most systems have very little interest in being changed. By its very nature, a system represents a collection of attitudes and experiences that characterize the "culture" of an organization or a group of interrelated organizations that share some common goals and methods of pursuing these goals. This culture evolves over time, gaining both complexity and inertia, and presents a natural barrier against those who promote "innovation" as a new way to solve old problems. As we unfold the story of the CTTM, the barriers presented by existing organizational cultures become evident, especially as these barriers pertain to the *sustainability* of our innovation once the initial impetus for its development had declined.

Development of the Model

The procedures that define the CTTM were implemented in local communities by a group of people known as a "community transition team." Membership on these teams involved the full array of people who were concerned about secondary special education and transition programs in their communities. This array of team members included representatives of four groups: (a) people with disabilities and their families, (b) school personnel, (c) adult agency personnel, and (d) members of the general public such as employers.

Although the planning procedures contained within the CTTM were designed to be implemented uniformly by teams throughout a state, the specific plans for program improvement efforts that emerged from each team were completely individualized, in response to local needs and local resources. This feature of the CTTM—uniform procedures yielding individualized outcomes—represented our attempt to respond to the dilemma of implementing a uniform federal policy in a manner that acknowledged and supported local values and adaptations. It can be very difficult to accomplish this "tender balance" between universal mandates and local adaptations, especially when the man-

dates are disruptive of prevailing organizational practices. This dilemma is apparent as we describe the CTTM, which we do from three different perspectives: (a) basic features of the model, (b) procedures for implementing the model, and (c) materials to support the model.

Basic Features

There were several essential features of the CTTM that provided structure for its successful implementation. These features included program standards as a frame of reference, local control for implementation, a developmental perspective on the process of change, a focusing of change efforts on program capacity, and a network for linking together the efforts of all participating teams.

Program Standards

The underlying foundation of the CTTM was a set of program standards that provided a frame of reference for guiding the process of systematic program change. The development and evolution of these standards emerged from a statewide survey of secondary special education and transition programs in Oregon (Benz & Halpern, 1986, 1987; Halpern & Benz, 1987) accompanied by a review of national literature in the field (Halpern, 1987). These inquiries identified five broad areas of need for program improvement, including the enhancement of (a) curriculum and instruction, (b) coordination and mainstreaming of instruction, (c) transition services, (d) documentation of student outcomes, and (e) comprehensive and adequate adult services. This taxonomy of needs eventually was translated into 38 program standards that became the frame of reference against which community transition teams gauged the availability and quality of programs and services within their local communities.

An example may prove useful for illustrating the central role of program standards as the foundation for the CTTM. Four standards eventually emerged within the broad area of transition services. One of these, Standard 21 in our set of 38, states the following: "Procedures exist for securing the appropriate involvement of parents in the transition process for their student with a disability."

This standard emerged from a consensus that parental involvement was usually desirable and not always available. As we describe later, transition team members were asked to reflect on the *relative importance* and *current status* of each of the 38 standards, eventually selecting a few high-priority standards to guide their program planning and development efforts.

Local Control

Even though a set of standards provided a framework for initiating change, local control was both presumed and systematically delegated with respect to the specific objectives, activities, and desired outcomes that community transition teams selected to implement any given standard. At an operational level, this meant giving team members the freedom to interpret, shape, and mold a given change from their own perspectives, without "external" pressures attempting to specify "right" and "wrong" methods for accomplishing the change. In fact, many teams chose vastly different ways of addressing the same standard, based on their own stage of development and local political realities. This feature of the CTTM represented our attempt to acknowledge the dilemma of universal mandates being modified to address the unique needs of local communities.

Developmental Perspective on Change

The commitment of teams to address and implement change meaningfully was presumed to be developmental with respect to both level of *concern* and level of *implementation* for any proposed change. Level of concern for a change can range from dim awareness of a problem to evangelistic fervor for innovation. Level of implementation can range from token efforts and lip service to complete alteration in the way things are done. Teams definitely varied along both of these dimensions, tending to become more and more involved in the process as they gained experience over time and responded to the benefits of their involvement. Counterbalancing such changes, of course, was the inertia of simply continuing to function within the parameters of their existing organizational cultures.

Focus on Program Capacity

The ultimate focus of any intervention is to improve the services, support, and/or advocacy that are provided directly to (and sometimes by) people with disabilities to enhance the quality of their lives. Even though this is the ultimate focus, there are two very different approaches to planning that can be followed to achieve this end: *person-centered* and *intervention-centered*. The person-centered approach to planning is implemented within the context of an IEP. The IEP process is believed to facilitate two very different ends: (a) it coordinates existing programs and services that are needed by the person being helped, and (b) it provides a context for identifying new programs and services that are required but not yet available to address satisfactorily the needs of the individual being helped.

The intervention-centered approach acknowledges that available programs and service opportunities are inadequate and that the capacity to provide high-quality interventions often must be addressed separately if IEPs are to be implemented completely and effectively. This focus on program capacity involves the development of new interventions that, if shown to be effective, can then become available as options for meeting individual needs. The CTTM focused on the intervention-centered approach to change, to build capacity for the person-centered approach.

Networking Among Teams

Networking was another important feature of the CTTM. Each team was encouraged to participate in a network of similar teams, the purpose of the network being to share information among teams and provide a vehicle for assisting one another. Such sharing occurred in several areas, including (a) procedures being used to pursue common objectives in annual plans, (b) problems encountered while implementing an objective, (c) approaches used to resolve the problems, and (d) accomplishments achieved and products developed. The process of networking was aided by a state-operated management information system (MIS) that gathered appropriate information from each team and produced and distributed appropriate reports from the information base. As we mentioned at the beginning of this chapter, this MIS represents the sole "technology" component of our innovation.

Procedures for Implementing the Model

Although structured by the set of standards described previously, the procedures for implementing the CTTM were organized around a typical management-by-objectives paradigm. The model had 5 basic components: (a) team building, (b) needs assessment, (c) program planning, (d) program implementation and evaluation, and (e) repetition of the cycle. A complete set of procedures and materials was developed and field-tested for assisting teams in using these components of the model to design and implement program changes. The procedures are described next, and the materials are described subsequently.

Team Building

Team building, which signaled the beginning of a local effort to implement the transition team model, was actually an ongoing process that evolved and improved continually over time. The first stage of team building, not surprisingly, involved identifying initial team members, selecting a team leader, and beginning the process of establishing a working rapport among team members. This was not as easy as it might seem. In many communities, the various people involved in addressing transition needs did not necessarily have a history of working well together. Failures were likely to be viewed as "someone else's" fault rather than as a shared responsibility. The process of breaking down these communication and attitudinal barriers took time and effort, but it was essential because the backbone of the CTTM required a group of common stakeholders working together to solve common problems.

Needs Assessment

This step involved selecting several of the program standards as goals requiring immediate attention at the local level. The process began with a rating exercise, using an instrument (Halpern, Lindstrom, Benz, & Rothstrom, 1990) in which each standard was evaluated along two dimensions: relative importance and current status. This mechanical but efficient exercise produced an immediate narrowing of the field of discourse to approximately 15 standards that team members regarded to be of immediate greatest concern. Additional evaluation of the 15 standards, including team member discussions of present feasibility, eventually resulted in their selection of two to four goals (standards) that became the focus of a current annual plan. The entire process required around 6 hours of structured interactions, guided by state agency facilitators, and provided each team with complete discretion in choosing the focus of its innovational efforts.

Program Planning

The next stage of model implementation involved program planning to provide a method of both operationally defining and eventually achieving the standards selected by team members for immediate attention. The process of developing an annual plan took between 1 and 1½ days of concentrated team effort, which included the following activities: (a) identifying specific objectives for addressing each selected standard; (b) identifying tasks, timelines, intended outcomes, resources, and people responsible for accomplishing each selected objective; (c) developing an annual calendar of activities, based on the set of task-analyzed objectives combined; and (d) developing an annual budget for implementing the plan. During this stage of the process, teams normally began to solidify their interpersonal relationships as their commitments and responsibilities, self-selected, began to crystallize.

Program Implementation/Evaluation

This phase of the model occurred over the 9 to 12 months that teams specified in their written plans. During this phase, the transition team typically divided itself into subcommittees to implement each objective in the plan. Meetings of the entire team were also held either monthly or bimonthly to monitor and coordinate efforts and also to make any midcourse corrections that became necessary. A structured evaluation at the end of this period of time, called a *year-end report,* provided team members with information about their level of accomplishment, and set the stage for repeating the cycle.

Repeating the Cycle

The next cycle began with a reassessment of needs, taking into consideration both past accomplishments and previously identified needs that had not yet been addressed. If de-

sired by team members, a brand-new needs assessment also could be done, looking afresh at the complete set of 38 standards. Whether or not this occurred, teams developed a new plan, which structured their next year of activities.

Support Structure for the Model

The statewide network of teams was supported by a state facilitation team comprised of staff from the Oregon Department of Education (ODE) and the University of Oregon. Support for the network of local teams involved providing direct training and technical assistance to local teams and developing materials that supported the entire network at both state and local levels.

Training and Technical Assistance

During their first year of participation, teams received direct technical assistance to help them (a) build membership that was representative of their respective communities; (b) identify and prioritize their highest priority needs; (c) develop and implement their action plans; (d) identify and secure resources to assist with their work; and (e) evaluate their accomplishments and continuing needs, using this information as the foundation for their next annual plan. Teams that completed their first year of work successfully received less direct technical assistance in subsequent years but continued to receive regular telephone consultation and occasional on-site visits. Continuing support for all teams also occurred through biannual (fall and spring) team leader meetings. These meetings were planned and conducted by the state facilitation team in consultation with team leaders to ensure that they addressed issues of concern to the network of local teams. Through these biannual meetings, teams were able to (a) obtain timely information on new federal or state initiatives that affected the delivery of secondary and transition services to youth,

(b) share ideas, products, and resources that local teams had developed and that could be adopted or adapted to help other communities address similar needs, (c) identify and solve generic problems affecting the performance and impact of teams in their local communities, and (d) establish a collective identity and common voice for influencing state policies and practices.

Support Materials

The procedures described previously for implementing the CTTM were supported by a set of materials and a computer program that we designed and developed specifically for this project. A *Team Leader's Manual* (Halpern, Nelson, Lindstrom, & Benz, 1990) described all aspects of the CTTM, providing team leaders with the information and supporting forms they needed to implement the model in a local community. A *Facilitator's Manual* (Benz, Lindstrom, Halpern, & Rothstrom, 1990) described various ways in which state agency facilitators could assist team leaders and members during each phase of CTTM implementation.

We also developed a computerized MIS, called the Transition Team Management Information System (TTMIS), to assist with the implementation of the model in several ways, including processing needs assessment information, developing annual plans, and processing year-end reports. These various functions within the TTMIS helped team leaders and facilitators engage local teams in the CTTM process, prepare reports summarizing team activities and outcomes, and facilitate the networking of information to teams throughout the state. The uses of the TTMIS were described in detail in a *Management Information System Manual* (Lindstrom, Ard, Benz, & Halpern, 1990). This set of materials proved to be useful not only in Oregon but also in the eight other states mentioned previously that chose to adopt and adapt the CTTM after its initial development in Oregon.

Status of the CTTM Over Time

The CTTM was developed, implemented, evaluated, and revised in Oregon over a period of 9 years, beginning in 1985. The effort began fairly modestly, with only 5 teams participating during the first year. By 1993, participation had expanded to 38 teams and included 1 or more teams in every county of the state. Total team membership ranged from 7 to 38 members per team, with an average 19 members participating per team. At its peak in 1993, the CTTM involved 722 school and community agency staff, parents, and community members in systematic efforts to improve services and outcomes for youth with disabilities in their local communities.

Funds to support the development and implementation of the statewide network of teams came from two sources. First, the University of Oregon received a 3-year (1986-1989) grant from the U.S. Department of Education, Office of Special Education Programs, that funded the development and evaluation of the procedures and support structure described previously. These funds also supported our involvement in the biannual meetings of team leaders and the delivery of technical assistance to teams in local communities. Second, the ODE committed both personnel and funds to support the development of the statewide network of local teams. During the early years of implementation, two people in the ODE worked together on developing and supporting the network of teams, contributing approximately 1.25 full-time equivalent (FTE) of effort to the program. In addition to this basic support, the ODE provided teams with small incentive grants to assist in the implementation of their annual plans and additional funds to support team participation in the biannual team leader meetings.

During 1993 to 1998, however, the trajectory of utilization was downward rather than upward. By 1998, only small vestiges of the original statewide network remained. This raises some intriguing questions. What contributed to the development and broad implementation of the model statewide? What contributed to the disintegration and eventual demise of the network? What can we learn about sustainability of the kinds of change efforts embodied in the CTTM? In the remainder of this chapter, we document the successes and failures of the CTTM as we experienced them over a decade. We also examine these outcomes from the perspective of theories of sustainability in an attempt to find some answers to these questions.

Accomplishments, Failures, and Implications for Supporting and Sustaining Change

When we began the articulation and development of the CTTM, we examined the literature on educational change for lessons and principles that were applicable to our efforts and that should guide the capacity-building procedures to be used by local teams and the support strategies to be used by the state facilitation team (e.g., Berman & McLaughlin, 1976; Cuban, 1988; Fullan, 1982; Hord, Rutherford, Huling-Austin, & Hall, 1987; Scott et al., 1989). In preparation for this chapter, we revisited this literature and more recent publications (e.g., Cuban, 1990; DeLone, 1990; Fullan, 1991, 1996; Fullan & Miles, 1992; McLaughlin, 1990) to help us better understand our accomplishments and failures from the perspective of educational change and sustainability. In the remaining sections of this chapter, we offer our reflections on what we discovered.

Our Accomplishments and Their Implications for Supporting Change

Based on our review of the educational change literature, we began the development of the CTTM with the strong belief that meaningful change in secondary and transition services for youth with disabilities required school personnel to reach outside school walls and build partnerships with key community members, including procedures that supported the collective efforts of these individuals over time in their local communities and a support structure that encouraged a statewide effort and respected the unique needs of local communities. We believe we achieved these goals and that local teams associated with the CTTM were quite successful in improving the capacity of their communities to support students' transition from school. Using information contained in the TTMIS database, we can document outcomes achieved by teams within and across 5 years, 1989 to 1993. The number of local community teams on which data were available included 18 in 1989, 25 in 1990, 29 in 1991, 32 in 1992, and 33 in 1993. We also present a vignette of a local team to illustrate the process of CTTM implementation in one community over time.

Local Team Accomplishments

As described earlier in this chapter, local teams followed a structured needs assessment and program planning process to develop individualized plans that addressed locally determined needs. Despite the highly individualized implementation of this process, several issues emerged consistently over the 5 years we examined as being high priorities for improvement across all participating teams. These issues reflected national concerns about secondary and transition programs during this timeframe, and included desires to improve (a) transition planning services for individuals; (b) school and community-based instructional options, especially in vocational and independent living content areas; (c) meaningful access to regular vocational and academic courses by students with disabilities; (d) options for obtaining a meaningful exit document; and (e) student outcomes and access to adult services, especially in employment, residential, and continuing education areas.

TABLE 10.1 Types of Outcomes Achieved by Transition Teams

Types of Outcomes Reported by Teams	1989		1990		1991		1992		1993	
	n	%	n	%	n	%	n	%	n	%
New curriculum materials	4	22	7	28	8	28	15	47	13	39
New instructional programs	4	22	13	52	19	66	19	59	12	36
Procedures for improving mainstreaming	12	67	6	24	13	34	12	38	13	39
Transition planning procedures	12	67	17	48	15	52	24	75	19	57
Media products to support the program	5	28	9	36	5	17	5	16	6	18
Users' guides to support students' transition	13	72	15	60	18	62	17	53	13	39
Inservice training	10	56	9	36	10	35	23	72	25	76
Surveys and feasibility studies	14	78	15	60	13	45	12	38	12	36
Increased access to adult services	3	17	6	24	8	28	8	25	9	27
Small business ventures to support programs	4	22	6	24	7	24	6	19	9	27
Information meetings to advertise programs	1	6	15	60	15	52	15	47	25	76
Total number of teams reporting outcomes	18		25		29		32		33	
Average number of outcomes per team	4.6		4.7		4.4		4.9		4.7	

The types of outcomes accomplished by teams in each of the 5 years we examined are presented in Table 10.1. During that time period, each team accomplished an average of four to five specific products or tangible outcomes that were related to their capacity-building goals.

As is evident from the types of outcomes accomplished by participating teams, many of these outcomes have direct financial support implications. It takes money to design a new collaborative program between schools and adult agencies, develop and print a resource manual, or conduct an inservice training workshop for all school staff. During each of the 5 years these data were collected, each team received a small discretionary grant (between $500 and $1,000) from the

TABLE 10.2 Amount of Additional Funds Secured by Transition Teams

Number of Teams	1989 (N = 18)		1990 (N = 25)		1991 (N = 29)		1992 (N = 32)		1993 (N = 33)	
Teams reporting additional funds (n, %)	5	28	11	44	13	45	14	44	14	43
Total amount of additional funds ($)	20,832		138,137		231,120		161,149		360,804	
Average amount of funds per team ($)	4,166		12,558		17,778		11,511		25,772	

ODE to help with the implementation of its approved program plan. Table 10.2 presents information on the additional funds that teams secured to help with the implementation of their plans.

As can be seen in Table 10.2, around 40% of participating teams reported securing additional funds beyond the discretionary grant provided by the ODE. The amount of funds teams secured increased steadily over the 5 years we examined these data. Teams were successful in securing funds from a variety of sources, including sponsoring school districts, adult agencies, and state and local charitable organizations. It should be noted that the funds reported by teams were not "in-kind" contributions but rather direct funding of team activities, products, and outcomes. This suggests that teams were successful in building both strong district administrative support and effective interagency collaborations as they implemented their local improvement efforts.

Vignette of a Team's Change Efforts Over Time

The findings presented previously provide a perspective on the outcomes accomplished across participating teams both within and across years. The following vignette provides a more in-depth description of the types of outcomes achieved by one team over time. It is illustrative of the ways in which a team's activities related to one another within any given year and the ways in which activities built cumulatively on one another to create change over time. We describe two areas of activity, both of which address this team's general concern for improving transition services within its community: developing transition planning procedures and increasing family involvement in transition.

Developing Transition Planning Procedures. Transition planning for students with disabilities was a priority for many local community teams even before the legislative mandates in the Individuals With Disabilities Education Act (P.L. 101-476) emerged in 1992. This team focused its attention on transition planning over a 5-year period, beginning in 1991 with the development of a "written transition planning document" and culminating with ongoing procedures for specially trained school district personnel to use with some very difficult students.

During the first year of effort in this area, a small subcommittee of school personnel worked with family members and adult agency representatives to create an individualized transition planning (ITP) form and procedures, reflecting an emphasis on preparing students for life after high school. Over the course of the school year, this new process was field-tested by a few teachers with a few students. The following year, Congress passed P.L. 101-476, and transition planning was mandated, requiring the school district to develop transition goals for all students on IEPs. To assist in this process, the community transition team applied for a Cooperative Personnel Planning Grant from the ODE. The team used the grant to support inservice training for a "working group" of secondary special education teachers in the schools represented by the community transition team. The training had two components: to inform participants of the new transition services component of IDEA and the new transition planning documents developed by the team. As a result of this inservice training, the original ITP forms and procedures were modified to meet the requirements of the new legislation. Over the course of the next 2 years, all of the district's certified special education staff (more than 200 people) were trained in using the new transition planning forms and procedures.

Now that all the special education teachers in the district had a set of written procedures and a form to guide them in their transition planning efforts, the transition team believed that more needed to be done to ensure that all students had the benefit of these procedures. As a final step in addressing this concern, the team secured another grant to train a group of "transition facilitators" (both teachers and support staff) who would work with students and families to assist them in the planning process. Their mission was to find students who were really struggling with (or who may have dropped out of) the existing school system and develop a relationship with these students and their families. The facilitators helped to "hook up" students with needed services and facilitate a process of developing a person-centered transition plan.

Increasing Family Involvement in Transition. During this same timeframe, another subcommittee of the transition team focused its efforts on increasing family involvement in the transition process. The team had ranked this issue near the top of the list in their formal needs assessment, based on the belief that families needed more and better information to support their students with disabilities during the transition years. With that goal in mind, the team decided to schedule several events to educate family members about the transition process as well as possible transition resources.

During the first year of implementing this plan, the team hosted a Transition Fair. The Fair was arranged in a "Home and Garden Show" format, in which various adult service agency representatives set up information tables around the school gym. Parents (and students) could wander around the room, collect materials, and ask questions about possible postschool resources. This Fair was a good way to provide introductory information to a lot of people at the same time. However, some parents wanted more in-depth information and a forum for sharing their concerns. The team designed parent "coffees" to address this need. The Parent Coffees were evening meetings (complete with pie and coffee) organized around a specific transition topic, such as "Applying for Social Security Benefits" or "Post-Secondary Education Options." At each meeting, a guest speaker from the community presented information, and school staff were available to answer questions and discuss how these resources might affect specific students.

The coffees were a great success. In fact, the team decided to hold them once a month over the following school year. Yet the team was not totally satisfied with the impact of this program on parent involvement. The next step in accomplishing this broad goal was to develop a class for parents of students with disabilities. This class, titled "A Parent's Survival Kit," was developed jointly and team-taught by a high school special education teacher and a local vocational rehabilitation counselor who volunteered her time in the evening. The class was revised based on parent input; continues to be offered as an ongoing course at the local community college;

and involves staff from several high schools, the community college, and adult service agencies. The class has been a wonderful opportunity for parents to get information and help prepare their students for the transition from school to the community. As one parent commented, "One of the things that helped me through this [transition] process was talking to other parents who have children with disabilities. . . . Another was having professionals who could describe the whole picture and offer educated advice."

Implications for Supporting Change

Local teams associated with the CTTM were successful in improving the effectiveness, efficiency, and breadth of secondary and transition services for youth with disabilities in their communities—improvements that we believe are similar to the kinds of "first-order" changes that have characterized many of the successful secondary education reform efforts in this century (Cuban, 1988). What contributed to these successes? As we reviewed the educational change literature and reflected on its implications for the CTTM, we concluded that the answers lie in the procedures employed by local teams to identify and address their high-priority needs over time and in the strategies used by the state-level facilitation team to support the entire network of teams.

Fullan and Miles (1992) offer several propositions for successful change that are exemplified by the procedures employed by local teams. First, they suggest that successful change requires an approach that views change as a guided journey rather than a blueprint. "The message is not the traditional 'Plan, then do,' but 'Do, then plan . . . and do and plan some more'" (p. 749). Second, the change process must encourage a systemic view and support a focus on the interrelationships among all of the main components of the system. Third, successful change requires the ability to garner additional, sufficient resources that are focused on local capacity

building. This is because change usually means "developing solutions for complex problems, learning new skills, arriving at new insights, all carried out in a social setting already overloaded with demands" (Fullan & Miles, 1992, p. 750). Finally, change must occur at the level of the local school or community. In the final analysis, implementation by local stakeholders is the only way that change happens.

By design, the needs assessment, planning, implementation, and evaluation procedures used by local teams in the CTTM were very consistent with these propositions. Teams were able to use these procedures to attack high-priority needs and build on their successes in an iterative and cumulative manner. Teams also were effective in identifying and securing additional resources that could be focused on their capacity-building efforts. As we described earlier in this chapter, the efforts of local teams were supported by a state-level structure that included targeted training, technical assistance, and materials. The formative and summative evaluations we conducted with teams indicated that these local and state-level procedures provided local communities with strategies for building effective school and community partnerships. Comments from three teams in the final assessment we conducted in 1993 are illustrative of the findings we obtained over time. When asked to comment on the most important feature of their team's accomplishments, they reported:

Bringing community leaders together around common issues. (Deschutes County Team)

Bringing a diverse group of people together to educate them to the needs of students in transition and to get their input and support. (Jefferson County Team)

Defining community resources and developing them to benefit our students countywide. (Polk County Team)

Our Failures and Their Implications for Sustaining Change

Of course, the question that begs to be asked is, If teams were so successful in bringing about changes in their local communities, then why aren't they still functioning? This question drove us back into the literature on educational change. Before discussing what we learned, we summarize what happened to the CTTM over the past 10 years.

Decline of the CTTM

One of the objectives in the federal grant we obtained originally to develop the CTTM admonished us to "secure state funding for continuation of the program once federal funds are terminated." This was no easy accomplishment at the time, given the existing (and unfortunately still current) track record of most federally funded projects with regard to continuation in implementation sites after termination of external funds. So, when the ODE made a commitment to continue the CTTM and the support structure for the statewide network of teams using state personnel and funds, we hailed our accomplishments in the final report we submitted in 1990 to the funding agency.

Unfortunately, this commitment began to wane over time. The first signs of attrition occurred in the assignment of staff time to the CTTM. In 1990, ODE assigned two staff to support the statewide network of teams, accounting for a total 1.25 FTE of staff time. Within 12 months, one of those staff persons retired, and ODE decided to assign this FTE to activities associated with other emerging educational initiatives in the state, leaving a total 0.75 FTE to support the entire network. Over the next 3 years, the remaining staff person's time devoted to on-site technical assistance to local teams was reduced and reassigned to monitoring local school districts for compliance with federal and state regulations related to special education, an activity that demands considerable attention in all state

education agencies across the country. During this same time frame, state-funded incentive grants to help local teams implement their annual action plans went from $1,000 to $500 to zero dollars. In addition, state support for the biannual team leader meetings was reduced, first by reducing the number of days for each meeting from 2 days to 1 day and eventually by reducing the number of meetings from two to one per year.

By 1994, state support for the network of teams consisted of funding to conduct one annual 1-day meeting and assignment of staff time to manage the paperwork associated with the needs assessment, planning, and evaluation functions of local teams. Staff time for providing local teams with technical assistance was dramatically reduced. By fall 1995, in a survey of the 33 teams remaining in the network (down from 38 in 1993), 16 teams described themselves as very active (defined as meeting regularly and playing an important role in developing transition services and policy), and the remaining 17 teams described themselves as somewhat active (defined as meeting but with little clear direction and focus). In 1995, the staff person with responsibility for assisting transition teams retired, and his replacement was not given any responsibilities for assisting the quickly declining network of teams. In 1998, the CTTM was no longer functioning in Oregon.

Implications for Sustaining Change

So what happened to the CTTM? What contributed to the disintegration of this once viable force for change in local communities throughout the state? Given the accomplishments of local teams and the initial commitment of the ODE to the statewide network, why was the CTTM not sustained over time? What we understood only vaguely at the time, and perhaps a little more clearly now, is that sustainability is not an event. In our early efforts to achieve our final project objective and secure continued state funding for the program, we may have failed to appreciate the distinction between transferring the CTTM to the ODE and integrating this approach to change into the structure and culture of the Department. On reflection, we believe we failed to appreciate fully the complexity of the sustainability process. We now offer the following three propositions for sustaining a process of change based on our experiences with the CTTM. We describe them separately, but, in practice, they are integrally related to one another.

Sustainability of Local Change Efforts Such as the CTTM Requires Specific Attention to the Integration of the Innovation Into Existing Programs at Both State and Local Levels

More than two decades ago, Berman and McLaughlin (1976) noted the importance of the concept of mutual adaptation for the sustainability of the innovations they studied. Mutual adaptation is a *process* through which the initial design of the innovation is adapted to fit the particular school and community in which it is being implemented, and the school and its staff adapt to the demands of the innovation. It is a process that can be influenced and that must begin during the early stages of implementation and continue into and through the stages when decisions are being made about the incorporation of the innovation (Berman & McLaughlin, 1976; Fullan, 1991). Ideally, the end result of the mutual adaptation process is a conscious set of decisions about whether the innovation will be continued, what components of the innovation will be incorporated and continued, and on what scale the innovation will be maintained.

Our failure to attend sufficiently to the mutual adaptation process and to help key policymakers at state and local levels make conscious decisions about the incorporation

of the CTTM may have contributed to the feelings of fragmentation and overload we heard reported by state staff and team members in local communities. Fragmentation and overload occur when multiple reform efforts are perceived to work—or in fact do work—at cross-purposes or in disjointed ways (Fullan, 1996). With regard to fragmentation, during the time the CTTM was developing in communities across the state, several other initiatives were begun within the ODE and within the Oregon Department of Human Resources.[1] Many of these initiatives also involved "local teams" that directly touched on the roles of local transition teams associated with the CTTM. Comments from focus group interviews with team members illustrate this point.

Lack of a clear mandate for collaboration from the state leaves local collaboration across agencies up to individual attitudes and personalities—which can be both good and bad. (Team Leader Meeting, December 1992)

Community transition teams do not exist in a vacuum. Other system change efforts are also operating in many communities (e.g., supported employment councils, interagency coordination councils from [the Department of Human Resources]), often involving the very same people who serve on transition teams. The relationships among these various entities is [sic] usually unclear. (Team Leader Meeting, April 1993)

The fragmentation experienced by local team members was exacerbated by their beliefs of being overloaded with responsibility, especially for local team leaders, and their beliefs that teams were operating at the periphery. These issues emerged strongly in several focus groups we conducted with teams, as illustrated by the subsequent comments.

Whenever possible, the work being done by transition team members should be construed as part of their paid jobs, rather than a voluntary add-on effort. This is especially important for team leaders, whose level of commitment must be substantial if the transition team is to thrive. (Team Leader Meeting, December 1992)

Many transition teams feel that they are tolerated rather than supported. This often translates into a feeling that their work is not perceived to be valuable enough to warrant a genuine effort on their part. Transition teams need to be "legitimized" by top policy makers, and perhaps even formalized through legislative mandate. (Team Leader Meeting, April 1993)

To our knowledge, these feelings of fragmentation and overload were never addressed satisfactorily. Change, especially complex change in education, is inherently nonlinear and fragmented (Fullan, 1996). Addressing these characteristics of change and reducing feelings of fragmentation and overload requires helping those responsible for implementing change efforts to "see the big picture" and to incorporate the fragments of change into this picture (Fullan, 1996). It also requires clear commitment from state and local administrators (McLaughlin, 1990) and strategies to respond to the "resource-hungry" nature of change (Fullan & Miles, 1992). For local team members in the CTTM, solutions to these issues were defined in part as building transition team responsibilities into their basic job duties. Would we have been able to address these issues satisfactorily if we had understood the mutual adaptation process more clearly and the distinction between transferring responsibility for the CTTM and integrating the critical components of the model into state and local structures? Perhaps.

Sustainability of Local Change Efforts Such as the CTTM Requires a Commitment Over an Extended Period of Time, Eventually Requiring the Support of Policymakers Who Were Not Themselves Responsible for the Innovation

It is obvious that change takes time and that complex change takes longer. But maintaining the momentum for the CTTM became difficult as new staff within the ODE assumed responsibility for an innovation they did not create. We believe 1993 became the watershed year for the CTTM in terms of a challenge for maintaining a consistent focus on local teams as instruments for local change and capacity building. By 1993, with only one exception, the creators and supporters of the CTTM in the ODE and the University of Oregon no longer had direct responsibility for the network. The State Director of Special Education, who had been instrumental in obtaining the federal and state funds to start the CTTM and who guided the initial development of local teams, had retired. As we described earlier, of the two staff in ODE who had direct responsibility for the network, one of these individuals had retired, and the other had the time he devoted to on-site technical assistance reduced substantially. Although this staff person retained responsibility for the CTTM until his retirement in 1995, his ability to provide direct support to local teams was severely limited. Our involvement in providing direct support to the network and the involvement of staff that worked with us at the University of Oregon ended in 1992.

In fall 1992, the ODE received a major federal grant to conduct systems-change activities in transition services for youth with disabilities. This new grant brought new staff who assumed responsibility for the statewide network of local teams. These new staff had not been involved in the creation of the CTTM. Based on our conversations with them during this time period, and on our review of documents from meetings held during that time, we believe they had two major concerns about the CTTM. First, they did not support philosophically the community capacity-building focus of the CTTM. They believed that teams should be focusing on the needs of individual students. Second, they were skeptical about the effectiveness of the local teams and the value of the state-level structure that supported teams' efforts. Several concept papers were written by these staff in late 1993, all aimed at addressing these concerns and creating alternative visions for the CTTM. The preambles from two of those papers illustrate these points:

> The following is a proposal to expand the mission of the community transition teams, currently operating throughout Oregon, to include more direct support to individual students and families. It is the intent of this proposal to combine the systems-change activities of community transition teams with activities which focus on community collaboration and facilitation of the transition service components of students' individual education plans. The outcome of this cooperative effort will be a network of community transition teams that are *self-supporting* [italics added] and responsive to the needs of individual students. (Concept Paper 1)

> Transition issues, being both global and specific in scope, present unique problems beyond any existing service system. By pairing a parent/community member and a member of an existing transition team, a powerful alliance could be forged. Through training in person-centered planning and the creative utilization of resources, these pairs

could be available as Community Transition Facilitators to schools, community, and families to develop plans leading to the student being situated upon leaving school. (Concept Paper 2)

Many of the concerns these new staff expressed about the CTTM—such as the inequitable participation of parents and other community members relative to school and agency staff—were valid. Several teams, in their annual evaluations, reported difficulty recruiting parents and other community members and retaining their active participation over time. To our knowledge, however, no conscious decision was made regarding the future of the CTTM. Instead, beginning in 1994, a new initiative was implemented through the systems-change grant to create "Community Building Groups." The purpose of the Community Building Groups initiative was to bring key school and community stakeholders together to identify resources and develop plans for improving transition services and outcomes for youth with disabilities. This initiative was implemented in six pilot communities with a modest level of support from grant-funded staff. Community Building Groups flourished for a period of time, but they did not remain as a legacy of the grant when it ended in 1997.

Was the dismantling of the CTTM inevitable with a change in personnel and the change in philosophy that occurred with these new staff? Can new personnel with differing philosophies embrace a long-term commitment to the steady work of change in local communities without first requiring dismantling the work of others who have gone before? Can we view the change process as part of a long-range reform plan that will survive changes in personnel? Is it possible to make a sustained commitment to sustainability? We do not have confident answers to these questions. We do know, however, that we are not the first to ask them (e.g., McLaughlin, 1990; Pipho, 1996).

Sustainability of Local Change Efforts Such as the CTTM Requires Ultimately That Fundamental Changes Occur in the Prevailing Cultures of Local Schools, State Education Agencies, and Institutions of Higher Education

Cultures do not, and probably should not, change easily. The tendency to support the status quo represents an appropriate desire not to tinker with something unless it is clearly broken. In other words, innovation rarely can occur without coming into direct confrontation with inertia. Furthermore, when this confrontation does occur under the banner of "change," the innovations usually must be accompanied by external support and legislative or judicial mandates, for a period of time, before the struggle between innovation and inertia is resolved. As this struggle unfolds, those responsible for implementing the innovation at all levels, front-line and administrative, eventually must coalesce in order for the innovation eventually to become integrated into the prevailing culture of the organizations responsible for its implementation. To what extent did the CTTM achieve such cultural integration? The journey toward each integration must begin with partnerships among stakeholders who have strong interest both in the status quo and in the innovations being explored.

We believe, at its heart, that the CTTM was about building effective partnerships. At the local level, schools were expected to build new partnerships with parents, students, and community members. At the state level, the ODE and the University of Oregon were required to build a partnership with one another to establish an effective state facilitation team and then build partnerships with the local teams that comprised the statewide network. These partnerships required new roles and

ways of thinking for the participants and changes in the expectations and structures of the participating agencies. Those of us involved in the CTTM at state and local levels viewed these changes as exciting and positive. What we may have failed to appreciate fully at the time is that "judgement of whether a change is an improvement rests in the mind of the beholder" (Cuban, 1988, p. 341).

The reality that stakeholders can view change through very different—even diametrically opposed—lenses may help explain the difficulties that local teams sometimes experienced in obtaining and maintaining active participation from parents and community members and in securing strong support from local school and adult agency administrators. It is possible that nonparticipating parents and community members and reluctant administrators did not view the change activities of the local team in the same positive light as did team members, especially because these changes called for the infusion of new resources. Differing perspectives on the desirability of change also may help explain the changes we described previously in the roles of the state-level CTTM facilitators. The proactive, on-site technical assistance to local teams provided by facilitators at the time the ODE assumed responsibility for the CTTM was unfamiliar to the state education agency. The shifting of this person's responsibilities during the next 4 years to monitoring compliance with federal and state regulations, conducting the 1-day team leader meetings, and managing paperwork associated with the network all were much more familiar to the agency, and in fact were highly consistent with the duties of other staff in the agency.

We were attempting to change prevailing school and community "systems" through these new partnerships at local and state levels. We were attempting to reshape the ways in which local schools interacted with key transition stakeholders in their communities and the ways in which the state education agency interacted with local schools. But, like a rubber band that returns to its original shape and size when it no longer is being pulled, these organizations returned relatively easily to familiar structures and patterns when the "pressure" of the CTTM began to wane. After delving back into the education change literature, we might now conclude like Fullan (1996) that "Systems have a better track record of maintaining the status quo than they have of changing themselves" (p. 423). Ultimately, Fullan noted, it is people who change systems. This change begins to occur when individuals with new attitudes and behaviors reach a sufficiently critical mass that they begin changing the culture (i.e., the values, beliefs, norms, and practices) of their agency.

So how can we help key stakeholders view change through similar sets of lenses, and how can we build the critical masses necessary to change the cultures of participating agencies in positive and enduring ways? The key may lie in a combination of external facilitation and legislative or regulatory mandates.

The importance of external facilitation of local capacity building is supported strongly in the educational change literature (e.g., DeLone, 1990; Fullan, 1991; Fullan & Miles, 1992; McLaughlin, 1990; Scott et al., 1989). Change is complex and difficult:

> During transitions from a familiar to a new state of affairs, individuals must normally confront the loss of the old and commit themselves to the new, unlearn old beliefs and behaviors and learn new ones, and move from anxiousness and uncertainty to stabilization and coherence. Any significant change involves a period of intense personal and organizational learning and problem solving. People need support for such work. (Fullan, 1996, p. 748)

Of course, acknowledging the importance of an external support structure to facilitate local change efforts brings us full circle to one of the original design principles of the CTTM. Responses by transition team members to a survey conducted in 1995 by staff associated with Oregon's systems-change grant affirm the importance of external facilitation and ongoing professional development. Despite the fact that support to sites had diminished considerably by that point, more than 90% of the 35 teams responding reported wanting on-site technical assistance, continued funding of team leader meetings, and opportunities to network with other teams in the state. Comments by several teams illustrate the importance of external facilitation:

> I think it is essential for the state-wide network of transition teams to continue. The support generated by this "peer group" is reinforcing and encourages creativity. (Eugene School District Team)

> Periodic meetings and support. We have really appreciated [the ODE facilitator]. He has given our program support and assistance. He will be missed. (North Clackamas School District Team)

> Very much want ODE to continue planning and facilitating Team Leader meetings. (Josephine County Team)

> We want to know that someone is at the ODE to help if we need it. (Central Point School District Team)

> We still need to be informed of changes ongoing at the State Department level and, no matter where we are, we should always be trying to improve and give better services to our students. (Burns County Team)

What will it take to ensure external facilitation is available to support the change efforts of local communities? Clearly, the support provided to local teams in the CTTM was effective and appreciated. Yet neither the ODE nor the University of Oregon was willing to continue this function over time. In the case of the ODE, the initial commitment of funds and personnel devoted to external facilitation and professional development activities was reduced gradually until it no longer supported the network in any direct, functional way. The provision of proactive, on-site technical assistance to local communities was—and remains—inconsistent with the prevailing culture of the agency. In the case of the University of Oregon, our involvement with the CTTM ended with the termination of external funds to support our activities. Assigning faculty time to supporting the change efforts in local communities is not consistent with the prevailing culture in higher education, especially in research universities. These issues are not unique to Oregon. Indeed, the lack of structures for providing consistent facilitation to local communities is an issue in many states.

Because the natural condition of agencies and organizations normally will support the status quo, we reluctantly have concluded that legislative or regulatory mandates may be required ultimately to change the inertia and culture of systems. This raises some intriguing questions. Should state education agencies be mandated to conduct proactive professional development and external facilitation activities in addition to or in place of the compliance monitoring activities that now consume so much time and effort? Should colleges of education that are supported by public tax dollars, including those at research universities such as the University of Oregon, be expected and mandated to participate in the steady work of change in local communities?

The educational literature is mixed in its support for mandated change. Fullan (1996) eschews regulatory reform as folly and argues instead for strategies that mobilize large numbers of people in new directions. This seems reasonable to us, but we are not sure what to do when agencies responsible for the external facilitation of these strategies fail to participate. Cuban (1988), in his analysis of different kinds of planned change, noted that over the past three decades many of the "first-order" changes that have been adapted and sustained in local schools have been sponsored by federal and state legislation (e.g., procedural and programmatic changes in schooling practices brought about by federal legislation in special education). This is encouraging because we would describe the accomplishments of the local teams in the CTTM as being largely first-order changes. McLaughlin (1990) suggests that belief can follow practice and that individuals who are required to change or take up new practices can become believers: "Belief or commitment to change can follow mandated or coerced involvement at both the individual and the system level" (p. 13). Of course, such a strategy is not foolproof. At some point, mandated change must merge with local will, and it is the results of this merger that determine the vitality with which practices are implemented (McLaughlin, 1990).

Summary and Conclusions

We opened this chapter by noting that systems change is a very tricky business, in that most systems have very little interest in being changed. By its very nature, a system represents a collection of attitudes and experiences that characterize the culture of an organization or a group of interrelated organizations that share some common goals and methods of pursuing these goals. This culture evolves over time, gaining both complexity and inertia, and presents a natural barrier against those who promote "innovation" as a new way to address long-standing problems.

In the area of secondary special education and transition programs, systems change is fairly complex because it involves the school system, the adult service system, the private sector system (e.g., employers), and the interactions among all three. The CTTM was an attempt to help appropriate members of local communities sharpen their visions, conceptualize program improvement, obtain needed resources, improve local services and resources, and network effectively with colleagues, all for the purpose of enhancing the transition of students with disabilities from high school as they begin to assume emerging roles as young adults in their communities. The CTTM included procedures and materials to structure the efforts of individual local teams and procedures and materials to facilitate and support the entire network of teams.

As we described in this chapter, the structure associated with the CTTM was successful in nurturing the development of local teams and supporting their program improvement activities, and it allowed the entire network of teams to grow and flourish for almost 10 years. Yet, as we also described, despite our successes, the statewide network of community transition teams no longer exists. So, what should we conclude about the rise and fall of the CTTM? What should we emphasize? Should we praise its accomplishments or mourn its failures? Most important, what can we learn about the conditions that are necessary to engage members of local communities in systems change and to support their activities over time?

Both our personal experiences and our reflections on relevant literature suggest that sustainability of a systems-change model is enhanced when the following conditions are present:

1. A carefully designed innovation is available that *addresses a problem of concern* to key state and local stakeholders.

2. Adequate and dependable *financial and personnel resources* are available to implement the innovation.

3. The innovation is supported by an *external structure* that legitimizes the efforts of local users and provides them with locally relevant training, technical assistance, and materials throughout implementation.

4. An evolving sense of *ownership* for the innovation develops, signifying a respect for the values that underlie the

innovation and a determination to *integrate* it into existing programs and the culture that supports these programs.

5. *Sufficient time* is available for the innovation to pass muster through a rigorous iterative process of implementation, evaluation, and modification that eventually leads to a well-seasoned program with demonstrable and desirable outcomes, incorporated into the existing cultures of the affected agencies.

Indeed, if these are some essential conditions for sustaining innovations within a statewide systems-change model, how long must the innovation be sustained in order for it to be deemed successful? Certainly not forever. For it would seem that very few innovations are strong enough to influence the beliefs and policy mandates of "any reasonable person" in a consistent and similar manner over an extended period of time. Any given problem usually can be approached in several different ways. The specific problems that capture our imagination and demand our attention also vary among individuals and over time.

Indeed, if the life span of most innovations is not forever, what does it mean to encourage the sustainability of any given innovation? Perhaps the lesson we have learned most clearly over the past 15 years of experience with the CTTM and other related initiatives we have conducted is that change is everchanging, innovations will spawn new innovations, and sustainability requires an organization's commitment to support local change efforts in a general way that transcends specific innovations. Under the best of circumstances, given the conditions we described previously, innovations will be developed, adopted, and adapted in response to specific problems of concern to state and local agencies. But the cycle will not end there. By design, innovations are specific to their problems. New and continuing problems inevitably must give rise to additional innovations, and these innovations also must be supported if they are to address adequately the presenting problem and leave a legacy within participating agencies. This legacy will include the incorporation of some components of a proven innovation into the agency's status quo, accompanied by a general receptivity to explore new opportunities for improvement.

In support of this notion that sustainability may be a never-ending, ever-evolving process and that the ultimate and inevitable manifestation of sustainability is metamorphosis, we close this chapter with a brief discussion of the legacy of the CTTM. You may recall from our earlier discussions that transition teams eventually became restless with the program *development* focus of the CTTM and wanted to spend more of their efforts on the *implementation* of new and promising programs. This shift in emphasis also was evident in the value orientations that emerged in 1992 when Oregon received its 5-year systems-change grant from the federal Office of Special Education Programs.

At the same time that this desire for implementing innovations was growing stronger, a new program concept also was emerging that would be designed to strengthen transition services through an effective collaboration between secondary special education and vocational rehabilitation programs. This potential innovation emerged in part from a sense of trust that developed as special educators and rehabilitation professionals sat around the same table on community transition teams and began to work together toward the identification of program needs in their local communities and the development of new programs to respond to these needs. When the ideas for this specific new program began to coalesce across the network of transition teams, the program was given a name, the Youth Transition Program (YTP), and two events occurred that gave birth to the YTP. The first event involved members of 38 transition teams across Oregon successfully lobbying the Oregon legislature to provide state funding for the YTP as a line item in the budget for the Oregon Vocational Rehabilitation Division. The second event involved staff from the University of Oregon securing a federal grant to develop the operational components and supporting materials for the YTP and providing training and technical assistance to new implementers of the program in local communities. From a modest beginning in 1990, enthusiasm and support for the program has grown dramatically, and the YTP is now operating in 75% of all high schools throughout Oregon (Benz, 1998; Benz & Lindstrom, 1997).

For better or for worse, enthusiasm and support for the CTTM in Oregon has been replaced by enthusiasm and support for its legacies. But the caveats still remain. If the YTP is to be sustained, it will need to be incorporated into the existing cultures of the vocational rehabilitation agency and the collaborating state and local education agencies.

The rise and fall of the CTTM, which spawned the YTP as an offspring, are only examples of innovations that purport to address long-standing problems with new insights. Such innovations always will be confronted with the inertia of the status quo. But the status quo itself will evolve, if ever so slowly, as truly effective innovations become adopted or adapted into the mainstream agency cultures. As we think about and promote sustainability, we must recognize that the confrontation between innovation and inertia is not likely to result in a "winner take all" outcome. Our responsibility is to pay attention to those conditions, described previously, that enhance the sustainability of proven innovations and facilitate useful offspring, recognizing that organizational cultures can (and should) only partially be changed as old ways are integrated with new ways of doing business.

Note

1. The Department of Human Resources is an umbrella agency in Oregon that consists of many community-based service agencies, such as vocational rehabilitation, developmental disabilities, and mental health programs.

References

Benz, M. R. (1998). *Project SUSTAIN: Strategies for understanding and sustaining educational innovations*. Washington, DC: U.S. Department of Education, Office of Special Education Programs.

Benz, M. R., & Halpern, A. S. (1986). Vocational preparation for high school students with mild disabilities: A statewide study of administrator, teacher, and parent perceptions. *Career Development for Exceptional Individuals, 9*, 3-15.

Benz, M. R., & Halpern, A. S. (1987). Transition services for secondary students with mild disabilities: A statewide perspective. *Exceptional Children, 53*, 507-514.

Benz, M. R., & Lindstrom, L. E. (1997). *Building school-to-work programs: Strategies for youth with special needs*. Austin, TX: PRO-ED.

Benz, M. R., Lindstrom, L. E., Halpern, A. S., & Rothstrom, R. (1990). *Community Transition Team Model: Facilitator's manual*. Eugene: University of Oregon.

Berman, P., & McLaughlin, M. (1976). Implementation of educational innovation. *Educational Forum, 40*, 345-370.

Brolin, D., Durand, R., Kromer, K., & Muller, P. (1975). Postschool adjustment of educable retarded students. *Education and Training of the Mentally Retarded, 10*, 144-149.

Cuban, L. (1988). A fundamental puzzle of school reform. *Phi Delta Kappan, 69*, 341-344.

Cuban, L. (1990). Reforming again, again, and again. *Educational Researcher, 19*, 3-13.

DeLone, R. H. (1990). *Replication: A strategy to improve the delivery of education and job training programs*. Philadelphia: Public/Private Ventures.

Edgar, E. (1987). Secondary programs in special education: Are many of them justifiable? *Exceptional Children, 53*, 555-561.

Fafard, M., & Haubrich, P. A. (1981). Vocational and social adjustment of learning disabled young adults: A followup study. *Learning Disability Quarterly, 1*, 122-130.

Fardig, D., Algozzine, R., Schwartz, S., Hensel, J., & Westling, D. (1985). Postsecondary vocational adjustment of rural, mildly handicapped students. *Exceptional Children, 52*, 115-121.

Fullan, M. G. (1982). *The meaning of educational change*. New York: Teachers College Press.

Fullan, M. G. (1991). *The new meaning of educational change*. New York: Teachers College Press.

Fullan, M. G. (1996). Turning systemic thinking on its head. *Phi Delta Kappan, 77*, 420-423.

Fullan, M. G., & Miles, M. B. (1992). Getting reform right: What works and what doesn't. *Phi Delta Kappan, 73*, 745-752.

Halpern, A. (1987). Characteristics of a quality program. In C. Warger & B. Weiner (Eds.), *Secondary special education: A guide to promising public school programs* (pp. 25-55). Reston, VA: Council for Exceptional Children.

Halpern, A. (1990). A methodological review of follow-up and follow-along studies tracking school leavers in special education. *Career Development for Exceptional Individuals, 13*(1), 13-28.

Halpern, A. S., & Benz, M. R. (1987). A statewide examination of secondary special education for students with mild disabilities: Implications for the high school curriculum. *Exceptional Children, 54*, 122-129.

Halpern, A., Lindstrom, L., Benz, M., & Rothstrom, R. (1990). *Community Transition Team Model: Needs assessment instrument*. Eugene: University of Oregon.

Halpern, A., Nelson, D., Lindstrom, L., & Benz, M. (1990). *Community Transition Team Model: Team leader's manual*. Eugene: University of Oregon.

Hasazi, S. B., Gordon, L. R., & Roe, C. A. (1985). Factors associated with the employment status of handicapped youth exiting high school from 1979 to 1983. *Exceptional Children, 51*, 455-469.

Hasazi, S., Gordon, L., Roe, C., Finck, K., Hull, M., & Salembier, G. (1985). A statewide follow-up on post high school employment and residential status of students labeled mentally retarded. *Education and Training of the Mentally Retarded, 20*, 223-234.

Heal, L. W., Copher, J. I., & Rusch, F. R. (1990). Interagency agreements (IAAs) among agencies responsible for the transition education of students with handicaps for secondary schools to post-secondary settings. *Career Development for Exceptional Individuals, 13*, 121-127.

Hord, S. M., Rutherford, W. L., Huling-Austin, L., & Hall, G. E. (1987). *Taking charge of change*. Alexandria, VA: Association for Supervision and Curriculum Development.

Humes, C. H., & Brammer, G. (1985). LD career success after high school. *Academic Therapy, 21*(2), 171-176.

Individuals With Disabilities Education Act of 1990, 42 U.S.C.A. § 12101 *et seq.* (West 1993).

Individuals With Disabilities Education Act Amendments of 1997, 20 U.S.C. §§ 1400-1487 (1997).

Kregel, J., Wehman, P., Seyfarth, J., & Marshall, K. (1986). Community integration of young adults with mental retardation: Transition from school to adulthood. *Education and Training of the Mentally Retarded, 21*, 35-42.

Lindstrom, L., Ard, W., Benz, M., & Halpern, A. (1990). *Community Transition Team Model: Management information system manual*. Eugene: University of Oregon.

McLaughlin, M. W. (1990). The Rand Change Agent Study revisited: Macro perspectives and micro realities. *Educational Researcher, 19*, 11-16.

Mithaug, D. E., Horiuchi, C. N., & Fanning, P. N. (1985). A report on the Colorado statewide follow-up survey of special education students. *Exceptional Children, 15,* 397-404.

O'Brien, P. J., & Schiller, W. J. (1979). Evaluation of a transitional training program for mentally retarded, multiply handicapped high school students. *Rehabilitation Literature, 40,* 232-235.

Pipho, C. (1996). Removing obstacles from the path of reform. *Phi Delta Kappan, 77,* 462-463.

Schalock, R. L., Wolzen, B., Ross, I., Elliott, B., Werbel, G., & Peterson, K. (1986). Postsecondary community placement of handicapped individuals:

A five-year follow-up analysis. *Learning Disability Quarterly, 9,* 295-303.

Scott, A. C., Yin, R. K., Zantal-Wiener, K., Cheung, O. M., Erlanger, W. J., & Yin, R. T. (1989). *Evaluation of discretionary programs under the Education of the Handicapped Act: Diffusion study final report.* Washington, DC: COSMOS Corp.

Will, M. (1984). *OSERS programming for the transition of youth with disabilities: Bridges from school to working life.* Washington, DC: U.S. Department of Education.

Zigmond, N., & Thornton, H. (1985). Follow-up of post-secondary age learning disabled graduates and dropouts. *Learning Disabilities Research, 1*(1), 50-55.

CHAPTER ELEVEN

How Does Technology Support a Special Education Agenda?

Using What We Have Learned to Inform the Future

MARLEEN C. PUGACH
University of Wisconsin-Milwaukee

CYNTHIA L. WARGER
Warger, Eavy, & Associates

For more than two decades, technology has been used to solve problems in the field of special education. The results of technology utilization in special education have been significant in improving the lives of students with disabilities (Woodward, Gallagher, & Rieth, Chapter 1, this volume; Woodward & Rieth, 1997). From assistive technology (AT) that enables students to participate in typical school settings, to computer-assisted instruction (CAI) that allows teachers flexibility in how they manage individualized education programs (IEP), to administrative tools that offer efficient management of paperwork, to programs that crunch assessment data and present profiles of individual student learning strengths and weaknesses—technology has proven its worth in supporting a special education agenda.

The value and potential of technology to advance special education has been recognized at the federal level as well. The U.S. Department of Education, Office of Special Education Programs, has provided considerable funding for research and development designed to improve the quality, availability, and effective use of technology in special education (Hauser & Malouf, 1996).

Until recently, technology in special education has supported a traditional agenda, one that has promulgated a separate system of education for students with disabilities. In this traditional special education paradigm, technology served an important curricular and instructional function—helping special educators primarily in self-contained and resource rooms provide individualized programs for their students. Today, that agenda is shifting.

This shift, which can be characterized as a serious movement to include increased numbers of students with disabilities in general education curriculum and classrooms, formally was supported at the federal level by the 1997 Reauthorization of the Individuals With Disabilities Education Act (1997) (IDEA '97). Under this legislation, students with disabilities are expected to participate in the neighborhood schools and general education classrooms in which they normally would and expected to learn in the standard curriculum (however that is defined locally) alongside their peers without disabilities. To the extent possible, students with disabilities also are expected to participate in large-scale assessments, extracurricular activities, and standard school routines. Should school personnel determine that such participation is not appropriate for a given student, they must produce sufficient evidence to justify their position.

For the vast majority of students with high-incidence disabilities, the general education curriculum is the starting point for any individualization or accommodation that is required to foster their success in learning. In addition, although a full continuum of supplementary supports and services is still at the core of special education, there has been an ideological shift to implementing the belief that "special education is a service, not a place." It is precisely this shift that represents the new paradigm that is guiding—and will guide—the delivery of special education services in the future and the role of technology in their delivery. This systemic change in how we view and provide special education ser-

vices requires us to reassess technology as a player in the change process. The situation is more complex because technology will have to expand far beyond traditional, segregated special education practice. The question we must ask today is, How does technology support this shifting special education agenda?

From a federal perspective, technology continues to be viewed as important to advancing special education. This is evidenced by the new mandate in IDEA '97 to require supplementary aids and supports—which may include technology—to accommodate student learning needs in general education school environments. Even more significant is the new IDEA requirement to consider AT for all students as part of their IEPs.

The purpose of this volume is to use the case of technology to illustrate some of the deeper issues facing special education today. At the core of this discussion is a consideration of the role technology utilization can play in advancing special education in this new paradigm, this context of special education as a service rather than simply a place. If it does not, then our efforts to implement it and increase its utilization most likely will be met with less than positive responses.

The chapters in this volume offer an entry point into understanding how technology might be used to assist students with disabilities in attaining high standards in the general education curriculum and, therefore, how technology can support contemporary special education practice. Many of the researchers featured in this volume used the general education curriculum portal to begin their technology implementation work; that is, rather than frame their work in the old special education paradigm—which separated students with disabilities and most often advocated for interventions that were decontextualized from general education classrooms and their concomitant curriculums—they instead mapped their particular projects onto what was already going on in the district or in the classroom curriculum. Their approaches were defined by the general education curriculum, and their purpose became one of figuring out how best to individualize and provide accommodations in that learning environment. When the curriculum represented an instance of reform, they matched their work to those reforms. This approach led them away from the traditional mode of looking at students and determining, for example, that they needed CAI to be successful. Rather, they looked at the curriculum, valued it, and asked, "How might technology be used to assist students in this classroom in accessing and learning this curriculum?" As such, we draw on the work of these authors for examples as we explore some of the issues that face special education in terms of the paradigm in which it is now operating.

One way to begin thinking broadly about whether technology supports this new special education agenda is to look at the potential role of technology in the prevailing general education curriculum and, therefore, at its potential use in solving problems and providing solutions to the kinds of instructional issues that face students with disabilities. We believe that this issue must be explored prior to any consideration of the complex implementation issues associated with technology. Indeed, technology has the potential to augment human capacities and provide instructional alternatives—but it is not at all clear if technology can do anything to make the general education curriculum more accessible. And although we recognize that not all students with disabilities will necessarily be expected to achieve in the general education curriculum, the trend is unmistakably moving in this direction. To encourage dialogue on this issue, we begin with a brief overview of some of the basic issues related to providing access to the general education curriculum to students with disabilities. We then move on to a general consideration of how technology may be of help. We conclude with a discussion of some of the emerging issues relevant to the question.

Access to the General Education Curriculum

Curriculum is at the heart of schooling. However, as many special educators have observed, students who are increasingly being included in general education classrooms are the same students who were excluded in the first place because of their unsuccessful performance in the standard curriculum. Unfortunately, the standard curriculum continues to pose problems for students with disabilities and thus affects the ease and success with which their integration into general education classrooms and into the general education curriculum can take place (Pugach & Warger, 1996).

When considering the question of access, special educators have moved beyond a consideration of mere proximity and presence-in-the-classroom goals. Access is more than having students with disabilities sitting in classrooms with their same-age peers working on separate curriculum goals and activities. Rather, the emphasis is on the diversification of curriculum and instruction to accommodate a wide range of student learning needs and abilities. In this context, access to the general education curriculum has two components: (a) participation in instruction alongside peers without disabilities, and (b) the opportunity actually to learn the curriculum outcomes.

Relative to participation, too often students are denied access to the curriculum simply because they do not have the prerequisite skills that will allow them to participate in the instructional lesson. For example, if the lesson includes a lecture, then students will need the skills of listening and focusing for sometimes extended periods of time, taking notes, sitting quietly, knowing how to interrupt to ask for clarification, and so forth. If the lecturer uses materials or writes information on the chalkboard, then students also will need to be able to see and, possibly, copy information. If the lesson requires group discussion, then, in addition to content knowledge, students will need a variety of social communication skills, such as listening, asking questions, disagreeing appropriately, sharing information, and waiting one's turn.

In the case of students with sensory and physical disabilities, the concept of access to instructional lessons is perhaps most familiar. If a student has difficulty with vision and the presentation requires the review of written information, instructional accommodations are made to ensure that the student can obtain the written information from another medium or source. Access to participation in the curriculum and instructional process for students with cognitive or behavioral difficulties involves a different kind of accommodation. For example, participating in group projects requires not only content knowledge and social skills but also independent learning skills such as being prepared and staying on task. Students will need all these skills if they are to participate in instruction, thereby deriving learning benefit from it.

In other cases, the problem for students with disabilities lies with the structure and content of the curriculum itself. In the past decade, concepts of what constitutes *good* curriculum have changed significantly. Most schools now have embraced a reformed curriculum, one that calls for more rigorous content and increased academic standards for all students by emphasizing in-depth coverage of content, students' abilities to think critically and to solve problems creatively, and integration into the curriculum of concepts that are connected across subject areas. Although the traditional curriculum may have posed problems because of its diffuse and disconnected structure, new difficulties can arise for students when the cognitive level of the content is too high, requires analytic skills that the student does not have, or assumes a certain knowledge base that is not present. So at both the participation and curriculum structure levels, challenges are posed for students with disabilities.

However, as curriculum reform has progressed, so too have views about technology use in these reformed curricula. Although reports like that of the Office of Technology Assessment (OTA, 1995) paint a bleak picture of teachers' embrace of technology, the potential clearly is evident. Rather than viewing technology as an "add-on," current thinking envisions technology embedded within curriculum and instruction as a tool—an "accommodation" that is necessary for all students—for meeting curriculum goals. In a recent chapter by Williams et al. (1998), the role of technology in reformed curriculum was summarized:

- ◻ Technology tools enable teachers to bring information about important, authentic problems into the classroom, in ways that support student understanding and foster student problem solving.

- ◻ Technology tools can support students in solving complex problems and sustaining interest by encouraging in-depth understanding of information.

- ◻ Technology tools can be used to provide frequent feedback, reflection, and revision, all strategies that improve student learning.

- ◻ Technology tools offer opportunities for students to communicate with each other, with teachers, and with the greater community. (p. 115)

In the curriculum standards for every major subject group, technology is identified as being essential to mastering that content area. In fact, in many cases, the standards are obtainable for any student only with the use of technology. Most often, technology is presented as vital to helping students access knowledge, process information, deepen their understanding, and produce evidence of their achievement in the particular subject area (Committee for Economic Development, 1995; Kendall & Marzano, 1996). This is a growing trend in district curricula as well, in which it is common to find standards, as early as elementary school, that include goals such as "The student will use computer application software and related technologies to communicate ideas and solve problems" and "The student will use computer software to reinforce, extend, enrich, and apply skills and concepts."

Furthermore, in these reformed classrooms, technology is considered to be most successful when it is linked with teaching strategies that encourage substantive student discourse and collaboration, strategies such as cooperative learning, thinking skills, guided inquiry, and thematic teaching. When students work with technology together, in pairs and in small groups, they are afforded the opportunity to become active participants in the learning process in many ways. For example, students also use technology to act on information, thus facilitating their learning. Technology stimulates more interactive teaching, effective grouping of students, and cooperative learning (Interactive Educational Systems Design, 1996). It also is important to note that successful implementation of technology does not remove teachers from the scene. Rather, it casts them in new roles as facilitators of learning.

In this new, more complex curricular and instructional context in which technology is already meant to be embedded, special education technology research will need to continue to parallel the existing concerns for access to the curriculum and achieving the learning outcomes of the curriculum. However, the kinds of questions special educators raise in these inquiries must necessarily take into account a full understanding of the reformed curriculum and its technological counterparts and begin where these technological uses leave off as they consider the full range of disabilities students may have.

New Questions and Issues for Technology and Special Education

The general education curriculum emphasized in IDEA is essential in the new paradigm of special education. Participation and access to the general education classroom and curriculum have become prime considerations in developing IEPs. As we consider a student's needs relative to access, is there a role for technology? If a reformed curriculum that promotes deep understanding for all students is in place, can we turn to technology as a viable accommodation for students with disabilities? As we have seen in this volume, technol-

ogy can support students both in participating in general education classroom environments and in accessing the curriculum.

Technology and the Goal of Participation

At its most basic level, technology regularly has supported the presence and participation of many students with disabilities in both segregated and general educational settings. In a sense, one of the traditional roles of AT has been to "fix" an external problem for students with mobility, sensory, and physical needs without worrying too much about the curriculum. AT has a well-proven track record in this regard—not to change the curriculum per se but rather to enable students with sensory or motor disabilities to participate in the existing one—whether it is the traditional or the reformed curriculum. The expectation is that whatever curriculum is in use is appropriate for students with these difficulties.

As it has been understood and implemented to date, this role for AT still functions, but it enables students with sensory and physical disabilities to participate in more inclusive education as well. As Todis (Chapter 2, this volume) points out, AT is an intervention that can increase students' independence, social participation, and academic participation. However, Todis (1996) has been forthright in acknowledging that unresolved problems with assistive devices exist that can impede rather than promote the independence and inclusion of students who rely on them.

Todis describes a number of barriers to full participation in classrooms, such as speed, access, preferences, and setting constraints as they directly relate to the AT. Additional contextual issues—such as how teachers, special educators, classmates, families, and others in the school community perceive and interface with the student and the technology—will need to be addressed as we learn more about how students and their AT interact in inclusive settings (Todis & Walker, 1993). For example, although the response time of a particular technology tool may not have been a detriment to communication between the student and teacher in a traditional special education self-contained classroom, it may put the child at risk in a general education classroom where the teacher's attention is shared among many students. Similarly, in more inclusive settings, students without disabilities will need to learn how to communicate with students who use communication aids; otherwise, students with disabilities may be present but not involved in social interactions.

It is evident that technology has solved many important problems in terms of providing students who have sensory or physical disabilities with the support they need to participate in the activities of schooling. However, solving the problems of participation in inclusive rather than segregated environments is more complex, particularly as those problems relate to cognitive access to the curriculum. Students not only must participate alongside their peers but must also will be expected to learn the curriculum content as well. Can technology use be extended to support this need?

Technology as an Accommodation for Accessing Curriculum

IDEA '97 marks a significant shift in how educators view technology and its relation to the curriculum. Previously, AT was viewed almost exclusively within a rehabilitative or remedial context; now, technology is being considered as a tool for expanding access to the general education curriculum. How can technology be used to accommodate special learning needs in the standard general education curriculum?

The concept of what constitutes an accommodation for a student with high-incidence disabilities—learning, cognitive, or behavioral—is at the forefront of discussions regarding how best to serve these students in a challenging curriculum. For example, many students with learning disabilities have inefficient

strategies for organizing, remembering, and attending to information. Many also lack skills and background knowledge, which often results in their falling further and further behind as new knowledge is built on earlier information they never mastered in the first place. Finally, a large number of these students have problems with self-regulation, or meta-cognitive strategies—problems that cause them great difficulty in evaluating their own performance and progress in the curriculum.

Earlier uses of technologies have addressed specific problems for students with high-incidence disabilities. For example, for some time now, students with learning disabilities that affect their writing have been accommodated with word processors, spell checkers, and word prediction software. Although these tools initially represented accommodations specifically for students labeled as having *disabilities,* today the use of spell checkers is universal in its application for all students, who now regularly rely on word processing programs to facilitate their writing in school.

But what other solutions can technology provide in terms of assisting students in accessing newer, reformed curricular practices, practices that already might embed the use of technology like CAI for basic skills but that demand much more complex cognitive processes on the part of students? What other ways, in addition to supports like the omnipresent spell checkers, can technology assist to ensure access to a challenging curriculum?

Researchers across the country are finding that technology tools, combined with effective instruction, extend learning opportunities for students with disabilities (Council for Exceptional Children, 1998). For some students, technology is being used as a cognitive tool that supports the learning process. For example, both Blackhurst (Chapter 8, this volume) and Woodward and Rieth (1997) discuss how technology is being used to anchor instruction for students who lack background knowledge and experiences—a typical need for many students with high-incidence disabilities who now are being included in the general education curriculum. One solution is to expose students to contextually based examples through the use of multimedia instruction. This approach situates learning in CD-ROM-based or videodisc environments and provides learners with examples of how experts use knowledge to solve problems—thereby allowing teachers to create contextually based experiences in the classroom (Cognition and Technology Group at Vanderbilt University, 1990).

Another way technology can assist in new curricular practices is by helping teachers and students manage the complexities of project-based learning. Project-based learning requires students to learn new information across content areas, to organize it, to integrate it, and to present it. As Okolo and Ferretti (Chapter 3, this volume) demonstrated, when project-based learning is enhanced with technology/multimedia, the quality of the students' written work improves. Students in their studies—both those with disabilities and those without—utilized multimedia authoring programs, scanning pictures and digitized sound in preparing their final reports and presentations. Requiring technology as a means of presenting the results of project-based learning is a way to enable a greater range of students to do well in this form of teaching and learning.

Zorfass (Chapter 5, this volume) utilized technology throughout each stage of the I-Search process to enhance and deepen all students' learning. In all cases, Zorfass seamlessly embedded technology-based accommodations within the instruction to ensure that students with disabilities would be full participants in the instructional environment. For example, using the software Inspiration, Zorfass and her colleagues assisted students with disabilities by using a cognitive organizer tool that provided them with a visual representation of their ideas. Although this tool was essential for students with disabilities, it also enhanced the work of nondisabled students. In another technology-based accommodation, rather than limit students' investigations to traditional texts—something

that typically proves troublesome for students with problems in the literacy area—Zorfass built in instructional opportunities for students to access information from a variety of sources (e.g., media, picture books, software, interviews). In addition, Zorfass developed the Search Organizer software—a tool that provided a concrete structure with prompts for processing information and organizing a research report. Although designed for students with learning disabilities, Zorfass found that the software helped all students complete the task successfully.

In mathematics, Woodward and Baxter (1997) have considered accommodations for middle school students with disabilities who lack basic skills. Using a spreadsheet application, teachers bypass the need for students to read story problems and perform laborious calculations—areas in which many students with cognitive disabilities experience difficulty—and have them focus instead on the mathematical thinking skills. Spreadsheets model or provide visual representations of the problem, crunch the calculations, and focus student attention on understanding the mathematical operations. This accommodation enables students with cognitive disabilities to learn higher-level, age-appropriate skills (i.e., mathematical problem solving) alongside their peers without being hampered by the lack of basic skills.

The work of researchers such as Okolo, Ferretti, Zorfass, Todis, and Woodward provides evidence that technology will continue to be a force in assisting students in accessing the curriculum, whether it be in the traditional role of AT or technology that serves as a cognitive partner. These uses of technology open up opportunities for students to access more complex projects that are often the hallmark of reformed curricula. Although technology continues to support students with sensory and physical disabilities, much of the newer technology provides supports not only for students with disabilities but for all students. Technological advances that in the beginning might be used as accommodations specifically for students with disabilities eventually may become commonplace practice for each student in a given classroom.

Technology as a Tool to Provide Individualization Within a Diversified Curriculum

The increased presence of students with disabilities in the general education curriculum typically extends the range of strengths and needs in the classroom and, thus, how technology might be used. This goes beyond thinking about technology as a special education *accommodation* or *intervention* and moves the conversation directly into reconceptualizing how technology may be viewed as an integral part of reconceptualizing who can be successful in school. In other words, How does technology promote deeper structural changes in schooling that enable all teachers to extend the range of students who can be successful achieving the curriculum? And, once such structural changes are in place and are supported by technology, what kinds of technological supports are needed for individualizing instruction in this new curricular environment?

For technology to help teachers provide more individualized support within the context of diversified instruction in general education instructional environments, applications far beyond CAI must be considered. Although CAI can be found across classrooms, it is rarely sufficient for helping students access the general education curriculum alongside their nondisabled classmates. Furthermore, unless all students in the class are working independently, setting a student with disabilities in front of a computer while his or her nondisabled classmates are engaged in other instructional endeavors does little to support the interaction of students with and without disabilities. As teachers organize their curriculum and instruction to support diverse groups of students, individualized technology accommodations must be embedded and delivered in the context in which students work together.

Greenwood et al.'s (Chapter 4, this volume) ClassWide Peer Tutoring is an example of how technology can support students working together. As the researchers show, such is an effective instructional strategy for diverse groups of learners. However, as they point out, outcomes of classwide peer tutoring are enhanced when teachers use data to inform instruction. In general education classrooms, in which large groups are the norm, technology can support individualization for students by making it possible for teachers to manage the data they need to maximize the effectiveness of the classwide peer tutoring strategy. For all practical purposes, teachers need the technology tool to manage the amount of data and to create the feedback students need—charts and graphs of progress—as well as to use that information for performance assessment. Thus, technology tools enable general education teachers to adopt different classwide strategies for individualizing instruction that require significant management of data. Classwide peer tutoring is no longer an intervention in this regard for some students only but a new way of doing business that has the potential to benefit all students.

The work of Englert and Zhao (Chapter 9, this volume) is another good example of a comprehensive approach that includes the use of technology both to diversify instruction and to provide individualization. In their work, the researchers refer to the "TELE-Web" project, which represents a comprehensive illustration of how technology can help in individualizing a comprehensive instructional program for students with differing abilities. TELE-Web is an outgrowth of the Early Literacy Project, another Englert initiative (Englert, Raphael, & Mariage, 1994). In this early initiative, Englert and her colleagues found that several issues warranted technology applications (Zhao et al., 1998):

1. Low-achieving students need a more concentrated set of experiences that unify literacy instruction across the curriculum domains (oral, listening,

reading, and writing). Technology addresses these areas by bridging these language domains in a simultaneous and fluid way.

2. When information is limited to texts, students typically view teachers and texts—rather than themselves—as authorities. Technology increases students' access to information from multiple sources, thereby increasing their sense of authority and ultimate independence.

3. A single classroom limits students' access to audiences and problems that are real to the students. Technology provides a functional and reality-based purpose for gathering, manipulating, and integrating information from multiple sources and authoring oral or written texts as part of a knowledge-constructing process. It also provides multiple ways to access, organize, visualize, link, and discover relations among various sets of ideas and opportunities to form interactions and encourage discourse among students and between teachers and students.

4. It is difficult for teachers to monitor and support students' performance on a moment-to-moment basis or to prompt the use of strategies when students are writing independently. With technology, teachers can provide prompts as needed.

IDEA '97 has forced us to move beyond traditional notions of curriculum and instruction. And, as the researchers in this volume have shown, new ways to view technology in the context of the new special education paradigm are emerging. When teachers are able to use technology to implement more complex approaches to curriculum and instruction, approaches that enable students to engage in highly motivating, highly contextualized work that is mediated by their peers, they undoubtedly will also be moving toward meeting the needs of those students who have had diffi-

culty learning in the standard, traditional curriculum.

Managerial Tasks, Technological Tools, and Special Education

By supporting practitioners in administrative and managerial tasks related to quality programming, technology serves a secondary role as well. As Woodward and Rieth (1997) reported, technology has long been an invaluable support with regard to helping special educators respond to the paperwork requirements of the law. Such technology-based applications are only likely to increase given the new reporting requirements in IDEA '97.

In addition, we may see an expanded role for managerial technology applications. A new area ripe for investigation is the role of technology in supporting special education services being brought to the student. Depending on the student's needs, services may span several agencies and/or programs both within the district and from outside community sources. In recent years, there has been a growing trend in schools to offer a continuum of student and family support services on school grounds and to provide school-district coordination for such services. For example, the concept of full-service schools—schools that provide basic health care, mental health services, educational enrichment, and social services on school grounds—is becoming more commonplace in diverse, urban districts.

When multiple agencies are involved, interagency collaboration and management are essential to ensure that services are delivered as intended. There is a real danger that without such collaboration, services may become fragmented or, worse, not provided. As Halpern and Benz (Chapter 10, this volume) showed, not only can technology assist educators in handling the increased paperwork and documentation required when collaborating with outside agencies, but technology can help manage the collaboration as well.

Finally, families have a major role to play in their children's education. The principle of family involvement has been a hallmark of special education and continues to be embellished on in each legislative reauthorization. For example, IDEA '97 now requires more formal reporting of student progress. IDEA '97 regulations (March 1999) also require that EP teams consider whether the child needs AT in the home to ensure a free and appropriate education. These requirements can be viewed as part of an educational agenda that supports a student's participation across home, school, and community settings. Communication between school and home can be enhanced with technology. But, more important, there is an implicit notion that families will understand and support their child's technology usage in the home. Practical considerations, such as training family members in how to use and maintain equipment and selecting technology that can transcend settings, will become increasingly important as this agenda become actualized.

Summary

There is no doubt that technology has benefited students with disabilities. Technology in the form of alternative communication and mobility aids has enabled students with physical and sensory disabilities to participate in classrooms. When applied appropriately to instruction, technology has helped students with cognitive disabilities achieve improved results in basic skills and, in some cases, the students have been supported in learning higher-level concepts. Also, educators have utilized the capacity of technology to enhance communications and decision making. Although the technology projects described in this volume cover a wide range of issues and needs, they all have implications for promoting a special education agenda.

To realize the full potential of technology as a means of supporting special education, it will be critical to consider not only the technological advances themselves but the ways in which these advances might best become part of new educational norms. In other words, a focus on the implementation of technology must be paired with a concern for what the technology is capable of doing within the context of supporting contemporary implementation of special education practice.

Emerging Implementation Issues

The researchers in this volume have identified a number of challenges in implementing technology tools with students with disabilities. They began by looking at the factors that limit the widespread use of technology (e.g., lack of awareness, lack of training, lack of funding, lack of administrative support, lack of time) and at strategies that may eliminate barriers. This line of inquiry regarding what it takes to integrate technology use into the educational setting—from making sure all parties have an awareness of effective tools, to making these tools readily available, to ensuring that all parties have sufficient training and ongoing support to utilize the tools—has been at the core of special education research in technology for nearly a quarter of a century. What the researchers in this volume have shown is that studying technology as an intervention for today's practice of special education requires an even more complex approach. The pattern of inquiry has evolved from looking at technology in isolation from the complex educational environment to exploring what it takes—with regard to the intersection of curriculum, professional development, technical support, administrative support, and policy issues—to implement innovative tools and services across settings.

If enduring change is to be realized, technology implementation will require more than attention to one or two elements. It is not enough to look only at gaining the support of the administrator or training a teacher. Although each element is essential, each is also part of a more comprehensive framework of interrelated elements that must be addressed in the course of technology implementation. In most cases, the full implementation of technology requires a comprehensive and complex look at integrating the technology into the curriculum, into instruction, and into the setting with substantive policy and professional development support.

In this volume, many of the authors provide examples of how technology can provide support for students with disabilities as they participate and access the general education curriculum and instructional program. But as Cuban (Chapter 7, this volume) reminds us, unless teachers see the instructional relevance of technology, they probably will not expend the time and energy to use it. Thus, how all stakeholders at each level of implementation view the relevance of a proposed change—in this case, technology use for students with disabilities—will affect implementation, for better or for worst. As Means et al. (1993) pointed out, we cannot simply provide a student with technology without considering the broader setting, including the classroom, school, district, state, and federal levels. If support is lacking at any of these levels for technology use, the likelihood of changing the status quo will be slim. Taken together, the chapters in this volume attest that if those multiple levels are not included in change efforts, then they most likely will pose significant barriers that impede use of technology in classrooms with even the most willing teachers.

Finally, implementation of technology also must be seen and understood within the context of a changing view of special education practice. Implementation of accommodations in traditional, segregated educational settings will yield different purposes and different results than will accommodations in inclusive settings. In the context of considering how technology supports special education, we must see if, in fact, technology supports the key goals of contemporary practice. If technology does not, then it probably will get lost in the curriculum reforms—and most likely it will not be considered a major alternative in supporting students with disabilities in accessing the curriculum.

Whether explicitly or implicitly, researchers in this volume started with a particular viewpoint on the emerging special education agenda as they addressed technology implementation from a systems-change perspective. As Cuban (1996) articulated so clearly, fundamental changes are those that aim to transform and alter, permanently, the basic structural framework for the system. When we think about changing the permanent structural framework of schools in relation to students with disabilities, it is including students in general education classrooms and curriculum that constitutes such a change. A more inclusive view of special education practice requires rethinking how schools and classrooms are organized and, more important, how curriculum and instruction are conceptualized. In some cases, this requires redesigning some of the fundamental norms of schooling and challenges traditional pedagogy. As the examples in this volume show, the success of how each researcher's viewpoint mapped onto the status quo in classrooms, in school buildings, and district/statewide was influenced by the congruency of how the researcher's approach fit with the status quo and the direction of those subsystems. It also was influenced by the resources that were available to shape new knowledge and skills for the participants.

To the extent that technology can advance such reform-minded agendas, it will be an important support. However, if teachers are not interested in pedagogical reform because they are not interested in meeting the needs of a wider range of learners, if teachers pine away for "the good old days when students did their work," technology is not likely to change their minds and their practices.

However, if technology is embedded into a state-of-the-art program of professional development that is focused on shifting pedagogies to meet the needs of all students, the likelihood of its implementation over the long haul increases. And this kind of professional development is something the field of teacher education has illuminated over the past decade.

A crucial feature in using technology to foster better special education results will be the identification of linkages to various levels of subsystems that are geared toward reform. At the classroom level, special education fits with the growing trend of more diverse classrooms. The greater challenge seems to be at the school level. In schools where this new view of special education is in place, there is a clear goal of including all children ("It is the right thing to do"), there is a culture for acceptance and learning that transcends the building, teachers are given time to collaborate and are afforded opportunities for professional development, and site-based management is in place that allows for organizational features that serve the specific school and neighborhood.

At the district level, technology use will be focused on creating and controlling local funding, ensuring professional development, and complying with all state and federal mandates (National School Boards Association/ U.S. Office of Special Education Programs, 1997). Both districts and policymakers will be held accountable for ensuring that AT is considered for every student with an IEP. As students are placed in general education classrooms and environments, technology will need to be flexible and manageable. Issues of access to technology, proximity of technology to the classroom instruction, and training of nondisabled students to interface with the student who uses technology all will need to be addressed as educators embrace a more inclusive conception of special education that is supported by technology.

Professional Development, Technology, and Contemporary Special Education Practice

Because the main entry point for new technology is the classroom, the professional development of teachers is key to its widespread use. However, professional development is more than just instruction in technology.

As Englert, Tarrant, and Rozendal (1993) point out, the literature in the professional development of teachers clearly weighs in on the side of providing sustained opportunities for risk taking with each new approach or method (in this case, technology use); for shared coaching, practice, and feedback regarding its use; and for multiyear expectations for learning to embed the new approaches in practice. Most important, technology needs to be viewed as a solution to real problems that teachers identify themselves so that their investment in learning how to use it and why to use it meshes with who they are as teachers. Innovation, then, cannot merely be appended to existing practice. Instead, it must make sense to teachers, and they must have a good sense of the results and outcomes it can yield in terms of the students they teach.

So, it is not merely technical support that is needed but the opportunity to reflect and plan for instruction with their colleagues—which was a major part of the work carried out by Zorfass (Chapter 5, this volume). Relative to including students with disabilities, teachers will need to understand the reformed curriculum itself, the needs the student has, and then how technology might accommodate those needs without impeding the success of others. This is not the same mind-set as having a student with a disability and "fixing" him or her with a piece of technology. Therefore today technology requires a complex approach to professional development and collaboration. As Englert et al. (1993) stressed, for teachers to change, they must have a voice in the process to promote their ownership of the innovation.

As Englert and Zhao (Chapter 9, this volume) have pointed out, professional development is a function of teachers as communities of learners and not as learners in isolation. Traditionally, special education teachers have not been included in professional development efforts. Even in many collaborative relationships among teachers, special education teachers have not always been comfortable giving up their roles as "experts" to become one of a group of professional "learners." Under a more inclusive education philosophy, it is not only the students who become part of the classroom community; teachers, too, must become part of one unified community of learners to improve instructional opportunities for all of the school's students. Englert and Zhao (Chapter 9, this volume) argue for professional development that is tied directly to the local context rather than professional workshops that prescribe how to use a particular innovation irrespective of context. To achieve deep changes in teacher practice and to sustain any innovation, teachers themselves must be highly involved in the process of implementation, rather than just be recipients of knowledge about the innovation. Unless a collaborative professional culture is established in a school or in a district, no change is likely to endure.

As MacArthur and Malouf (1991) summarized, projects that actively engaged teachers of special education students in long-term professional development focused on change in their instruction and curricula. Thus to separate technology training from the context in which it will be used—helping diverse groups of youngsters succeed in a challenging curriculum—not only will have limited results but may, in fact, undermine progress and impede change.

In addition, if teachers are going to think of technology in terms of solving problems, then they must have sufficient knowledge of it and skill in using it, not to mention the equipment to carry it out. As Blackhurst (Chapter 8, this volume) attested, these competencies are significant. When skill is lacking, school administrators will need to provide opportunities for teams of teachers and specialists to work together. For example, Zorfass (1998) has been studying an approach that regularly brings together teachers, science specialists, special educators, and technology specialists to plan, act, and reflect on technology and how to support student learning in inclusive classrooms.

Implementation of technology, then, is a multifaceted challenge that spans mastering the technology itself and putting into place a defensible program of professional development for teachers who will use it. In the absence of these two components, it is unlikely that technology will be integrated to a level that will enable students with disabilities to profit from a reformed curriculum.

Conclusion

We began this chapter by asking how technology can support a special education agenda. Although the jury is still out regarding whether the new direction special education has taken will result in improved achievement for students with disabilities, technology use in special education exists today in a context much different from that which existed when the notion of AT was first introduced. Technology today holds the promise of advancing special education in which students with disabilities participate and learn to high standards in the general education curriculum alongside their nondisabled peers. Is it worth the effort? As the researchers in this volume unanimously show, technology can improve learning opportunities for students with disabilities and help them achieve to high standards.

From a curriculum reform perspective, technology as an accommodation for students with disabilities can be a real solution to access and participation when it is embedded in the curriculum. There is ample support in this volume from researchers who provided clear instructional models focused on important academic and cognitive curriculum outcomes that were supported by technology. These researchers took outcomes that were advanced by reformed curriculum and showed how technology could accelerate and enhance student learning. In so doing, teachers were able to provide diversified instruction within the mandated curriculum.

We have come a long way from seeing technology as an end-all to using it as a tool to support teaching and learning. Special educators have long been adept at both applications and inventiveness. Today, the more special educators work with general educators to embed technology into their instruction, the more individual accommodations can be linked to curriculum outcomes, and the more we demonstrate that technology accommodations can help all students learn, the higher the probability that technology will be utilized to its maximum potential.

References

Cognition and Technology Group at Vanderbilt University. (1990). Anchored instruction and its relationship to situated cognition. *Educational Researcher, 19,* 2-10.

Committee for Economic Development. (1995). *Connecting students to a changing world: A technology strategy for improving mathematics and science education.* Reston, VA: Author.

Council for Exceptional Children. (1998). *Integrating technology into the standard curriculum: Extending learning opportunities for students with disabilities.* Reston, VA: Author.

Cuban, L. (1996). Myths about changing schools and the case of special education. *Remedial and Special Education, 17,* 75-82.

Englert, C. S., Raphael, T., & Mariage, T. (1994). Developing a school-based discourse for literacy learning: A principled search for understanding. *Learning Disability Quarterly, 17,* 2.

Englert, C. S., Tarrant, K. L., & Rozendal, M. S. (1993). Educational innovations: Achieving curricular change through collaboration. *Education and Treatment of Children, 16,* 441- 473.

Hauser, J., & Malouf, D. (1996). A federal perspective on special education technology. *Journal of Learning Disabilities, 29,* 504-511.

Individuals With Disabilities Education Act Amendments of 1997, 20 U.S.C. §§ 1400-1487 (1997).

Interactive Educational Systems Design. (1996). *Report on the effectiveness of technology.* Washington, DC: Software Publishers Association.

Kendall, J. S., & Marzano, R. J. (1996). *Content knowledge: A compendium of standards and benchmarks for K-12 education.* Aurora, CO: Mid-Continent Regional Educational Laboratory.

MacArthur, C., & Malouf, D. (1991). Teachers' beliefs, plans, and decisions about computer-based instruction. *Journal of Special Education, 25*(5), 44-72.

Means, B., Blando, J., Olson, K., Middleton, T., Morocco, C., Remz, A., & Zorfass, J. (1993). *Using technology to support educational reform.* Washington, DC: U.S. Department of Education.

National School Boards Association/U.S. Office of Special Education Programs. (1997). *Technology for students with disabilities: A decision maker's resource guide.* Washington, DC: Authors.

Office of Technology Assessment. (1995). *Teachers and technology: Making the connection.* Washington, DC: Author.

Pugach, M. C., & Warger, C. L. (1996). *Curriculum trends, special education, and reform: Refocusing the conversation.* New York: Teachers College Press.

Todis, B. (1996). Tools for the task? Perspectives on assistive technology in educational settings. *Journal of Special Education Technology, 13,* 49-61.

Todis, B., & Walker, H. (1993). User perspectives on assistive technology in educational settings. *Focus on Exceptional Children, 26*(3), 1-16.

Williams, S. M., Burgess, K. L., Bray, M. H., Bransford, J. D., Goldman, S. R., & Cognition and Technology Group at Vanderbilt University. (1998). Technology and learning in schools for thought classrooms. In C. Dede (Ed.), *ASCD yearbook 1998: Learning with technology* (pp. 97-119). Alexandria, VA: Association for Supervision and Curriculum Development.

Woodward, J., & Baxter, J. (1997). The effects of an innovative approach to mathematics on academically low achieving students in inclusive settings. *Exceptional Children, 63,* 373-388.

Woodward, J., & Rieth, H. (1997). An historical review of technology research in special education. *Review of Education Research, 67,* 503-536.

Zhao, Y., Englert, C. S., Ferdig, R., Jones, S., Chen, J., & Shah, M. (1998, April). *Supporting writing on the Internet: A dialogue between technology and pedagogy.* Paper presented at the annual meeting of the American Education Research Association, San Diego, CA.

Zorfass, J. (1988). *Successful science for every student: How technology helps.* Newton, MA: Education Development Center, Inc.

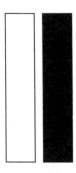

Index

CORWIN
PRESS

The Corwin Press logo—a raven striding across an open book—represents the happy union of courage and learning. We are a professional-level publisher of books and journals for K–12 educators, and we are committed to creating and providing resources that embody these qualities. Corwin's motto is "Success for All Learners."